Innovation in Public Se

CW00349009

In response to changes in internal needs, external organizational environments and the expectations of shareholders – most notably, citizens and politicians – innovation is now an important commonplace aspect of governance and the running of public service organizations (PSOs). Given the ongoing financial and economic crisis, which presents a significant challenge to PSOs, there is a growing need to establish innovative strategies to survive the crisis and provide the basis for future sustainable growth.

This book contributes towards the discussion of PSO innovation through theoretically informed empirical studies of innovation across a range of theories, topics and fields. Studies examine the role of citizens, managers and PSOs; the adoption, diffusion, implementation and management of innovations; collaboration, communication and information technologies; and decision-making, ethical principles, HR management, leadership and procurement. The studies – which examine the situation in a range of countries in Europe and Asia – cover a range of different organizations such as non-profits, health service organizations and local governments. This book was originally published as two special issues of *Public Management Review*.

Stephen P. Osborne is Chair of International Public Management and Director of the Centre for Service Excellence at the University of Edinburgh Business School, Edinburgh, UK.

Louise Brown is a Reader in the Department of Social and Policy Sciences at the University of Bath, UK.

Richard M. Walker is Chair Professor of Public Management in the Department of Public Policy and Associate Dean in the College of Liberal Arts and Social Sciences at the City University of Hong Kong, Hong Kong.

Innovation in Public Services

Theoretical, managerial and international perspectives

Edited by
Stephen P. Osborne, Louise Brown and Richard M. Walker

Routledge
Taylor & Francis Group

LONDON AND NEW YORK

First published 2016
by Routledge
2 Park Square, Milton Park, Abingdon, Oxon, OX14 4RN, UK

and by Routledge
711 Third Avenue, New York, NY 10017, USA

First issued in paperback 2017

Routledge is an imprint of the Taylor & Francis Group, an informa business

British Library Cataloguing in Publication Data
A catalogue record for this book is available from the British Library

ISBN 13: 978-1-138-29526-1 (pbk)
ISBN 13: 978-1-138-94982-9 (hbk)

Typeset in Adobe Garamond Pro
by diacriTech, Chennai

Publisher's Note
The publisher accepts responsibility for any inconsistencies that may have arisen during the conversion of this book from journal articles to book chapters, namely the possible inclusion of journal terminology.

Disclaimer
Every effort has been made to contact copyright holders for their permission to reprint material in this book. The publishers would be grateful to hear from any copyright holder who is not here acknowledged and will undertake to rectify any errors or omissions in future editions of this book.

Contents

CONTENTS

Citation Information

The chapters in this book were originally published in *Public Management Review*, volume 16, issue 1 (January 2014) and issue 2 (February 2014). When citing this material, please use the original page numbering for each article, as follows:

Chapter 1
Internal and external antecedents of process innovation: A review and extension
Richard M. Walker
Public Management Review, volume 16, issue 1 (January 2014) pp. 21–44

Chapter 2
The innovation imperative: An analysis of the ethics of the imperative to innovate in public sector service delivery
Sara R. Jordan
Public Management Review, volume 16, issue 1 (January 2014) pp. 67–89

Chapter 3
Multiple institutional logics in health care: 'Productive Ward: Releasing Time to Care'
Judith van den Broek, Paul Boselie and Jaap Paauwe
Public Management Review, volume 16, issue 1 (January 2014) pp. 1–20

Chapter 4
Strategies for introducing organizational innovation to public service organizations
Alexandra Collm and Kuno Schedler
Public Management Review, volume 16, issue 1 (January 2014) pp. 140–161

Chapter 5
Innovation-oriented culture in the public sector: Do managerial autonomy and result control lead to innovation?
Jan Wynen, Koen Verhoest, Edoardo Ongaro and Sandra van Thiel, in cooperation with the COBRA network
Public Management Review, volume 16, issue 1 (January 2014) pp. 45–66

CITATION INFORMATION

Chapter 6
From hero-innovators to distributed heroism: An in-depth analysis of the role of individuals in public sector innovation
A. J. Meijer
Public Management Review, volume 16, issue 2 (February 2014) pp. 199–216

Chapter 7
Innovation in the public procurement process: A study of the creation of innovation-friendly public procurement
Hans Knutsson and Anna Thomasson
Public Management Review, volume 16, issue 2 (February 2014) pp. 242–255

Chapter 8
Evaluation of the impacts of innovation in the health care sector: A comparative analysis
Maria Cucciniello and Greta Nasi
Public Management Review, volume 16, issue 1 (January 2014) pp. 90–116

Chapter 9
Mandate versus championship: Vertical government intervention and diffusion of innovation in public services in authoritarian China
Xufeng Zhu
Public Management Review, volume 16, issue 1 (January 2014) pp. 117–139

Chapter 10
Determinants of innovative behaviour in Flemish nonprofit organizations: An empirical research
Bram Verschuere, Eline Beddeleem and Dries Verlet
Public Management Review, volume 16, issue 2 (February 2014) pp. 173–198

Chapter 11
Exploring managerial mechanisms that influence innovative work behaviour: Comparing private and public employees
Rune Bysted and Kristina Risom Jespersen
Public Management Review, volume 16, issue 2 (February 2014) pp. 217–241

Chapter 12
Diffusion and assimilation of government microblogging: Evidence from Chinese cities
Liang Ma
Public Management Review, volume 16, issue 2 (February 2014) pp. 274–295

For any permissions-related enquiries please visit
http://www.tandfonline.com/page/help/permissions

Notes on Contributors

Eline Beddeleem is a former Researcher in the department of Business and Public Administration at Ghent University, Belgium. Her research focuses on innovative behaviour in social profit organizations. She is currently the coordinator of a multidisciplinary network organization in health care in the city of Ghent.

Paul Boselie is a Professor in the School of Governance at Utrecht University, the Netherlands. His research traverses human resource management (HRM), institutionalism, strategic management and industrial relations, and is published in various international journals. His teaching involves executive training in strategic HRM for HR and non-HR professionals, a master's course in HR Studies and a bachelor's course in strategic HRM. He was the European Editor of *Personnel Review* until 2012, and is a member of the editorial board of both the *Journal of Management Studies* and *Human Resource Management Journal*.

Judith van den Broek is a Ph.D. candidate at the Institute of Health Policy and Management, Erasmus University Rotterdam, the Netherlands, and in the department of Human Resource Studies, Tilburg University, the Netherlands. Her research focuses on human resource management innovations in the Dutch health care sector. To study these innovations, she uses different theoretical perspectives such as institutionalism, human resource management, innovation processes and public management.

Louise Brown is a Reader in the Department of Social and Policy Sciences at the University of Bath, UK.

Rune Bysted is a Ph.D. student in the Department of Economics and Business at Aarhus University, Denmark. His research focuses on creativity, innovative work behaviour, business economics and motivational differences between public and private sector employees.

Alexandra Collm is a Research Associate and Program Manager (Innovative Public Managing) at the Institute for Systemic Management and Public Governance, University of St Gallen, Switzerland. Her research interests include public management reform and innovation management; strategic management and change management; and electronic government.

NOTES ON CONTRIBUTORS

Maria Cucciniello is Assistant Professor in the Public Management and Policy Department, Bocconi University, Milan, Italy, where she is involved in many projects and teaching activities concerning the innovation process in the public and health care sectors, focusing on the adoption, implementation and evaluation of information and communication technologies. Her research areas are e-government, innovation in government, change management in the public sector, collaborative public management, the impact of technology on the public and health sectors, social capital in the public sector and networks of public interest.

Kristina Risom Jespersen is Associate Professor in the Department of Economics and Business at Aarhus University, Denmark. Her research focuses on open innovation, user involvement in innovation, employee-driven innovation and information use for innovative learning. She has published in international journals such as the *Journal of Product Innovation Management* and the *International Journal of Innovation Management*.

Sara R. Jordan is an Assistant Professor in the Department of Politics and Public Administration at the University of Hong Kong, Hong Kong. Her research addresses issues of ethics in the management of academic research as well as cross-cultural and historical comparisons of ethics concepts in political and management theory.

Hans Knutsson is an Assistant Professor in the School of Economics and Management at Lund University, Sweden. His research focuses on strategic management and public procurement in the public sector. He is also involved in projects concerning the food industry, with a special focus on public procurement and innovation within health care.

Liang Ma is a Lecturer at the MPA Education Center, School of Humanities, Economics, and Law, Northwestern Polytechnical University, Xi'an, China. He earned his Ph.D. from the School of Management, Xi'an Jiaotong University, China. His research interests are public organizational innovation and performance management, and he has published research in *Public Management Review* and *Public Administration*.

A. J. Meijer is Associate Professor in the School of Governance at Utrecht University, the Netherlands, where he teaches public administration and policy sciences. His research focuses on public accountability, informatization in public administration and the use of e-mail by government organizations. He has published frequently in journals such as *Public Administration Review*, the *International Review of the Administrative Sciences* and *Public Management Review*. He is co-chair of the permanent study group on the informatization of the European Group for Public Administration, and sits on the editorial board of *Information Polity*.

Greta Nasi is Associate Professor at the Institute of Public Administration and Health Care Management Carlo Masini (IPAS), assistant to the Director of the CLAPI

Master of Science program and a teacher in the SDA Bocconi Public Management and Policy Department, all at Bocconi University, Milan, Italy. She is also a lecturer for the Project Management module of the Master's in Health Information Management course at Erasmus University Rotterdam, the Netherlands. Her research interests are in e-government, innovation in government, change management in the public sector, collaborative public management, the impact of technology on the public and health sectors, social capital in the public sector and networks of public interest.

Edoardo Ongaro is Professor of International Public Services Management at Northumbria University, Newcastle, UK. He is also a Visiting Professor at Bocconi University, Milan, Italy. His research work is on the dynamics of administrative reforms at the national and European level, and on the organization and strategic management of public service organizations.

Stephen P. Osborne is Chair of International Public Management and Director of the Centre for Service Excellence at the University of Edinburgh Business School, Edinburgh, UK.

Jaap Paauwe is Professor of Human Resource Studies at Tilburg University, the Netherlands, and is involved in supervising Ph.D. students in the area of human resource management (HRM) and performance in health care at Erasmus University Rotterdam, the Netherlands. He has written and co-authored books on HRM, and published more than 150 papers/chapters in international refereed journals and books. His main research interests are in the area of HRM, performance and well-being, HR function and delivery, corporate strategy, governance and risk management, organizational change and industrial relations. As well as his academic work, he is also involved in more practice-oriented research, coaching and acting as a moderator for a leading group of HR directors.

Kuno Schedler is Professor for Public Management at the University of St Gallen, Switzerland. His research interests include management accounting (public and private sector), public management (including financial, human resources and performance management); national and international (new) public management; business-government relations; public institutions and location management; and electronic government and public governance.

Sandra van Thiel is a Professor of Public Management at Radboud University, Nijmegen, the Netherlands. She has published, edited and lectured internationally on Public Management and Public Administration. Her articles have appeared in several journals, such as *Governance*, *Public Management Review* and the *Journal of Public Administration Research and Theory*.

Anna Thomasson is an Assistant Professor in the School of Economics and Management at Lund University, Sweden. Her research focuses on management and corporate governance in public sector services, public procurement and privatization of public sector services.

Koen Verhoest is a Research Professor affiliated with the Research Group on Public Administration and Management in the Department of Political Science at the University of Antwerp, Belgium. He is also co-chair of EGPA SG on Governance of Public Sector Organization and the ECPR Standing Group of Regulatory Governance. He has published in journals such as *Governance*, *Public Management Review*, *International Review of Administrative Sciences*, *Policy Studies*, *Public Performance* and *Management Review and Organizational Studies*. The chapter published in this volume is based on research done within the Flemish Research Foundation project to compare and explain the effects of organizational autonomy in the public sector.

Dries Verlet is Policy Evaluation Advisor to the Research Centre of the Flemish Government, and Visiting Professor in the Faculty of Economics and Business Administration at Ghent University, Belgium, where he teaches methodology and statistics. As an advisor, he is involved in a wide variety of policy evaluation programs.

Bram Verschuere is Assistant Professor in Public Management at the Faculty of Economics and Business Administration, Ghent University, Belgium. His research focuses on management of public and social profit organizations, government organization, coproduction of public services and welfare policy.

Richard M. Walker is Chair Professor of Public Management in the Department of Public Policy, Director of the Laboratory for Public Management and Policy and Associate Dean in the College of Liberal Arts and Social Sciences at the City University of Hong Kong, Hong Kong.

Jan Wynen is based at the Public Management Institute, Katholieke Universiteit Leuven, Belgium, and is working on a project examining the effect of autonomy in the public sector. He has a master's degree in Commercial Sciences and an advanced master's in International Business Economics. His main research interests are econometrics and public sector management.

Xufeng Zhu is a Professor in the School of Public Policy and Management at Tsinghua University, Beijing, China. His major research interests are policy process, policy analyses and governance. He is the author of *The Rise of Think Tanks in China* (Routledge, 2012). His recent publications include articles in *Public Administration*, *The China Quarterly*, *Policy Sciences*, *Nature*, *Public Administration and Development* and *Asian Survey*.

Introduction

Growth in the study of public service innovation

Richard M. Walker, Stephen P. Osborne and Louise Brown

Innovation is now commonplace in public service organizations around the globe. Innovation is used to create public value in citizen collaborations, through civil society and non-profit organizations and with private partners (Ansell and Torfing 2014). Innovations range in scale from behavioural prompts to tackling recycling rates, increasing energy conservation and promoting better health, to radical transformations in the ways technology alters the delivery and consumption of public services. These changes in public services are recognized and rewarded though a range of award programs, some of which are directly supported by governments and others at arm's length. For example, the 'Innovation of American Government Awards' scheme run by Harvard University's JFK School of Government, the China Government led 'Innovations and Excellence in Chinese Local Governance', the English government's 'Beacon Council Scheme' and the 'CPSI Public Sector Innovation Awards' sponsored by the South African Government. These important changes to the public service innovation landscape require new ways to conceive of public service innovation, conduct research and consider the societal impacts.

An important place to start when considering new approaches to the study of public service innovation is its definition. Definitions of innovation in public service studies typically draw upon a number of concepts including the generation (development) or adoption (use) of new ideas, objects or practices that are new to the unit of analysis (Amabile 1988; Damanpour and Schneider 2006; O'Toole 1997; Rogers 1995). More recently Chen, Walker and Sawhney (2015) have offered a slightly more nuanced definition: The development and implementation by a public service organization of a new idea to create or improve public value and change its relationship(s) with ecosystem partners. This definition of public service innovation recognizes that it is different from that for traditional goods derived from a product-dominant logic, where a transfer of ownership takes place in exchange. The intangibility of services is different to products in that 'production and consumption occur simultaneously' (Osborne et al. 2013, 139). Because production and consumption are simultaneous, no two service experiences are identical, and users are central to the way in which the service is experienced. Thus, the role of the user is that of a co-producer of the service.

Chen et al.'s (2015) definition places service at its core. It offers five characteristics. First, it maintains an important emphasis upon novelty or newness. Second, it recognizes innovation as a dynamic process that requires development on the way to implementation. The act of innovation acknowledges that there are relationships in the process of developing innovation, and these can be with a range of partners

INTRODUCTION

in the public, private and non-profit sectors. These relationships are conducted in an ecosystem. The ecosystem is the institutional context for innovation where the relationships between actors are played out. Critically, this includes citizens in the co-production of innovation. Ansell and Torfing (2012) refer to this as collaborative innovation. Finally, public service innovation is driven towards the creation of public value, the defining characteristic of public services. These themes are found throughout this book.

In the remaining parts of this chapter we take the opportunity to ask questions about the nature of research on public service innovation published in public administration journals. The analysis, drawing on journal articles published and held in the Web of Science's Social Sciences Citation Index, examines the number of articles published, the topics examined, the journals the articles appear in and the authors. This analysis reveals a substantial growth in scholarship on public service innovation over recent years, but an uneven coverage of topics that suggests much knowledge still has to be generated. The nature of the contributions to this edited volume is then outlined and placed in context of growing interest and attention in understanding the nature of public service innovation.

The Study of Public Service Innovation

The evaluation of the study of public service innovation focuses on articles published in the Web of Science in the period 1976–2014. The search term innovat* was used to capture the range of studies on innovation. The search focused on titles only – to search wider would risk identifying articles that mention innovation (or its derivatives) but it is not the core concept in the article. For example, an article may present an innovative new methodology to measure collaboration, which does not place the study of innovation at the centre of the study. This search across the Social Sciences Citation Index led to the identification of 17,999 articles. The majority of the studies of innovation were in management (5,620), business (3,481), economics (3,227) and planning development (1,699). In the field of public administration, 492 articles were identified.

Number of articles

The number of articles published each year, between 1976 and 2014, is shown in Figure 1. Figure 1 indicates a consistent if slightly rising number of articles published each year until around the mid-2000s. In the late 1970s, from 1976 to 1979, there were 23 articles published with a mean of 5.75 per year. In the 1980s this increased to a mean of 6.7 articles per year, or 67 in total. The 1990s saw similar output by public administration scholars with a mean of 6.2 articles per year. The 2000s hint at some change in scholarly output with the mean rising to 11.9 and over 100 articles. However, in the first five years of the decade commencing in 2010 the total number of articles shot up to 197 with a mean of 39.4 per annum. These data suggest much keener attention has been paid to the study of innovation in recent years.

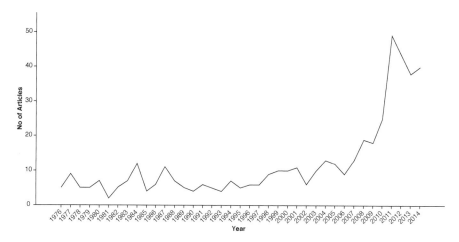

Figure 1: Number of articles published each year with 'innovation' in the title: 1976–2014.

Source: Web of Science search, June 2015.

Journals publishing public service innovation studies

Public administration is a board interdisciplinary field encompassing administration, behaviour and social psychology, economics, political science, sociology and so forth. In the Web of Science, journals that enter the index are free to cross-list in multiple disciplines. Table 1 indicates that of the 47 journals listed in the public administration field of the Social Sciences Citation Index, 24 published more than 5 articles with innovation in the title. This leaves just below 50 per cent of journals publishing fewer than 5 articles. Of the journals publishing over 5 papers, the majority focused on core questions of public administration and produced 252 articles. The eight journals taking policy as their core topic published 151 articles, with *Science and Public Policy* publishing the largest number of articles on innovation, 69.

Topics

Innovation research typically focuses upon a number of questions relating to diffusion and adoption, organizational characteristics, the management of innovation and the consequences of innovation adoption (Wolfe 1994). A large number of the studies did not seek to answer questions germane to the 'process of innovation'. Rather studies sought to problematize or understand the nature of the innovation phenomena and its covariates. For example, in *Policy Studies Journal* we find Mahroum (2013) discussing an analytic framework for policy innovations and Carlson (2011) examining trends and innovations in public policy analysis.

In relation to studies examining the 'process of innovation', the largest number of studies focused on questions of the diffusion of innovation and the antecedents of adoption (44). Thirteen studies, spanning the 30 plus years of our search, examined

Table 1: Journals publishing more than 5 articles with 'innovation' in the title, 1970–2014

Journal	N
Science and Public Policy	69
Environment and Planning C-Government and Policy	43
Public Administration Review	25
Policy Studies Journal	23
Australian Journal of Public Administration	18
Public Management Review	18
Public Money & Management	17
Administration in Social Work	16
Local Government Studies	16
Administration & Society	14
Journal of Policy Analysis and Management	13
Policy Sciences	13
Public Administration	13
Public Administration and Development	13
Journal of Public Administration Research and Theory	12
Canadian Public Administration	11
International Review of Administrative Sciences	10
Journal of European Public Policy	9
Policy and Politics	9
American Review of Public Administration	8
Canadian Public Policy	8
Cato Journal	8
Governance	8
Public Personnel Management	8

Note: Journals publishing five or less articles:
5 = *Climate Policy.* 4 = *International Public Management Journal.* 3 = *Contemporary Economic Policy, Journal of State Government, Innovar, Revista de Ciencias Administrativas y Sociales, Nonprofit Management & Leadership, Public Performance & Management Review, Public Policy, State Government, Transylvanian Review of Administrative Sciences.* 2 = *International Journal of Public Administration, Journal of Collective Negotiations in the Public Sector, Journal of Comparative Policy Analysis, Policy Studies, Regulation & Governance, Review of Public Personnel Administration, Social Policy & Administration, Social Security Bulletin.* 1 = *Journal of Public Policy, Journal of Social Policy, Public Finance/Finances Publiques, Review of Policy Research.*

Source: Web of Science search, June 2015.

questions about the diffusion of innovation across a population. Studies examining the diffusion of information technologies have featured strongly in this literature. For example, Perry and Kraemer (1978) explored the diffusion of computer-applications. In the 2000s Korteland and Bekkers (2008) examined e-policing, and more recently Chen (2014) focused on the effectiveness of e-learning in local government. Antecedent studies were varied in the factors that they examined, though the majority focused on internal antecedents – based upon the titles, no study focused on an examination of how the organizational environment might influence the adoption of innovation. Surprisingly few articles focus on the characteristics of innovative public service organizations.

The management of innovation within organizations sees only passing attention from public administration scholars, with three studies touching on this topic: Mitchell (2001) examines how innovation is managed in business improvement districts; Yin (1981) studies how the innovation practices become routine in organizations; and Walker (2003) focuses on the complex iterative process of managing innovation in non-profit housing associations. Lastly, only a limited number of studies focus on the consequences of innovation. Walker, Damanpour and Devece (2011) find that management innovation only has a positive relationship with performance when performance management mediates it. Rask, Maciukaite-Zviniene, and Petrauskiene (2012) examine performance in public participation in the science and technology policy and use multi-country data to build a model participatory performance. Clearly more studies are needed in this area.

Another important area of enquiry has been to develop innovation types, a topic addressed by Wu et al. (2013) in the Chinese context. Understanding different types of innovation is important in establishing a common language among innovation scholars, and it permits generalization of findings to different settings. The definition of innovation advanced here points towards the importance of innovation as a service rather than a product. Presumptions about product innovation are driven strongly by a private sector–derived model of innovation that does not fully capture the unique characteristics of services, notably intangibility, simultaneous production and consumption and coproduction (Gronroos 1978; Norman 1991; Osborne et al. 2013). The balance of the knowledge generated on innovation in the journals in the Web of Science for the period 1976–2014 focuses on product and technological innovation, with 43 articles examining these questions. By contrast, 20 articles have taken administrative, management or organizational innovation as their core topic of investigation. It is, however, instructive to note that over 50 per cent of the technologically focused articles are published in policy journals including *Science and Public Policy, Policy Sciences, Climate Change*, etc., whereas all the studies investigating administrative, management or organizational innovation were published in mainstream public administration journals.

INTRODUCTION

About the Book

Innovation responds to changes in needs, the external organizational environment and the expectations of stakeholders, notably citizens and politicians. This book contributes towards the discussion of public service innovation through theoretically informed empirical studies of innovation across a range of theories, topics and fields. The studies are diverse, pushing forward knowledge across a range of units of analysis and innovation themes.

The roles of citizens, managers, public service organizations and the state in public service innovation are considered in a number of ways. For example, Jordan (Chapter 2) draws parallels between the innovation imperative in public organization and the research imperative in bio-medical science to offer a framework for public servants to think about their innovative behaviour and ensure that the needs and interests of citizens are protected. In Chapter 9 Zhu notes the need to modify hypotheses on geographical proximity, diffusion, vertical integration and competition when studying innovation in authoritarian China. Zhu argues, through comparative case studies, that the complex processes of vertical authority (vertical administration and decentralized financial system) and horizontal competition (the personnel performance evaluation system for cadres) creates a new set of dynamics, which he terms 'championship policy diffusion'. Meijer (Chapter 6) brings our attention to the role of individuals in innovation and paints a picture of 'distributed heroism' based on his longitudinal case study on the Dutch police. Bysted and Jespersen (Chapter 11) continue the focus on individuals in their public–private comparison in Scandinavian countries, and offer insightful findings on the perceptions of innovation for public and private sector workers. In the public sector, innovation is seen as something beyond normal work and, as such, it should be compensated. By contract, private sector employees view innovative work as part and parcel of their normal employment and, thus, necessary for career advancement.

The adoption, diffusion, implementation and management of innovations in a range of settings are examined in a number of chapters. Van den Broek et al. (Chapter 3) examine decision-making and implementation in the face of competing institutional logics that complicate the innovation adoption. In Chapter 1 Walker provides an integration of the antecedents of process innovations, noting the importance of internal variables of organizational size, administrative capacity and organizational learning for the adoption of innovation in local governments. Walker does not, however, uncover any strong evidence for the role of external antecedents in the adoption of process innovations. In Chapter 8 Cucciniello and Nasi provide a multidimensional framework for assessing the impacts of innovation on organizational performance as perceived by stakeholders. They note the way in which organizational conditions and characteristics, alongside the implementation process, influence these assessments. Verschuere and colleagues (Chapter 10) address factors determining the innovative behaviour of Flemish nonprofit organizations noting the complex interaction between organizational and environmental variables.

Wolfe, R. 1994. Organizational innovation: Review, critique and suggested research agenda. *Journal of Management Studies*, 31:3, 405–431.

Wu, J. N., Ma, L. and Yang, Y. Q. 2013. Innovation in the Chinese public sector: Typology and distribution. *Public Administration* 91:2, 347–365.

Yin, R. K. 1981. Life histories of innovations – How new practices become routinized. *Public Administration Review*, 41:1, 21–28.

Abstract

Innovation in public organizations is widely documented and has increasingly been the subject of empirical scrutiny. This article integrates the empirical evidence of the internal and external antecedents of process innovations in local governments and proposes directions for future research. The importance of the internal antecedents of organizational size, administrative capacity and organizational learning is uncovered using the meta-analytic support score method, but not in relation to external antecedents. Directions for further research are presented on the independent, joint and non-linear effects of antecedents on the adoption of innovation, and the implications of these arguments on the future study of innovation in local governments are considered from a structural contingency perspective.

INTERNAL AND EXTERNAL ANTECEDENTS OF PROCESS INNOVATION
A review and extension

Richard M. Walker

Richard M. Walker
Department of Public Policy
City University of Hong Kong
Hong Kong
People's Republic of China

1

INTRODUCTION

Evidence shows that public organizations regularly implement new services and service delivery methods. These innovations occur in response to changes in the external environment – deregulation, resource scarcity and customer demands – and are based on internal organizational choices, such as perceived performance gaps, pursuit of a higher level of aspiration and increasing the extent and quality of services (Aiken and Alford, 1970; Borins, 1998; Light, 1999; Osborne and Brown, 2005). The evidence base on the factors influencing the adoption and implementation of innovation is longstanding (Mohr, 1969) and has been growing in public organizations over recent years (Berry, 1994; Borins, 1998; Light, 1999; Newman *et al.*, 2000; Wu *et al.*, forthcoming). It is important to take stock of the antecedents of innovation, to integrate and synthesize the existing knowledge and to identify a research agenda that populates the gaps in the evidence base.

Researchers have examined the innovativeness of organizations, the patterns of diffusion and the consequences of innovation across a range of different types of public agencies (Berry, 1994; Borins, 1998; Light, 1999; Salge and Vera, 2009). The dominant line of enquiry in the social sciences literature has been driven by a technological imperative that examines the organizational and environmental conditions that lead to innovative products and services (Gallouj and Weinstein, 1997; Miles, 2005). Given this bias, this review contributes to public management and innovation literatures by focusing on process innovations. Process innovations are concerned with how services are rendered. They include the organizational and technological components of organizations, together with inter-organizational relationships. Recent changes in the management of public organizations have heightened the importance of internal organizational changes. Such changes include the New Public Management (NPM) movement of the late twentieth century, which placed emphasis on process innovation through its focus on business and managerial practices, and the more-recent changes associated with networked governance (Pollitt and Bouckaert, 2004; Agranoff, 2007). Furthermore, process innovations are anticipated in older organizations such as local governments.[1]

This article seeks to make two contributions. The first is to examine and integrate empirical findings from studies on the internal and external antecedents that lead to the adoption and implementation of process innovations at organizational level. The second is to suggest future directions for research in this field. The organizations examined are local governments – a suitable unit of analysis because they are responsible for the delivery of many of the public services that people use on a daily basis and support many of the basic aspects of human existence. This ensures healthy environments through garbage removal, clean food and water supply, the education of children destined to become future citizens and the support of those most vulnerable in society. Focus is on the antecedents most widely examined in the studies reviewed – administrative capacity, organizational size, organizational learning, slack resources and deprivation, urbanization and wealth (e.g. Damanpour, 1987; Boyne et al., 2005; Fernández and Wise, 2010; Jun and Weare, 2010).

To meet these aims, this article commences by defining innovation and discussing innovation types, noting the importance of clear and comparable definitions to ensure that the results are comparable and, thus, generalizable. The published empirical academic evidence on the internal and external antecedents that influence adoption is subsequently reviewed. The review focuses on empirical journal articles on innovation in local governments, published and recorded in the Public Administration section of the Web of Science database. The examination of this evidence points towards the importance of organizational size and administrative capacity, but offers less-compelling evidence for other determinants. To advance the field directions for future research on the independent effects of internal characteristics, the joint effects of internal and environmental antecedents and likely non-linear relationships in the organizational environment are discussed within a structural contingency framework.

PROCESS INNOVATIONS

Innovation occurs when new ideas, objects and practices are created, developed or reinvented for the first time in an organization (Aiken and Hage, 1971; Kimberly and Evanisko, 1981; Rogers, 1995). Because public organizations may innovate to secure their legitimacy, they may not fully adopt an innovation. Thus, the implementation and use of an innovation is a critical aspect of its definition (Damanpour and Evan, 1984; Boyne et al., 2005).[2] Given this imperative, scholars have identified models of innovation adoption that range from sequential stages, such as initiation, adoption decision and implementation, to complex iterative process models (Zaltman et al., 1973; Van de Ven et al., 1999).

Social scientists generally concur that inconsistent results arise from variations in the definition and operationalization of concepts. Previous studies have sought to address this problem by distinguishing between innovation types to overcome problems of limited cumulative knowledge development (Aiken and Alford, 1970; Damanpour, 1991; Wolfe, 1994). Researchers have, for example, examined radical and incremental innovations as an essential aspect of understanding the adoption of innovation (Ettile et al., 1984).[3] Product and process innovations are the most commonly distinguished (see Edquist et al., 2001). Product innovations can be understood as what is produced or, more appropriately in public sector settings, what service is delivered. Processes innovations pertain to how a service is rendered. It is also possible to distinguish between ancillary and inter-organizational innovations; that is, those that are developed at the organization-environment boundary (Damanpour, 1987; Armbruster et al., 2008).

Process innovations affect management and organization. They change relationships amongst organizational members and affect rules, roles, procedures and structures, communication and exchange among organizational members and between such members and the environment (Abernathy and Utterback, 1978; Damanpour and

Gopalakrishnan, 2001). Given these wide-ranging effects, Edquist *et al.* (2001) drew attention to the organizational and technological aspects of process innovations.

Organizational process innovations occur in structure, strategy and administrative processes (Damanpour, 1987; Armbruster *et al.*, 2008). They include improvements in an organization's practices, the introduction of new organizational structures and the coordination of human resources (Borins, 1998; Edquist *et al.*, 2001; Light, 1999). Within the public sector, such changes embrace methods of purchasing, delivering services and generating revenue and include themes such as contracting, externalization and the market pricing of public services reflecting the NPM (see Hansen [2010] on Danish local government and Morgan [2010] on economic development). Organizational process innovations include new approaches to personnel (motivating and rewarding organizational members), tasks and units (searching out new approaches and structure) and modifying the organization's management processes (Daft, 1978; Kimberly and Evanisko, 1981; Light, 1999). For example, Fernández and Wise (2010) examined the personnel innovations arising from changes in employment visas, and Teodoro (2009) explored a number of innovations, including workforce succession planning.

Technological process innovations are new elements introduced into an organization's production system or service operation to render its services to users and citizens (Knight, 1967; Abernathy and Utterback, 1978; Damanpour and Gopalakrishnan, 2001). The drivers of these innovations are, primarily, reduction in delivery time, increase in operational flexibility and decreased production costs (Boer and During, 2001), and they are typically associated with information technology (IT) in public organizations. Researchers initially examined the use of IT in public organizations (Perry and Kraemer, 1978), but have recently shifted towards e-government (Jun and Weare, 2010). Technological process innovations, therefore, modify the organization's operating processes and systems (Schilling, 2005).

Innovations can be intra- or inter-organizational in character (Armbruster *et al.*, 2008). Inter-organizational or ancillary innovations are differentiated from other innovations because they are 'organisation-environment boundary innovations' (Damanpour, 1987, 678). An ancillary innovation is distinguished by the fact that successful adoption is dependent on factors outside an organization's control and their successful implementation is reliant on other actors in the organizational environment. Given that ancillary innovations involve a public organization working across organizational boundaries (i.e. business, users, citizens or non-profit), the growth of governance and the networked relations that have come to dominate service delivery mean that process innovations abound and are concerned with partnerships and joint efforts across sectors. Studies have examined tutorial services and adult continuing education programmes in libraries (Damanpour, 1987) and the development of external partnerships and internal coordination between departments (Walker, 2008).

ANTECEDENTS

Internal antecedents

The internal antecedents examined include organizational size, slack resources, administrative capacity and organizational learning.[4] Arguments about the role of organizational size as a determinant of innovation are presented from two diametrically opposed perspectives, and supported by inconsistent results. First, the public choice theory holds that large public organizations are monopolistic, inefficient and driven by the interests of bureaucrats rather than users or political sponsors. They are characterized as sluggish and unable to respond to changes in the environment, and as such are not likely to innovate (see Downs 1967; Niskanen 1971). The alternative perspective on size presents it as an antecedent of innovation because larger organizations are associated with access to more-complex and diverse facilities, professional and skilled workers and higher technical potential and knowledge (Hage and Aiken, 1970; Rogers, 1995; Damanpour et al., 2009). Furthermore, process innovations are more readily associated with older organizations (such as local governments) that use them to enhance efficiency. These theoretical arguments point towards a possible non-linear U-shaped relationship, with smaller and larger organizations offering optimal structural conditions for innovation.

During the adoption and implementation of innovations, organizations must assign staff and resources to manage what can be a difficult and turbulent time (Van de Ven et al., 1999). If an organization is cash strapped, it may not have the flexibility to deploy resources for the task of innovating. In resource-scare environments, levels of formalization may be higher and control over the budget and other resources sufficiently tight enough to hinder innovation. Slack resources provide organizations with the ability to innovate, bear the costs of innovation and experiment (Damanpour, 1991; Berry, 1994; Walker, 2003). Although the availability of slack resources is not consistently associated with all types of innovation, the case has been made for process innovations because they are more typically associated with efficiency gains that may, in turn, release further resources (Borins, 1998; Light, 1999).

The administrative intensity or capacity of public organizations has long been associated with their ability to adapt to circumstances for maintaining effectiveness, of which innovation is a key mechanism (Burgess, 1975). Studies of capacity and intensity vary in their focus. For example, the Government Performance Project painted administrative capacity as the ability of public organizations to direct and control human, physical and informational resources to achieve policy goals (Ingraham et al., 2003). In relation to innovation, it has long been maintained that a strong administrative core or a large number of managers are positively associated with the adoption of innovation because they provide the leadership, support and coordination necessary for innovation to succeed (Daft and Becker, 1978). Put another way, Andrews and Boyne (2011, 895) note 'low capacity governments would struggle to develop and implement innovations'. In studies of local government, capacity has been operationalized as administrative intensity or administrative overheads (ratio of managers to employees, see Fernández and Wise 2010) and financial, personnel and managerial capacity (see Moon and Bretschneider 2002). The term administrative capacity is used to capture the capacity and intensity facets of this notion in this study, and it is associated with the adoption of innovation.

Scholars addressing questions of innovation adoption in local governments have drawn on concepts of professionalism, boundary spanning and external communication. These concepts are central to organisational learning, 'social interaction' and 'shared thought and action in an organisational context ... which can be the sources of collective knowledge stimulating organisational change' (Rashman et al., 2009, 470).[5] Organizational learning is seen to be particularly suited to the public sector due to high levels of professionalism and learning through collective action. In studies of innovation in public organizations, authors have argued that professionalism reflects individual managerial and organizational experience (Walker, 2008). Higher levels of education and experience have been argued to increase the boundary-spanning activities of managers and a commitment to move beyond the status quo. The concept of professionalism is very closely associated with external communication. For example, the 'environmental scanning and extraorganisational professional activities of members can bring innovative ideas' and 'innovative organisations exchange information with their environments effectively' (Damanpour, 1991, 559). External communication through professional associations has been shown to lead to the adoption of innovation in studies of US states, the model laws and the knowledge transfer systems (Walker, 1969; Balla, 2001; Rashman and Radnor, 2005). Given the very close association with these variables used in studies on innovation and the concept of organizational learning, the label organizational learning is used, and it is presumed that this is associated with the adoption of innovations in local governments.

External antecedents

The external organizational environment can offer opportunities for, or place constraints on, the adoption of innovation. Contingency theorists argue that adaptation to the external environment takes place to enhance organizational efficiency and effectiveness, and that innovation is one such route to these outcomes (Donaldson, 2001). Consequently, the external organizational context will have bearing on the adoption of innovation.

Three external antecedents are examined: needs, wealth and urbanization.[6] The primary function of public organizations is to meet needs, be they expressed as demands for service from particular groups or the level of deprivation in a jurisdiction. Ensuring that goals are met is likely to motive them to innovate and provide appropriate and necessary levels of service. Public organizations are therefore motivated to innovate for meeting basic service needs. However, need alone might not be sufficient to facilitate the adoption of innovation, and thus two additional perspectives have been developed. The first proposes that innovation adoption will be easier in more-munificent external environments because more-affluent, economically skilled and socially enterprising households can use their resources alongside those of a public agency to coproduce services, increasing the opportunity for innovation (Armstrong and Taylor, 2000). Hence, researchers have included measures of affluence and wealth in models of adoption (Moon and deLeon, 2001). Second, the benefits of a supportive or malleable external environment have been identified as a mechanism to overcome obstacles to innovation (Light, 1999; Meyers and Goes, 1986). Urbanization has also been a subject of enquiry as a practical expression of malleable environments. The presumption is that urban environments are more amenable to innovation due to population concentrations that are relatively easy to access (Aiken and Alford, 1970).

The relationship between the environment and adoption is likely to be non-linear. Technical organizational environments place limits on organizations that are likely to constrain organizational outcomes (Pettigrew et al., 1992; Andrews et al., 2005). Public organizations cannot maintain innovation in the face of growing need because its adoption is disruptive (Van de Ven et al., 1999) and, at some point, organizational failure is likely to be substituted for innovation (Boyne and Meier, 2009).

METHODS

Empirical literature on innovation in local governments was located in the Thompson Reuters Web of Science database. Searches of titles, abstracts and keywords were conducted for the 1956 to 2010 period (inclusive), and supplemented by searches in the 'advance access' sections of journal websites in the public administration section of the Web of Science. The search terms used included: innovation AND local government, counties, cities and public (and derivatives thereof). The search terms were kept broad, so as not to omit studies. Once articles had been identified using these terms, the articles were examined in further detail and only studies that included the local government as the unit of analysis and process innovation were included. The search focused on the disciplinary areas of business, management, political science and public administration. Careful reading of the articles led to a final sample of seventeen empirical studies that contained full tables of statistical results. Articles were excluded from the review if they were not empirical, innovation was not the dependent variable, they did not include independent variables of internal and external antecedents, they contained partial statistical data, case studies were presented or they were conceptual pieces.

The review strategy adopted in this article benefits from focusing on peer-reviewed journal articles that were judged to be of suitable quality for publication by editors following a blind review and, therefore, should meet the basic requirements of theoretical and methodological rigor. However, it excludes unpublished papers on the antecedents of innovation in local government and work sponsored by government and national and global organizations, such as the Organization for Economic Cooperation and Development, with an interest in innovation in public organizations, along with books and book chapters. This approach may lead to bias if the relationship between antecedents and innovation adoption is overstated because articles that contain statistically significant results are more likely to be published. Estimates from other fields suggest that the magnitude of such a bias is small (Rosenthal, 1991). The publication of weak research findings is generally limited, although there are wider examples from the innovation and management literature (Damanpour, 1990; West and Schwenk, 1996).

The studies examined span the four most-recent decades of the search period. The distribution of these articles over time suggests that although not a mainstream topic, innovation adoption in local government is one that scholars have revisited with

Table 1: Measurement of innovation, context, sample, analysis and antecedents in reviewed articles

Study	Innovation	Context	Sample	Data source	Time	Analysis	Antecedents Internal P	Antecedents External P
Bingham (1978)	Y/N	US	310	Both	CS	r	X	X
Perry and Kraemer (1978)	Y/N	US	112	Survey	CS	β		X
Damanpour (1987)	Y/N	US	75	Survey	CS	r, β	X	
Brudney and Selden (1995)	Y/N	US	297	Survey	Lag	β	X	
Moon and Bretschneider (2002)	Perception	US	285	Survey	CS	β	X	
Boyne et al. (2005)	A&U	UK	79	Both	Lag	r, β	X	X
Damanpour and Schneider (2006)	A&U	US	1276	Survey	CS	r, β	X	X
Walker (2006)	Perception	UK	120	Both	CS	r, β	X	X
Walker (2008)	Perception	UK	101	Both	Lag	β	X	X
Damanpour and Schneider (2009)	Y/N	US	725	Both	CS	r, β	X	X
Kwon et al. (2009)	Y/N	US	233	Survey	Lag	β	X	X
Teodoro (2009)	Y/N	US	139	Survey	CS	β	X	
Bhatti et al. (2010)	A&U	Denmark	3931	Secondary	L	β	X	X
Fernández and Wise (2010)	A&U	US	532	Both	Lag	r, β	X	X
Hansen (2010)	A&U	Denmark	585	Both	CS	r, β	X	X
Morgan (2010)	Y/N	US	217	Both	CS	β	X	X
Jun and Weare (2010)	Y/N	US	2110	Both	L	β	X	X

Note: Y/N = dichotomous yes/no adoption, Perception = perception of innovativeness, A&U = measure of adoption and utilization, L = longitudinal, Lag = lagged, CS = cross-sectional, r = correlation and β = multiple regression.

increased interest in the twenty-first century. Table 1 shows that studies were typically undertaken in the US (twelve of the seventeen studies) with three in the UK and two in Denmark. The non-US samples focused on general-purpose local governments that delivered a range of services. For example, the services surveyed in English local governments included corporate services, benefits and revenues, education, housing, land use planning, leisure and culture, social services and waste management (Walker, 2006). The service provision of Danish municipalities includes education and culture, social services, technical services and city managers (Hansen, 2010). The structure of government in the US reveals many single-purpose local governments. Bingham (1978), Damanpour (1987), Teodoro (2009) and Fernández and Wise (2010) examined single-purpose authorities whereas the remainder investigated city, municipal and county governments. The large number of US studies in the sample is likely to bias results – a point that is addressed in the conclusion.

The average sample size is 655 and ranges from in the 70s (Damanpour, 1987; Walker, 2008; Teodoro, 2009) to over 1,000 (Damanpour and Schneider, 2006; Bhatti et al., 2010; Jun and Weare, 2010) (see Table 1). The majority of the studies examined surveyed one respondent from each organization, the exceptions being those in Demark, England and Wales (Boyne et al., 2005; Walker, 2006, 2008; Hansen, 2010).[7] The rest of the studies use a combination of secondary and survey data, with seven using only survey data, whereas the article by Bhatti et al. (2010) relies exclusively on secondary data. The studies were marginally more likely to report associations because their research design was cross-sectional. However, seven studies were able to build some semblance of time into their research design, of which two used longitudinal datasets. The remaining five studies (Brudney and Selden, 1995; Boyne et al., 2005; Walker, 2008; Kwon et al., 2009; Fernández and Wise, 2010) built a time lag between the dates that the independent and dependent variables were recorded. Twelve of the studies included explanatory variables of both internal and external characteristics, whereas Perry and Kraemer (1978) focused on external antecedents alone and the remaining four internal determinants (Damanpour, 1987; Brudney and Selden, 1995; Moon and Bretchneider, 2002; Teodoro, 2009).

Support score

The method used to combine and synthesise the results of the empirical evidence is based on the percentage of statistical tests that support the hypothesis that internal and external antecedents, positively or negatively (depending on the hypotheses presented), influence innovation adoption. The support score approach is adopted because the majority of studies implemented multiple regression techniques and do not report correlations (Boyne, 2002; Damanpour, 2010). To count as supporting the hypothesis, two conditions must be satisfied. First, the results must be in the predicted direction.

Second, the results must be statistically significant; that is, greater than would be likely to arise by chance alone ($p < .05$). If these criteria are applied to all the tests in a single study, then a support score can be calculated as a percentage of all of the tests that are reported (ranging from 6 to 105).

Following this, an aggregate support score can be calculated across all the studies, in at least two ways (Rosenthal, 1991; Boyne, 2002). First, the support score for each study can be treated equally, regardless of whether it contains 1 or 300 tests. Second, each study can be weighted (multiplied) by the number of tests in that study so that an equal weight is attached to each test, rather than to each study. The method can be illustrated using two hypothetical studies. Study A has one test that is statistically significant and positive at .05 or better. Study B has ten tests, of which five are positive and statistically significant. The unweighted positive support score would be 75 per cent (100 [per cent of positive statistically significant tests in Study A] + 50 [per cent of positive statistically significant tests in Study B]/2 [number of studies]). The weighted support score would be 55 per cent (Study A 100 [per cent of positive statistically significant tests in study] * 1 [number of tests] = 100. Study B 50 [per cent of positive statistically significant tests in study] * 10 [number of tests] = 500. Sum per cent of positive statistically significant tests: 100 + 500 = 600. Calculate the weighted percentage as 600/11 [number of tests in total] = 55 per cent). As this example reveals, the weighted mean has the advantage; that is, studies that report only a small number of tests do not have a disproportionate influence on the analysis. The advantage of the unweighted mean is that studies that conduct a large number of tests on the same data set are not given undue importance. The real level of support for the antecedent-innovation hypothesis probably lies somewhere between the unweighted and weighted figures. The text reports both support scores, but the more-conservative weighted score is reported first.

Alternative approaches can be adopted for the purpose of critical review. However, the majority of these techniques require the reporting of correlation matrices, and as Table 1 shows, only eight of the seventeen studies reported these. Unlike studies using correlation coefficients, the support score method reports statistically significant associations at the $p = .05$ level from regression models that control for other variables, thereby reducing concerns about bias arising from spurious relationships (Damanpour, 2010).

RESULTS

The results are presented in two parts. The first section presents the support scores for organizational size, administrative capacity and organizational learning. In each case, a positive relationship with innovation adoption is anticipated. The second section examines the external antecedents. Again, it is anticipated that deprivation, wealth and urbanization will be positively associated with adoption. To determine what counts as support for the hypotheses, Boyne (2002) and Damanpour (2010) proposed that a support score of 50 per cent shows strong support for a hypothesis – higher than chance alone. This decision rule is implemented in this study.

Internal antecedents

The findings commence with organizational size. Table 2 shows that organizational size affects the adoption of process innovations in local governments. The weighted support score for statistically significant positive results is 62 per cent (unweighted is 54 per cent). These results show that process innovations are associated with larger organizations and, as such, the findings reflect evidence of the size-innovation hypothesis in the management literature (Damanpour, 1991, 2010; Camison-Zornoza et al., 2004) without supporting the public choice arguments. In reaching this conclusion, the Camison-Zornoza et al. (2004) meta-analysis noted the importance of consistency in the measurement of size. Size is typically measured using employees or a proxy measure of population.[8] A sub-analysis indicates that the measure of population is

Table 2: The influence of the size and slack on the adoption of process innovations

	Size			Slack			
	N	+	ns	–	N	+	ns	–
Bingham (1978)	4	75	25	0				
Damanpour (1987)	2	50	50	0	3	33	67	0
Brudney and Selden (1995)					2	0	100	0
Moon and Bretschneider (2002)	1	0	100	0				
Boyne et al. (2005)	1	0	100	0				
Damanpour and Schneider (2006)	4	50	50	0				
Walker (2006)	4	25	75	0				
Walker (2008)	3	33	0	67	3	0	67	33
Damanpour and Schneider (2009)	1	100	0	0				
Teodoro (2009)	4	100	0	0				
Bhatti et al. (2010)	2	0	100	0				
Fernández and Wise (2010)	3	67	0	33	1	100	0	0
Hansen (2010)	5	80	20	0				
Jun and Weare (2010)	3	100	0	0				
Total number of tests	37				9			
Weighted support score %		62	30	8		22	67	11
Unweighted support score %		54	38	8		33	59	8

likely to marginally underestimate this relationship (weighted 53 per cent and unweighted 46 per cent) compared with all of the studies, whereas using the actual number of employees (Moon and Bretschneider, 2002; Boyne et al., 2005; Damanpour and Schneider, 2006, 2009; Teodoro, 2009; Fernández and Wise, 2010) increases the level of the weighted support score (64 per cent, unweighted 57 per cent).[9]

Table 2 also presents the results for slack resources. The support score results do not indicate a positive or a negative association between slack resources and the adoption of innovation in local governments. The weighted support score for a positive relationship was 22 per cent and fell to 11 per cent for a negative association. This leaves the balance of scores at nearly two thirds, suggesting non-significant relationships (67 per cent weighted, 59 per cent unweighted). This is in contrast to the line of reasoning that slack resources provide the capacity and space to bear the costs of innovation and experimentation. There are a number of possible explanations for this contrast, including that the number of studies measuring slack resources may be too small. In addition, different approaches were used to operationalize slack, ranging from simple budget surplus (Fernández and Wise, 2010) to a ratio against nationally determined spending guidelines (Walker, 2008). These results raise questions about the importance of measurement consistency.

An analysis of the effect of administrative capacity on the adoption of innovation is presented in Table 3. The findings for administrative capacity show a positive simple majority. The 62 per cent positive weighted support score (58 per cent unweighted) strongly supports the role of this variable as an antecedent of process innovation. All of the measures are of the number or proportion of staff as a ratio of administrators or supervisors over other personnel, or a portion of staff dedicated to a particular task or function. The exception is for Moon and Bretschneider (2002), who used a perceptual measure that included financial, personnel and managerial capacities. Thus, there is some consistency in

Table 3: The influence of administrative capacity on the adoption of process innovations

	N	+	ns	−
Damanpour (1987)	3	67	33	0
Moon and Bretschneider (2002)	3	100	0	0
Boyne et al. (2005)	1	0	100	0
Kwon et al. (2009)	1	0	100	0
Bhatti et al. (2010)	1	100	0	0
Fernández and Wise (2010)	1	100	0	0
Jun and Weare (2010)	1	100	0	0
Morgan (2010)	2	0	100	0
Total number of tests	13			
Weighted support score %		62	38	0
Unweighted support score %		58	42	0

Table 4: The influence of organizational learning on the adoption of process innovations

	N	+	*ns*	−
Bingham (1978)	5	20	40	40
Damanpour (1987)	2	50	50	0
Brudney and Selden (1995)	2	50	50	0
Damanpour and Schneider (2006)	3	100	0	0
Walker (2008)	3	0	100	0
Teodoro (2009)	4	50	50	0
Total number of tests	23			
Weighted support score %		45	45	10
Unweighted support score %		48	45	7

the approach to measurement across the articles reviewed here. The evidence implies that a larger number of managers in an organization provide capacity and play an important role in providing leadership and coordination in the pursuit of process innovation.

The relationship between organizational learning and the adoption of innovation is presented in Table 4 (operationalized as level of professionals employed and external communication, environmental scanning and involvement in professional organizations). The weighted support scores point towards a positive association with 45 per cent of the aggregate support scores tending in this direction.[10] Although the balance of evidence leans towards no significant relationship, indicating neither a positive nor a negative association between organizational learning and the adoption of innovation, scores near 50 per cent do indicate that a variable is likely to play an important role beyond chance alone (Boyne, 2002). This finding suggests that organizations that engage in social interaction through collaborative action tend to practice organizational learning, which has positive consequences on the adoption of innovation.

External antecedents

An analysis of the technical environment was undertaken for studies that examined need, wealth and urbanization (Table 5). Nine of the studies examined included a measure of deprivation or poverty, producing a relatively low positive weighted support score of 28 per cent (unweighted 21 per cent). Five of the studies included measures of community wealth and produced similar support scores: 29 per cent weighted and 40 per cent unweighted. Finally, four studies included urbanization as an external antecedent of innovation, prompting lacklustre results with a weighted support score of 30 per cent and an unweighted score of 38 per cent.

Table 5: The influence of urbanization, deprivation and wealth on the adoption of process innovations

	Urbanization				Deprivation				Wealth			
	N	+	ns	–	N	+	ns	–	N	+	ns	–
Bingham (1978)					8	25	62	13				
Boyne et al. (2005)	1	0	0	100	1	0	100	0				
Damanpour and Schneider (2006)	3	33	67	0	3	0	100	0	3	100	0	0
Walker (2006)					4	0	100	0				
Walker (2008)					4	50	50	0				
Damanpour and Schneider (2009)	1	0	100	0	1	0	100	0				
Kwon et al. (2009)									3	0	100	0
Bhatti et al. (2010)									1	100	0	0
Fernández and Wise (2010)												
Hansen (2010)	5	20	80	0	5	0	80	20	5	0	100	0
Morgan (2010)					2	0	100	0				
Jun and Weare (2010)					5	100	0	0	2	0	100	0
Total number of tests	10				32				14			
Weighted support score %		30	60	10		28	66	6		29	71	0
Unweighted support score %		38	37	25		21	75	4		40	60	0

It is possible that measurement is, once again, an important factor influencing these results. Measures of deprivation varied widely, ranging from indices of multiple measures of deprivation (Walker, 2006, 2008), to the poverty rate taken from the US census (Morgan, 2010) to the 'unemployment rate (the full-time unemployed as a percentage of the municipal population of working age)' (Hansen, 2010, 11). These tap different dimensions of deprivation, such as income and activity in the labour market. Similar variation exists in the operationalization of wealth. Urbanization is slightly more consistent in that studies measure either population density (Boyne et al., 2005), with larger numbers indicating more urban local governments, or the percentage of inhabitants in a municipality within a city (Hansen, 2010). Until more researchers can agree on and implement consistent measurement, it is likely that the lack of reliability and validity of measures will continue to produce inconsistent findings.

DIRECTIONS FOR FUTURE RESEARCH

Independent effects on internal antecedents

The evidence base that generated the presumption that size matters for process innovation was developed in technology-driven models. The technological imperative presumes that process innovations follow product innovations and are associated with more-mature organizations that have moved beyond the search for effectiveness to efficiency gains that stem from internal administrative, managerial and organizational changes (Abernathy and Utterback, 1978). The applicability of technological models of innovation is increasingly questioned because local governments are more likely to adopt innovations from other sectors that can be intangible (Barras, 1986; Miles, 2005; Damanpour et al., 2009). Although future studies can now more convincingly argue that larger organizations – associated with more-complex and diverse facilities – are more readily able to adopt process innovation, new theory and research is required that examines the dynamics of the adoption of process innovations in larger public organizations.

Aspects of this theoretical elaboration may come from examining process innovation types. Innovation types can have different relationships with antecedents. Organizational process innovations focus on basic work activities, structures, strategies and administrative processes, whereas technological process innovations relate to the organizations' production systems or service operation in relation to providing services to users. Damanpour's (1987) study of libraries is an example of a study that included an examination of technological process innovation, and it found a positive association with slack resources. Further theoretical and empirical work could examine the relationship between slack financial resources and technological process innovation. Another fruitful area to examine could be e-government, a growing area of research in its own right (Moon, 2002; Jun and Weare, 2010). For example, new IT hardware and software is expensive and, as such, innovation in this field, as opposed to the adoption of administrative and organizational practices, may require organizations to make substantial investments. Indeed, longstanding enquiry into this field may address such questions relatively quickly.

The budgeting processes of public organizations lend additional weight to this proposition. Most public organizations work on annualized budgeting cycles based on patterns of previous expenditure and the need for the support of higher political authorities. Typically, organizations that develop financial slack are not rewarded, but rather may be punished for 'under spending'. Consequently, the level of slack resources available in public agencies would be expected to be low and only contribute towards the adoption of innovation in limited ways. This may have resulted in largely non-significant results. Thus, the circumstances of public organizations may be at odds with much of the evidence on this topic, typically derived from the management literature (Bourgeois, 1981). However, as Fernández and Wise (2010) noted, innovation requires that costs be implemented, whereas future improvements are only promised. Further research is necessary to unpack the role of slack in studies on local government.

Building on the notion that differing antecedents will engage in varying relationships with innovation types, it is possible that administrative capacity will be more important in organizational process innovations. In public organizations, administrative capacity represents a critical area of 'slack' because public agencies can build slack in human resources more readily than in dollar terms (see above). The adoption and implementation of organizational innovations is likely to be more successful in organizations with a larger cadre of managers that can be diverted from other projects to focus on innovation without adversely affecting the day-to-day operation of the organization, including the delivery of services to the public. For example, Bhatti *et al.* (2010) looked at new organizational forms and Fernández and Wise (2010) studied personnel reforms. Both identified a positive association with administrative capacity. Furthermore, these innovations are concerned with motivating and rewarding staff, strategy and structure and the core tasks of organization and management that are accorded to managers, which creates a stronger association with the successful adoption of innovation.

Administrative capacity is also likely to be important in ancillary organizational process innovations. Kwon *et al.* (2009) and Morgan (2010) examined innovative approaches to local economic development that required local governments to work with other organizations; private sector firms in this case. The networking literature also points to the resource intensity of managing across organizational boundaries, and the ways in which doing so can take managers away from immediate and core organizational issues (Agranoff, 2007).

Joint effects on innovation antecedents

All of the studies examined in this review test for the independent effects of internal and external antecedents on the adoption of process innovations. A number of areas present themselves for empirical exploration. For example, it would be possible to examine whether larger organizations have the internal capacity to develop administrative volume and engage in organizational learning practices that systematically work across organizational boundaries to create the climate for change and innovation. One aspect of organizational learning – environmental scanning – points towards the joint effects of organizational environments and internal capacities. Managers who undertake environmental scanning may be better able to judge the technical environment their organization faces through an understanding of how it influences them, thereby responding to these pressures. Although it is possible that size may correlate with these other variables, they are conceptually distinct and empirical studies would serve to clarify such relationships.

Non-linear relationships

The bulk of the innovation evidence on the technical environment assumes a linear relationship between the pressures that emanate from the social-economic or political content. Only two of the studies included in the sample examined here explored these relationships; thus, it was not possible to apply the support score method (Walker, 2008; Jun and Weare, 2010). If the relationship between the environment and adoption were linear, it would imply increasingly greater external pressures, which would result in ever-higher levels of innovation adoption, the limits to which are noted above.

Empirical effort should be directed towards examining non-linearities with an inverted-U shape. Very low levels of need in the external environment will not place sufficient pressure on an organization to innovate. As the scale and diversity of need accumulates, organizations will read the external environment and begin to implement innovations to meet the demands. However, as pressures grow, the context becomes too demanding and organizations, while seeking to maintain service levels, find it very difficult to innovate. The downward slope of the inverted-U shape is likely to be found in turbulent technical environments, which are typified by uncertainty, complexity and change on change, all of which stifle attempts at innovation (Buganza et al., 2009). The proposed non-linear relationship points towards moderate levels of need being positively associated with the adoption of process innovations. A similar argument can be made for munificent environments. The reviewed evidence points towards some support for wealth as a driver of innovation. However, in situations of very high wealth, there is unlikely to be an incentive for public organizations to innovate because services are less likely to be required. Future research could examine where these tipping points occur.

Finally, it is noted in the review section that the relationship between size and innovation adoption may not be non-linear. Future studies should include a quadratic size term to ascertain whether there is an optimal size for an organization looking to develop process innovations.

Structural contingency theory

The aforementioned questions are largely empirical, and must be located within a framework. Suggested theories have included open system theories, which posit organizations as adaptive systems that introduce change to function effectively, and the resource-based view of the firm (Scott, 2003; Bryson et al., 2007; Damanpour et al., 2009). However, it has been proposed that a longstanding paradigm – the structural contingency theory – be applied to these questions of innovation (Qiu et al., 2011). At the centre of this theory is the notion of fit. Fit between structure and key contingencies results in higher performance. Innovation is an outcome designed to assist in achieving fit, and it drives higher levels of organizational outcomes by embodying adaptation to new circumstances put in place to ensure that high performance is attained. In moving towards goal achievement, organizations respond to contingencies in the environment. Seminal management research on the contingency theory has examined technology, tasks, strategy and size (Burns and Stalker, 1961; Woodward, 1965; Thompson, 1967; Child, 1975; Miles and Snow, 1978). While these studies were of firms, there is a public sector local government focused tradition that includes research from the Institute for Local Government Studies at the University of Birmingham in the 1970s (Greenwood *et al.*, 1975; Greenwood, 1987). A second illustration of a contingency framework applied to local government is Miles and Snow's (1978) strategy framework. Miles and Snow argued for fit between strategy content, structure, process and external context. For example, an innovative prospecting strategy was associated with decentralised structures, incremental processes and uncertain environments. Facets of these contingent relationships have been upheld in studies of local government (Greenwood, 1987; Andrews *et al.*, 2012).

Donaldson's (2001) Structural Adaptation to Regain Fit (SARFIT) contingency theory provides a framework that could facilitate the testing of the independent, joint and non-linear suggestions posed above. Figure 1 shows Donaldson's 'organisation in fit' model, adapted to include innovation as a key element in the process of achieving fit and organizational performance. The figure suggests that the relationship between structure and contingency moderates the achievement of acceptable levels of performance. Changes in a contingency or contingencies may upset this relationship. For example, the external context may become less munificent or malleable. Change takes place within the organization, but structures remain unmodified, resulting in misfit and reduced performance. As performance falls to an unacceptable level (real or perceived), the organization must make adaptive changes and a new structure is sought to bring the

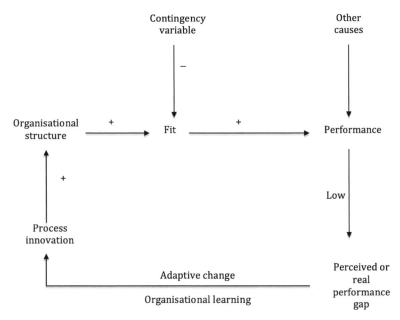

Figure 1: Structural adaptation to regain fit through innovation.
Adapted from Donaldson (2001).

organization back into fit, which restores performance. In seeking to attain fit and acceptable levels of performance, process innovation is implemented (technological e-government innovation or partnerships with external agencies). Innovations lead to change in structure that could include large-scale shifts from mechanistic to organic or subtler changes in organizational size. The mechanisms used to bring about innovations are what Donaldson referred to as adaptive change, but which innovation researchers working on questions of public services innovation have implicitly called organizational learning. Given the strong support score, this review has shown that organizational learning can be conceived of as a variable that mediates organizational responses to changes in contingencies.

Such a model enables innovation scholars to consider and clearly articulate the key contingences that must be studied to better understand the factors resulting in the adoption of innovation in local governments. These factors may be individual effects (such as slack) or joint relationships between internal variables, such as formalization and specialization, or non-linear effects, including variables such as size. Further research from a structural contingency perspective would lead to proposed contingencies between key variables to achieve the adoption of innovation in local governments. It would require researchers to tackle some of the aforementioned questions while extending the range of internal and external antecedents examined. Such work would likely contribute towards innovation configuration frameworks, similar to that proposed by Walker (2008), to assist in advancing the field in this important area.

A range of methods, data and analytical techniques will need to be mustered to tackle these questions within a structural contingency framework. Crisp and clear measurements of the adoption of different types of innovation and antecedents across time and contexts will be needed. This was notable for organizational size. Across all of the studies reviewed, those using the number of employees resulted in higher positive support scores than those using population measures. The number of employees may be less accurate a measure because of practices such as contracting and partnership, which may reduce the number of employees on the payroll. The examination of moderated and mediated relationships will require robust data that can withstand detailed investigation through interactions or regression-based moderation techniques (see Brewer et al. (2012) for an application in public management). If organizational learning mediates an organization's response to a change in contingencies, then future studies may need to use structural equation models to tease out the subtleties in these relationships. In short, research will need to summon a range of social science and analytical techniques to advance this research agenda.

CONCLUSIONS

This article has integrated quantitative studies of the antecedents of innovations in local government. The search rubric uncovered seventeen articles that were analysed by the support score technique, recording the proportion of statistically significant relationships in multiple regression models and thereby controlling for other variables (Rosenthal, 1991; Boyne, 2002). The main finding from this review is that internal antecedents matter more than their external counterparts do, and that the internal determinants reviewed – organizational size and administrative capacity – are particularly important explanatory variables.

The findings of this review must be tempered by the limitations of the small size of the dataset and the geographical distribution of the examined studies. Notable here was that twelve of the seventeen studies were located in the US, indicating a strong orientation towards studies conducted in the US. Thus, the artifacts of the structure, politics and varying organizational forms of local government – special purpose districts and small multiple purpose organizations – together with a tradition of non-professional management, may influence the findings.

The directions for future research as initially developed reaffirmed the importance of some key arguments from the literature such as in relation to organizational size, while pointing towards likely variations in internal antecedents and different process innovation types. Theory and evidence, often from the management literature, has suggested that the capacity for innovation is likely to come through slack resources. However, administrative capacity is more likely to be an important concept for public organizations. The importance of joint effects was highlighted as a way to further draw out important relationships and inconsistencies between antecedents, and arguments were made about the non-linear effects of the technical environment. Future research on the antecedents of innovation adoption in local governments can build on these propositions as long as the work is located within structural contingency frameworks that identify the potential relationships between variables and have the capacity to tease out causal relationships. Such frameworks should be tested across a range of innovation types (service, process and intra- and inter-organizational), differing sectors and localities and in studies designed to obviate or reduce concerns about causality and measurement bias.

NOTES

1 This emphasis on process innovations in public organizations can be seen in the local government studies reviewed here – only three studies examining service innovations were uncovered in the literature search, an insufficient number for review.

2 Adoption is used throughout the remainder of this article to infer adoption and implementation.

3 For a review of radical and incremental innovation in the public sector, see Osborne and Brown (2005).

4 More than thirty internal antecedent variables were identified in conducting this review. Those included were considered in at least four of the studies examined.

5 I am grateful to one of the anonymous reviewers for suggesting the value of the organizational learning literature.

6 At least four studies examining a variable applied the same decision rule to internal and external antecedents.

7 In the case of Hansen (2010), an organization is the unit of analysis, but the actual empirical research is undertaken on managers, with each manager representing a unit of local government.

8 Population is used because the size of a local government's labour force will vary by the population being served, given that they have statutory responsibilities to provide a given range of services.

9 Two studies are excluded from this sub-analysis: Damanpour (1987) used budget and Bingham (1978) did not report how size was measured.

10 These results are not unduly affected by the two different approaches to the operationalization of organizational learning. Sub-analysis shows that the three articles used measures of employees (qualification or full-time) and three professional activities. They had support scores of 44 and 45 per cent, respectively.

REFERENCES

Abernathy, W. J. and Utterback, J. (1978) Patterns of Industrial Innovation. *Technology Review*, June–July: pp40–47.

Agranoff, R. (2007) *Managing within Networks*, Washington, DC: Georgetown University Press.

Aiken, M. and Alford, R. R. (1970) Community Structure and Innovation: The Case of Public Housing. *American Political Science Review*, 64:3 pp843–64.

Aiken, M. and Hage, G. (1971) The Organic Organization and Innovation. *Sociology*, 5:1 pp63–82.

Andrews, R. and Boyne, G. A. (2011) Corporate Capacity and Public Service Performance. *Public Administration*, 89:3 pp849–908.

Andrews, R., Boyne, G. A., Law, J. and Walker, R. M. (2005) External Constraints on Service Standards: The Case of Comprehensive Performance Assessment in English Local Government. *Public Administration*, 83:4 pp639–56.

Andrews, R., Boyne, G. A., Law, J. and Walker, R. M. (2012) *Strategic Management and Public Service Performance*, Basingstoke: Palgrave Macmillan.

Armbruster, H., Bikfalvi, A., Kinkel, S. and Lay, G. (2008) Organizational Innovation: The Challenge of Measuring Non-Technical Innovation in Large-Scale Surveys. *Technovation*, 28:4 pp644–57.

Armstong, H. W. and Taylor, J. (2000) *Regional Economics and Policy*, Oxford: Blackwell.

Balla, S. J. (2001) Interstate Professional Associations and the Diffusion of Policy Innovations. *American Politics Research*, 29:3 pp221–45.

Barras, R. (1986) Towards a Theory of Innovation in Services. *Research Policy*, 15:2 pp161–73.

Berry, F. S. (1994) Innovation in Public Management: The Adoption of Strategic Planning. *Public Administration Review*, 54:4 pp322–30.

Bhatti, Y., Olsen, A. L. and Pedersen, L. H. (2010) Administrative Professionals and the Diffusion of Innovations: The Case of Citizen Service Centres. *Public Administration*, doi: 10.1111/j.1467-9299.2020.01882.x.

Bingham, R. D. (1978) Innovation, Bureaucracy, and Public Policy: A Study of Innovation Adoption by Local Government. *The Western Political Quarterly*, 31:2 pp178–204.

Boer, H. and During, W. E. (2001) Innovation, What Innovation? A Comparison between Product, Process, and Organizational Innovation. *International Journal of Technology Management*, 22:1 pp83–107.

Borins, S. (1998) *Innovating with Integrity: How Local Heroes are Transforming American Government*, Washington, DC: Georgetown University Press.

Bourgeois III, L. J. (1981) On the Management of Organizational Slack. *Academy of Management Journal*, 6:1 pp29–39.

Boyne, G. A. (2002) Public and Private Management: What's the Difference? *Journal of Management Studies*, 39:1 pp97–129.

Boyne, G. A., Gould-Williams, J. S., Law, J. and Walker, R. M. (2005) Explaining the Adoption of Innovation: An Empirical Analysis of Management Reform. *Environment and Planning C: Government and Policy*, 23:3 pp419–35.

Boyne, G. A. and Meier, K. J. (2009) Environmental Turbulence, Organizational Stability, and Public Service Performance. *Administration and Society*, 40:8 pp799–824.

Brewer, G. A., Walker, R. M., Bozeman, B., Avellaneda, C. N. and Brewer Jr, G. A. (2012) External Control and Red Tape: The Mediating Effect of Client and Organizational Feedback. *International Public Management Journal*, 15:3 pp288–314.

Brudney, J. L. and Selden, S. C. (1995) The Adoption of Innovation by Smaller Governments: The Case of Computer Technology. *American Review of Public Administration*, 25:1 pp71–85.

Bryson, J. M., Ackermann, F. and Eden, C. (2007) Putting the Resource-Based View of Strategy and Distinctive Competencies to Work in Public Organizations. *Public Administration Review*, 67:5 pp702–17.

Buganza, T., Dee'Era, C. and Verganti, R. (2009) Exploring the Relationship between Product Development and Environmental Turbulence: The Case of Mobile TLC Services. *The Journal of Product Innovation Management*, 26:3 pp308–21.

Burgess, P. M. (1975) Capacity Building and the Elements of Public Management. *Public Administration Review*, 35:6 (Supplement) pp705–16.

Burns, T. and Stalker, G. M. (1961) *The Management of Innovation*, London: Tavistock.

Camison-Zornoza, C., Lapiedra-Alcami, R., Segarra-Cipres, M. and Boranat-Navarro, M. (2004) A Meta-Analysis of Innovation and Organizational Size. *Organization Studies*, 25:3 pp331–61.

Child, J. (1975) Managerial and Organizational Factors Associated with Company Performance, Part 2: A Contingency Analysis. *Journal of Management Studies*, 12:1 pp12–27.

Daft, R. L. (1978) A Dual-Core Model of Organizational Innovation. *Academy of Management Journal*, 21:2 pp193–210.

Daft, R. L. and Becker, S. W. (1978) *The Innovative Organization*, New York: Elsevier.

Damanpour, F. (1987) The Adoption of Technological, Administrative, and Ancillary Innovations: Impact of Organizational Factors. *Journal of Management*, 13:4 pp675–88.

Damanpour, F. (1990) 'Innovation Effectiveness, Adoption and Organizational Performance' in M. A. West and J. L. Farr (eds) *Innovation and Creatively at Work. Psychological and Organizational Strategies*, London: Wiley, pp125–41.

Damanpour, F. (1991) Organizational Innovation: A Meta-Analysis of Effects of Determinants and Moderators. *Academy of Management Journal*, 34:3 pp555–90.

Damanpour, F. (2010) An Integration of Research Findings of Effects of Firm Size and Market Competition on Product and Process Innovations. *British Journal of Management*, 21:4 pp996–1010.

Damanpour, F. and Evan, W. E. (1984) Organizational Innovation and Performance: The Problem of 'Organizational Lag'. *Administrative Science Quarterly*, 29:2 pp392–409.

Damanpour, F. and Gopalakrishnan, S. (2001) The Dynamics of the Adoption of Product and Process Innovations in Organizations. *Journal of Management Studies*, 38:1 pp45–65.

Damanpour, F. and Schneider, M. (2006) Phases of the Adoption of Innovation in Organizations: Effects of Environments, Organization and Top Managers. *British Journal of Management*, 17:2 pp215–36.

Damanpour, F. and Schneider, M. (2009) Characteristics of Innovation and Innovation Adoption in Public Organizations: Assessing the Role of Managers. *Journal of Public Administration Research and Theory*, 19:3 pp495–522.

Damanpour, F., Walker, R. M. and Avellaneda, C. N. (2009) Combinative Effects of Innovation Types and Organizational Performance: A Longitudinal Study of Service Organizations. *Journal of Management Studies*, 46:4 pp650–75.

Donaldson, L. (2001) *The Contingency Theory of Organizations,* Thousand Oaks, CA: Sage.

Downs, A. (1967) *Inside Bureaucracy*, Boston: Little, Brown.

Edquist, C., Hommen, L. and McKelvey, M. D. (2001) *Innovation and Employment: Product versus Process Innovation*, Cheltenham: Edward Elgar.

Ettile, J. E., Bridges, W. P. and O'Keefe, R. D. (1984) Organization Strategy and Structural Differences for Radical versus Incremental Innovation. *Management Science*, 30:4 pp682–95.

Fernández, S. and Wise, L. R. (2010) An Exploration of Why Public Organizations 'Ingest' Innovations. *Public Administration*, 88:4 pp979–98.

Gallouj, F. and Weinstein, O. (1997) Innovation in Services. *Research Policy*, 26:4–5 pp537–56.

Greenwood, R. (1987) Managerial Strategies in Local Government. *Public Administration*, 65:2 pp295–312.

Greenwood, R., Hinnings, C. R. and Ranson, S. (1975) Contingency Theory and the Organization of Local Authorities. Part I: Differentiation and Integration. *Public Administration*, 53:1 pp1–23.

Hage, J. and Aiken, M. (1970) *Social Change in Complex Organizations*, New York: Random House.

Hansen, M. B. (2010) Antecedents of Organizational Innovation: The Diffusion of New Public Management into Danish Local Government. *Public Administration*, doi: 10.1111/j.1467-9299.2010.01855.x.

Ingraham, P. W., Joyce, P. G. and Donahue, A. K. (2003) *Government Performance: Why Management Matters*, Baltimore: John Hopkins University Press.

Jun, K.-N. and Weare, C. (2010) Institutional Motivations in the Adoption of Innovations: The Case of E-Government. *Journal of Public Administration Research and Theory*, doi 10.1093/jopart/muq020.

Kimberly, J. R. and Evanisko, M. (1981) Organizational Innovation: The Influence of Individual, Organizational, and Contextual Factors on Hospital Adoption of Technological and Administrative Innovations. *Academy of Management Journal*, 24:4 pp679–713.

Knight, K. E. (1967) A Descriptive Model of the Intra-Firm Innovation Process. *Journal of Business*, 40:4 pp478–96.

Kwon, M., Berry, F. S. and Feiock, R. C. (2009) Understanding the Adoption and Timing of Economic Development Strategies in US Cities Using Innovation and Institutional Analysis. *Journal of Public Administration Research and Theory*, 19:4 pp967–88.

Light, P. C. (1999) *Sustaining Innovation. Creating Nonprofit and Government Organizations that Innovate Naturally*, San Francisco: Jossey-Bass.

Meyers, A. D. and Goes, J. B. (1986) Organizational Assimilation of Innovation: A Multilevel Contextual Analysis. *Academy of Management Journal*, 31:4 pp897–923.

Miles, I. (2005) 'Innovation in Services' in J. Fagerbery, D. Mowery and R. N. Nelson (eds) *The Oxford Handbook of Innovation*, Oxford: Oxford University Press.

Miles, R. E. and Snow, C. C. (1978) *Organizational Strategy, Structure, and Process*, London: McGraw Hill.

Mohr, L. B. (1969) Determinants of Innovation in Organizations. *American Political Science Review*, 63:2 pp111–26.

Moon, M. J. (2002) The Evolution of E-Government among Municipalities: Rhetoric or Reality?. *Public Administration Review*, 62:3 pp424–33.

Moon, M. J. and Bretschneider, S. (2002) Does the Perception of Red Tape Constrain IT Innovativeness in Organizations? Unexpected Results Form a Simultaneous Equation Model and Implications. *Journal of Public Administration Research and Theory*, 12:2 pp273–91.

Moon, M. J. and deLeon, P. (2001) Municipal Reinvention: Managerial Values and Diffusion amongst Municipalities. *Journal of Public Administration Research and Theory*, 11:2 pp327–51.

Morgan, J. Q. (2010) Governance, Policy Innovation, and Local Economic Development in North Carolina. *Policy Studies Journal*, 38:4 pp679–702.

Newman, J., Raine, J. and Skelcher, C. (2000) *Innovation and Best Practice in Local Government*, London: The Stationery Office.

Niskanen, W. (1971) *Bureaucracy and Representative Government*, Chicago: Aldine-Atherton.

Osborne, S. P. and Brown, K. (2005) *Managing Change and Innovation in Public Service Organizations*, London: Routledge.

Perry, J. L. and Kraemer, K. L. (1978) Innovation Attributes, Policy Intervention, and the Diffusion of Computer Applications among Local Governments. *Policy Sciences*, 9:2 pp179–205.

Pettigrew, A., Ferlie, E. and McKee, L. (1992) *Shaping Strategic Change*, London: Sage.

23

Pollitt, C. and Bouckaert, G. (2004) *Public Management Reform*, Oxford: Oxford Univ. Press.

Qiu, J., Donaldson, L. and Lou, B. N. (2011) The Benefits of Persisting with Paradigms in Organizational Research. *Academy of Management Perspectives*, 26:1 pp93–104.

Rashman, L. and Radnor, Z. (2005) Learning to Improve: Approaches to Improving Local Government Services. *Public Money and Management*, 25:1 pp19–26.

Rashman, L., Withers, E. and Hartley, J. (2009) Organizational Learning and Knowledge in Public Service Organizations: A Systematic Review of the Literature. *International Journal of Management Reviews*, 11:4 pp463–94.

Rogers, E. M. (1995) *Diffusion of Innovations*, New York: Free Press.

Rosenthal, R. (1991) *Meta-Analytic Procedures for Social Research*, London: Sage.

Salge, T. O. and Vera, A. (2009) Hospital Innovativeness and Organizational Performance: Evidence from English Public Acute Care. *Health Care Management Review*, 34:1 pp54–67.

Schilling, M. A. (2005) *Strategic Management of Technological Innovation*, New York: McGraw Hill.

Scott, W. R. (2003) *Organizations: Rational, Natural, and Open Systems*, Thousand Oaks, CA: Sage.

Teodoro, M. P. (2009) Bureaucratic Job Mobility and the Diffusion of Innovations. *American Journal of Political Science*, 53:1 pp175–89.

Thompson, J. D. (1967) *Organizations in Action*, New York: McGraw-Hill.

Van de Ven, A. H., Polley, D. E., Garud, R. and Venkataraman, S. (1999) *The Innovation Journey*, Oxford: Oxford University Press.

Walker, J. (1969) The Diffusion of Innovation among the American States. *American Political Science Review*, 63:4 pp880–99.

Walker, R. M. (2003) Evidence on the Management of Public Services Innovation. *Public Money and Management*, 23:2 pp93–102.

Walker, R. M. (2006) Innovation Type and Diffusion: An Empirical Analysis of Local Government. *Public Administration*, 84:2 pp311–35.

Walker, R. M. (2008) An Empirical Evaluation of Innovation Types and Organizational and Environmental Characteristics: Towards a Configuration Framework. *Journal of Public Administration Research and Theory*, 18:4 pp591–615.

West Jr, C. T. and Schwenk, C. R. (1996) Top Management Team Strategic Consensus, Demographic Homogeneity and Firm Performance: A Report of Resounding Nonfindings. *Strategic Management Journal*, 17:7 pp571–76.

Wolfe, R. (1994) Organizational Innovation: Review, Critique and Suggested Research Agenda. *Journal of Management Studies*, 31:3 pp405–31.

Woodward, J. (1965) *Industrial Organization: Theory and Practice*, Oxford: Oxford University Press.

Wu, J., Ma, L. and Yang, Y. (forthcoming) Innovations in the Chinese Public Sector. Typology, Distribution, and Characteristics. *Public Administration*.

Zaltman, G., Duncan, R. and Holbek, J. (1973) *Innovation and Organizations*, New York: Wiley.

Abstract

Innovating to improve public service is regarded as potentially obligatory, not merely laudable, part of good public management. However, the moral content of an obligation to innovate is not well understood. How can we innovate ethically? In academic bioethics and research ethics, the obligatory nature of the 'research imperative' is discussed and criticized. In this article, I outline the content of what I call the 'innovation imperative' and draw a parallel between the innovation imperative and the research imperative, arguing that the ethical principles that govern innovation in public service are similar to those governing research imperative in bio-medical sciences.

THE INNOVATION IMPERATIVE

An analysis of the ethics of the imperative to innovate in public sector service delivery

Sara R. Jordan

Sara R. Jordan
Department of Politics & Public Administration
University of Hong Kong
Hong Kong
Hong Kong SAR

Citizens, their representatives and other clients of public services, such as immigrants or public servants in other nations, rely on public officials to improve their service delivery strategies to satisfy the demanding goals of today's state. In recent years, innovation has come to be the symbolic term to describe excellence in service delivery, product improvement or public value engagement efforts in both the public and private sectors (Borins, 2008). However, change, or innovation, is more than merely a laudable goal, supererogatory act or felicitous outcome of high-performing agencies' managers. Innovation is a form of applied research into improvements to the provision of public goods, particularly when coupled with the tasks of gathering and analysing performance data to judge the efficacy of the service changes, whether for the clients or for cost saving efforts. Within the public sector, quality improvement and innovation have become unwritten duties of public employees. What is the content of this duty and from when does this obligation come? And how might the discharge of this duty be policed, *ex ante,* by ethical principles?

Few critics offer a sustained and explicit challenge to the assumption that innovation *ought* to be pursued by public agencies. Instead, the importance of innovation is as given. Arising from the debates on how to make government 'not the problem' or how to make government 'good' or 'better', innovation proponents suggest that the demands of making public business more efficient, or the pressures of technological change, or the obligations of a responsive bureaucracy in a democracy are a de facto obligation of public servants (Walters, 2008). In making sweeping claims for innovation as integral to public performance, proponents of innovation, often unwittingly, make the subsidiary claim that an obligation to innovate ought to override other considerations, such as protecting citizens from the consequences of policy failures. If innovation is a scientific (or even pseudo-scientific) process of experimentation and evaluation to fulfil an objective, particularly an objective with myriad causal paths, then failure is a likely outcome of many experiments. And, failures are risky and costly.

Unfortunately, by advocating innovation as a normal part of everyday public service, those that champion innovation and those that dismiss it as merely an example of conventional practice inadequately capture the problems that can attend efforts to innovate. While lauding the benefits of innovation, it appears that some scholars have been dazzled by the promises of innovation to the point that possible positive changes are presumed to support the employment of almost any means necessary to achieve change (Osborne and Gaebler, 1992). As Kobrak points out, few works on innovation and entrepreneurship touch willingly upon the *failures* that must inevitably bedevil a sincere attempt at innovation (1996: 211–12, see also Ireland *et al.*, 2003; Luke *et al.*, 2010). Further, other scholars suggest that innovation is a 'calculative practice linked to performance management systems and effective/efficient achievement of outcomes', thus arguing that innovation does not describe a practice that is any different than ordinary good management in public organizations, thus contending that innovation is a non-issue that scarcely merits separate attention (anonymous reviewer, 2013). Instead, hearkening back to the founding debates on government performance (e.g. the Brownlow Report), innovation is merely change in the processes of government production that is incumbent upon good government.

If innovation is excellence in the ordinary practices of government, then what might explain the increase in scholars' advocacy of an 'innovations approach' or the establishment of the Innovations in American Government Awards and related programmes (Hartley, 2008: 167–71; Santos-Farah and Spink, 2008)? In this article, I outline how, if the obligation to innovate were to become an 'innovation imperative' as is seemingly pointed to in the scholarly literature of governance and public management for the practice of public service, what might be the source of this imperative and what ethical principles might govern its deployment?

I borrow the phrase 'innovation imperative' from the bioethics and research ethics literature that makes a claim for a 'research imperative' or an obligation of clinical health professionals to conduct research to find the best, most scientifically valid, treatment options for an individual patient's or public's health condition. The argument that there is a clinical duty to conduct research based upon a duty to rescue and that the derogation of this duty renders a professional morally complicit in evil acts, such as promoting suffering and untimely deaths of others, gives the research imperative its imperative structure. Starting with the heroic assumption that the discussion of innovation in public service literature has as its purpose the advocacy of innovation in street-level bureaucracy and that this advocacy has an imperative structure like the research imperative, then a failure to innovate would be a dereliction of duty and that an achievement of innovation without prior ethical considerations would also be a dereliction of duty.

In this paper, I address two interrelated problems that bedevil public sector innovation – the innovation imperative and principles for innovation in public organizations. I present a critique of the innovation imperative on the grounds that this is only an imperfect obligation of public managers, rooted in a particular conceptualization of the role of bureaucracy in a democracy. Through this critique, I outline the problems of the innovation imperative, examining the rhetoric, ideology and tentative arguments for this imperative to show that the obligation to innovate is ethically weak. I also show how the links between the innovation imperative in government service and the research imperative in biomedicine overlap in important ways that point toward a set of ethical principles that ought to govern efforts to innovate in public sector service provision. Importantly, however, I do not present an argument from the basis of empirical evidence that 'bureaucrats behave this way', where this way means that they feel pressured to conform to an innovation imperative. I describe the nature of the innovation imperative as related to the research imperative, show an example of a public service experiment (described as innovative) that had unintended and negative consequences (urban and rural income maintenance experiments in the United States) and then discuss how the rules governing biomedical researchers' up-take of the research imperative might potentially govern public managers' and public management scholars' inclination to the innovation imperative.

THE RESEARCH IMPERATIVE AND THE INNOVATION IMPERATIVE

Arguments for innovation in public administration and management do not often state the case in life or death terms, but instead describe innovation in laudatory terms that are normatively rich in positive connotations. Described as 'heroic' (Bernier and Hafsi, 2007; Borins, 2008), tied to government 'legitimation' (Klein *et al.*, 2010: 1), 'motivated by social and political goals, which are often numerous, varied and difficult to quantify' (citations removed, Bernier and Hafsi, 2007: 489), positively associated with 'national economic growth' and causal for both 'economic and non-economic benefits' (Luke *et al.*, 2010: 138), public sector innovation is proposed as the critically necessary element to contemporary survival and flourishing of states and citizens. Some scholars, in both public management and medical ethics, even describe innovation and entrepreneurship and the associated imperatives to pursue both of these as part of the quest for the 'Holy Grail' (c.f. Annas, 1996; Schay, 1993).

That modern public and private professionals work in a tangled web of presumed imperative obligations is not a new idea. Medical professionals, particularly medical researchers, are argued by bioethicists and lay observers alike to have an imperative obligation to research. An imperative obligation to engage in research is an expectation, based upon a strong notion of moral duty − such as stems from the supposed moral 'duty to rescue' − that members of the medical research field *must* engage in research that alleviates suffering of present and future patients. As Devolder and Savulescu contend in their argument for an imperative for scientists to engage in 'cloning for the purposes of research and therapy' and for policy makers to create a regulatory environment that allows this research to proceed with minimum restrictions, 'declarations, laws and policies that prevent or retard this [therapeutic stem cell cloning] research may prove in the future to have been a death sentence to our children' (2006: 19). They make the case that failure to engage in this research − widely heralded as cutting-edge innovation − or establishment of policy barriers that prevent research entrepreneurs from pursuing the clinical and commercial application of this research would render scientists and policy makers morally complicit in all deaths that could have, hypothetically, been prevented from occurring if these innovations had been permitted and undertaken. Public management scholars who laud innovation should be cautious to note the instrumentalist logic and strong teleological tenor of Devolder and Savulescu's argument; are public managers complicit in citizens' deaths if they do not innovate in service delivery? A closer examination of the concept of the research imperative may provide some clues for answering this question.

The research imperative

'To what extents can we go ethically with sets of humans, animals or tissues to produce a beneficial therapy for other humans?' is a central question for medical research ethicists. Noted bioethicist Paul Ramsey introduced the phrase 'research imperative' to the literature in his 1976 debate with Richard McCormick on the morality of allowing children (and other persons whose autonomy is compromised) to participate in non-therapeutic medical research. The research imperative, he describes, stems from the 'view of the necessity sometimes claimed for non-therapeutic research with uncomprehending subjects' (Ramsey, 1976: 21). Ramsey described research with children as one of a range of '"borderline situations" in which moral agents are under the necessity of doing wrong for the sake of the public good … it is immoral not to do the research. It is also immoral to use children who cannot themselves consent and who out not to be presumed to consent to research unrelated to their treatment' (Ramsey, 1976: 21). This view still permeates arguments for medical research today, but has extended to cover situations beyond non-therapeutic research with compromised participants to cover arguments for advancing high-technology research such as embryonic stem-cell research and human cloning research.

Reflecting on Ramsey's early formulation and Daniel Callahan's extensive analysis of Ramsey, Wayne and Glass (2010: 375) describe that, 'conceptually, the term [research imperative] entails both a value claim that (legitimate) medical research is an unmitigated good, and a moral claim that it is obligatory to pursue and support'. Wayne and Glass further elaborate that, 'the claim [of the research imperative] is that given the scientific soundness of any given project (in other words, its legitimacy *as* research), medical research is *always* good to pursue. Research that is not good is so only because it is not good medical science' (Wayne and Glass, 2010: 375, n1). In short, the research imperative makes the impetus to conduct research into potentially therapeutic medicines, devices and procedures a non-optional part of being a moral physician or part of a moral society even. This is not a wholly esoteric argument confined to the provinces of bioethical journals. In less philosophical language, some authors have gone so far as to suggest that ordinary citizens – patients – have a moral obligation to enrol in research to improve their lives and the lives of disease co-sufferers, what we may call a research-participation imperative (Harris, 2005). Further still, and important for managers of public health agencies and hospitals, the Affordable Care Act (ACA) (2010) mandates that healthcare institutions engage in 'comparative effectiveness research' to establish which treatment or course of treatments is most efficacious, most 'patient centered' and produces the greatest overall benefits to society (c.f., PCORI or Patient Centered Outcomes Research Institute; PCORI, 2012). Under the aegis of the ACA, health providers have a policy-driven imperative to conduct clinical effectiveness inquiries and health administration research.

Contemporary bioethicist Daniel Callahan, whose research attempts to update thinking on the research imperative, suggests that the research imperative can be described in two formulations – the morally hazardous version and the benign version. The hazardous or strong version, which outlines that research is a non-optional imperative, suggests that:

> The proposed research is called morally obligatory, and it is either said or implied that the chosen research direction is the only or the incontestably superior way to go; its proponents dismiss critics of the research as ignorant, fearful, or biased and make only superficial changes to mollify them; and when the research fails to pan out or is slow in coming, they take that fact to show that more research money is needed to that ethical hand-wringing and groundless anxieties have stood in its way. (Callahan, 2003: 177; quoted in Wayne and Glass, 2010: 375)

The weak or benign version suggests that research is a part of the design science necessary to produce the good life, and that, if we intend to promote a good life, we must promote scientific research as part of it. However, conducting research is not morally necessary for individuals to participate as good partners in the delivery of this good life.

Callahan's distinction between the strong and weak versions of the research imperative highlights a critical point for the definition of an innovation imperative. A strong innovation imperative would imply that it is mandatory – a job condition or code of ethics mandate – for public servants to innovate with service design or delivery. This would also mean that public servants would be mandated to treat public funds as a pool of experimental resources and to envision citizens as a pool of participants in experiments in service design or delivery. Presuming that the goal of public sector innovation is to design 'the one best way', or to develop a basis for generalizeable knowledge and practice, then public sector innovation becomes a type of 'human subjects research'. As I will outline below, there are US federal regulations that have 'exempted' public service delivery experimentation from human research participants protection policies, seemingly paving the way for an innovation pathway to be cut in public sector management, irrespective of the instrumentalism implied in the stronger version of the innovation imperative. Whether an innovation pathway is risk free and whether this public service experimentation should be exempted from ethical oversight is a matter for address in the discussion and conclusion (see also Sugarman, 2012).

Scientific research and innovation

Research and innovation are linked in common speech, often referring to the development of new technology, particularly hardware. These two concepts are also linked through their definitions, philosophies, inputs and outputs. In this section, I explore these links briefly and take up the importance of these links as the argumentative basis for adapting research ethics principles as principles for innovation.

Research is defined by the United States Department of Health and Human Services, in the widely known Common Rule or 'Basic HHS Policy for Protection of Human Research Subjects', as 'a systematic investigation, including research development, testing and evaluation, designed to develop or contribute to generalizeable knowledge' (45CFR46.102(d)). Interpretation of this regulatory definition often hinges on the systematic nature of the research or the conduct of experimental, quasi-experimental, formal or logical inquiries designed to answer questions that have a basis in the physical or social scientific literature. Some scholars in fields such as oral history have argued that their research is not systematic in this way and that their work ought to be excluded from the categories of social scientific or humanities inquiry that are ordinarily governed by the Common Rule.

There is no such clear regulatory definition of innovation in the US regulatory context. The Australian Government, via the Department of Industry, Innovation, Science, Research and Tertiary Education, defines a 'capacity to innovate' as '[a capacity] to create new knowledge, find new ways of doing business, and transform great ideas into great results' (Innovation, n.d). The term innovation can be found in the disciplinary and lay literature associated with everything from products to processes, cars to cosmetics, R&D to management (Daily *et al.*, 2002). In much of the literature on innovation, the concepts of entrepreneurship (Drucker [1986] 1993; Ireland *et al.*, 2003), competitive advantage (Day and Wendler, 1998), leadership (Hitt and Ireland, 2002; McGrath and MacMillan, 2000), opportunity exploitation (Shane and Venkataraman, 2000) and strategic management are used as synonyms (Hitt *et al.*, 2001). Given this background, constructing a singular, rigorous definition of innovation would be beyond the bounds of this article, so I select the definition of the widely cited and widely used (in teaching settings) work of Peter Drucker.

In his 1986 classic, *Innovation and Entrepreneurship*, Drucker links innovation and entrepreneurship in ways that have later been reiterated, explicitly or implicitly, in the innovation literature. Drucker inextricably links innovation and entrepreneurship, 'Entrepreneurs innovate. Innovation is the specific instrument of entrepreneurship. It is the act that endows resources with a new capacity to create wealth. Innovation, indeed, creates a resource' ([1986] 1993: 30). Later, authors such as Shane and Venkataraman uphold the innovation entrepreneurship link with use and creation of resources, but for generating corporate wealth (2000).

Importantly for the exploration of innovation in public organizations, Drucker attempted to define a general theory of innovation and entrepreneurship that goes beyond a model of innovation as the investment of private equity into development of products to promote shareholder value. In Drucker's work, innovation and entrepreneurship are what any good manager does, regardless of their position in private or public organizations. This perspective anticipates by almost a decade the work of public management theorists who argue a similar point (e.g. Borins, 2008).

The link between innovation and amassing resource or wealth surplus is not lost in the supposed translation of innovation from private to public management. The logic of *Reinventing Government* and its predecessor arguments start with an axiomatic principle that entrepreneurship and innovation will lead to gains in wealth, even where wealth is measured as gains in input–output efficiency and thus budget conservation (Osborne and Gaebler, 1992). Nor is the instrumentalism of innovation lost in the transition from private to public management. Innovation is the tool of entrepreneurial leaders –

' "change masters" and "quiet entrepreneurs" who can play a wide gamut of critical roles, such as systems builders, loss cutters, socially conscious pioneers or sensitive readers of cues about the need for strategy shifts. These leaders seek to improve their organizations and recognize, perhaps most significant, "the need to exercise skills in obtaining and using power in order to accomplish innovation"' (Kanter, 1983: 212; quoted in Kobrak, 1996: 218). Control in the deployment of skills and resources is one of the essential skills of entrepreneurial innovation often lauded by innovation scholars. As Dodgson and Gann (2010) point out, innovators, like Thomas Edison, are systematic, meticulous, well organized and focused (2010: 86–112). They are, in a word, scientific about their pursuits. Drucker synthesizes the systematic nature of innovation in the following definition: 'Systematic innovation therefore consists in the purposeful and organized search for changes, and in the systematic analysis of the opportunities such changes might offer for economic and social innovation' ([1986] 1993: 35). Drucker's systematic entrepreneurs engage with the social and economic world in a way that mimics the systematic inquiry paradigm captured in the regulatory definition of research found in 45CFR46.

Scholars of public management are unlikely to take exception with either Druckers' entrepreneurial innovation or an innovation as systematic inquiry perspective, although pressure against 'scientism' may be found from post-modern or post-structuralist schools of thought. Like scientists, however, innovators are also playful, creative and press the boundaries of conventions, seeking opportunities for 'breaking up old, and creating new tradition' (Schumpeter quoted in Dodgson and Gann, 2010: 46). An innovator will prod the boundaries of knowledge, seeking an opportune moment to challenge, then overthrow, the dominant paradigm. Such descriptions are similar to conventional descriptions of the work of natural scientists by philosophers of science, notably Thomas Kuhn and Imre Lakatos. Both of these canon thinkers in the philosophy of science emphasize the importance of boundary spanning, testing heroic assumptions, challenging opportunities systematically and accepting the generative power of failure. What public management scholars might rightfully question though is whether the public sector can tolerate the riskiness of innovation as frequent, even catastrophic failure.

THE INNOVATION IMPERATIVE

Most readers of *Public Management Review* are fortunate to live in a time and location where the situation of supreme emergency will not likely arise. Given the relative peace, prosperity and tranquility of contemporary liberal-democratic life, the strong language of an imperative, such as self-defense in war, seems like so much hyperbole. In a way that only imperfectly captures Kant's use in the formulation of categorical imperative, the term imperative means something that must, without fail, be done to prevent (material or moral) calamity. To the extent we deny our imperative, we risk calumny. In a situation where supreme emergencies do not arise, the moral and empirical drivers for an imperative are weakened. Weak imperatives, however, are what are implied in the instrumentalist language of consequentialist ethics – we risk moral sanction if we do not use the best tools (means) to bring about the best ends. There is not an imperative to do our duty as a causal agent of good, but to do our duty to select from a range of other causal agents (tools) to perform the stated duty in the best way. Public managers are duty bound to use the process of innovation and entrepreneurship as a means to a higher, public good, end. Innovative products or processes are not, in themselves, ends. It is the instrumentalism of descriptions of innovation as a tool for resource creation or enhancement that lend it, in part, the basis for a weakly imperative use.

The overwhelming value ascribed to increases in participation, enhanced services, better use of budgets and streamlining service provisions described by scholars of innovation in public service are not questioned widely. Instead, to innovate in the public sector is seen as a path to an unalloyed good, only held up by fearful, conservative, entrenched interests, recalcitrant politicians and obstinate moralists. In this guise, negative portrayals of procedures, processes or products described as innovative are branded as curmudgeonly, hostile and even evil. Note, for example, the strongly positive language used in this description by Luke, Verreynne and Kearnis:

> Entrepreneurship within the public sector has been presented as a deliberate search for innovative change, the generation of new revenue sources and provision of enhanced service through the involvement of citizens, and on-going innovation to achieve increased efficiency and effectiveness. Other approaches to public sector entrepreneurship in both theory and practice include downsizing staff and operations, refocusing the efforts of existing staff towards purposeful objectives, selling government assets through privatization, operating with a strong customer focus under competitive market forces, and adopting an entrepreneurial role through creative and risk-taking activity versus maintaining an administrative role which aids entrepreneurship within the private sector. (Citations removed; 2010: 39–140)

What might provoke the use of the rhetoric and imperative of innovation? The imperative to innovate might be expressed as a steady drive to change service provisions or product development. The drive to change, however, may be weak and may not constitute an imperative to change that is substantive, indeed the change may be merely a change in vocabulary. However, even these minor changes demonstrate the power of the felt obligation to demonstrate work, movement and competence in the public sector. As such, the innovation imperative may provide a rationale for 'pork projects' that are of doubtful utility, but represent flashy changes that do not seem *prima facie* harmful, which may play a part in a public relations campaign to justify increases in budgets or other resources that may have otherwise been allocated to programmes serving similarly important community values (Callahan, 2003: 3–4). Akin to 'green-washing', claiming a programme is innovative or that a manager is entrepreneurial lends positive normative connotations to the programme or person, even if there is little new or different for either. For example, the ACA promoted the establishment of a quasi-governmental body – PCORI. The purpose of PCORI is to 'Assesses the benefits and harms of preventive, diagnostic, palliative, or health delivery system interventions to inform decision making, highlighting comparisons and outcomes that matter to people'; to be 'inclusive of an individual's preferences, autonomy and needs, focusing on outcomes that people notice and care about such as survival, function, symptoms, and health related quality of life'; in a way that 'incorporates a wide variety of settings and diversity of participants to address individual differences and barriers to implementation and dissemination'; by delivering patients and providers information based upon rigorous research that 'investigates (or may investigate) optimizing outcomes while addressing burden to individuals, availability of services, technology, and personnel, and other stakeholder perspectives'. Although patient-centred outcomes research is heralded as a necessary public innovation, it is scarcely different in scope, method and purpose from and evidence-based medicine (EBM), a strong component of healthcare improvement efforts since the 1990s. Note, for example, the description of EBM by Straus *et al.* (2005):

> Evidence based medicine (EBM) requires the integration of the best research evidence with our clinical expertise and our patient's unique values and circumstances. By *best research evidence* we mean valid and clinically relevant research, often from the basic sciences of medicine, but especially from patient-centered clinical research into the accuracy of diagnostic tests …, the power of prognostic markers, and the efficacy and safety of therapeutic, rehabilitative, and preventive regimens …. By *clinical expertise* we mean the ability to use our clinical skills and past experience to rapidly identify each patient's unique health state and diagnosis, their individual risks and benefits of potential interventions, and their personal circumstances and expectations. By *patient values* we mean the unique preferences, concerns and expectations each patient brings to a clinical encounter and which must be integrated in to clinical decisions if they are to serve the patient. By *patient circumstances* we mean their individual clinical state and the clinical setting (2005: 1).

Reflecting on the terms used in these definitions, there is little apparent difference between PCORI's mandate and the on-going practice of EBM, save for promotion of the former in the ACA and development of a subsequent institution to support its mandate. What gives innovation in public services an imperative character, however, is unclear. One clue lies in the language of innovation. The terms used to describe innovation and entrepreneurship as the cure for ills in public organizations echo the terms used to describe the drive to gain scientific knowledge about, and thus traction over, ill health or poverty. For example, while proponents of the research imperative often use the terms of war to describe the imperative nature of their research – for example the fight against cancer, the battle of the bulge – proponents for innovation and entrepreneurship also use the same language – for example the War on Drugs, the

War on Poverty, combating fraud, waste and abuse. As Wayne and Glass point out, echoing the lament of William James in his classic 'The Moral Equivalent of War' (1995), using the language of war is a powerful rhetorical device used by proponents of research to justify the instrumentalist view of medicine as a weapon used to combat a powerful enemy, damn the consequences (2010: 377). Does this a scholar's use of the language of support the idea of an innovation imperative? Or, does combat rhetoric cloak instrumentalism or provide cover for public management scholars or bureaucrats themselves to promote the same performance initiatives they have always undertaken in stronger terms?

Instrumental logic and the logic of imperatives

The imperative to innovate is not well supported by combat rhetoric; emotive appeals to the novelty of change do not by themselves justify changes to programmes that have potential adverse consequences for individuals enrolled in those programmes or those that are indirect participants (community members) in those programmes. A true imperative to innovate must be upheld by serious philosophical arguments. Two potential sources for supportive arguments include the arguments of pragmatists for engagement and experimentation in democracy and the arguments of ethicists, like James Rachels, and other proponents of the 'rule of rescue', who posit that failing to act to improve or save lives is as morally reprehensible as taking them. In this section, I examine both of these potential arguments.

For most people living in liberal-democratic nations, government services are not only one part of a good life, they are an absolute necessity for the good life. Consider, for example, arguments for the moral importance of the ACA, which places healthcare (and by extension health insurance) at the centre of a dignified life. However, provision of government services alone is insufficient – services must be democratically approved, liberally allocated and democratically sanctioned. The democratic, deliberative impulse in public services provision includes a significant pragmatist and experimental mindset. As described by some of the pragmatist philosophers of democracy, like John Dewey, whose works heavily influenced the American schools of thought in public administra-tion and public management, public services should be infused by a spirit of bold experimentation chastened by the participation of an educated, civic-minded and enlightened public. The participation of the public in demanding, orchestrating and reviewing public service provision is critical, as democratic participation is both a source of ideas for innovation, a source of evidence of innovation efficacy and a legitimating force for approving innovation. Innovations that do not meet the test of democratic legitimacy may be rightfully rejected as technocratic domination or, depending on the success of the programme or process, waste and abuse. While the spirit of pragmatism in public service provision provides a basis for conducting experimentation and developing or implementing innovations in a democracy, arguments based upon the Rule of Rescue provide some principled basis for innovations as promoting the moral principle of beneficence. The rule of rescue, coined by Jonsen in 1986, describes an 'imperative to rescue identifiable individuals facing avoidable death, without giving too much thought to the opportunity cost of doing so' (quoted in McKie and Richardson, 2003: 2407). The sentiment to rescue without appreciation of the consequences to oneself is motivated by a psychological imperative based on a 'shock-horror' reaction that is motivated also by a '"sense of perceived duty", "a perceived duty", "an ethical imperative", or a "powerful human proclivity"' (McKie and Richardson, 2003: 2411). This rule of rescue is used by proponents of the research imperative to argue that research that has the possibility to save lives, whether they are identifiable or not, must be done, lest those who had the capacity and opportunity to perform the research with rescue potential be held morally liable for their acts of omission.

James Rachels argued that those with the means and opportunity to provide benefits to others at no excessive costs to themselves could be held morally blameworthy if they fail to marshal those resources or exploit those opportunities. For example, if a researcher has a hypothetical cure for drug-resistant tuberculosis, but fails to pursue that research or provide others qualified to pursue that research with the hypothesis, because she/he feels that drug-resistant tuberculosis is not a disease that would produce the most publications or opportunities for blockbuster drug patents, then she/he could be held morally blameworthy for the failure to act. Following the logic of Rachels' arguments, as Devolder and Savalescu make clear:

> To fail to do beneficial research can be as wrong as doing harmful research. Imagine that a scientific team, after 10 years, develops a cure for a disease that kills 100,000 people per year. Imagine that for one year, the team fights over who will have what fraction of the profits. As a consequence, the release of the drug is delayed by one year. Those scientists are as responsible for those deaths as if they had killed those sick people. (2006: 12)

Apropos of the link made between research and innovation above, the duty to rescue means that to fail to innovate when one has a reasonable chance to do so and there is a reasonable possibility of success, even in a long-term future, then the person who does not innovate could be held to be morally complicit in the suffering and deaths of those the innovation could have helped. Arguments could be made that the degree of moral complicity that public service innovators have for failing to implement change is low; public servants who fail to pursue a line of programmatic change that could help others due to concerns about professionalism, such as overreaching rather than boundary spanning, may only be remote material complicit in the deaths of those who did not receive the help. As Brown describes:

> remote material complicity attaches if one or more intermediaries stand in the causal pathway between those who cooperate and those who engage in wrongdoing. If those intermediaries block aid and

encouragement to morally wrong actions or practices, then a responsibility firewall has been erected that shields cooperators from culpable material complicity; if on the other hand, they intermediaries convey or amplify the effects of material cooperation and these effects are foreseeable, then material complicity is transmitted regardless of the length or complexity of the causal network. (2009: 5)

In other words, if public servants intentionally block innovations, whether by word or deed, which could assist others to avoid premature deaths or suffering, then they are complicit in wrongdoing and should be held morally blameworthy for failing to heed the innovation imperative.

How might public employees avoid the stink of moral complicity in hypothetical deaths by innovating, but do it in a way that does not risk instrumentalizing the lives of those who would be part of the process of testing the feasibility of innovations in the public setting? It is to this matter – how to ethically innovate – that I now turn.

ETHICS AND THE INNOVATION IMPERATIVE

As described above, innovation is a laudatory term used by scholars of public management and politicians alike to describe their aspirations for public service change. Although innovation may be a rhetorically useful term to cover ordinary practices of governing change in public institutions, it is important to explore the ethical ramifications of public service change. Ethical exploration is important because change can produce both winners and losers or those who accept undue risks for change and those who may be granted benefits unwittingly that are sullied by the harms done to those who risked their own safety and health for innovation. Ethical exploration is also important in the case of innovation as it involves purposive action that intervenes on the lives of individuals who may not have the knowledge or understanding of the full effects of what changes in service provision may mean to their livelihoods. As such, innovation may entail uses of power that need to be checked against the possibility of abuses, *ex ante* by ethical principles and *ex post* by democratic processes. In simple terms, public sector innovations are experiments with the provision of public services conducted with citizens as the participants, funders and beneficiaries of the service innovation. Unfortunately, innovation, like research, can both succeed or fail, and failed or successful innovation produces costs, risks and benefits whose just allocation must be considered.

Since innovation is risky and can produce harms and benefits, it ought to provoke ethical concerns for public management scholars. However, if we do not engage in innovation or research projects, we cannot ascertain whether existing programmes or treatments are as safe as possible or as efficacious as possible. Like research with human participants, a situation under which researchers must demonstrate to a research ethics committee that the research is reasonably safe and beneficial, innovation presents a quandary to public servants who must validate to their superiors, both elected officials and citizens, that their projects and proposals are reasonably safe. And, problematically, in the case of both research and innovative public service projects, it is not possible to *ex ante* insure safety or success.

Devolder and Savulescu summarize well the quandary of regulating the safety of research, a type of innovation:

> What research turns up may be very different from what is promised. But it may be very important nonetheless. There is an important distinction between the regulation of research and the formation of social policy and law. Research should be prevented only if it harms people or exposes them to unreasonable risks. We must do the research, then form the policy on the basis of the results, not in advance of them, not in prediction of them, and not in fear of them. Scientific research is like trying to pick the winner of a horse race. There can be favorites, but one can never know in advance which horse will win. The race has to be run. (2006: 19)

The core problem of ethically managing public sector innovation becomes: if we are obligated to run the race of public sector innovation, how might we do so without exposing the public to unacceptable risks, whether those risks are costs to public finance, service continuity or to the lives of individual participants?

To govern the implementation of the imperfect duty to innovate, I suggest that public managers turn to the ethical principles governing research with human participants. However, managers must ensure that they do not lose sight of the object of innovation as merely a tool to an ideal end of better service. As public sector innovation is applied research, or in more technical terms, a form of translational research that moves the techniques of basic research to the 'bedside', I add that the principles of patient care in a patient-centred outcomes environment ought to motivate the conduct of ethical innovation in public services. I outline below how principles of medical research and practice form a sound basis for an ethics of innovation for bureaucrats in a democracy.

THE PRINCIPLES OF ETHICS FOR BIOMEDICAL RESEARCH AND PRACTICE

Within the research ethics literature, a few principles for governance of human participants research stand out, which govern the intersection of biomedical practice and research. For example, Beauchamp and Childress, in their classic text *Principles of Biomedical Ethics*, list five principles, which are consistent across other normative biomedical ethics texts, such as the Belmont Report, the Nuremburg Code and the Council for International Organizations of Medical Sciences. These principles are respect for autonomy, Non-maleficence, beneficence, justice and the four principles that support professional–patient relationships (veracity, privacy, confidentiality and fidelity). An exhaustive examination of each of these concepts, which are heavily debated in the bioethics literature, is beyond this article, but a list of these principles and their definitions appears in Box 1 below.

Box 1. Beauchamp and Childress' principles of biomedical ethics

Principles of Biomedical Ethics

Respect for Autonomy: 'To respect an autonomous agent is, at a minimum, to acknowledge that person's right to hold views, to make choices and to take actions based on personal values and beliefs. Such respect involves respectful *action*, not merely a respectful *attitude*' (125). 'The principle of respect for autonomy can be stated, in its negative form, as follows: *Autonomous actions should not be subjected to controlling constraint by others*' (125–6).

Non-maleficence: 'One ought not to inflict evil or harm' (*primum non nocere*) (190).

Beneficence: '*Beneficence* refers to an action done for the benefit of others; *benevolence* refers to the character trait or virtue of being dispose to act for the benefit of others; and *principle of beneficence* refers to a moral obligation to act for the benefit of others' (260). There are two principles of beneficence: '*Positive beneficence* requires the provision of benefits. *Utility* requires that benefits and drawbacks be balanced' (259).

Justice: '... fair, equitable, and appropriate treatment in light of what is due or owed to persons' (327). '*Distributive justice* refers to fair, equitable and appropriate distribution in society determined by justified norms that structure the terms of social cooperation' (327). '*Rectificatory justice*, which refers to just compensation for transactional problems such as breaches of contracts and malpractice ...' (327).

Principles Governing Professional–Patient Relationships

Veracity: 'Veracity can pertain to any truthful and honesty management of information that may affect a patient's understanding or decision-making' (398).

Privacy: '... a state or condition of physical or informational inaccessibility ...' (407), 'Privacy as inaccessibility also extend to bodily products and objects intimately associated with the person, as well as to a person's intimate relationships with friends, lovers, spouses, physicians and others' (408).

Confidentiality: 'Confidentiality is present when one person discloses information to another, whether through words or through an examination, and the person to whom the information is disclosed pledges not to divulge that information to a third party without the confider's permission. In schematic terms, information I is confidential if and only if A discloses I to B, and B pledges to refrain from disclosing I to any other party C without A's consent' (420).

Fidelity: '... the obligation to act in good faith to keep vows and promises, fulfill agreements, and maintain relationships and fiduciary responsibilities' (430). 'Professional fidelity or loyalty has been traditionally conceived as giving the patient's interests priority in two essential respects: (1) the professional effaces self-interest in any conflict with the patient's interests and (2) the patient's interests take priority over others' interests' (431).

Note: Beauchamp and Childress enumerate five principles of biomedical ethics: respect for autonomy, non-maleficence, beneficence, justice and professional–patient relationships. Professional–patient relationships are governed by these four 'sub-principles': veracity, privacy, confidentiality and fidelity.
Source: Adapted from Beauchamp and Childress (1994).

A research-centred perspective on innovation suggests that the ethics of innovation should dovetail with research ethics to establish an ethic for public sector innovation. However, the research ethical principles for innovation must be compatible with the ethical commitments of the context – delivery of goods and services to citizens in a democratic state – if they are to be viable as a corrective to the innovation imperative (Pellegrino, 2008).

Accountability and veracity

The foremost principles of ethical conduct for bureaucrats in a democratic state are accountability, responsibility, respect for the constitution and respect for citizens (Cooper, 2004).[1] As an ethical principle, or a statement that organizes our behaviour towards one another, accountability means to be prepared to answer completely and without hesitation what it is that we, and those individuals who are in our supervision, have done with which resources and for what purpose. In his book *Rethinking Democratic Accountability*, Robert Behn captures well the central question of accountability – 'how will we hold whom accountable for what?' Kobrak synthesizes the sum of Behn's answer to this question as 'elected officials, political appointees, members of the accountability establishment, and yes, citizens too must consider "how empowered, entrepreneurial, responsive civil service can make innovative decisions in a decentralized yet democratic government"' (Behn, 2001: 64; quoted in Kobrak, 2002: 417). Accountability, in this way, is closely linked to the principle of veracity.

As Beauchamp and Childress put it, 'veracity can pertain to any truthful and honesty management of information that may affect a patient's understanding or decision-making' (398). To abide by a principle of veracity, physicians must be prepared to give their patients (clients) all information that is pertinent to their case and their care. This may include information about the risks and benefits of care, of problems and anticipated side effects from treatments and, importantly, information about unforeseen adverse events in care (e.g. medical errors).

Employed as principles for innovation ethics, accountability and veracity mean that public managers should be prepared, as far as their circumstances allow them to do so, to present, truthfully and honestly, information that is relevant for citizens' to engage in informed decision-making about their participation in alternative methods of public service delivery.

Fidelity and bureaucratic responsibility to role and constitution

Calls for responsible government abound, but it is often unclear who should be responding to whom and how. Ultimately, an official is responsible to those who authorize and provide appropriations for her role – elected officials and citizens. To be responsible means to take actions that are causally related to the accomplishment of goals and tasks assigned to a specific role. In the sense that bureaucrats must be responsible to their professional roles, it could be said that they must act with professional fidelity, a principle for ethical medical practice.

Beauchamp and Childress define professional fidelity in the following way:

> Professional fidelity or loyalty has been traditionally conceived as giving the patient's interests priority in two essential respects: (1) the professional effaces self-interest in any conflict with the patient's interests, and (2) the patient's interests take priority over others' interests (431).

In ways that echoes the views on responsibility of later theorists on the responsibility of public officials, Beauchamp and Childress emphasize that responsibility may mean taking as paramount the interests of others over one's self interest. Thompson (1981: 283, n14) points to the definition of role responsibility offered by Hart:

> A 'responsible person', 'behaving responsibly' (not 'irresponsibly') requires for their elucidation a reference to role-responsibility. A responsible person is one who is disposed to take his duties seriously; to think about them, and to make serious efforts to fulfill them. To behave responsibly is to behave as a man would who took his duties in this serious way. (1968: 213)

Thompson describes two types of responsibility for public servants – causal and volitional. Causal responsibility, Thompson argues, can only be weakly ascribed to an official who is but 'a candidate for the ascription of moral responsibility, usually along with many other people'. Weak causal responsibility means that the official must be '*a* cause of an outcome in the sense that the outcome would not have happened but for one's act or omission' (1981: 268). Volitional responsibility is more difficult to describe, given the constraints of the role of officialdom upon any given official. As scholars of the constitutional perspective on public administration ethics, such as John Rohr make clear, the constitution of a state is to be its north star, offering organizing tenets for the good life to which administrators are obligated professionally to imple- ment. To be an ethical administrator, Rohr challenges, the public employee must consider themselves responsible for the institutions enshrined by the constitution and for implementing policies in accord with the normative premises of the constitution. As Rohr astutely summarizes:

> Our religious and philosophical traditions teach us to think of morality in universal terms, but in a world of nation-states, ethics in government means thinking in particularistic terms of what is good for a certain nation and within that nation what is good for certain subdivisions such as states, provinces, cities, towns, counties, communes, boroughs, and so forth. (1996: 549)

The tradition governing a state is its constitution or the source of the 'regime values' that govern the allocation of administrative responsibilities to each of the 'constitutional masters' and the 'common good' as enumerated in the founding document (Rohr, 1988: 171, 175).

Employed as principles for innovation ethics, fidelity and responsibility mean that public managers should refer to their obligations as enumerated in the constitution and public or common law arguments of their state. Where the obligations of public officials are left unspecified by the founding documents, officials should refer to the duties enumerated in the codes of practice of their selected profession (e.g. accountancy) and the codes of ethics for public servants (e.g. ASPA code of ethics). A responsibly innovating public servant should carefully consider the inputs (e.g. funds and personnel) and outputs (e.g. service changes) and outcomes (e.g. client satisfaction) of their proposed changes from the perspective of the founding principles and clients' interests.

Respect for citizens and respect for persons

The *sine qua non* of ethical bureaucracy in a democratic state is the respect of bureaucrats for citizens. The content of 'respect', however, is not well understood. The principle of respect for autonomy, enshrined in each of the codes of ethics for medical research, offers some illustrative guidance.

> To respect an autonomous agent is, at a minimum, to acknowledge that person's right to hold views, to make choices, and to take actions based on personal values and beliefs. Such respect involves respectful *action*, not merely a respectful *attitude*. The principle of respect for autonomy can be stated, in its negative form, as follows: *Autonomous actions should not be subjected to controlling constraint by others.* (Beauchamp and Childress, 125–6)

A perennial question for bureaucratic respect, though, is 'respect for whom'? As described well by theorists of bureaucracy in the United States, for example, bureaucrats have a 'multiple principals problem'. Public servants are doubly accountable to the citizens' elected representatives and responsible to the citizens themselves. In order for bureaucrats to be respectful of citizens, they must be attentive to the autonomous choices of citizens, expressed directly (through street-level contact) or indirectly through policy-makers pronouncements. Respect, however, is not paternalistic; to respect citizens requires that public servants recognize, reflexively, themselves as citizens as well. As Cooper puts it:

> The public administrative role is viewed as derived from that of the citizen, thus making administrators representative citizens, professional citizens, fiduciary citizens, or citizens in lieu of the rest of us. Public administrators hold the role of citizen in trust as they conduct the public business previously done by citizens, but now handed over to professional citizens who have the time, technical training, and resources to carry it out. Their ethical obligations are associated with the good citizen in American society. (2004: 397)

As an ethical principle for innovation, an ideal public manager will respect citizens meaning that she or he will acknowledge the autonomy of citizens to express their views fully in ways that are meaningful to them, and to respond to those expressions attentively, with candour, and with an ear to listen for evidence of impending harm to citizen as citizens and citizens as neighbours and co-creators of the community.

Beneficence, non-maleficence and justice

Beneficence and justice are two principles that are at the heart of both medical care and research and public service. Medical care, medical research and implementation of regulation and other public policies have the potential to both help and harm. For the purpose of this paper, the crux of the ethical problem of innovation is that innovations in public service can cause unforeseen harms.

That innovation invites harm and benefit suggests that a natural principle of ethics for innovation is beneficence or maximizing benefits while minimizing harms. However, stated in its reverse, non-maleficence or the commitment to do no harm, beneficence may be read as a principle that strongly cautions against innovation. Innovation, like science, invites failures and, in the context of public service delivery where harm can be measured as misspending public funds or inadequately delivering a public service, failures invite harm. If non-maleficence is introduced as an ethic of innovation, then public servants are committed to preventing known harms from befalling their organizations or their clients, which may preclude introducing innovative techniques that may, as they are untested, be harmful. Any innovation that could be reasonably expected to affect negatively the health, educational opportunities, economic viability or general welfare of individuals, groups or an entire community should be avoided. If harm to others is a known probability that will arise from a programme, the expected harm must be minimized, according to the associated principle of beneficence as utility, to the lowest possible levels and harms revealed to citizens. Within a democratic government, implementation of policies without the consent, at least the tacit consent vis-à-vis election of representatives, of the governed is impermissible. Public sector innovations should not be implemented without the consent of the governed.

An example where public managers may need to consider the harmful costs of an innovation would be the establishment of programmes to minimize environmental degradation. For example, a deposit-site for recyclable goods within a community serves the laudable long-term goals of recycling programmes – to minimize waste and preserve future resources. However, these long-term goods must be balanced against the long- and short-term costs associated with location of environmental disamenities, such as waste deposit locales.

Public managers must cope with the tradeoffs between short- and long-term goals and innovative programmes or processes will adversely affect the interests of some party, identifiable or hypothetical. To minimize these harms, the principle of rectificatory justice should be considered and harmed individuals duly compensated for harms. But, to implement a programme of compensation, public managers must ensure that the harms claimed by citizens are legitimate and that a regress of harm does not occur, wherein the cure for the ailment perpetuates or compounds the ailment further. In short, ethical innovation requires constant evaluation for ensuring that harm is not done and that justice is perpetuated.

Innovations in public management or health services delivery, as scholars of innovation like Drucker (1986) or Gawande (2008) point out, require continuous evaluation for their efficacy and effects upon cherished principles such as efficiency. Evaluation, however, requires amassing information on the effects of processes or procedures that may include sensitive data about individual clients' lives, needs and feelings. Evaluation of programme innovations, for example video monitoring of home conditions in child welfare programmes, requires significant intrusions into clients' lives and private matters. Client's expectations of privacy in areas not related to programme evaluation and the maintenance of confidentiality standards and agreements should be considered as a matter of fidelity and respect for the autonomous choices of clients to determine which information is used and shared openly. Moreover, in all situations, the respect for clients' autonomous choice to remain in programmes and to contribute data for evaluations should be respected. As Beauchamp and Childress (1994: 125–6) make clear, 'autonomous actions should not be subjected to controlling constraint by others', even if those others seek to control choice for the purpose of such a laudable standard as the public interest.

As an ethical principle for innovation, beneficence obligates public managers to take precautions against any potential harms, to maximize opportunities for benefits, and to ensure that all citizens (and bureaucrats) harmed in the process of implementing innovative programmes are duly compensated according to principles of justice in redistribution.

Taken together, adoption of these principles will not automatically insure public programmes against fraud, waste or abuse. Likewise, designing public programme changes with these principles in mind is not going to ensure that no public manager or client is harmed in the process of programmatic change. As with the principles of research ethics for human participants' research, these principles for ethical innovation in public organizations set out the aspirations according to which the public can expect the conscientious public sector innovator to govern their inquiries.

CONCLUDING REMARKS AND A TRAJECTORY FOR FUTURE RESEARCH

The innovation imperative is the implicit or explicit belief that public servants must engage in innovation or entrepreneurial activity to be considered as doing good and to fulfil the expectations of a bureaucracy in a democracy, even if the innovations implemented are unproven and ultimately cause harm. The innovation imperative shares rhetorical, logical, ideological and philosophical similarities with the research imperative, which is a belief that there is a duty for researchers to conduct research, even with vulnerable populations, if it serves an overriding public good. The shared rhetoric, logic and philosophical foundations of these two imperatives points to a shared group of ethical principles to motivate ethical conduct of innovation in public services.

In this article, I introduced the concept of the innovation imperative in public management and offered an exposition on the possible applications of the logic and ethics of the research imperative in medicine to the situation of ethical innovation in public service. Following the argument offered by Borins (2008), the contours of innovation and the innovation imperative are best studied through two channels – theoretical and empirical. In lieu of a formal conclusion, I propose a number of possible avenues for both below.

Vis-à-vis theoretical research, the concept of the innovation imperative should be more extensively examined from the perspective of public management theory and applied ethical analysis. Public management scholars may explore more fully the contours of the imperative nature of innovation and entrepreneurship in public management theory. A more complete theory of entrepreneurship and performance in public management would ideally include discussion of the imperative to innovate.

From the perspective of applied ethics, a more rigorous examination of the conceptual symmetry between principles of ethics for bureaucrats and ethics for biomedical research should be conducted. Further, an expansion of the range of ethical principles for innovation in public services, possibly originating in the principles appointed for other researcher-practitioners, such as healthcare workers, engineers and educators, would be a profitable expansion to this analysis.

Vis-à-vis an empirical research agenda, additional research into the question 'do bureaucrats behave as if innovation is an imperative?' would advance this area of research markedly. Also, discovery of those areas where the innovation imperative is strongest felt by public managers (e.g. innovating for efficiency, fairness, or efficacy) would begin fruitfully a programme of empirical research into the composition of an innovation imperative. Likewise, an examination of service areas where an innovation imperative is most palpable would point to scholars to a more refined analysis of the concept and its consequences.

Understanding the normative and perceptual contours of innovation, including the views of those on the front lines of innovative projects and struggling to innovate ethically, is the next step in the comprehensive study of innovation in public management.

ACKNOWLEDGEMENT

I would like to thank the organizers of this special issue, members of the faculty at the Maxwell School at Syracuse University, and Phillip Gray for their comments on this paper.

NOTE

1 The content and contestations surrounding each of these terms is voluminous, thus to cut down the volume of conceptual exegesis here, I offer the following definitions, drawn from the work of experts on each of these concepts as a guiding ethical principle for public administrators or public managers.

REFERENCES

Annas, G. J. (1996) Questing for Grails: Duplicity, Betrayal and Self-Deception in Postmodern Medical Research. *Journal of Contemporary Health, Law and Policy*, 12:2 pp297–324.

Beauchamp, T. L. and Childress, J. F. (1994) *Principles of Biomedical Ethics* (4th edn), New York: Oxford University Press.

Behn, R. D. (2001) *Rethinking Democratic Accountability*, Washington, DC: Brookings Institute Press.

Bernier, L. and Hafsi, T. (2007) The Changing Nature of Public Entrepreneurship. *Public Administration Review*, 67:3 pp488–503.

Borins, S. (ed.) (2008) *Innovations in Government: Research, Recognition, and Replication*, Washington, DC: Brookings Institute Press.

Brown, M. T. (2009) Moral Complicity in Induced Pluripotent Stem Cell Research. *Kennedy Institute of Ethics Journal*, 19:1 pp1–22.

Callahan, D. (2003) *What Price Better Health: Hazards of the Research Imperative*, Berkeley, CA: University of California Press.

Cooper, T. L. (2004) Big Questions in Administrative Ethics: A Need for Focused, Collaborative Effort. *Public Administration Review*, 64:4 pp395–407.

Daily, C. M., McDougall, P. P., Covin, J. G. and Dalton, D. R. (2002) Governance and Strategic Leadership in Entrepreneurial Firms. *Journal of Management*, 28:3 pp387–412.

Day, J. D. and Wendler, J. C. (1998) The New Economics of Organization. *The McKinsey Quarterly*, 1:1 pp5–18.

Devolder, K. and Savulescu, J. (2006) The Moral Imperative to Conduct Embryonic Stem Cell and Cloning Research. *Cambridge Quarterly of Healthcare Ethics*, 15:1 pp7–21.

Dodgson, M. and Gann, D. (2010) *Innovation: A Very Short Introduction*, Oxford, UK: Oxford University Press.

Drucker, P. F. ([1986] 1993) *Innovation and Entrepreneurship*, New York: Harper.

Gawande, A. (2008) *Better: A Surgeon's Notes on Performance*, New York: Picador.

Harris, J. (2005) Scientific Research is a Moral Duty. *Journal of Medical Ethics*, 31:4 pp242–8.

Hart, H. L. A. (1968) *Punishment and Responsibility*, 211–30. Oxford, UK: Oxford University Press.

Hartley, J. (2008) 'Does Innovation Lead to Improvement in Public Services? Lessons from the Beacon Scheme in the United Kingdom' in S. Borins (ed.). *Innovations in Government: Research, Recognition, and Replication*, 159–87. Washington, DC: Brookings Institution Press.

Hitt, M. A. and Ireland, R. D. (2002) The Essence of Strategic Leadership: Managing Human and Social Capital. *Journal of Leadership and Organization Studies*, 9:1 pp3–14.

Hitt, M. A., Ireland, R. D., Camp, S. M. and Sexton, D. L. (2001) Strategic Entrepreneurship: Entrepreneurial Strategies for Wealth Creation. *Strategic Management Journal*, 22:Special Issue pp479–91.

Ireland, R., Hitt, M. and Sirmon, G. (2003) A Model of Strategic Entrepreneurship: The Construct and its Dimensions. *Journal of Management*, 29:6 pp963–89.

James, W. ([1910] 1995) The Moral Equivalent of war. *Peace and Conflict: Journal Of Peace Psychology*, 1:1 pp17–26.

Kanter, R.M. (1983) *The Change Masters*. New York: Simon & Schuster.

Klein, P. G., Mahoney, J. T., McGahan, A. M. and Pitelis, C. N. (2010) Toward a Theory of Public Entrepreneurship. *European Management Review*, 7:1 pp1–15.

Kobrak, P. (1996) The Social Responsibilities of a Public Entrepreneur. *Administration & Society*, 28:2 pp205–37.

Kobrak, P. (2002) Review of Rethinking Democratic Accountability by Robert D. Behn. *The American Political Science Review*, 96:2 pp417–18.

Luke, B., Verreynne, M.-L. and Kearins, K. (2010) Innovative and Entrepreneurial Activity in the Public Sector: The Changing Face of Public Sector Institutions. *Innovation: Management, Policy & Practice*, 12:2 pp138–53.

McGrath, R. M. and MacMillan, I. C. (2000) *The Entrepreneurial Mindset*, Boston, MA: Harvard Business School Press.

McKie, J. and Richardson, J. (2003) The Rule of Rescue. *Social Science & Medicine*, 56:12 pp2407–19.

Osborne, D. and Gaebler, T. (1992) *Reinventing Government*, Reading, MA: Addison-Wesley.

PCORI (2012) "About Us". Available at www.pcori.org/about (accessed 10 December 2012).

Pellegrino, E. (2008) *The Pellegrino Reader*, Notre Dame, IN: Notre Dame University Press.

Ramsey, P. (1976) The Enforcement of Morals: Nontherapeutic Research on Children. *The Hastings Center Report*, 6:4 pp21–30.

Rohr, J. A. (1988) Bureaucratic Morality in the United States. *International Political Science Review*, 9:3 pp167–78.

Rohr, J. A. (1996) An Address. *Journal of Public Administration Research and Theory: J-PART*, 6:4 pp547–58.

Santos Farah, M. F. and Spink, P. (2008) 'Subnational Government Innovation in a Comparative Perspective: Brazil' in S. Borins (ed.). *Innovations in Government: Research, Recognition, and Replication*, 71–92. Washington, DC: Brookings Institution Press.

Schay, B. W. (1993) In search of the Holy Grail: Lessons in Performance Management. *Public Personnel Management,* 22:4 pp649–68.

Shane, S. and Venkataraman, S. (2000) The Promise of Entrepreneurship as a Field of Research. *Academic of Management Review*, 25:1 pp217–36.

Straus, S. E., Richardson, W. S., Glasziou, P. and Haynes, R. B. (2005) *Evidence-based Medicine: How to Practice and Teach EBM* (3rd edn), New York: Elsevier.

Sugarman, J. (2012) Questions Concerning the Clinical Translation of Cell-Based Interventions under an Innovation Pathway. *Journal of Law, Medicine, and Ethics*, 40:4 pp945–50.

Thompson, D. F. (1981) 'Moral Responsibility and the New York City Fiscal Crisis' in J. L. Fleishman, L. Leibman and M. H. Moore (eds) *Public Duties: The Moral Obligations of Government Officials*, 266–85. Cambridge, MA: Harvard University Press.

Walters, J. (2008) 'Twenty Years of Highlighting Excellence in Government' in S. Borins (ed.) *Innovations in Government: Research, Recognition, and Replication*, 13–27. Washington, DC: Brookings Institution Press.

Wayne, K. and Glass, K. C. (2010) The Research Imperative Revisited: Considerations for Advancing the Debate Surrounding Medical Research as Moral Imperative. *Perspectives in Biology and Medicine*, 53:3 pp373–87.

Abstract

Health care organizations are often confronted with multiple institutional logics. In this study, a longitudinal case study method was used to gain insights into the adoption decision-making and implementation process of an apparently hybrid innovative practice when multiple logics are present. The case study focuses on the adoption and implementation of 'Productive Ward: Releasing Time to Care' in a Dutch hospital. This is a quality improvement programme developed by the National Health Service (NHS) in the United Kingdom. The results show that institutional logics complicate the adoption and implementation process.

MULTIPLE INSTITUTIONAL LOGICS IN HEALTH CARE

'Productive Ward: Releasing Time to Care'

Judith van den Broek, Paul Boselie and Jaap Paauwe

Judith van den Broek
Institute of Health Policy and Management
Erasmus University Rotterdam, Rotterdam
The Netherlands
Department of Human Resource Studies
Tilburg University, Tilburg
The Netherlands

Paul Boselie
Utrecht School of Governance (USG)
Utrecht University, Utrecht
The Netherlands

Jaap Paauwe
Department of Human Resource Studies
Tilburg University, Tilburg
The Netherlands
Department of Applied Economics
Erasmus University Rotterdam, Rotterdam
The Netherlands

INTRODUCTION

As a result of developments in their sector, public organizations are being confronted with competing values (Van der Wal *et al.*, 2011). The health care sector is a striking example of a public organizational field where multiple values and demands are at play. Hospitals in many countries are confronted with the challenge to simultaneously enhance the quality and reduce the costs of care. One of the drivers of this development in the Netherlands is the 2006 health care act, forcing Dutch hospitals to consider the cost aspects of care. These developments are also taking place in other countries, such as New Zealand and the United Kingdom. In these countries, New Public Management-inspired reforms are restructuring health care (Doolin, 2001). Bekkers *et al.* (2011: 9) illustrate this by referring to the health care sector when discussing the 'introduction of a stronger market orientation' (9). In addition, Noordegraaf (2007: 773) notices that 'businesslike managerialism' and 'traditional professional values' are being combined in public organizations. From a theoretical point of view, the institutional logics perspective might be used to analyse these developments in public sector organizations such as hospitals (Thornton *et al.*, 2012). Institutional logics can be defined as 'the belief systems and associated practices that predominate in an organizational field' (Scott *et al.*, 2000: 170). Scott *et al.* (2000) observed a shift from dominance of a professional logic to dominance of a managerial logic through market mechanisms in health care. Furthermore, several authors suggest that health care is an organizational field where multiple institutional logics exist (e.g. Reay and Hinings, 2005, 2009), i.e. an institutional complex field. Reay and Hinings (2009) for example show that both professional and business-like logics coexist in a Canadian health care system. It is expected that in hospitals, physicians and nurses might be acting in accordance with a professional logic that emphasizes the quality of care, while managers and directors might take on a more business-like logic, which is mainly occupied with efficiency (Ruef and Scott, 1998).

Several researchers conclude that research is needed to increase our knowledge about the ways in which organizations respond to multiple institutional logics (e.g. Greenwood *et al.*, 2011; Lounsbury, 2007). While research has been undertaken to explore the adoption and implementation processes of innovations in the health care sector (e.g. Greenhalgh *et al.*, 2004; Jespersen *et al.*, 2002), the adoption and implementation of innovative practices from a multiple institutional logics perspective is still relatively unexplored. Therefore, this study aims to contribute to the existing knowledge by studying the adoption and implementation of an apparently hybrid practice in a context where multiple institutional logics are at play.

In the literature, several clues are provided that make it likely that institutional complexity affects innovation adoption and implementation. First of all, the linkage between logics and practices is well established; organizational practices are seen as manifestations of institutional logics (Greenwood *et al.*, 2010; Lounsbury, 2007). In addition, logics are expected to determine the appropriateness of practices (Greenwood *et al.,* 2011). Moreover, it is expected that institutional logics affect organizational decision-making by steering the attention of decision-makers (e.g. Ocasio, 1997; Thornton, 2002). For example, Thornton (2002) expects that when one logic is dominant, the attention of decision-makers is directed towards issues and practices consistent with this logic. This makes us wonder what would happen when an organization experiences multiple logics. Adoption and implementation could result in possible tensions, contradictions and ambiguities, because different organizational stakeholders will be influenced by different logics. This study combines the innovation and the institutional logics perspective to study the adoption and implementation of an innovative practice in an institutional complex context where both business-like and professional logics are expected to be present, namely the health care sector. More specifically, we focus on the innovative practice 'Productive ward: Releasing Time to Care', which in its appearance is a hybrid practice combining the business-like (productive ward) and professional (releasing time to care) logic. We use the institutional logics perspective as our prime theoretical focus, because we aim to address public sector developments from a different perspective and thereby add to the debate on health care management and governance.

The research question of this study is 'How does the presence of multiple logics affect the adoption decision-making and implementation process of an innovative practice in health care?' By focusing on multiple institutional logics, this study extends public management, innovation and institutional logics research.

To explore these issues, a longitudinal case study of 'Productive Ward: Releasing Time to care' in a Dutch hospital was performed. First of all, this article will proceed with theoretically embedding this study in the literature and introducing the context. After describing the methods, the results of the study will be presented. This will be followed with a discussion of the results and concluding remarks.

THEORETICAL FRAMEWORK

Institutional logics

The institutional logics perspective represents a research stream within new institutionalism (Friedland and Alford, 1991). While new institutionalism is being criticized for the limited attention for agency in studying organizations, the institutional logics perspective emphasizes the role of actors (e.g. Thornton *et al.,* 2012). As Scott *et al.* (2000: 170) state: 'Institutional logics refer to the belief systems and associated practices that predominate in an organizational field'. Greenwood *et al.* (2010: 2) explain that 'logics underpin the appropriateness of organizational practices in given settings and at particular historical moments'. Research on this topic has for example focused on the ways institutional logics can guide the attention of organizational decision-makers (Ocasio, 1997) and paid attention to shifts in dominant logics in organizational fields (e.g. Scott *et al.,* 2000; Thornton and Ocasio, 1999).

Thornton *et al.* (2012: 4) state that 'individuals and organizations, if only subliminally, are aware of the differences in cultural norms, symbols, and practices of different institutional orders and incorporate this diversity into their thoughts, beliefs and decision making. That is, agency, and the knowledge that makes agency possible, will vary by institutional order'. Markets and professions are examples of institutional orders (Thornton *et al.*, 2012). Often organizations experience multiple and sometimes conflicting institutional logics (Pache and Santos, 2010; Thornton and Ocasio, 2008). Research on this topic shows how organizations respond to and manage competing institutional logics (e.g. Pache and Santos, 2010; Saz-Carranza and Longo, 2012). Pache and Santos (2010) explain that organizations in organizational fields that are moderately centralized and highly fragmented are most likely to experience multiple institutional logics. Research (e.g. Reay and Hinings, 2009; Scott *et al.*, 2000) shows that health care is highly fragmented, i.e. that health care organizations are dependent on a high number of actors with possibly different logics (Pache and Santos, 2010). Also, this field appears to be moderately centralized because there is a dual authority structure, with public authorities and health care professionals as central actors (Pache and Santos, 2010). Therefore, it is expected that health care organizations are confronted with multiple institutional logics. In addition, Greenwood *et al.* (2011) state that in hospitals many different occupations are present that are likely to be influenced by different logics and that hospitals should be able to balance professional and business goals in order to be perceived as legitimate. Several authors indicate shifts in institutional logics in the health care field from a professional logic to a business-like logic. In addition, it is acknowledged that multiple institutional logics might coexist (e.g. Kitchener, 2002; Reay and Hinings, 2009; Ruef and Scott, 1998; Scott *et al.*, 2000). According to Kitchener (2002), the professional logic entails that 'legitimacy was judged against criteria of prestige and the technical quality of the services provided' (391). Goodrick and Reay (2011) emphasize that autonomy is an important aspect of a professional logic. The core aspects of the professional logic are high quality of care, sufficient time to spent directly on patients and autonomy (e.g. Goodrick and Reay, 2011; Kitchener, 2002). Alternatively, the business-like logic ascribes importance to practices that could lead to cost reduction (Raey and Hinings, 2009).

Competing or compatible institutional logics

Based on their review of empirical studies on institutional complexity, Greenwood *et al.* (2011: 332) conclude that most studies implicitly assume that logics are 'inherently incompatible'. This is illustrated by their own definition of institutional complexity as situations where organizations are confronted with 'incompatible prescriptions from multiple institutional logics' (318).

However, there are indications that multiple logics can coexist and maybe even be combined within an organization or an organizational practice: so-called hybrids (e.g. Battilana and Dorado, 2010; Dunn and Jones, 2010; Goodrick and Reay, 2011).

A hybrid organization is an organization that combines different institutional logics (Battilana and Dorado, 2010). Next to the hybridization of an organization, it is also possible that organizational practices become hybridized, i.e. that multiple logics will be combined within one practice. An example of a hybrid innovative practice in the health care context is the clinical management role implemented in health care organizations (e.g. Kirkpatrick *et al.*, 2009). 'Productive Ward: Releasing Time to Care' also appears to be such a hybrid practice.

Innovation

Scholars define innovation in several ways (Crossan and Apaydin, 2010). These definitions all emphasize a newness aspect, primarily in terms of new to the organization that adopts it. For example, Damanpour (1991) defines innovation as 'adoption of an internally generated or purchased device, system, policy, program, process, product, or service that is new to the adopting organization'(556). In their review on innovation in health care, Länsisalmi *et al.* (2006) define innovation as 'the intentional introduction and application within a role, group, or organisation, of ideas, processes, products or procedures, new to the relevant unit of adoption, designed to significantly benefit the individual, the group, or wider society' (67). Very early on, Schumpeter (1934) distinguished product innovation (a new good), process innovation (a new production method), market innovation (opening of a new market), input innovation (new source of input) and organizational innovation (new organization or industry). Another well-known distinction is that between technological and administrative innovations. Technological innovations refer to product, process and service innovations, whereas new procedures, policies and organizational forms can be regarded as administrative innovations (Damanpour and Evan, 1984; Damanpour, 1991). In this article, the definition of Damanpour (1991) is adopted. Therefore, 'Productive Ward: Releasing Time to Care' is viewed as an innovation, because it is a new practice for the adopting hospital. This innovation can be characterized as an administrative innovation, because it represents a new way for hospitals to enable nurses to make changes in their wards. Because little is known about the role of multiple logics in innovation processes of these types of innovations, the focus of this article will be on the role of multiple institutional logics in the adoption and implementation phases of this innovative practice. We use these phases as a heuristic framework to guide our research.

Institutional logics and the innovation adoption decision process

Adoption of an innovative practice can be defined as 'the decision to make full use of an innovation as the best course of action available' (Rogers, 2003: 177). According to the rational economic perspective, organizations will adopt innovations based on information about their contribution to performance. This perspective explicitly takes into account the role of human agency and strategic choice in adoption decision processes (Child, 1972). Alternatively, research indicates that institutional logics could also influence adoption decisions. As Ocasio (1997) explains, institutional logics are capable of guiding the attention of organizational decision-makers to specific issues and affect decisions. This means that organizational actors convert the logics into action. Thornton (2002) and Goodrick and Reay (2011) support this view by explaining that logics play an important role in steering the attention of organizational actors. Goodrick and Reay (2011: 375) state that 'logics shape individual and organizational practices because they represent sets of expectations for social relations and behavior. A core assumption is that the interests, identities and values of individuals and organizations are embedded in logics and provide the context for decisions and outcomes'. Therefore, institutional logics could play an important role in the adoption process by steering the attention of actors towards innovations that fit with their logic.

In public management literature, the distinction is made between logic of consequence and logic of appropriateness. The logic of consequence emphasizes the efficiency and effectiveness of innovations (Bekkers et al., 2011; Bekkers and Korteland, 2008). In this view, adoption decisions are rational decisions based on balancing the cost and benefits of the innovation (Korteland, 2011). This logic shows many similarities to the rational economic perspective explained above. The logic of appropriateness emphasizes legitimacy and trustworthiness (Bekkers et al., 2011; Bekkers and Korteland, 2008). Taking on this perspective, it is believed that the context of the organizations has a tremendous influence on the adoption decisions (Korteland, 2011), which is related to the institutional logics perspective. In this study, the institutional logics perspective will be used to study innovation adoption and implementation, because little research uses this perspective to focus on these processes. The adoption decision-making process might be complicated through the potential conflict between the different logics.

Institutional logics and the innovation implementation process

After the adoption decision has been made, the implementation process follows. The implementation of an innovation can be defined as 'the early usage activities that often follow the adoption decision' (Meyers et al., 1999: 295). Kostova and Roth (2002: 217) distinguish two elements in this response to the adoption decision. First of all, the behavioural element, which is reflected by what they label implementation: 'Implementation is expressed in the external and objective behaviors and the actions required, or implied, by the practice' (217). Second, the attitudinal element, internalization, is the 'internalized belief in the value of the practice' (216) and represents an important predictor of the persistence of an innovation. According to these authors, 'Internalization is that state in which the employees at the recipient unit view the practice as valuable for the unit and become committed to the practice' (Kostova and Roth, 2002: 217). Different combinations of internalization and implementation are proposed. For example, ceremonial adoption is the 'formal adoption of a practice on the part of the recipient unit's employees for legitimacy reasons, without their believing in its real value for the organization' (220). Ceremonial adoption combines a high level of implementation with a low level of internalization. A related concept is decoupling, which can be defined as 'a situation where compliance with external expectations is merely symbolic rather than substantive, leaving the original relations or practices within an organization largely intact and unchanged' (Han and Koo, 2010: 31). Both decoupling and ceremonial adoption refer to the superficial implementation of a new practice, possibly affected by institutional pressures to adopt the practice (e.g. Kostova and Roth, 2002). The presence of multiple institutional logics, both in the institutional context and in the innovative practice, might play an important role in determining the extent to which a new practice becomes implemented in the organization. This adopted practice might be only superficially implemented on the one hand or become actually internalized by organizational actors on the other hand. As Dearing (2009: 504) states, 'often in complex organizations, the users are not the choosers of the innovations. Implementers often subvert or contradict the intentions of the adopters'. This is especially relevant when the organization is confronted with multiple logics, because then it is more probable that the decision-makers will adhere to a different logic than the users of the new practice. For example, in health care organizations decision-makers are often the board members and directors, adhering to a business-like logic, while the users are primarily nurses, adhering to a nursing professional logic. These multiple logics might complicate the implementation process and affect the extent of implementation of innovative practices.

'Productive Ward: Releasing Time to Care'

In order to unravel the adoption and implementation processes of an innovative practice in a institutional complex context, we study a hospital that was among the first to adopt 'Productive Ward: Releasing Time to Care' in The Netherlands. This programme was developed in 2006 by the NHS Institute for Innovation and Improvement in the United Kingdom (NHS, 2010). The core assumption of the programme is that nursing staff organizes their own ward and improve processes themselves. This could increase the amount of time for direct patient care, which would result in a higher quality of care, more satisfied patients and nurses and a decreasing amount of waist. One of the core components of the programme was to enhance the empowerment and autonomy of nurses. Evaluations of the programme in the United Kingdom showed that empowerment of ward staff has increased due to the programme (Lipley, 2009). Empowerment can be defined as 'the psychological state of a subordinate perceiving four dimensions of meaningfulness, competence self-determination and impact, which is affected by empowering behaviours of the supervisor' (Lee and Koh, 2001: 686). Research shows that empowerment is important for positive nursing outcomes, such as retention (e.g. Erenstein and McCaffrey, 2007).

This practice represents an innovative way for Dutch hospitals to initiate changes, by empowering nurses. It is especially interesting to investigate the adoption and implementation of this programme using an institutional logic perspective, because at first glance, the programme seems to combine the multiple logics health care organizations are confronted with. Research shows that communication plays an important role in the implementation of innovations in health care organizations (e.g. Damschroder *et al.*, 2009; Rogers, 2008). In this specific case, the way the programme is communicated throughout the organization refers to multiple institutional logics. That is, the labelling of the programme, 'Productive Ward: Releasing Time to Care', suggests that this could be an example of a hybrid practice that incorporates both the nursing professional logic (Releasing Time to Care) and the business-like logic (Productive Ward).

METHODS

Case study context

The pilot project 'Productive Ward: Releasing Time to Care' in the focal hospital is about implementing the first three modules (of a total of eight) within approximately 9 months in two wards. We decided to focus on this pilot phase, because we expected that the role of institutional logics in the adoption and implementation of the practice manifested itself especially in the early phases of implementation when the innovation is introduced. The first module is called 'Knowing how we are doing', where ward based measures are developed to make better informed decisions. The second module is called 'Well-organized Ward', which is about reorganizing and rearranging the ward. The third module, 'Patient status at a glance', aims to improve patient communication and flow. A project organization was set up to facilitate the implementation process, supported by an external consultancy agency.

This study was performed in a Dutch hospital. Dutch hospitals are not-for-profit organizations. Different types of hospitals (academic, top-clinical and general) exist, each with their own characteristics. The hospital under study is a top-clinical hospital, which performs highly specialized medical care. A two-tier governance model is adopted in these organizations, consisting of a board of directors and an independent board of supervisors. Traditionally, Dutch hospitals have a functional organization structure. However, more and more hospitals are changing their design towards a more process oriented structure (Veld, 2012).

Data collection and analysis

Two in-depth longitudinal case studies were carried out (Yin, 2008), because this enables the in-depth study of a real-life phenomenon and its context, which suits the research question. Both pilot wards are under study to be able to compare these wards.

Several data collection methods were used: semi-structured interviews, focus groups, document studies and observations. First of all, semi-structured interviews were conducted with project leaders, project team members and workgroup members (including ward nurses) from both wards, as well as the hospital director, communication advisor and an external consultant that facilitated the implementation process. In total, fifteen interviews were conducted, of which eight were conducted at the start and seven in the middle of the pilot programme. The key actors in the process were selected, and from each key actor group, one or more respondents were interviewed in order to provide a complete overview of the process from all perspectives. The interview questions primarily focused on the adoption decision process and the implementation process of the programme. Interviews lasted approximately 1.5 hours. Second, at the end of the pilot programme, two focus groups were conducted, in order to collect information on the implementation process with focus group members interacting with each other. One focus group of approximately 2.5 hours was organized for each pilot ward, with seven nurses, internal advisors and managers participating. In addition, relevant documents were analysed, such as the project plan, communication plan, presentations and brochures. Finally, the researcher was able to attend workgroup meetings during the implementation period and the evaluation meeting of the steering group at the end of this period. Observational notes from these meetings were made.

In sum, a multi-actor approach was adopted to generate a complete picture of the process. Multiple data collection methods were used to triangulate the data. Furthermore, a longitudinal research design was used to be able to detect potential changes throughout the process. Three data collection rounds were performed; at the start, the middle and the end of the pilot project.

The collected interview, focus group and document data was analysed using Atlas.ti (ATLAS.ti Scientific Software Development GmbH, Berlin, Germany), following thematic analysis (Braun and Clarke, 2008; Grbich, 1999; Rapley, 2011). First, the researchers familiarized themselves with the data, by transcribing all the interview material and rereading the transcribed material. Second, initial codes were generated, which were used to search for themes. These initial codes formed an initial list of ideas about what information is in the data. As Braun and Clarke (2008) state, these codes 'identify a feature of the data ... that appears to be interesting to the analyst' (88). When searching for initial codes, the research question was kept in mind, but codes were primarily data driven. These initial codes were then organized in broader categories based on repeated patterns across the data set: the themes. In this phase, the analysis was refocused at a broader level and codes were sorted into subthemes and themes. After that, the (sub)themes were reviewed in the light of the coded data extracts. Finally, the themes were defined and renamed. Examples of initial codes were business, economizing, budget, efficiency, productivity and time pressure. These codes resulted in the subtheme business-like logic. The resulting theme, this subtheme, belongs to its multiple institutional logics. In addition, this process of identifying codes, subthemes and themes resulted in the themes communication, labelling, empowerment and internalization. These resulting themes are used to structure the findings section of this article.

FINDINGS

In order to answer the research question, 'How does the presence of multiple logics affect the adoption decision-making and implementation process of an innovative practice in health care?', the main themes derived from the data analysis are used in this section.

Multiple institutional logics

Several respondents refer to the two-sided nature of the programme, including both efficiency and quality of care, when discussing motives for adoption. Respondents from the nursing population as well as managers refer to the multiple logics reflected in the programme.

> Well, one of the reasons to introduce it is finding a way to improve the quality of care. But not only quality of care, also how you can realize efficiency in the ward. (internal guide, ward A)

> Increasing direct patient care, but also working more efficiently...I think how can you use rooms in the best and most efficient way will benefit us. Less walking, and less searching. (senior nurse, ward B)

However, we can also see some differentiation in adoption motives that are mentioned by respondents stemming from different disciplines. First of all, nurses reported to the Nursing Advisory Board that they increasingly experience more work pressure. They feel that many additional administrative tasks are being forced upon them and they do not understand why these tasks, that withhold them from direct patient care, are necessary. The fact that they are unable to spend enough time on direct patient care is perceived as a problem and results in lower job satisfaction.

> Nurses felt that they were almost communicating with the patient via checklists. That is not what nurses want, it is not nice. (Nursing Advisory Board chair)

Due to the fact that administrative tasks are being imposed on nurses, they experience a lack of empowerment. They feel that other people determine how they do their job. This results in a lot of resistance from the nurses when management tries to implement something new. Therefore, the chair of the Nursing Board searched for a programme that would give the control over work to nurses. Exactly the fact that the 'Productive Ward: Releasing Time to Care' is not a top-down change programme, but that nurses are being empowered to reorganize and restructure their ward themselves in order to improve patient care is what appeals to her.

> They [nurses] feel that a lot of work is improper and forced upon them. This causes dissatisfaction and resistance about every innovation and change. (project plan, p. 3)

> If you talk about innovation in health care, it is often top-down or a management tool....employees say nice for you, but we can't work with that. (Nursing Advisory Board chair)

> They [Nursing Advisory Board] were enthusiastic about involving the team in thinking along instead of letting everything come from the top ... I think that will eventually result in a better running hospital. (senior nurse, ward B)

Quality of care, another indicator of the nursing professional logic, is also reflected in reactions from the nursing perspective on the programme.

> That is why the Nursing Advisory Board went looking for possibilities to improve the quality of care, but then for and by nurses. (project plan, p. 3)

> There is nothing worse for a nurse than being unable to do your work right, resulting in lower quality of care. (nurse, ward A)

Besides these indicators that were closely linked to the nursing professional logic, the project plan also reflects a motive that could be linked to the business-like logic.

> The Nursing Advisory Board also wanted to contribute to the strategy of the hospital by looking for more efficient ways of working. (project plan)

The hospital director, who was involved in making the adoption decision, primarily refers to rational economic motives for adoption and shows a more business-like logic. He mentions motives such as working more efficiently.

> More from a business perspective, of course hospitals are confronted with economizing ... We will have to work with the people we have, there will be no additional staff. That means that you will have to work more efficiently. (hospital director)

Next to that, he also refers to problems within the organization that could be improved by the project, such as the high-perceived work pressure and agitation within the wards. Similar to the Nursing Advisory Board chair, he also refers to fact that the programme is a bottom-up implementation that empowers nurses is one of the main reasons for adopting 'Productive Ward: Releasing Time to Care', because this addresses the needs of nurses.

> What I as director find important is that this is a bottom-up innovation. Thus, I only facilitate and steer. They [nurses] are the directors and have to do the project....they embraced the project. (hospital director)

When evaluating the project at the end of the pilot period, the two logics are also represented. The health care manager refers to both logics when expressing his opinion at the end of the pilot.

> It [Productive Ward: Releasing Time to Care] results in better patient care and I believe in the business case of the programme. (health care manager)

The hospital director primary refers to the business-like logic, by stressing the importance of the return on investment to project could generate. In evaluating the pilot, the director emphasizes the importance of whether the investment brings benefits towards the organization in terms of money.

> We started this project with the idea that it is an economic instrument; that you can skip a dayshift because of the project. (hospital director)

On the other hand, a physician and nursing representative evaluating the programme are more drawn towards the implications the programme has for the work and care processes in the ward.

> I think it is special that the project gives something back to people that deliver care, which can't be expressed in financial value. (physician, ward A)

> I consider what the project brings, empowerment of nurses to be of much more importance than that it results is mayor efficiency gains. (nursing representative)

In summary, these findings suggest that 'Productive Ward: Releasing Time to Care' might indeed be perceived by the respondents as a practice that combines nursing professional logics and business-like logics.

Communication and labelling

The labelling and communication of the programme also reflects these multiple logics. The communication of the programme was adjusted to the different audiences within the hospital. The communication plan reveals that different messages were composed to explain the programme, according to the logics of the audiences. The message to the directors and managers is 'Productive Ward is a good way for nurses to structure and organize their work themselves, fitting with the mission and vision of the hospital'. The message to the health care professionals, nurses and physicians, emphasizes the effects of the programme in terms of increased time for patient care, safety and quality of care, which fits well with the professional logic. To illustrate this, the message for nurses of the pilot wards is Productive Ward is the way you, together with your colleagues, can organize your ward in order to eventually again, within the mission and vision of the hospital, have more time for the patient. By organizing the wards well, patient safety and quality of care will improve. The project is not used to economize, it is not the intention to cut back on personnel.

In addition, the labelling of the project appears to be important. The fact that not only the logics of efficiency and productivity side of the project are being emphasized, but also the aspect of 'Releasing Time to Care' is important to engage nurses. The director even prefers not to call it 'Productive Ward', but 'Releasing Time to Care'.

> I thought "Productive Ward" was a difficult label. "Releasing Time to Care" is more friendly and points out the direct customer interest....I prefer that latter name instead of productive ward or enhancing efficiency, because the latter are terms that do not ground easily with that kind of professionals. (hospital director)

The double label of the programme used in the organization, 'Releasing Time to Care: Productive Ward', seems to create some suspicion among nurses. Before the start of the project, when hearing the double label of the programme, nurses were afraid that the time they would save because of the more efficiently organized ward they would create during the project would result in cutbacks on personnel. They thought the programme would be a disguised economizing method. To prevent this perception form becoming an obstacle for implementation, the director guaranteed that any time that would be saved, could be invested in direct patient care, at least in the first year of the project. This reassured nurses and enhanced their commitment to the project.

> It is not only focused on efficiency, also not in its appearance. And it works well that all the time it brings in extra will not be used for economizing. That really creates support among nurses; that they know that if they gain time they don't have to hand it in terms of shifts of hours, but that they can really put it back in patient care. That is very important for them. (internal guide, ward A)

Nevertheless, during the focus groups at the end of the pilot programme, it appeared that the labelling of the programme had some drawbacks. Several respondents, primarily from the nursing discipline, indicate that the label 'Releasing Time to Care' was misleading in the sense that because of this label they expected to see an increase in direct patient time, while in fact there were no large changes observed at the end of the pilot. In the beginning, the project title motivated them, because they presumed direct patient time would be increased. However, the title backfired when nurses did not experience an increasing amount of time they could spend on direct patient time. Moreover, they often were more occupied with rearranging closets and measuring the efficiency of their ward for the project, than actually providing care.

> The name of the project should be different next time. With the current name, wrong expectations are being created. (nurse, ward B)
> However, more time for direct patient care is not visible....The title suggests something else. That is still a struggle for our team. The title suggests that you will have more time for the patients, but you're actually working on organizing your ward well. (senior nurse, ward A)

Empowerment and internalization

While empowerment of nurses is one of the core components of the programme, some ambiguities were revealed. First of all, the implementation process was top-down. While one of the core principles of the project is that nurses are empowered to make their own decisions, the decision to participate in the pilot programme was made by their supervisors.

> If you're going to say that the ward team has influence in such a project, so they can decide for themselves what the ward is going to look like and have control over it, than they should also have that in the choice to participate. (internal guide, ward A)

This might have caused nurses to perceive this project as yet another top-down intervention that they did not choose for, while 'Productive Ward: Releasing Time to Care' was introduced into the organization to empower nurses. The top-down implementation of this project contradicts with this aim and with the autonomy component of the nursing professional logic.

Nurses seemed to appreciate the fact that they were finally able to determine themselves how to organize and change their ward, instead of listening to managers. Nevertheless, internal guides and project leaders notice that it is very difficult for nurses to propose solutions themselves.

> They all say, finally we can decide for ourselves. But you notice that if they just get a plan how to do something that they also find that very convenient. (project leader 2)

This was supported by findings that show that nurses need a lot of support and need to be motivated by the workgroup members to be actively involved in the implementation process. An illustration of this can be found when analysing the events during the summer holiday break. This was a difficult period for both wards to remain working on the project, because a lot of the project members were on holiday. In ward B, the motivation of nurses was extremely low during this period. Nurses were very busy with patient care because of a staffing shortage and did not feel like working on the project. Not many concrete results were visible yet, and they questioned the mertis of investing so much time and effort in the project. Without many project ambassadors on site, it was difficult for them to find the motivation to keep working on the project. This is a clear signal the project was not completely internalized in that ward. Also in other periods during the implementation, nurses did not seem to be very proactive in addressing issues they wanted to improve and much of the project results depended on the work group.

> If we [workgroup] ask nurses to volunteer to participate we get very little response ... I hope that nurses will feel more committed and will come up with topics themselves. And also for example go to a workgroup member and say I see you are working on this topic and I would like to contribute. (internal guide, ward B)

When evaluating the implementation process, committed and enthusiastic ambassadors of the project appear to be crucial. Many respondents express their satisfaction with the project team and workgroup members and the important role they play in successfully implementing the project. They stimulate others by showing a lot of energy and enthusiasm.

> Your workgroup need to be enthusiastic and needs to be able to make the team enthusiastic. (care coordinator, ward A)

During the evaluation of the programme, this observation was confirmed by responses of workgroup members. When discussing whether nurses make use of the opportunity to be involved in decision-making, the reactions of workgroup members point in the direction that this was rarely done.

> When you sit and wait, not much is coming from the ward. (nurse, ward B)

In sum, the findings indicate that institutional logics play an important role during the adoption and implementation of the programme. In the next section, these findings will be discussed.

DISCUSSION AND CONCLUSION

The goal of this study is to unravel the adoption and implementation processes of a new practice when multiple logics are present in both the organizational field and the practice itself.

First of all, the findings verified that the health care organization is indeed being confronted with multiple logics; both the nursing professional logic and the business-like logic are reported by respondents when discussing the 'Productive Ward: Releasing Time to Care' programme.

With respect to the adoption process, some respondents, managers and project leaders as well as nurses, refer to both logics simultaneously when discussing the motives of adoption of the programme. However, we can see that motives related to the nursing professional logic are dominant in the responses of nursing staff, while managers and directors primarily referred to motives related to the business-like logic. Nurses referred to aspects related to improvement in the quality of care and enhancing their own autonomy, while managers primarily mentioned arguments related to the enhancement of efficiency. Similar results were found in the evaluation of the programme. These findings are consistent with the conclusions from other researchers (e.g. Reay and Hinings, 2009).

The labelling and communication of the programme throughout the organizations seemed to play an important role in addressing these multiple logics. More specifically, the project was called 'Productive Ward: Releasing Time to Care' in the hospital, which reflects both logics. Besides that, the communication of the programme was adjusted towards the target audience. This resulted in a description of the programme stressing aspects related to the nursing professional logics, such as quality of care, empowerment and more direct patient care time, when communicating towards nurses. These elements were not explicitly mentioned in communication towards managers. These labelling and communication strategies might explain the appearance of multiple logics in the findings mentioned above. In addition, these results indicate that the programme might be a hybridized practice, incorporating multiple logics. The double labelling of the practice seemed to motivate nurses on the one hand, because 'Releasing Time to Care' appealed to their professional logic. However, this backfired when only very limited increases in direct patient time were observed. In addition, nurses struggled to make use of the room for manoeuvre they were supposed to get due to the programme. Moreover, the results show that double label also appeared to create suspicion among nurses whether it was not just another tool to enhance the productivity and efficiency which would eventually result in downsizing.

Our findings indicate that 'The Productive Ward: Releasing Time to Care' in its initial appearance is indeed an example of the hybridization of multiple logics, but in reality is primarily aimed at accomplishing goals that fit the business-like logic instead of adhering to both logics. The organization presented the programme as empowering nurses to make changes to their ward in order to increase the direct patient time, although the bottom line of the programme was increasing efficiency. Furthermore, several respondents did point at the fact that the pressure to economize in this hospital is increasing. In addition, respondents indicate that it is very difficult to engage nurses in change programmes aiming at efficiency and that these initiatives lead to a lot of resistance in this professional group. 'Productive Ward: Releasing Time to Care' seems to be used to commit nurses to the change programme by appealing to their professional logic, while it was actually another economizing programme.

However, engaging nurses through presenting the programme as fitting with their logic did not deliver the intended results. In the beginning of the implementation process, nurses were enthusiastic and saw this innovative programme as a means for them to be empowered and improve the quality of care they deliver. Nevertheless, this perception changed. Due to the suspicion of nurses about the sincerity of the aims of the programme, accompanied with the problematic implementation process and the lack of concrete results with regard to releasing time to care, it resulted in a lack of commitment of nurses towards the programme. In the end, the nurses in the wards that participated in the pilot programme did not appear to see the value of the programme. Therefore, the programme was implemented, but not internalized by the nurses. Hence, this case of 'Productive Ward: Releasing time to care' seems to be an example of ceremonial adoption of a new practice (Kostova and Roth, 2002). This is problematic, because internalization is an important precondition for the sustainment of the innovation (Kostova and Roth, 2002).

Some limitations of this study can be indicated. First of all, we focused our study on the implementation of the pilot phase of the programme. Therefore, we are unable to observe whether our findings are consistent throughout the implementation of the full programme. However, we decided to focus on this pilot phase, because we expected that the role of institutional logics in the adoption and implementation of the practice would be most observable in the early phases of implementation. Due to the fact that only two wards were studied, external validity of this study is low. It is difficult to generalize the finding from this study to other contexts, though this was not the aim of this study. It might be interesting for future studies to investigate similar issues in other public service sectors, such as education and social care, in order to find out what logics are present in those sectors and whether they affect the innovation process. Future research on innovation in public services could take the complexity of the institutional environment into account, because this study indicated that this could affect the innovation process. Furthermore, future research is needed to enhance our understanding of hybridized practices and the ways internalization instead of only ceremonial implementation of these practices could be achieved.

In summary, the multiple logics that are expected to be present in the health care sector, nursing professional and business-like, are reflected in the findings. To answer our research question, it does seem to be more complex to successfully adopt and implement a new practice when multiple logics are at play. By hybridizing the logics in a practice, one runs the risk of sending conflicting messages that cause confusion. At the same time, focusing on one logic and neglecting the other might result in less commitment from the group adhering the neglected logic. Our results show that practices appealing to the logic of the users initially enhances their commitment and degree of internalization of the practice, which is beneficial for the implementation process. However, in a context where multiple logics are at play, one should be careful when trying to implement a hybrid innovative practice aimed to appeal to multiple logics, because sending out multiple messages might create suspicion among the recipients of this message, which might decrease the amount of commitment and internalization.

REFERENCES

Battilana, J. and Dorado, S. (2010) Building Sustainable Hybrid Organizations: The Case of Commercial Microfinance Organizations. *Academy of Management Journal*, 53:6 pp1419–1440.

Bekkers, V. J. J. M., Edelenbos, J. and Steijn, B. (2011) *Innovation in the Public Sector*, New York: Palgrave Macmillan.

Bekkers, V. J. J. M. and Korteland, E. H. (2008) The Diffusion of Electronic Service Delivery Innovations in Dutch E-policing: The Case of Digital Warning Systems. *Public Management Review*, 10:1 pp1–28.

Braun, V. and Clarke, V. (2008) Using Thematic Analysis in Psychology. *Qualitative Research in Psychology*, 3:2 pp77–101.

Child, J. (1972) Organizational Structure, Environment and Performance: The Role of Strategic Choice. *Sociology*, 6:1 pp1–21.

Crossan, M. M. and Apaydin, M. (2010) A Multi-Dimensional Framework of Organizational Innovation: A Systematic Review of the Literature. *Journal of Management Studies*, 47:6 pp1154–91.

Damanpour, F. (1991) Organizational Innovation: A Meta-analysis of Effects of Determinants and Moderators. *Academy of Management Journal*, 34:3 pp555–90.

Damanpour, F. and Evan, W. M. (1984) Organizational Innovation and Performance: The Problem of 'Organizational Lag'. *Administrative Science Quarterly*, 29:3 pp392–409.

Damschroder, L. J., Aron, D. C., Keith, R. E., Kirsh, S. R., Alexander, J. A. and Lowery, J. C. (2009). Fostering Implementation of Health Services Research Findings into Practice: A Consolidated Framework for Advancing Implementation Science. *Implementation Science*, 4:50 pp1–15.

Dearing, J. W. (2009) Applying Diffusion of Innovation Theory to Intervention Development. *Research on Social Work Practice*, 19:5 pp503–18.

Doolin, B. (2001) Doctors as Managers: New Public Management in a New Zealand Hospital. *Public Management Review*, 3:2 pp231–54.

Dunn, M. B. and Jones, C. (2010) Institutional Logics and Institutional Pluralism: The Contestation of Care and Science Logics in Medical Education, 1967–2005. *Administrative Science Quarterly*, 55:1 pp114–49.

Erenstein, C. F. and McCaffrey, R. (2007) How Healthcare Work Environments Influence Nurse Retention. *Holistic Nursing Practice*, 2 pp303–07.

Friedland, R. and Alford, R. R. (1991) 'Bringing Society Back in: Symbols, Practices, and Institutional Contradictions' in W. W. Powell and P. J. DiMaggio (eds) *The New Institutionalism in Organizational Analysis*. Chicago, IL: University of Chicago Press.

Goodrick, E. and Reay, T. (2011) Work of Pharmacists Constellations of Institutional Logics: Changes in the Professional Work of Pharmacists. *Work and Occupations*, 38:3 pp372–416.

Grbich, C. (1999) *Qualitative Research in Health: An Introduction,* London: Sage.

Greenhalgh, T., Robert, G., MacFarlane, F., Bate, P. and Kyriakidou, O. (2004) Diffusion of Innovations in Service Organizations: Systematic Review and Recommendations. *The Milbank Quarterly*, 82:4 pp581–629.

Greenwood, R., Díaz, A. M., Li, S. X. and Lorente, J. C. (2010) The Multiplicity of Institutional Logics and the Heterogeneity of Organizational Responses. *Organization Science*, 21:2 pp521–39.

Greenwood, R., Raynard, F., Micelotta, E. R. and Lounsbury, M. (2011) Institutional Complexity and Organizational Responses. *The Academy of Management Annals*, 5:1 pp317–71.

Han, J. and Koo, J. (2010) Institutional Isomorphism and Decoupling among Korean Firms: Adoption of Performance Compensation System. *Korean Journal of Sociology*, 44:3 pp27–44.

Jespersen, P. K., Nielsen, L. M. and Sognstrup, H. (2002) Professions, Institutional Dynamics, and New Public Management in the Danish Hospital Field. *International Journal of Public Administration*, 25:12 pp1555–74.

Kirkpatrick, I., Jespersen, P. K., Dent, M. and Neogy, I. (2009) Medicine and Management in a Comparative Perspective: The Case of Denmark and England. *Sociology of Health & Illness*, 31:5 pp642–58.

Kitchener, M. (2002) Mobilizing the Logic of Managerialism in Professional Fields: The Case of Academic Health Centre Mergers. *Organization Studies*, 23:3 pp391–420.

Korteland, E. H. (2011) 'Diffusie en Adoptie van Interorganisationele Innovaties in de Publieke Sector: Een Onderzoek binnen de Beleidssectoren Onderwijs en Veiligheid'. Unpublished PhD thesis, Erasmus University Rotterdam, The Netherlands.

Kostova, T. and Roth, K. (2002) Adoption of an Organizational Practice by Subsidiaries of Multinational Corporations: Institutional and Relational Effects. *The Academy of Management Journal*, 45:1 pp215–33.

Länsisalmi, H., Kivimäki, M., Aalto, P. and Ruoranen, R. (2006) Innovation in Healthcare: A Systematic Review of Recent Research. *Nursing Science Quarterly*, 19:1 pp66–72.

Lee, M. and Koh, J. (2001) Is Empowerment Really a New Concept? *The International Journal of Human Resource Management*, 12:4 pp684–95.

Lipley, N. (2009) Productive Wards Hailed for Transforming Care. *Nursing Management*, 16:4 p4.

Lounsbury, M. (2007) A Tale of Two Cities: Competing Logics and Practice Variation in the Professionalization of Mutual Funds. *Academy of Management Journal*, 50:2 pp289–307.

Meyers, P. W., Sivakumar, K. and Nakata, C. (1999) Implementation of Industrial Process Innovations: Factors, Effects, and Marketing Implications. *Journal of Product Innovation Management*, 16:3 pp295–311.

NHS Institute for Innovation and Improvement. (2010) *Improving Healthcare Quality at Scale and Pace. Lessons from the Productive Ward: Releasing Time to Care Programme*, Coventry: NHS Institute for Innovation and Improvement. Available at http://www.institute.nhs.uk/quality_and_value/productivity_series/productive_ward.html.

Noordegraaf, M. (2007) From "Pure" to "Hybrid" Professionalism: Present-Day Professionalism in Ambiguous Public Domains. *Administration & Society*, 39:6 pp761–85.

Ocasio, W. (1997) Toward an Attention-based View of the Firm. *Strategic Management Journal*, 18:S1 pp187–206.

Pache, A. C. and Santos, F. (2010) When Worlds Collide: The Internal Dynamics of Organizational Responses to Conflicting Institutional Demands. *Academy of Management Review*, 35:3 pp455–76.

Rapley, T. (2011) 'Some Pragmatics of Qualitative Data Analysis' in D. Silverman (ed.), *Qualitative Research* (3rd ed.). London: Sage.

Reay, T. and Hinings, C. R. (2005) The Recomposition of an Organizational Field: Health Care in Alberta. *Organization Studies*, 26:3 pp351–84.

——— (2009) Managing the Rivalry of Competing Institutional Logics. *Organization Studies*, 30:6 pp629–52.

Rogers, E. M. (2003) *Diffusion of Innovations*, New York: Free Press.

Ruef, M. and Scott, W. R. (1998) A Multidimensional Model of Organizational Legitimacy: Hospital Survival in Changing Institutional Environments. *Administrative Science Quarterly*, 43:4 pp877–904.

Saz-Carranza, A. and Longo, F. (2012) Managing Competing Institutional Logics in Public–Private Joint Ventures. *Public Management Review*, 14:3 pp331–57.

Schumpeter, J. A. (1934) *The Theory of Economic Development. An Inquiry into Profits, Capital, Credit, Interest, and the Business Cycle,* London: Oxford University Press.

Scott, W. R., Ruef, M., Mendel, M. and Caronna, G. (2000) *Institutional Change and Healthcare Organizations: From Professional Dominance to Managed Care,* Chicago, IL: University of Chicago Press.

Thornton, P. H. (2002) The Rise of the Corporation in a Craft Industry: Conflict and Conformity in Institutional Logics. *Academy of Management Journal*, 45:1 pp81–101.

Thornton, P. H. and Ocasio, W. (2008) 'Institutional Logics' in R. Greenwood, C. Oliver, K. Sahlin- Andersson and R. Suddaby (eds) *Handbook of Organizational Institutionalism*, Thousand Oaks, CA: Sage.

Thornton, P. H., Ocasio, W. and Lounsbury, M. (2012) *The Institutional Logics Perspective: A New Approach to Culture, Structure, and Process*, Oxford: Oxford University Press.

Van der Wal, Z., De Graaf, G. and Lawton, A. (2011) Competing Values in Public Management. *Public Management Review*, 13:3 pp331–41.

Veld, M. F. A. (2012) 'HRM, Strategic Climate and Employee Outcomes in Hospitals: HRM Care for Cure?'. Unpublished PhD thesis, Erasmus University Rotterdam, The Netherlands.

Yin, R. K. (2008) *Case Study Research, Design and Methods* (4th ed.). Thousand Oaks, CA: Sage.

Abstract

As social systems, organizations need to ensure connectivity between established and deviant communication streams to accomplish organizational innovation. This article explores elements and systemic strategies of connectivity formation for the introduction of an organizational innovation such as the concept of crowd innovation in the public sector. For public administrations, crowd innovation represents an organizational innovation since it implies broad participation and the integration of external ideas, and thus often opposes prevalent organizational structures. Our findings contribute to the knowledge on systemic innovation management and suggest that public managers can enhance connectivity formation by addressing semantics, routines, practices, roles, and redundancies.

STRATEGIES FOR INTRODUCING ORGANIZATIONAL INNOVATION TO PUBLIC SERVICE ORGANIZATIONS

Alexandra Collm and Kuno Schedler

Alexandra Collm
Institute for Systemic Management and Public Governance
University of St. Gallen
St. Gallen
Switzerland

Kuno Schedler
Institute for Systemic Management and Public Governance
University of St. Gallen
St. Gallen
Switzerland

INTRODUCTION

This article approaches innovation in public sector organizations from a *systemic management* perspective (Schwaninger 2009), which assumes that organizations are complex adaptive systems (Stacey 1995) that cannot be controlled entirely by hierarchical methods. Instead, systemic management requires the use of decision models that have the required variety commensurate with the management of a public sector organization (Rios and Suárez 2012). Prominent representatives of a systems theory approach regard organizations as social systems that consist of specific communication: the communication of decisions. Communication between members of the organization creates the distinction between the organization and its environment and thus creates and re-creates the organization itself (Luhmann 2000). Organizations persist through connecting communication on decisions to other communication on decisions. In other words, communication on new decisions (e.g., on innovation) needs to be connected to established communication. Thus, organizational innovation can only happen if an external stimulus is considered to be a piece of meaningful information for the system. Stimuli without any meaning for the organization will not be taken into consideration because they are neither understood nor could they support the ongoing flow of communications of decisions. Therefore, in order to deal with innovation while safeguarding its own existence, an organization implicitly manages its conditions of connectivity between different communications of decisions by discerning, observing, and establishing meaningful information (Luhmann 2000). The existing communication in a system, based on an ongoing mutual reconstruction of meaning (Berger and Luckmann 1966), separates meaningful from meaningless information, and thus acts like a filter for incoming information. Consequently, a systemic manager will try to find strategies to form connectivity which respect the self-organizing and sense-making processes in a system and intervene in these processes adequately, respectfully, and continuously. In this article, we will use the term 'communication stream' for a number of communication activities that are linked to a specific decision.

Innovation in the public sector, and specifically policy innovation, has been addressed frequently in the literature in the last three decades (Berry 1994; Grady 1992; Osborne and Brown 2005; Windrum et al. 2008). Innovations can be created internally, enforced by external pressure, or generated collectively in collaboration with stakeholders. It is especially the third kind of innovation process which is both promising and demanding due to a higher level of uncertainty and complexity (Sørensen and Torfing 2011). The idea of collaborative innovation implies the participation of actors outside organizational boundaries and thus a minimal level of openness of the innovation process. The new practice, which has been defined as 'crowd innovation' (Collm and Schedler 2012), goes even further by suggesting broad and equal participation, especially during the idea generation phase of the innovation process rather than during the following idea design and idea implementation phases (Osborne and Brown 2005; Roberts and King 1996; Tushman 1977).

This article focuses on systemic strategies to form connectivity between communication streams in an organizational innovation process in the public sector. As mentioned, we assume that public sector organizations can only respond to stimuli of innovation if they are able to perceive them as meaningful and shape them into discernible information. Connectivity between communication streams, therefore, is a crucial link and a precondition for adequate responses to stimuli of innovation by the organization (Figure 1). The article adds to existing work on systemic innovation management and public sector innovation by providing insights into two aspects: first, we analyse elements of and strategies used for connectivity formation as discussed in the literature. Second, based on a longitudinal case study, we explore the role of elements of connectivity formation and strategies used by actors to enhance connectivity formation in the context of a crowd innovation project. We argue that the focus on communications improves our understanding of managerial strategies in innovation efforts. Therefore, the central research questions to be examined in this article are

1.   What are the elements of connectivity formation that foster the introduction of an organizational innovation?
2.   Which strategies do public managers apply to trigger the formation of connectivity in the context of an innovation project?

In order to analyse the formation of connectivity in the public sector, we will refer to systems theory and the concept of autopoiesis as coined by Maturana and Varela (1980)

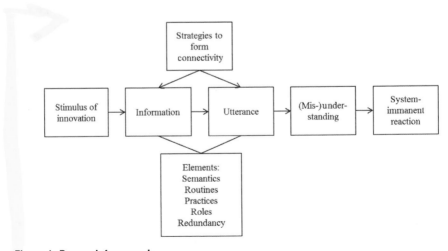

Figure 1: Research framework

and advanced by Luhmann (1986) and others. So far, the systems theory approach has been used in public management research to understand the complexity of a social system (Bielecki and Stocki 2010), to analyse the transformation of public governance (Esmark 2009), and to examine public sector performance (Andersen 2005; Boland and Fowler 2000).

From a systems theory perspective, the formation of connectivity between communication streams is crucial for achieving disruptive change: an innovative organizational concept such as crowd innovation is assessed and selected based on the existing structures of an organization. The reason for such an innovation usually lies in the recognition that traditional forms of change management, such as hierarchical orders or bureaucratic formal ruling, have not proven to be effective. We assume that crowd innovation is a new and radical approach that creates tensions with established closed processes, which gain legitimacy from formal rules (e.g., the principle of legality). Additionally, while the idea of opening up public policy processes for external ideas is not new, first practical experiences show that, if taken seriously, broad participation, transparency, and openness will lead to profound organizational innovation.

This article is divided into five sections. Following the introduction, the next section outlines innovation from a systems theory perspective. We emphasize the need for connectivity by introducing the concept of communications, consisting of information, utterance, and (mis-)understanding, as well as five central elements of connectivity. The third section explains the challenge of introducing crowd innovation in the public sector. The fourth section illustrates how the concept of crowd innovation was introduced into a public organization using a longitudinal case study and explores strategies employed to enhance connectivity. Finally, we discuss the different results on elements of connectivity and strategies to form connectivity. We close with concluding remarks on elements of connectivity and strategies to form connectivity, as well as notes on further research.

CONNECTIVITY FORMATION FOR INTRODUCING INNOVATION

Organizations such as public administrations are based on a special type of communication which occurs around decisions. The communication of decisions consists of different themes, which are reflected in the memory of the organization, based on documents, files, and archives (Luhmann 2000). This in turn leads to the development and re-creation of organizational structures. The organization, though, can only exist as a social system if a difference between the organization and its environment is visible and if the decisions are perceived as decisions by its members. In other words, the distinction between who or what is inside and who or what is outside the organization is indicated through decision communication (Luhmann 1984).

Communication only evolves if information that has been uttered is understood or misunderstood. Understanding evolves if members of organizations co-create meaning by referring the information to the organizational past or present state and express the information by referring to themselves (Luhmann 2000). By doing this, a social system creates and re-creates its specific logic of action and communication, and it reduces complexity – at the cost, however, of producing blind spots of perception (Prahalad 2004). With communication, social systems also generate specific ways to perceive information from the environment: even though the environment cannot determine its effects on the system (Brans and Rossbach 1997), each system will inherently distinguish noise from external stimuli that make sense to the system and its members by discerning, observing, and finally establishing them as meaningful information based on the systems' own structures (Luhmann 2000). Luhmann (2000) describes this as operative closure: systems are closed with respect to their own organization and structure but they are not environmentally closed. In sum, external stimuli that cannot be interpreted and shaped into meaningful information on the basis of the organization's communication streams will be ignored by the organization and remain outside the organization – they fall through the cracks of an organization's perception ability.

Persisting organizations live in an equilibrium of connected decisions. Any definite request for innovation is – at first glance – considered to be a disruption to this connectivity. In other words, innovations are impulses which irritate the organization as a social system (Luhmann 2009). The formation of *connectivity* is a means to limit the level of irritation to a tolerable extent in order to avoid rejection reactions by the organization. Luhmann (2000) stressed that organizations often underrate the risk of retaining existing 'successful' structures. In a similar sense, Gassmann (2006) pointed out that such 'organizational orthodoxies' need to be overcome in order to increase innovativeness. This leads to an inherent dilemma: innovations have to appear novel enough to attract attention as innovations, but they also have to connect to the existing structures. It is that which exists which enables the organization to recognize what is new. As Hargadon and Douglas put it: 'Without invoking existing understandings, innovations may never be understood and adopted in the first place. Yet by hewing closely to existing institutions, innovators risk losing the valued details, representing the innovation's true novelty, that ultimately change those institutions' (Hargadon and Douglas 2001, p. 478).

So far, only a few authors have analysed the role of connectivity for managing organizational innovation from a systems theory perspective. Authors have described *semantics, routines, sociomaterial practices,* and *roles* (Mayr and Siri 2010; Nassehi 2005; Schoeneborn 2011) as elements that could serve as a medium for constructing connectivity. Even fewer studies can be found on systemic management strategies used by (public) managers to support the recognition of new communication and thus the development of connectivity. Nassehi's work (2005) is a rare example that describes strategies to construct connectivity based on systems theory. In addition to the strategies of visibility creation and complexity reduction identified by Nassehi (2005), we consider the approach of establishing objectivity as described by Luhmann (2000).

The first strategy we refer to is to make the decision-making process visible. Part of this is the management of decisions in 'meetings, in special rooms, at special times, with special rites, and on special documents' (Nassehi 2005, p. 186). This also includes the communication of goals and objectives, which aims at 'rationalizing' decisions in order to obtain legitimacy from internal and external stakeholders. This strategy emphasizes the role of organizational semantics, routines, and practices for the formation of connectivity. *Semantics* can be described as powerful and traditionally constant schemes of ideas which connect terms and symbols with meaning and which have to be preserved (Mayr and Siri 2010). They are mutually constructed informal rules for the interpretation of terms which enable communication in a social system. The higher the level of professionalization has developed in a social system, for example, the higher the specificity of its semantics. An organization's prevalent communication streams will usually be characterized by a typical set of semantics, which forces champions of innovative ideas to adapt to these semantics in order to be heard and understood in the organization.

Routines, like decision routines, can arise in organizations, according to Nassehi (2005), when forms of decisions are concentrated and repeated. Routines allow for higher efficiency in organizational collaboration since they make it unnecessary to re-agree on the specific form of collaborating in a situation. When routinized behaviour becomes taken for granted, it may develop into an institution (Meyer and Rowan 1977). Structuration theorists would argue that routinized behaviour forms and re-affirms organizational structures. This 'duality of structure' comes into effect when actors communicate their expectations regarding existing organizational structures on the basis of these structures and thus confirm or generate new structures (Giddens 1984). In a systems perspective, routines allow for efficient communication on decisions as they are based on the embedded experience of the social system.

Sociomaterial *practices* such as certain documents or media can stabilize the organiza-tion in its continuous reproduction from one communicative event to the next (Schoeneborn 2011). For organization members who took part in decisions, these practices act as manifestations of the decision process, including the communication of arguments, values, fears, and hopes. For those who did not take part in decisions, documents and media transport information that will be interpreted on the basis of individual values, fears, and hopes.

A decision communication, however, implicitly or explicitly includes the commu-nication of rejected alternatives and thus creates a paradox for organizations. On the one hand, the selected alternative might not appear as justified and definite, even more so if it is communicated that there are possible alternatives to it. On the other hand, the decision will appear less as a decision and the possible alternatives will appear less as alternatives, the more the chosen alternative is justified as the single correct selection (Seidl and Becker 2006). This paradox is often faced and absorbed by deciders, described by Nassehi (2005) as a second prominent strategy to form connectivity. The decider is a constructed *role* assigned to individuals who are to be held accountable for the decision (Luhmann 2000). The construction of the role of a decider helps the organization to overcome the problem of dealing with choice by 'describing the limited resources of individual deciders in complex organizations' (Nassehi 2005, p. 186). Thus, the role of the decider reduces complexity by assigning choice to a role under bounded rationality.

In addition, *redundancy* in communication streams leads to the re-confirmation of expectations concerning existing codes and concepts. In order to create legitimacy for new concepts in a social system, it needs to be included in all kinds of communication media and streams in parallel. This third strategy creates pressure for the social system to acknowledge the relevance of the innovation and to include it in its everyday sense-making processes. Thus, repeated communication can lead to new themes based on common knowledge and attitudes amongst organizational members and thus form connectivity between new and orthodox communication streams and organizational structures. Hence, this strategy is directed towards establishing a form of objectivity based on shared knowledge and attitudes. Thus, organizational innovation is legitimated through the redundancy of recognized communications based on the use of detailed semantics (Luhmann 2000) employed for practices, routines, and the construction of roles (Table 1).

To sum up, in order to examine innovation from a systems theory perspective, it is necessary to ask 'how the organization engages with the novelty that presents itself as a possibility, but without "losing itself"' (Bakken et al. 2009, p. 174). For public managers attempting to introduce innovation in organizations, the role of semantics, practices, routines, roles, and redundancy suggest 'they should choose their designs carefully to present some details as new, others as old, and hide still others from view altogether' (Hargadon and Douglas 2001, p. 499). The challenge for public managers lies in finding a strategy that combines familiar cues and new ideas without binding actors too closely to the old ways of doing things. Therefore, public managers must find a 'balance between novelty and familiarity, between impact and acceptance' (Hargadon and Douglas 2001, p. 499).

CROWD INNOVATION AS ORGANIZATIONAL INNOVATION

Borrowing approaches from systems theory to analyse the introduction of organizational innovation allows us to explore how decision communications influence the way public

Table 1: Formation of connectivity: strategies and elements from the literature review

Strategy	Semantics	Routines	Practices	Roles	Redundancy
Visibility creation	x	X	x		
Complexity reduction				x	
Formation of objectivity					x

administrations deal with organizational innovation. In this article, we use a crowd innovation project as an example of an innovative management practice that has the potential to affect the organization, its culture, and processes as a whole. Crowd innovation has been described as being rooted in the concepts of open innovation (Chesbrough 2003) and crowdsourcing (Brabham 2008). Both source concepts can be advanced through the use of information and communication technologies (ICT), which permit a direct and fast communication between organizational and external actors. Collm and Schedler describe crowd innovation as follows: 'Consequently, a public administration that practices crowd innovation invites its stakeholders to participate in a weakly structured, public process of generating and developing innovations in the administration. All the participants basically have equal rights and are equally legit-imized to inject their contributions into the process. In order to allow for quick, transparent and interactive communication, Web 2.0 technologies are used.' (Collm and Schedler 2012, p. 5). To sum up, crowd innovation describes a fast and effective way of opening up the innovation process to gather ideas from large numbers of external actors and to make internal ideas accessible to external actors by the use of ICT.

With observations of alternative ways of idea generation and design, different concepts emerged, such as high involvement innovation (Bessant 2003), democratiza-tion of innovation (Von Hippel 2005), crowd collaboration (Brown 2007), and collaborative innovation (Bommert 2010). The concept of innovation relates to the organization and contains elements that are perceived as new by the organization and its stakeholders (Rogers 1995). Since aggregating ideas from many sources, as well as interacting and collaborating with a large number of people, is at the heart of crowd innovation, openness and transparency are its two main principles. Crowd innovation can be employed to achieve citizens' acceptance of major changes, to improve service and customer orientation, and to strengthen public sector innovativeness. With a higher degree of public trust and accountability and a greater number of citizens served, crowd innovation can even be an opportunity to reform public innovation management towards enhanced publicness. However, it is a great challenge to traditional public administration, especially in a *Rechtsstaat* culture, which is based on closed-system practices and routines (Collm and Schedler 2012).

Based on studies on open innovation and crowdsourcing, we assume that the motivation for introducing crowd innovation is a reaction to increased actor complex-ity, new participatory practices by citizens, or to a lack of trust in government (e.g., Nam 2010). Further proactive motives are harnessing scarce resources, improving problem solving, attaining representation and legitimacy, or increasing innovativeness and creativity (e.g., Bason 2010). The benefits of crowd innovation could be described as a faster, more effective, and cheaper initiation of the innovation process whilst getting to know customer needs (Brabham 2009; Fuglsang 2008). In other words, while innovation in itself may be perceived as a threat by the members of an organization, the benefits are obvious and should legitimize the change process. Four different main fields exist where crowd innovation can be seen as an opportunity: idea generation, product development, problem solving, and collaborative creation (Gassmann et al. 2010).

A broadly based collection of ideas is adequate for determining public opinion or a trend. Examples are ideas competitions using Web 2.0 solutions that enable participants to enter an idea but also to evaluate ideas from other actors. The initiation of a new product or service, its development and design, calls for a more intense interaction between the crowd and the organization. The same is true for the solution of a given problem that the organization works on. In most cases, these two fields require time and expert knowledge from the crowd. The area of collaborative creation demands even higher and continuous engagement from the crowd and the organization since both actors develop a product or service together. Many examples can be found in the common creation of knowledge, such as wikis, where content is user-generated and the organization mainly moderates the process.

Following this argumentation, the implementation of crowd innovation implies a great challenge for public managers. Ongoing dialogue and interactions, as well as increasing openness understood as the free flow of ideas, knowledge, information, and experiences combined with broad and equal actors' participation, represent a change of organizational structures. The structures that need to be changed include (a) breaking rules and conventional management routines, (b) becoming accustomed to upside-down thinking to amplify organizational boundaries, (c) process facilitation, (d) developing sophisticated networking evolution skills, and (e) establishing an effective stakeholder management system (Hafkesbrink and Scholl 2010). According to West and Gallagher (2006), it represents a paradigm shift for most public administrations in order for them to find ways to exploit internal innovation, incorporate external innovation, and motivate outsiders to provide external innovations. Many public officials thus question the idea of extensive public involvement and 'the capacity of citizens to come to a sound judgment on public policy matters' (Lukensmeyer and Torres 2008, p. 226), since broad participation could also lead to the submission of inconvenient ideas and unwanted comments.

Taking a systems theory perspective, different challenges to implement crowd innovation can be identified. Crowd innovation opens up formerly closed processes of idea generation, idea evaluation, and decision-making about new ideas, and it allows for new actors to contribute to these processes. New actors introduce new semantics, their practices are different from any existing structures, they may not necessarily be key stakeholders with routinized legitimacy claims, and they may jeopardize the monopoly of powerful deciders in public administration to generate and enact innovation. According to Luhmann (2000), in such a situation the construction of connectivity to existing communication streams is essential in order to generate common knowledge and attitudes amongst organizational members. Since it is based on an ongoing dialogue and interaction, crowd innovation needs to be implemented as an ongoing process, possibly in combination with closed co-creation processes integrating the best spin doctors of the crowd (Slowinski and Sagal 2010) and enhancing the formation of communities and social capital.

The following sections illustrate how a large city in Switzerland considers the implementation of crowd innovation and show how certain strategies relate to the formation of connectivity between communication streams using a longitudinal case study.

METHOD

To explore the formation of connectivity between communication streams for organizational innovation, we use the method of an in-depth longitudinal case study. The case study describes and analyses the employment of the crowd innovation concept in one major Swiss city: an internet platform was implemented and extended to allow for intense interaction, participation, and the integration of ideas from external actors. The whole process from the initiation of the platform to its extension according to the crowd innovation concept lasted from July 2009 to July 2011. We conducted extensive document analysis, participant observation, and expert interviews. For the document analysis, we had access to more than 40 minutes, drafts and other relevant documents like policies and regulations from the whole period. Participant observations included five meetings of the central IT steering committee and twenty one meetings of the project management team in charge of the implementation of the platform. All observations took place during the platform extension from September 2010 until August 2011. For each observation, minutes were produced. Members of the IT steering committee included the heads of the IT and the communication departments, the mayor, the town clerk, and four other top managers from major departments. The IT steering committee was in charge of deciding upon strategic IT projects, such as the Internet platform. The project management team included three members from the IT and the communication department as well as the external consultant. Validating interviews with the project management team members were conducted at the beginning, during, and shortly after the extension of the platform.

We analysed our data in two steps: first, we identified the communication streams on decisions of the IT steering committee and the project management team. Second, we focused on the five elements and analysed the communication streams with regards to semantics, routines, roles, and practices constructed, as well as redundancy. As a consequence, our empirical findings are descriptions of communication streams, which shed light on the five elements that both shape communicative sequences and are a result of communicative sequences (Besio and

Pronzini 2010). In the following, we will describe the process of introducing organizational innovation using the concept of crowd innovation and its relevant decision communications.

CONNECTIVITY FORMATION: THE CASE OF A LARGE SWISS CITY

The city of XX is – in Swiss terms – a large city with a politico-administrative system that can be ascribed to a *Rechtsstaat* tradition. All important decision processes are formalized and closed to a high degree. In other words, both political and administrative decisions are taken behind closed doors, with some formal elements of participation such as consultation with selected external actors. Although there is a well-functioning system of direct democracy, many decisions still remain in the administration. Not only are decision processes formalized but communications on decisions also remain in well-structured processes both towards the inner and the outer world of the administration. As a consequence, responsibilities for policy fields are fragmented, and it has become part of politico-administrative life to try and channel communication streams in order to keep control over the topics dealt with in the media and in politics.

In 2009, the management of the IT department of the city of XX had the idea of an Internet platform to complement existing efforts in the fields of electronic government and social media. The platform was seen as an opportunity to establish the city's image as an innovator. Regarding the objectives, the platform was in line with the city's 'Online Strategy'. The online strategy did not only include the improvement of services and an enhanced provision of information online but also the intent to have a constant dialogue with external actors and to strengthen the image of the city as an innovative public actor. However, the management of the IT department could not convince the city council initially. The members of the council expressed their doubts concerning the risks of openness, the need for the platform, and the controllability of external input. Therefore, the city council suggested setting up the platform as an 'experimental project'. After the platform had been re-defined as a 6-month-long experiment, which could be abandoned should it not meet expectations, the city council approved the project in late October 2009.

When the project had been approved, the IT department was appointed to implement the platform. Together with the communication department, they developed the functional requirements, made a design draft, solved legal aspects, discussed contract specifications with the IT solution provider, planned marketing activities, and informed the employees of the city using the usual channels and forms of communication. The semantics chosen were similar to those in prevalent communication streams on electronic government. The platform was described as the 'first local electronic participation solution' to offer the opportunity to send feedback to the administration, a 'clear structured web-based platform' that allowed for 'collecting and retrieving information' in a simple manner, and a digital scrapbook of the city where everybody could upload data, for example, pictures. New opportunities for intense interaction on local topics between users, or the development of a community, were not emphasized. Finally, the platform was launched in October 2010, supported by several online and offline marketing activities. The initial functionalities of the platform comprised an open discussion forum, a section where users could announce local events, recommend and comment on locations, as well as upload videos and pictures. In order to write a comment in the forum or to upload a picture, the user had to register on the platform. After the launch of the platform, the communication department was appointed to operate the platform. Since the city intended the content on the platform to be user-generated, the city did not engage in the online discussions and no further marketing activities were granted.

Two months after the launch of the platform, the communication department made a first report on the status of the platform and its future development. Due to the high media coverage, up to 1,500 Internet users per day visited the platform during the first two weeks. On average, 400 Internet users per day visited the platform and 600 users registered during the first two months. Since the city had approached many companies in order to register and introduce their business, only two-thirds of the registered users were individuals. The communication department assumed that the platform faced high risks if seen as a regulars' table because the additional value of generating content was not obvious to the public. In addition, users criticized that the platform was not attractively designed and did not support social networking functions. Furthermore, it was criticized that the role of the city was not clear since the city was not actively involved on the platform and did not join in the discussions. At that moment, it became clear that innovative practices were needed that had not been seen before were the project to survive its trial period. In order to increase the popularity of the platform and attract more users, the communication department launched an ideas competition towards the end of the year. However, this contest only increased the number of users for the time of the competition. Several users criticized that they were left alone with their questions and assumed that local officials were not joining in any discussions since they had not received any answer in the forum. Several users expressed their resentment, like the following user who stated in the forum on 17 November 2010:

> Nobody will answer anything here [on this platform]. I thought I would receive a statement but nothing happened. Nobody knows if they [public officials of the city] will respond to us. They said that they would use the forum to get to know the citizens' concerns. That's why I will hardly write anything here anymore, I expected something different.

At the end of 2010, an external consultant was appointed by the IT steering committee to analyse the situation and suggest further activities in order to increase the acceptance of the platform. The consultant pointed out that the platform lacked a clear objective. The platform was portrayed to internal and external actors as an instrument to monitor the pulse of the general public, as a regulars' table, or as an experiment the city could learn from. Furthermore, different opinions about the role of the city existed in the city: members of the public administration favoured the city either to solely moderate discussions or to initiate and moderate discussions or even participate in discussions. In addition, the online strategy of the public administration was insufficient as an overall strategy to link the platform and its functions to the organization since it did not take into consideration the new openness of decision and communication that is provoked by crowd innovation. Due to the highlighted problem fields, the IT steering committee feared that the platform would fail and harm the image of the city.

As a solution to the problem, the consultant drafted a pathway for developing the platform by means of four scenarios towards a community-based online approach fostering crowd innovation. The community-based online approach included an overall strategy with clear objectives linked to organizational structures, the use of social media, and the proactive acquisition of external ideas. Based on the suggestions, the IT steering committee agreed that the platform should not be seen as a regulars' table but as a prioritized project promoting openness, transparency, and direct interaction. Consequently, the consultant was assigned the role of developing a strategy for the creation of a community-based online approach that emphasized crowd innovation.

In order to develop the strategy, the consultant analysed user profiles and activity rates, prepared a comparative analysis of similar approaches on an international scale, conducted interviews with promoters of the platform, and worked closely together with the project management team. A first draft of the strategy was established in January 2011. The consultant presented the first draft of the strategy before the IT steering committee in February 2011. The main components of the strategy were a vision, four main objectives, three guiding principles, the components of the online approach, and four development stages with concrete activities. As a reaction to the draft, intense discussions took place in the IT steering committee (Table 2). The opinions of the IT steering committee members stressed different topics. The town clerk emphasized that 'the strategy should take into account the existing communication policy and its central values'. Several members emphasized that it was necessary to clarify how organizational members should communicate and what their future role would be. One top manager made it clear that it 'is important that we know how to deal with it, with faster communication, more interaction, and fewer organizational boundaries'. The discussions led to a revised strategy, which was complemented by an implementation plan and presented in April 2011. In order to implement the strategy, organizational requirements were identified and presented in June 2011.

Discussions in the project management team developed in between the milestones presented at the IT steering committee meetings (Table 3). After the internal report and an analysis of the status quo, the project management team mainly worked on the objectives of the approach, an attractive design of the platform and the acceptance of users. By the time of the presentation of the first draft of the analysis, the project

Table 2: Decision communications during the implementation process

Decision communications	Date	Themes	Selected alternative (decision)
Internal report Analysis of status quo	November 2010 December 2010	Role of the city; future development of the platform Objectives of the platform; fear of failure	External analysis and support needed Implementing first actions and quick-wins, strategy
1st draft of the strategy	February 2011	Role of the official homepage; who is in charge; commitment of employees; interaction across boundaries; official or personal opinions; focus not only on citizens	Revision of the strategy
2nd draft of the strategy	April 2011	Organization of tasks and responsibilities; attractiveness of the approach to users; new approach leads to additional costs; terms used in the strategy are not consistent with existing terms	Members of the committee revise the strategy individually
Implementation plan	April 2011	Many tasks have to be conducted together with other departments; existing regulations have to be revised	Strategy has to be revised first
Organizational requirements	June 2011	Integration of functions, technologies, and homepage; additional resources; complex organizational development task; political decision necessary; different board needed	Board to continue with organizational development

Table 3: Phases of project management team decision communications

Decision communications	Time	Themes	Selected alternative (decision)
After internal report	November–December 2010	Activities to raise acceptance	Ideas competition; support of consultant
After analysis of status quo	January 2010	Sustainability of events; platform is not an experiment but an approach of interaction and innovation; what kind of communication/what objectives does the city focus on	Implementation of quick-wins; development of strategy; identity of the approach
After 1st draft of the strategy	March–April 2011	Platform as a combination of different functions; differentiation: platform and official homepage; responsibilities and tasks; role of human resource development; acceptance of members of the IT steering committee	Theme-oriented design and combination of functions; user analysis; analysis of good practices; integration of human resource development; concretizing responsibilities and tasks; implementation plan, illustration of status quo, simplify concepts, meaningful connection to other strategies, regulations, and norms
After 2nd draft of the strategy	May–June 2011	Members of the IT steering committee's acceptance of ambitious approach	Common terms; structuring comments; suggestion for dealing with different comments; position of the approach not in opposition to existing communication values and channels; integration of external ideas is not uncontrolled – employees do not communicate autonomously
After implementation plan	May–June 2011	Members of the IT steering committee's acceptance of ambitious approach.	Implementation of quick-wins.
After organizational requirements	July 2011	Continuation of the process: organizational development, communication processes, human resource development	Social media workshops; implementation of quick-wins; marketing activities

management team had become aware of the fact that the members of the IT steering committee had different views on the strategy's main elements. Communication between the two teams had not taken place as the existing routines were driven by formal project management relations. In addition, the technical rationality of the project management team was in conflict with the legal-administrative rationality of the steering committee. Some members of the latter feared the creation of an open and uncontrollable organization in which any member could communicate anything. Other members appreciated the opportunity to increase public responsiveness. Yet other members worried about the exposure of prevalent norms, rules, and structures. The project management team sought to increase the acceptance of the IT steering committee members by illustrating the lack of alternatives due to the decreasing numbers of users and the importance of the city's image as an innovative city. In addition, the project management team outlined additional expenses as an investment in improved innovation processes, enhanced social capital, and the development of an active Internet community dealing with public topics. They also pointed out meaningful connections to existing strategies, regulations, and norms.

After the presentation of the second draft of the analysis and the implementation plan in April 2011, the members of the IT steering committee received a revised version of the strategy and the implementation plan to comment on. Many comments were made in relation to organizational development tasks, communication processes, and human resource development activities. As one top manager put it: 'What we are looking at is a dramatic organizational change with high expectations towards the departments and agencies regarding strategy, structure, and culture [...] therefore, the city council has to be involved more directly'. Another top manager added that 'expectations are high, departments and agencies have to provide necessary resources [...] thus, we have to let them participate'. The town clerk stated that 'the city has a communication policy that is still valid [...] and that it uses different communication channels [...] to implement crowd innovation we need a political decision not additional paper'.

Since the comments did not only deal with fundamental topics but regarded the approach as very ambitious, the project management team feared that the strategy would be rejected. Therefore, the project management team tried to make it clear that the approach should not be seen as being in opposition to existing structures and regulations. In addition, they illustrated that the approach would not lead to an uncontrolled process either in relation to internal communication processes or in terms of the integration of external ideas. The project management team also made it clear which comments could be solved right away in the IT steering committee meetings and which questions had to be decided in a different setting.

The final presentation of organizational requirements in June 2011 led to two different reactions. The members of the IT steering committee agreed that several questions of organizational development, communication processes, and human resource development had to be discussed but in a broader context. The mayor emphasized that 'we need to develop the organization as a whole but we have to be less rigid […] and overcome departmental boundaries […] at the same time we have to continue developing the platform in an incremental way'. The proposed quick-wins were approved and made it possible to implement an attractive platform design and enhance existing marketing activities. In addition, the communication department became more involved in public discussions and triggered topics and themes. However, the complete employment of the strategy and the development of a community-based online approach were postponed until the organizational requirements were met.

The analysis of documents, data from participant observations, and interview transcripts led to the following results regarding the evolvement of connectivity and the five elements. Recapitulation and repeated explanation of new ideas, concepts, and terms led to *redundancy* and enabled the construction of common knowledge and attitudes amongst the IT steering committee members. Due to the operative closure of the organization, new themes like 'interaction', 'participation', and 'innovation' were acknowledged over time and legitimized further decisions. Existing organizational structures such as organizational values (e.g., communication values) were confirmed by ensuring their compatibility with new themes. The same was true for existing rules, norms, and regulations, which the IT steering committee considered and integrated into the strategy document.

As for decision communication *routines*, the IT steering committee insisted on revising documents like the strategy draft or the implementation plan several times in order to ensure connectivity with the system and its structures. The project management team felt a continuous challenge to raise the acceptance of the IT steering committee for the Internet platform and the community-based online approach.

Important *roles* were constructed over time: the head of the communication department became an important mediator to construct meaning between the political rationalities existing in the IT steering committee and the management rationalities of the project management team. While the mayor took on the role of decider, the external consultant provided external stimuli, which the organization partly constructed into information and thus decision communications. In order to introduce, repeat, and finally legitimize new ideas, concepts, and terms, members of the project management team and the IT steering committee used meetings and the strategy document as main *practices*.

Turning towards *semantics*, the usage of familiar and simple terms connected to existing strategies, documents, and routines proved to be powerful corporate codes, which drew distinctions between the organization and its environment. In comparison, the use of radical terms such as openness, dynamic, autonomy, and independence was limited. Further strong semantics were positive references to – even very small – achievements made during the process. The management of the IT department, and later on the project management team, also used positive connotations to 'sell' the

Internet platform and the later community-based online approach to the IT steering committee. However, they also pointed out that there was no alternative to the selected solution: every other solution would be inadequate for integrating external ideas and creating a sustainable approach. Since the city had already created a new innovative image supported by massive media attention, the Internet platform was no longer a reversible experiment the city could have abandoned without losing its new image.

DISCUSSION

The analysis of the formation of connectivity for organizational innovation from a systems theory perspective allows us to shed light on different aspects than well-known drivers of change. From a systems theory perspective, innovations take place between the past and the future. Since the future is still unknown, promoters of innovations often use positive connotations to describe the effects of new ideas and projects. As shown in the case study, these positive *semantics* are used as powerful corporate codes, which help them to develop *legitimacy in advance*. Apart from the legitimacy of innovations, the risk of keeping established structures is often under-estimated and thus still favoured by many actors: familiar and simple terms connected to existing strategies, documents, and routines are thus used. Therefore, innovations are often introduced as experiments: depending on the results, the innovation would be reversible (Luhmann 2000).

Based on the use of *semantics* and *redundancy*, existing rules, regulations, and norms were confirmed as a legitimate part of the *organization's memory*. According to systems theory, organizations try to reduce the loss of control by synchronizing decisions with what happened in the past and what might happen in the future regarding the organization and its environment. Since the future effects of decisions are not pre-dictable and organizations and their environment exist at the same time, organizations at least try to retain a detailed memory in order to hold on to past decisions. Therefore, self-reference is very important for organizations as each decision has to qualify as part of the future past (Luhmann 2000).

As illustrated in the case study, it was most important for several members of the IT steering committee as well as for the decider that compatibility with organizational values, as well as existing rules, norms, and regulations, was clearly *visible*. The project management team tried to draw linkages between new communications and established structures as well as to push the repetition of new ideas, concepts, and terms by using certain *practices*. This was especially observable when it came to the usage of new terms in contrary to well-established terms describing the communication principles of the organization. However, criticism was not resolved completely. *Routines*, which were recognized and used during the process, mainly represented either new decision communications or established structures that helped to reduce complexity. *Roles*,

Table 4: Formation of connectivity: strategies and elements identified in the case study

Strategy	Semantics	Routines	Practices	Roles	Redundancy
Visibility creation	X	X	X	X	
Complexity reduction		X		X	
Formation of objectivity					X
Construction of legitimacy	X		X		
Creation of organizational memories	X				X

like the mediator, the decider, or the external consultant as external stimuli, which were constructed and assigned during the process also helped to reduce complexity by assigning different levels of accountability to certain individuals (Table 4).

The construction of innovations as decision communications requires connectivity to the system and its structures based on redundancy. As shown in the case study, it is crucial that roles trigger the formation of common knowledge and attitudes to develop a sense of objectivity by using repeated communications (Luhmann 2000). Based on this objectivity, actors can construct themes like decision premises, which are building blocks of organizational structure (Luhmann 1995). Regarding the intensity of communications, we noticed important differences in the case study: intense communication existed amongst members of the project management team and single members of the IT steering committee and the project management team. A common knowledge of and attitude towards the implementation of crowd innovation were observed amongst these members. However, communication was low between the IT steering committee and the project management team as a whole, as well as in the IT steering committee. This made it difficult to mutually develop a new set of semantics, routines, and practices which would have helped the system to make sense of and adjust to the innovation. The IT steering members only agreed on a few aspects such as enhanced participation, the necessity of innovation, and more direct interaction. Overall objectivity thus evolved only in parts: there was no agreement regarding the complete implementation of the community-based online approach and thus decision communications remained without major effects on the organizational structure.

CONCLUSION

This article approaches innovation in the public sector from a systemic management perspective. Unlike hierarchical management, systemic management treats the organization as a social system that develops activities on the basis of its own rules and norms. As a result of our study, we define a *systemic management of innovation* as a chain of decision communications that provoke maximum possible irritation while maintaining connectivity to the existing system and its structures. This should be done in an orchestrated manner which enables new semantics, routines, practices, and roles to evolve in the organization.

As we have seen in our study, there is a shift of focus away from heroic entrepreneurs, capacities, or capabilities and towards systemic communication. The case has shown that routines, practices, roles, redundancy, and semantics are important elements which should be taken into regard by systemic managers when constructing strategies to achieve connectivity between communication streams. In addition to the two strategies identified by Nassehi (2005) and the formation of objectivity, we were able to observe strategies for the construction of legitimacy and the creation of organizational memories. The strategies *of visibility creation* and *complexity reduction* were identified and put to intensive use. While visibility creation derived from the use of semantics, routines, practices, and roles, the reduction of complexity was achieved through roles and routines. The *formation of objectivity* was needed but existed only in parts in our case study. It is based on the use of intense communication in order to construct common knowledge and attitudes. The *construction of legitimacy in advance* is based on the use of semantics and structures for expressing positive connotations, selling the innovation as an irreversible experiment, and establishing connectivity to corporate codes, as well as formalized strategies, regulations, and norms. The *creation of organizational memories* is based on the use of semantics and intense communications, and thus the construction of redundancy, in order to qualify as part of the future past. Both strategies were identified as crucial for the formation of connectivity.

Summing up, we agree with Luhmann's statement that the greatest challenge in implementing an organizational innovation lies in the construction of connectivity between the innovation and the existing organizational system. Public managers who want to introduce crowd innovation in their organization already need to consider the duality of structures at an early stage of the innovation process.

Since an organization needs time to develop new organizational structures and moreover to regain stability after innovations have been introduced, it is possible that the time frame of our case study for the implementation of crowd innovation was too limited. Further studies are needed to analyse the strategies used for the formation of connectivity and to confirm or complement our results.

REFERENCES

Andersen, S. C. (2005) How to Improve the Outcome of State Welfare Services. Governance in a Systems-Theoretical Perspective. *Public Administration*, 83 pp891–907.

Bakken, T., Hernes, T. and Wiik, E. (2009) 'Chapter 4 Innovation and Organization: An Overview From the Perspective of Luhmann's Autopoiesis' in R. Magalhães and R. Sanchez (eds) *Advanced Series in Management*, Vol 6. Bingley: Emerald Group Publishing Limited. pp69–88.

Bason, C. (2010) *Leading Public Sector Innovation: Co-Creating for a Better Society*, Bristol: Policy Press.

Berger, P. L. and Luckmann, T. (1966) *The Social Construction of Reality: A Treatise in the Sociology of Knowledge*, Garden City, NY: Anchor.

Berry, F. S. (1994) Innovation in Public Management: The Adoption of Strategic Planning. *Public Administration Review*, 54: pp322–30.

Besio, C. and Pronzini, A. (2010) Inside Organizations and Out. Methodological Tenets for Empirical Research Inspired by Systems Theory. *Forum: Qualitative Social Research*, 11:3 pp1–22.

Bessant, J. (2003) *High-Involvement Innovation: Building and Sustaining Competitive Advantage Through Continuous Change*, Chichester: Wiley.

Bielecki, A. and Stocki, R. (2010) Systems Theory Approach to the Health Care Organization on National Level. *Cybernetics & Systems*, 41 pp489–507.

Boland, T. and Fowler, A. (2000) A Systems Perspective of Performance Management in Public Sector Organisations. *International Journal of Public Sector Management*, 13 pp417–46.

Bommert, B. (2010) Collaborative Innovation in the Public Sector. *International Public Management Review*, 11 pp15–33.

Brabham, D. C. (2008) Crowdsourcing as a Model for Problem Solving. *Convergence: The International Journal of Research Into New Media Technologies*, 14 pp75–90.

Brabham, D. C. (2009) Crowdsourcing the Public Participation Process for Planning Projects. *Planning Theory*, 8 pp242–62.

Brans, M. and Rossbach, S. (1997) The Autopoiesis of Administrative Systems: Niklas Luhmann on Public Administration and Public Policy. *Public Administration*, 75 pp417–39.

Brown, C. (2007) Open Sourcing Social Solutions (Building Communities of Change). *Innovations: Technology, Governance, Globalization*, 2 pp125–36.

Chesbrough, H. W. (2003) *Open Innovation: The New Imperative for Creating and Profiting From Technology*, Boston, MA: Harvard Business Press.

Collm, A. and Schedler, K. (2012) Managing Crowd Innovation in Public Administration. *International Public Management Review*, 13:2 pp1–18.

Esmark, A. (2009) The Functional Differentiation of Governance: Public Governance Beyond Hierarchy, Market and Networks. *Public Administration*, 87 pp351–70.

Fuglsang, L. (2008) Capturing the Benefits of Open Innovation in Public Innovation: A Case Study. *International Journal of Services Technology and Management*, 9 pp234–48.

Gassmann, O. (2006) Opening up the Innovation Process: Towards an Agenda. *R&D Management*, 36:3 pp223–28.

Gassmann, O., Daiber, M. and Muhdi, L. (2010) 'Der Crowdsourcing-Prozess' in O. Gassmann (ed) *Crowdsourcing – Innovationsmanagement Mit Schwarmintelligenz*. München: Hanser.

Giddens, A. (1984) *The Constitution of Society. Outline of the Theory of Structuration*, Berkeley, CA: University of California Press.

Grady, D. O. (1992) Promoting Innovations in the Public Sector. *Public Productivity & Management Review*, 16: pp157–71.

Hafkesbrink, J. and Scholl, H. (2010) 'Web 2.0 Learning – A Case Study on Organizational Competences in Open Content Innovation' in J. Hafkesbrink, H. U. Hoppe and J. Schlichter (eds) *Competence Management for Open Innovation*. Köln: Josef Eul. pp239–54.

Hargadon, A. B. and Douglas, Y. (2001) When Innovations Meet Institutions: Edison and the Design of the Electric Light. *Administrative Science Quarterly*, 46:3 pp476–501.

Luhmann, N. (1984) *Soziale Systeme. Grundriss Einer Allgemeinen Theorie*, Frankfurt am Main: Suhrkamp.

Luhmann, N. (1986) 'The Autopoiesis of Social Systems' in F. Geyer and J. Van Der Zouwen (eds) *Sociocybernetic Paradoxes*. London: Sage.

Luhmann, N. (1995) *Social Systems*, Stanford, CA: Stanford University Press.

Luhmann, N. (2000) *Organisation Und Entscheidung*, Wiesbaden: Westdeutscher Verlag.

ORGANIZATIONAL CULTURE AND NEW PUBLIC MANAGEMENT

Most scholars would agree that although the heyday of new public management (hereafter NPM) lies behind us, it remains one of the most powerful reform doctrines to have reshaped the public sector in OECD countries and beyond. A core idea of NPM is that task specialization results in performance gains (Hood, 1991). Following this logic, governments have structurally disaggregated major public sector organizations into smaller parts, with some degree of autonomy (Laegreid and Verhoest, 2010). NPM entailed the introduction of managerial autonomy, performance management and incentives, competition and other reform elements (Dunleavy, 1996). Basically, NPM envisaged creating a stimulating environment, as much as possible, similar to the private market, for senior civil servants so that they would push their organizations and staff to perform better, to take risks and to innovate (e.g. Hood, 1995; Lane, 2001; Pollitt and Bouckaert, 2011). In exchange for autonomy, public organizations (or their CEOs) would be held accountable by their minister and parliament for their performance and sanctioned or rewarded accordingly. The process by which the political principal of a public organization sets the objectives and corresponding performance targets in performance contracts, keeps the organization and its management accountable for achievement of these performance targets with respect to these standards, and, if necessary, applies sanctions to the organization or its managers will be referred to in this article as result control. It was believed that an increase in managerial autonomy combined with result control would, among others, stimulate a more innovation-oriented culture and ultimately lead to an increase of performance (see e.g. OECD, 1994, 1997).

While the notion of organizational culture is well developed in the literature, it remains a highly complex phenomenon whose interconnections with other organizational dimensions, like performance, still need to find a fully developed theoretical framing (Glick, 1985; Chia and Koh, 2007; Jenkins *et al.*, 2008). Culture is often understood to comprise shared basic assumptions, customs, myths and ceremonies that communicate underlying beliefs about the use and distribution of power and privilege and is evidenced by values reflected in individual and group behaviours (Pettigrew, 1979; Reigle, 2001). NPM claims that the 'right' culture is a trigger for efficiency and effectiveness (often objectives of reforms in the public sector) and that culture is a malleable component of organizations (Ongaro and Rodolfi, 1998; Schedler and Proeller, 2007). In this perspective, organizational culture is treated as an organizational feature which managers can manage and therefore change. Following this logic, managerial autonomy and result control can be determinants of organizational culture. There is, however, little or no empirical evidence available on this relation.

Consequently, this article studies to what extent managerial autonomy combined with result control does affect the development of an organizational culture conducive to innovation. Do managerial autonomy and/or managerial pressures, such as result control, induce public organizations to create an innovation-oriented culture, as assumed by NPM doctrines?

In the literature there are various definitions of innovation-oriented culture. Key aspects from a cultural perspective can be described as creativity, openness and receptiveness to new ideas, risk taking and entrepreneurial mindset (Koberg and Chusmir, 1987; Deshpandé et al., 1993; Brettel and Cleven, 2011). In short, an innovation-oriented culture encompasses both the intention to be innovative and the creation of a supportive climate for innovation (Dobni, 2008; Laegreid et al., 2011). Innovation, in turn, can be regarded as the adoption of an existing idea for the first time by a given organization (Damanpour, 1991; Borins, 2002; Rogers, 2003; Laegreid et al., 2011). Accordingly, innovative behaviour is defined as the initiation and application of new and useful ideas, processes, products or procedures (Farr and Ford, 1990) and captures all behaviours through which employees can contribute to the innovation process.

Unfortunately, a positive correlation between managerial autonomy and organizational culture does not say much about the direction of causality; it could be that more autonomy leads to a more innovation-oriented culture, or that agencies with an innovative culture are more capable of 'extorting' a higher autonomy from oversight authorities over time (Carpenter, 2001). To solve this issue, the concept of Granger causality[1] can be used to test for causal relationships in both directions. This would, however, require longitudinal data, which are not available either publicly or in our dataset. We will therefore have to develop theoretical arguments about the direction of the relationship.

Furthermore, we will examine the innovation-oriented culture of a specific type of public sector organization, which we refer to as 'public sector agency'. Basically, 'agencies' are those organizations in the public sector which have higher levels of autonomy or discretion in decision making, compared to normal ministerial departments (Verhoest et al., 2012). Following Pollitt et al. (2004) and Verhoest et al. (2010), we focus specifically on public sector agencies which have the following features: (1) they are public law bodies, (2) they are structurally disaggregated from other organizations or from units within core ministries, (3) they have some capacity for autonomous decision making with regard to management or policy, (4) they are formally under at least some control of ministers and ministries, (5) they have some expectation of continuity over time and (6) they have some resources on their own. Companies and corporations with a commercial focus which have to closely observe the laws regulating private companies or which are registered under company law as a company as well as governmental foundations, trusts and charities are excluded from our understanding of agencies.

THEORETICAL APPROACHES

Research has shown that administrative reforms not only need a match with organizational culture, but also that reforms can change organizational culture (Bouckaert, 2007;

Ongaro, 2009, 2011; Laegreid *et al.*, 2011). Basically, the NPM argument on this point boils down to two conditions that create such a culture (Kettle, 1997; Pollitt and Bouckaert, 2004; Verhoest *et al.*, 2007). First, 'let public managers manage, and hence innovate' by giving them enough managerial autonomy to develop new ways of processing and handling their business. Secondly, 'make managers innovate' by incentivizing public managers through result control by the government (OECD, 1997). In general, as Osborne (1998) states: 'It [the literature on innovative capacity of the public organizations and the voluntary sector] has thus been in terms of how to make them more like for-profit organizations, and consequently as more likely to be innovators' (Osborne, 1998: 159). We will discuss these two lines of argument first separately and then together.

'Agencification' is referred not just to a process of specialization (setting up novel organizations with narrower tasks) but to the contemporaneous process of both specialization and autonomization (further accompanied by the setting up of systems of steering and control, and possibly by forms of re-regulation – see Pollitt and Talbot, 2004; Verhoest *et al.*, 2004; Fedele *et al.*, 2007; Verhoest *et al.*, 2010). More precisely, we refer to agencification as the creation of semi-autonomous organizations that operate at arms' length of the government, to carry out public tasks (regulation, service delivery and policy implementation) in a relatively autonomous way, i.e. there is less hierarchical and political influence on their daily operations, and they have more managerial freedoms. Autonomy is thus a constitutive component of agencification, enabling the adage of 'letting managers manage' in NPM.

More specifically, managerial autonomy is defined here as the extent to which an organization can decide independently from political and administrative principals on the choice and use of resources (Verhoest *et al.*, 2004). The assumed beneficial effect of managerial autonomy for innovation in public sector organizations can be deduced from different theoretical angles. First, it relies strongly on the managerialist school of thought (Maor, 1999; Pollitt, 2004), which advocates the idea of 'business-like government'. In essence, this school expects public bureaucrats to behave like private sector managers in exploring new ways of combining production factors, provided they are given sufficient flexibility and autonomy to manage as they see fit. Under conditions of sufficient managerial autonomy and flexibility, senior civil servants will adopt an innovation-oriented behaviour, leading to customer orientation and enhanced performance (Osborne and Gaebler, 1993) – very much like private sector managers do. The attitude of senior management towards change and risk-willingness is a strong determinant for the extent of innovation in public sector and other organizations (Damanpour, 1991; Vigoda-Gadot, 2009).

A second related argument draws from research findings showing that in autonomous agencies political signals are attenuated and possibilities for horizontal control by peers and customers are enlarged (Egeberg, 2003; Egeberg and Trondal, 2009; Thiel and Yesilkagit, 2011). To retain organizational legitimacy from customers and political principals (and thus to safeguard their existence and future resources), senior agency managers will encourage the development of a customer-oriented and innovative organizational culture (see e.g. Osborne, 1998; Verhoest et al., 2007).

Another related argument looks at social identity theory which claims that to stimulate group identification by individuals groups will try to emphasize their differences from other similar groups, claiming superiority by stimulating other behaviour than in the other groups. For instance, Demuzere (2012) uses this theory to explain the effect of enlarged managerial autonomy to the adoption of quality management techniques in public sector organizations (Demuzere, 2012). Following Pettigrew (1979), one could assert that the process of disaggregation from a parent administration may in fact be interpreted as a social drama, which refers to critical events whereby the opportunity to recast an organizational culture arises. In the case of agencification, the newly created autonomous agencies will emphasize those features that distinguish themselves from the parent departments where they originate from (Veenswijk and Hakvoort, 2002). Van Thiel (2008) has referred to this process of differentiation, between newly created agencies and their parent departments, as the human process of adolescence in which adolescents distance themselves from the values of their parents to shape and assert their individuality. As ministerial departments are still more infused with traditional cultures emphasizing compliance, details and precision, newly created agencies will emphasize organizational cultures which are sufficiently different: based on customer-orientation, flexibility, innovation and risk-taking behaviour. Indeed, van Thiel and van der Wal (2010) find that Dutch agencies with more managerial autonomy exhibit more managerial values, including innovation, than traditional departments or public sector bodies with less managerial autonomy. Lyons et al. (2006) find that work values differ between employees from core public and parapublic organizations. This is in line with the findings of van der Wal and Huberts (2008), which indicate that managers from executive agencies and parapublic organizations with more managerial autonomy are more inclined to adopt business-like values and also portray a desire to function more business-like in the near future. De Bruijn and Dicke (2006) come to similar conclusions and indicate that market-like values become increasingly more important for public sector organizations that have been autonomized, liberalized or privatized. Consequently, following business-like values is expected to be valued higher in agencies than in their parent ministries (Hood, 1991, 1995; Maesschalck, 2004; van der Wal and Huberts, 2008)

Some evidence does indeed seem to suggest that agencification and managerial autonomy lead to more innovation or an innovative culture (Verhoest et al., 2007). Moreover, organizational innovativeness studies emphasize the positive influence of less centralization of decision-making capacity and less formalization (Thompson, 1965; Slater and Narver, 1995; Koch and Hauknes, 2005; Vigoda-Gadot, 2009) for innovation. However, not all empirical studies show clear patterns (Damanpour, 1991; NAO, 2006; Laegreid et al., 2011).

INNOVATION IN PUBLIC SERVICES

The second 'line of argumentation' within NPM about what conditions may create or foster an innovation-oriented culture may be boiled down to the 'making managers manage' argument. Besides managerial autonomy, pressure is needed to stimulate innovation. According to NPM, such pressure can be created internally in the public sector by means of harsh performance standards in performance contracts with government, to which the agency is held accountable and to which sanctions or rewards are linked. At the delivery level, the imposition of challenging performance targets on public sector organizations and their management encourage or even force the latter to strive increased levels of efficiency and service quality, leading to a search for innovative ways to deliver services and to organize processes. Put, more positively, Behn (1999) argues that goals and performance targets can redefine the meaning of success, get everyone thinking and behaving innovatively, foster leaders at all levels and encourage organizations to reach out to other institutions whose work is helpful, or even necessary, in achieving these goals. Linking result-achievement with sanctions and rewards even increase this pressure to innovate in order to achieve high performance, because public organizations and their managers are assumed to be self-interested actors (Boorsma and Halachmi, 2008; Laegreid *et al.*, 2011). Indeed, a National Audit Office (NAO) study found that efficiency goals, performance targets to improve service quality, as well as organizational performance reviews and individual performance evaluations were strong drivers for organizational innovation in the British public sector (NAO, 2006). Similarly, Verhoest *et al.* (2007) found a positive effect of result control, including sanctions and rewards on innovation within public sector organizations in a study on state agencies. However, result control does not always directly result in higher level of innovativeness. Laegreid *et al.* (2011) did not find a direct effect of result control but concluded that result control can have an indirect effect as an instrument to 'make managers manage' – i.e. as a cultural feature. Moreover, Publin researchers found that performance indicators and targets were often used in too static a way, thereby entrenching existing ways of working and inhibiting performance (Koch and Hauknes, 2005). Taking into account this nuances, we expect result control to have a positive effect on the innovation-oriented culture within public sector organizations.

In sum, NPM claims that managerial autonomy and result control are *both* needed to stimulate innovation-oriented culture and to ultimately bring about a better performance. Managerial autonomy combined with result control provides public managers with both the possibility and the incentive to experiment and innovate. This allows public managers to explore more and novel options, develop and adapt new products, services and management techniques and produce better performance (Dunleavy *et al.*, 2006). Based on this line of reasoning, we expect managerial autonomy and result control to foster an organizational culture emphasizing innovation. In view of these mixed findings, we pose the following central question: do managerial autonomy and/ or result control induce public organizations to create an innovation-oriented culture, as assumed by NPM doctrines?

The next section discusses our research design. The 'Results' section presents the results of our analyses and the 'Conclusion and discussion' section concludes this article.

METHODS AND DATA

Data used for the analysis have been provided by the Comparative Public Organization Data Base for Research and Analysis or COBRA network. The COBRA network aims to encourage and enable comparative research into public sector organizations (for more information, see http://soc.kuleuven.be/io/cost/index.htm). It developed a common questionnaire to survey senior managers of public sector organizations. The questionnaire focuses on issues of autonomy, control and management of public sector organizations, in particular, (semi)-autonomous agencies. The joint dataset comprises unique agency-level survey data spread across fifteen different countries and seven years. For this article, we will use data on agencies from five countries: Belgium (Flanders), Italy, The Netherlands, Hong Kong and Romania.

Measuring innovation-oriented culture

The main variable of interest, the degree to which an agency has an innovation-oriented culture, is based on an aggregation of variables which are available in the COBRA data and which specifically gauge the innovative culture of an organization. A measurement instrument for organizational culture with thirty-six items and nine dimensions, as developed and tested by Tepeci (2001), was used in the survey. Following Tepeci's clustering of culture-items (2001), the following set of variables is used to construct the aggregation:

- Innovation
- Risk taking
- Willingness to experiment
- Creativity.

Each organization was asked to indicate on a scale of 0–6 how distinctive each of these features was for their organization as a whole. These responses have been aggregated, after which they have been divided by 24, resulting in a value between 0 and 1.[2] The index is found to be reliable (Cronbach's Alpha is 0.8033).

Autonomy and result control as independent variables

Two types of managerial autonomy are taken into account: personnel management autonomy (PA) and financial management autonomy (FA). Personnel management autonomy relates to the autonomy of an agency to take decisions concerning salary level, promotion and evaluation of staff, in general (so beyond individual decisions), without interference from ministries (see appendix, Table A1, for the precise wording of these questions). For each of the three items, organizations can either have no autonomy (score 0) or full autonomy (score 1). A dummy score is calculated, based on the aggregation of the three items; whereby score 1 indicates full autonomy on all three items.

Financial managerial autonomy is measured in a similar way. An index is constructed, based on the aggregation of the scores on three items: the extent to which the organization is able to shift personnel and running cost budgets, to set tariffs for services and products, and to shift personnel-running cost and investment budgets (cf. Table A1 in the appendix). However, unlike the indicators for personnel management autonomy, organizations can either have no autonomy (score 0), needing prior approval from parent ministries (score 1) or without prior approval from above (score 2). Each variable is recoded to a dummy (dummies are set to 0 if score equals 0 or 1 and set to 1 otherwise) and then aggregated. After which this sum is again transformed to a dummy, whereby score 1 indicates full autonomy on all three items.

The measurement of result control is based on (1) the accountability of the agency CEO for agency performance (results) to the government and (2) the extent to which the organization faces sanctions or rewards for its performance. Again a dummy variable is constructed which measures the extent to which the organization is subject to a high level of result control by government. A high level of result control in this case equals a 'hard' form of performance contracting, in which under- or over-performance leads to not only the accountability of the agency CEO, but also to sanctions or rewards (see Verhoest, 2005; Verhoest et al., 2010). A score of 0 refers to no result control or 'soft' result control (meaning CEO is accountable for the results, but without sanctions or rewards being given).

As we expect that the effect of management autonomy is linked with result control, we construct an interaction term of high personnel management autonomy and high result control and one of high financial management autonomy and high result control. This allows us to clearly distinguish the individual and combined effects of management autonomy and result control.

Control variables

In our analysis, we will also control for a number of other variables, which have proven to influence innovation or organizational culture in one way or other in earlier studies (e.g. Verhoest et al., 2010; Laegreid et al., 2011).

One such variable is size in terms of number of staff, which is measured in full time equivalents (FTE) and included as a continuous variable. In organizational innovativeness studies, organizational size is said to have a negative effect, because it increases the number of communication channels, formalization and centralization and inhibits the flow of innovative ideas (Hull and Hage, 1982; Borins, 2001), although Damanpour et al. (1989) and Damanpour (1991) finds a positive relation.

Another variable is budget, which is also included as continuous variable. Budget is expected to have a positive effect since large budgets allow an organization to support mechanisms for innovations in public sector organizations (e.g. Koch and Hauknes, 2005; NAO, 2006; Windrum, 2008; Borins, 2010), although others say that financial stress encourages agencies to change routines and consequently organizational behaviour. Note that Laegreid et al. (2011) do not find a relationship between budget size and innovation-oriented culture in agencies in Norway and Flanders.

Furthermore, also agencies age, and age is measured in years since founding is included as a continuous variable. According to the literature (e.g. Krause, 2003; Koch and Hauknes, 2005), age is clearly linked to organizational culture since the development of a distinct culture and tradition within an organization takes some time (Laegreid et al., 2011).

Because the distributions of size, budget and age are highly skewed, we use the logarithms such as ln(Size), ln(Budget) and ln(Age) in our models.

Moreover, we add dummies to examine the effects of agency type: a unit within government with no managerial autonomy (Type1), a unit with no legal independence but some managerial autonomy (Type2), a unit with legal independence, vested in public law (Type3) and a dummy for private law agencies (Type4). 'Unit of government without managerial autonomy (Type1)' is used as reference category and consequently omitted from the analyses. According to the literature (Bouckaert and van Dooren, 2003; Bach and Jann, 2010), organizations closer to government are less in direct contact with citizens and are more politicized, which is typically seen as hampering managerial instruments. Likewise, organizations further away from the government are more likely to develop innovation-oriented cultures.

Task-related factors are also taken into account by the inclusion of a dummy (Services). The dummy equals 1 if the agency's primary task includes general public services or business and industrial services. It equals 0 for primary tasks related to regulation, exercising public authority and policy formulation. Agencies having service delivery as primary task have been found to have a greater focus on innovation since they interact most with citizens and private organizations as customers (Borins, 1998; Vigoda-Gadot, 2009; Laegreid et al., 2011).

Descriptives

Table 1 shows the descriptive statistics for the dependent and explanatory variables. On average, agencies in our sample employ, in number of FTE, 1460 employees and have on average been in existence for 22 years. The median budget equals 10.42 million

Table 1: Summary statistics

Variable	Description	Mean	Std. Dev.	Median
Dependent variables				
Innovation-oriented culture	Proportion	0.64	0.19	0.67
Independent variables				
High pers. man. aut.	Dummy	0.44	0.50	0.00
High fin. man. aut.	Dummy	0.22	0.42	0.00
High res. contr.	Dummy	0.21	0.41	0.00
Primary task				
services	Dummy	0.61	0.49	1.00
Age	Continuous	22.05	28.83	12.00
Type				
Unit of national government (ref. cat.)	Dummy	0.12	0.32	0.00
No legal independence but some autonomy	Dummy	0.06	0.24	0.00
Legal independence	Dummy	0.51	0.50	1.00
Not- for- profit or private law based	Dummy	0.31	0.47	0.00
Budget (million €)	Continuous	1,564.97	15,056.46	10.42
Size (FTE)	Continuous	1,460.97	5,469.71	118.50

Note: $N = 222$. All variables are available for the following countries: Belgium (81 obs.), Italy (24 obs.), The Netherlands (54 obs.), Hong Kong (33 obs.) and Romania (30 obs.).

euros. When it comes to type, we notice that only 6 per cent of the examined agencies report to have no legal independence but some autonomy, while 51 per cent report to have legal independence; 12 per cent of the examined agencies are a unit of national government and 31 per cent is not-for-profit or private law based. From the statistics with regard to the organizational task, it becomes clear that a small majority of agencies (61 per cent) is involved in services. In general, more agencies have high personnel management autonomy (44 per cent) than financial management autonomy (22 per cent). Furthermore, only 21 per cent of agencies report having high result control. Finally, the average score on innovation-oriented culture equals 0.64.

Econometric model

As previous sections have shown, we expect that the degree of an innovation-oriented culture Y depends on personnel and financial management autonomy (PA & FA), result control (RC), other observable agency characteristics (Z) as well as non-observable factors (ε)[3]

$$Y = \beta_0 + \beta_1 PA + \beta_2 FA + \beta_3 RC + \beta_4 PA \times RC + \beta_5 FA \times RC + \Sigma_k \beta_6 Z_k + \varepsilon.$$

Z includes the control variables defined in previous section and a set of four country dummies. To estimate the relationship between the variables outlined above and Y, a specific econometric model is required. Ordinary least squares (OLS) is not suitable because it does not take into account that Y is bounded between 0 and 1, which can result in impossible predictions. We use a Tobit model, where one can set the lower and upper bounds, to deal with this kind of dependent. The assumptions of homo-scedasticity and normality were not violated.[4] The coefficients in the Tobit model can however be interpreted in a number of ways, depending upon one's interest. We are only interested in the latent variable, following Cameron and Trivedi (2005) the marginal effect is the following:

$$\frac{\partial E\{y_i^*\}}{\partial x_{ik}} = \beta_k$$

Since agencies are nested in different countries, we have to take this country clustering into account. Failing to do so will lead to biased results. We therefore include country dummies. This way we are able to investigate relations while controlling for the influence of country characteristics.

Our analyses include interaction terms, which are difficult to interpret in non-linear models such as the Tobit model. However instead of interpreting them in terms of the probability of being censored, or the expected outcome on not being censored, we only interpret them in terms of the latent outcome. In this case the interaction terms are relatively easy to interpret. The logic is that a Tobit model is non-linear in terms of the probability of being censored or the expected outcome condition on not being censored, but is a linear model in terms of the latent variable. Consequently we can interpret the coefficient of the interaction term as we would in a linear regression.

Robustness test: Reliability of the innovation index

There may however be a bias in the measurement of innovation-oriented culture; organizations may see themselves as innovative, but this doesn't necessarily mean that they also exhibit innovative behaviour. In other words, what organizations say should be reflected in what they do. Therefore we also include a correction of our main variable of interest for the actual use of 'new' and 'innovative' management techniques. By doing so, we are able to check the reliability of the index of innovation-oriented culture. An aggregation of the following set of management techniques is used as an indicator of innovative behaviour:[5]

- Internal allocation of resources of resources to organizational units on the basis of results
- Internal steering of the organizational subunits and lower management levels on objectives and results

- Assessment of results: development of internal reporting and evaluation systems to enable the governing board and the management to assess results with regard to the set objectives
- Extension of service delivery for pay
- Cost-calculation systems
- Result-oriented human resource management (e.g. result-oriented pay, setting of objectives and targets to achieve)
- Extended internal management autonomy of lower management levels concerning financial and human resources management
- Development of innovative products and services.

For each of these management techniques, the survey asked the agency CEO to which extent these techniques were implemented and used in their organization. These scores were aggregated and transformed to a variable with ten categories. Apart from a score on innovation-oriented culture, each agency thus also receives a score on the use of the above-mentioned management techniques, as a measurement of their innovative behaviour. To make both scores comparable, the score on innovation-oriented culture is also transformed to a variable with ten categories. If there is a deviation of more than three categories between the indexes, a penalty is given. This is only done in one way, namely when agencies have a higher score for innovation-oriented culture compared to their score for the use of innovative management techniques. We thus correct for an overestimation of the value for innovation-oriented culture or, in other words, for innovation-oriented culture which does not manifest itself clearly in innovative behaviour at an equal level. For each difference higher than three categories, the score of innovation-oriented culture is reduced by 10 per cent. Table 2 gives an overview of the used penalties.

Table 2: Used penalties

Innovation-oriented culture							
10	9	8	7	6	5		
−10%						6	
−20%	−10%					5	
−30%	−20%	−10%				4	Use of management
−40%	−30%	−20%	−10%			3	techniques as manifestations
−50%	−40%	−30%	−20%	−10%		2	of innovative behavior
−60%	−50%	−40%	−30%	−20%	−10%	1	

For example, when an agency has a very high score for innovation-oriented culture and falls within category 9, but does not use a lot of management techniques and consequently only falls within category 1, the initial score on innovation-oriented culture is reduced by 50 per cent.

In the following section, we will discuss the results for the original and corrected index of innovation-oriented culture.

RESULTS

The results of the Tobit estimations are presented in Table 3. Models 1–4 make use of the original index for innovation-oriented culture while model 5 uses the corrected index. Models 2, 4 and 5 include all explanatory variables while models 1 and 3 include only the main effects of managerial autonomy and result control. Models 3, 4 and 5 include the interaction terms. When comparing models, we notice that the inclusion of extra variables has no effect on the statistical significance of autonomy-related variables. Furthermore, when comparing model 4 (original index) and model 5 (corrected index), we notice no difference in signs or significance of the independent variables, indicating that the original index of innovation-oriented culture is reliable.

High financial management autonomy proves to have a positive significant effect on the innovation-oriented culture of an agency. In other words, higher financial management autonomy will lead to a more innovation-oriented culture. High result control and high personnel management autonomy, on the other hand, are not statistically significant for models 1 and 2. However, these variables prove to be positive and significant for models 3, 4 and 5. These are the models that contain the interaction terms. The interaction term between high financial management autonomy and high result control is not statistically significant, but, surprisingly, the interaction term between personnel management autonomy and high result control is statistically significant but negative. The negative coefficients of the interaction term indicate that the effect of high personnel management autonomy on innovation-oriented culture decreases when it is combined with high result control (alternatively, one could say that the effect of high result control on innovation-oriented culture decreases when it is combined with high personnel management autonomy). Therefore, the effect of high personnel management autonomy on the innovation-oriented culture is ambiguous, causing models without interaction terms to fail in observing the precise effect of high personnel management autonomy. This does not seem to be the case with high financial management autonomy: high result control does not alter its effect.

When examining the control variables (models 2, 4 and 5), we notice significant effects of budget and size. Larger agencies with a smaller budget will be more likely to have an innovation-oriented culture. Primary task and legal type of an agency have no statistically significant effects. Although agencies with legal independence are less likely to have an innovation-oriented culture than agencies being a unit of government

Table 3: Tobit estimations

Variables	Original index				Corrected index
	Model 1 dF/dx	Model 2 dF/dx	Model 3 dF/dx	Model 4 dF/dx	Model 5 dF/dx
High pers. Man. Aut. (1)	0.029	0.047	0.071*	0.095**	0.103***
	(0.030)	(0.032)	(0.037)	(0.038)	(0.037)
High fin. Man. Aut. (2)	0.114***	0.103***	0.114***	0.101***	0.086**
	(0.032)	(0.036)	(0.037)	(0.039)	(0.037)
High res. Con. (3)	0.033	0.036	0.083**	0.093**	0.120***
	(0.028)	(0.028)	(0.036)	(0.036)	(0.035)
Interaction (1) & (3)			−0.113**	−0.125**	−0.140***
			(0.054)	(0.053)	(0.051)
Interaction (2) & (3)			−0.020	−0.016	−0.039
			(0.071)	(0.070)	(0.068)
Services		0.030		0.028	0.037
		(0.030)		(0.030)	(0.029)
Age		−0.023		−0.024	−0.018
		(0.015)		(0.015)	(0.014)
Type2		0.002		−0.013	−0.009
		(0.063)		(0.062)	(0.060)
Type3		−0.076*		−0.093**	−0.088**
		(0.044)		(0.044)	(0.043)
Type4		−0.061		−0.071	−0.053
		(0.053)		(0.053)	(0.051)
Budget		−0.017**		−0.016**	−0.014**
		(0.007)		(0.007)	(0.007)
Size		0.018**		0.016*	0.019**
		(0.008)		(0.008)	(0.008)
Country dummies	Included	Included	Included	Included	Included
Observations	222	222	222	222	222
Log-likelihood	57.680	65.282	60.222	68.371	75.368
McKelvey & Zavoina's R2: R^2	0.104	0.124	0.124	0.186	0.200
Joint significance of country dummies	3.26**	3.92***	3.38**	4.41***	3.41**
Joint significance of type dummies	–	1.33	–	1.80	1.81

Notes: Significance levels: *10%; **5%; ***1%. All models contain a constant and four country dummies. Standard errors in parentheses.

(reference category), the overall effect of agency type is not significant. As mentioned previously, country dummies have been included to control for differences across countries. Not surprisingly, these dummies prove to be significant. In other words country-specific characteristics significantly affect the innovation-oriented culture of an organization.

CONCLUSION AND DISCUSSION

N·B

The results indicate that the link between managerial autonomy and result control, on the one hand, and innovation-oriented culture, on the other hand, is not as clear cut as expected. High financial management autonomy, high personnel management autonomy and high result control each proved independently to have strong positive effects on innovation-oriented culture. However, when high result control is combined with high financial management autonomy, no enforcing effects were observed. On the other hand, when agencies have high personnel management autonomy while being under high levels of result control by government, they will be less likely to exhibit an innovation-oriented culture. Studies analysing the effect of reforms on change of organizational cultures have not taken the effect of the interaction between result control and managerial autonomy on organizational culture into account, which can explain the ambiguous effects of managerial autonomy and result control on innovative behaviour and culture found in literature. This article contributes to the literature in at least three ways.

First, our conceptual setup allows us to examine the different effects of managerial autonomy and result control, separately and in interaction, on organizational culture in detail. Furthermore, by controlling for innovative behaviour, we are able to verify the reliability of the index of innovation-oriented culture.

Second, the results support the assumption that granting a high level of managerial autonomy to these agencies is likely to bring about a more innovation-oriented culture in these agencies, which could be seen as a support for managerialist theories, arguments related to specialization, organizational legitimacy (Verhoest et al., 2007) or identity building. More managerial autonomy allows for more flexibility in the use of staff and finances, more free resources for innovation and experimenting. Moreover, also 'hard' forms of result control by government, entailing performance-related sanctions and rewards, induces higher levels of innovation-oriented organizational cultures, compared to no or 'soft' result control. Clear performance targets linked to sanctions or rewards seemingly may induce more risk taking and experimenting (NAO, 2006). However, the core of NPM that both managerial autonomy and hard result control are simultaneously and in combination needed to get agencies to become more risk-willing and innovative is not supported by our data. In case of financial management autonomy, the effect stays the same with or without result control. A possible explanation can be that agencies seldom suffer the financial consequences of their risk-taking behaviour; sanctions are selectively foreseen by design (e.g. 42 per cent reported them in the case of Italian agencies, see Ongaro, 2008) and quite seldom set in action (Fedele et al., 2007; Ongaro, 2009), making result control obsolete.

Another explanation can be that if managers enjoy financial management autonomy, they will support innovative activities as indicated by our data. Yet to remain autonomous, they will try to increase performance by using innovative activities as a source of legitimacy or trust in the eyes of superior bodies or the general public (see Verhoest et al., 2007). This would make the use of result control in combination with financial management autonomy ineffective.

However, when high personnel management autonomy is combined with high result control, a lower level of innovation-oriented culture is achieved. Similarly, hard forms of result control have a positive effect but only when this is not combined with a high level of personnel management autonomy. There are two potential explanations for this. First, high personnel autonomy enables and induces managers and their staff to embark upon risky experiments, but the threat of sanctions in case of bad performance may stifle this urge to take risks. For experimenting, risk taking and innovations may fail, leading to declining performance (see Thaler et al., 1997). Hence, the threat of looming sanctions may enforce risk-aversive behaviour of the agency managers and their staff. A second potential explanation is the role of professionals in the (non)-diffusion of innovation (Ferlie et al., 2005). Professionals, who thrive in organizations with high levels of personnel management autonomy, are particularly sensitive for hard result control and related instruments, like performance targets and incentives, and may develop counteracting strategies.

A third contribution of this article lies in the lack of effects of primary task, age and type of agency, which partially refutes previous research (e.g. Borins, 1998; Krause, 2003; Koch and Hauknes, 2005; Vigoda-Gadot, 2009; Laegreid et al., 2011). For example, we found that larger agencies exhibit a stronger innovation-oriented culture compared to smaller agencies. Apparently, the higher degree of formalization, centralization, longer communication channels and hierarchical levels which is central to large organizations does not impede innovation-orientedness. On the other hand, we found that larger budgets result in a less innovation-oriented culture – which also is in contrast with existing empirical studies. The potential consequences of failed innovations and experiments are perhaps larger in such agencies, which are known to be relatively more politically salient and hence under more scrutiny (Pollitt et al., 2004). Moreover, budgetary stress, which could be associated with smaller budgets, could enhance innovation-seeking attitudes.

Our results have some policy implications as well. Granting agencies managerial autonomy is beneficial to innovation-oriented cultures. However, the use of result control will lead to ambiguous results and should therefore be well considered. Policymakers should be aware that combining high levels of personnel management autonomy and sanctioning or rewarding them for their results (e.g. by contracts) may in fact hinder innovation. However, not only managerial autonomy and result control are important determinants of innovation-oriented culture, policymakers should also take into account that the size of the agency's budget has an important role on the innovation-oriented culture. The higher the budget, the less likely an agency will have an innovation-oriented culture. Finally, policymakers should be aware that an innovation-oriented culture is more likely to exist in larger organizations. When trying to encourage an innovation-oriented culture within the public sector, policy makers should thus focus on the precarious balance between managerial autonomy and result control, while taking into account the budget and size of the organization. Policy makers should thus develop different strategies for different (individual) agencies when they want to stimulate innovation because straightforward NPM recipes may be counterproductive.

ACKNOWLEDGEMENTS

The COBRA network developed a joint survey instrument to study the autonomy and control of semi-autonomous agencies. COBRA members of the following countries were involved in the collection of survey data which was used for this article: Belgium (Flanders) (Koen Verhoest, Bram Verschuere and Geert Bouckaert – University of Leuven), Italy (Eduardo Ongaro, Dario Barbieri – Bocconi University, Paolo Fedele – Udine University; and Davide Galli – Catholic University of Milan), The Netherlands (Sandra van Thiel – Radboud University Nijmegen and Kutsal Yesilkagit – University of Utrecht), Hong Kong (Martin Painter – City University of Hong Kong), and Romania (Prof Calin Hintea and Dr Adrin Hudrea – Babes-Bolyai University). We owe many thanks to these colleagues.

NOTES

1 The Granger causality test is a statistical hypothesis test for determining whether one time series is useful in forecasting another. See: Greene (2003).
2 In principle the level of measurement of a Likert-type index is ordinal. However, we are treating the measurement as if it were interval. This practice allows us to create an index and it is our opinion that treating Likert-type scales as if they were interval measures provides more advantages than disadvantages in this case (7-point Likert scales).
3 For simplicity, we suppress agency subscripts i.
4 See Appendix for a more detailed discussion of the model.
5 Cronbach's Alpha for the index of management techniques equals 0.76.

REFERENCES

Bach, T. and Jann, W. (2010) Animals in the Administrative Zoo: Organizational Change and Agency Autonomy in Germany. *International Review of Administrative Sciences*, 76:3 pp443–68.
Behn, R. (1999) 'Do Goals Help Create Innovative Organizations?' in H. G. Frederickson and J. M. Johnston (eds) *Public Management Reform and Innovation: Research, Theory, and Application*, pp70–88. Tuscaloosa, AL: University of Alabama Press.

Boorsma, P. and Halachmi, A. (2008) *Inter and Intra Government Arrangements for Productivity: An Agency Approach*, Boston, MA: Kluwer Academic Publishers.

Borins, S. (1998) *Innovating with Integrity: How Local Heroes Are Transforming American Government*, Washington, DC: Georgetown University Press.

Borins, S. (2001) *The Challenge of Innovating in Government*, Arlington, VA: The PricewaterhouseCoopers Endowment for the Business of Government.

Borins, S. (2002) Leadership and Innovation in the Public Sector. *Leadership & Organization Development Journal*, 23:8 pp467–76.

Borins, S. (2010) Strategic Planning from Robert McNamara to Gov 2.0. *Public Administration Review*, 70 pp220–1.

Bouckaert, G. (2007) 'Cultural Characteristics from Public Management Reforms Worldwide' in K. Schedler and I. Proeller (eds) *Cultural Aspects of Public Management Reforms*. Amsterdam: Elsevier.

Bouckaert, G. and van Dooren, W. (2003) 'Performance Measurement and Management in Public Sector Organizations' in T. Bovaird and E. Löffler (eds) *Public Management and Governance*. London: Routledge.

Brettel, M. and Cleven, N. J. (2011) Innovation Culture, Collaboration with External Partners and NPD Performance. *Creativity and Innovation Management*, 20 pp253–72.

Cameron, A. C. and Trivedi, P. K. (2005) *Microeconometrics*, Cambridge: Cambridge University Press.

Carpenter, D. P. (2001) *The Forging of Bureaucratic Autonomy: Reputations, Networks, and Policy Innovation in Executive Agencies*, Princeton, NJ: Princeton University Press.

Chia, Y. M. and Koh, H. C. (2007) Organizational Culture and the Adoption of Management Accounting Practices in the Public Sector: A Singapore Study. *Financial Accountability and Management*, 23:2 pp189–213.

Damanpour, F. (1991) Organizational Innovation: A Meta-Analysis of Effects of Determinants and Moderators. *Academy of Management Journal*, 34 pp555–90.

Damanpour, F., Szabat, K. A. and Evan, W. M. (1989) The Relationship Between Types of Innovation and Organizational Performance. *Journal of Management Studies*, 26:6 pp587–601.

de Bruijn, H. and Dicke, W. (2006) Strategies for Safeguarding Public Values in Liberalized Utility Sectors. *Public Administration*, 84:3 pp717–37.

Demuzere, S. (2012) 'Verklarende factoren van de implementatie vankwaliteitsmanagementtechnieken. Een studie binnen de Vlaamse Overheid'. Catholic University Leuven (Katholieke Universiteit Leuven), Doctoral dissertation.

Deshpandé, R., Farley, J. U. and Webster, F. E. (1993) Corporate Culture, Customer Orientation, and Innovativeness in Japanese Firms – A Quadrad Analysis. *Journal of Marketing*, 57 pp23–7.

Dobni, C. B. (2008) Measuring Innovation Culture in Organizations: The Development of a Generalized Innovation Culture Construct Using Exploratory Factor Analysis. *European Journal of Innovation Management*, 11:4 pp539–59.

Dunleavy, P. (1996) 'Political Behaviour: Institutional and Experiential Approaches' in R. E. Goodin and H. D. Klingemann (eds) *A New Handbook of Politics*, vol. 9. Oxford: Oxford University Press.

Dunleavy, P., Margetts, H., Bastow, S. and Tinkler, J. (2006) New Public Management Is Dead – Long Live Digital-Era Governance. *Journal of Public Administration Research and Theory*, 16:3 pp467–94.

Egeberg, M. (2003) 'How Bureaucratic Structure Matters: An Organizational Perspective' in B. G. Peters and J. Pierre (eds) *Handbook of Public Administration*. London: Sage.

Egeberg, M. and Trondal, J. (2009) Political Leadership and Bureaucratic Autonomy. Effects of Agencification. *Governance*, 22:4 pp673–88.

Farr, J. L. and Ford, C. M. (1990) 'Individual Innovation' in M. A. West and J. L. Farr (eds) *Innovation and Creativity at Work*. Chichester: John Wiley & Sons.

Fedele, P., Galli, D. and Ongaro, E. (2007) Disaggregation, Autonomy and Re-Regulation, Contractualism: Public Agencies in Italy (1992–2005). *Public Management Review*, 9:4 pp557–85.

Ferlie, E., Fitzgerald, L., Martin, W. and Hawkins, C. (2005) The Non-Spread of Innovation: The Mediating Role of Professionals. *Academy of Management Journal*, 48:1 pp117–34.

Glick, W. H. (1985) Conceptualizing and Measuring Organizational and Psychological Climate: Pitfalls in Multilevel Research. *Academy of Management Review*, 10 pp601–16.

Greene, W. (2003) *Econometric Analysis*, Upper Saddle River, NJ: Prentice Hall.

Hood, C. (1991) A Public Management for All Seasons. *Public Administration*, 69 pp3–19.

Hood, C. (1995) Contemporary Public Management: A New Global Paradigm? *Public Policy and Administration*, 10:2 pp104–17.

Hull, F. M. and Hage, J. (1982) Organizing for Innovation: Beyond the Burns and Stalker's Organic Type. *Sociology*, 16:4 pp564–77.

Jenkins, G. J., Donald, R. D., Bedard, J. C. and Curtis, M. B. (2008) Accounting Firm Culture and Governance: A Research Synthesis. *Behavioral Research in Accounting*, 20:1 pp45–74.

Kettle, D. F. (1997) The Global Revolution in Public Management: Driving Themes, Missing Links. *Journal of Policy Analysis and Management*, 16 pp446–62.

Koberg, C. S. and Chusmir, L. H. (1987) Organizational Culture Relationships with Creativity and Other Job-Related Variables. *Journal of Business Research*, 15 pp397–409.

Koch, P. and Hauknes, J. (2005) *On Innovation in the Public Sector: Academic Summary Report of Publin*, Oslo: NIFU STEP, Publin Report No. D20.

Krause, G. A. (2003) 'Agency Risk Propensities Involving the Demand for Bureaucratic Discretion' in G. A. Krause and K. J. Meier (eds) *Politics, Policy and Organizations: Frontiers in the Scientific Study of Bureaucracy*. Ann Arbor, MI: University of Michigan Press.

Laegreid, P., Roness, P. G. and Verhoest, K. (2011) Explaining the Innovative Culture and Activities of State Agencies. *Organization Studies*, 32:10 pp1321–47.

Laegreid, P. and Verhoest, K. eds. (2010) *Governance of Public Sector Organizations*, Basingstoke: Palgrave Macmillan.

Lane, J. E. (2001) *New Public Management*, London: Routledge.

Lyons, S. T., Duxbury, L. E. and Higgins, C. (2006) A Comparison of the Values and Commitment of Private Sector, Public Sector, and Parapublic Sector Employees. *Public Administration Review*, 66:4 pp605–18.

Maesschalck, J. (2004) The Impact of New Public Management Reforms on Public Servants' Ethics: Towards a Theory. *Public Administration*, 82:2 pp465–89.

Maor, M. (1999) The Paradox of Managerialism. *Public Administration Review*, 59 pp5–18.

NAO (2006) *Achieving Innovation in Central Government Organisations: Detailed Research Findings*, London: National Audit Office HC 1447-II, Session 2005–2006.

OECD (1994) *Performance Management in Government: Performance Measurement and Results Oriented Management*, Paris: Public Management Committee, OECD.

OECD (1997) *In Search of Results: Performance Management Practices in Ten OECD Countries*, Paris: Public Management Committee, OECD.

Ongaro, E. ed. (2008) *L'Organizzazione Dello Stato Tra Autonomia E Policy Capacity*, Soveria Mannelli: Rubbettino.

Ongaro, E. (2009) *Public Management Reform and Modernization: Trajectories of Administrative Change in Italy, France, Greece, Portugal and Spain*, Cheltenham, UK: Edward Elgar.

Ongaro, E. (2011) The Role of Politics and Institutions in the Italian Administrative Reform Trajectory. *Public Administration*, 89:3 pp738–55.

Ongaro, E. and Rodolfi, E. (1998) L'innovazione Nella Gestione Delle Università Italiane: Uno Studio Di Casi Di Introduzione Del Controllo Di Gestione [Innovation in the Management of Italian Universities: A Multiple Case Study of Introduction of the Management Control System]. *Azienda Pubblica*, 1–2 pp77–101.

Osborne, S. (1998) *Voluntary Organizations and Innovation in Public Services*, London: Routledge.

Osborne, D. and Gaebler, T. (1993) *Reinventing Government: How the Entrepreneurial Spirit Is Transforming the Public Sector*, New York: Penguin.

Papke, L. E. and Wooldridge, J. M. (1996) Econometric Methods for Fractional Response Variables with an Application to 401(k) Plan Participation Rates. *Journal of Applied Econometrics*, 11 pp619–32.

Pettigrew, A. M. (1979) On Studying Organizational Cultures. *Administrative Science Quarterly*, 24:4 pp570–81.

Pollitt, C. (2004) 'Theoretical Overview' in C. Pollitt and C. Talbot (eds) *Unbundled Government. A Critical Analysis of the Global Trend to Agencies, Quangos and Contractualisation*. London: Routledge.

Pollitt, C. and Bouckaert, G. (2004) *Public Management Reform: A Comparative Analysis*, 2nd ed, Oxford: Oxford University Press.

Pollitt, C. and Bouckaert, G. (2011) *Public Management Reform: A Comparative Analysis – NPM, New Public Governance and the Neo-Weberian State*, 3rd ed, Oxford: Oxford University Press.

Pollitt, C. and Talbot, C. eds. (2004) *Unbundled Government*, London: Routledge.

Pollitt, C., Talbot, C., Caulfield, J. and Smullen, A. (2004) *Agencies. How Government Do Things with Semi-Autonomous Organizations*, Basingstoke: Palgrave Macmillan.

Reigle, R. F. (2001) Measuring Organic and Mechanic Cultures. *Engineering Management Journal*, 13:4 pp3–8.

Rogers, E. M. (2003) *Diffusion of Innovations*, 5th ed, New York: Free Press.

Schedler, K. and Proeller, I. eds. (2007) *Cultural Aspects of Public Management Reform*, Oxford: Elsevier.

Slater, S. and Narver, J. (1995) Market Orientation and the Learning Organisation. *Journal of Marketing*, 59:3 pp63–74.

Tepeci, M. (2001) *The Effect of Personal Values, Organizational Cultures, and Person–Organization Fit on Individual Outcomes in the Restaurant Industry*, University Park, PA: School of Hotel, Restaurant and Recreation Management, Pennsylvania State University, Doctoral dissertation.

Thaler, R., Tversky, A., Kahneman, D. and Schwarz, A. (1997) The Effect of Myopia and Loss Aversion on Risk Taking: An Experimental Test. *Quarterly Journal of Economics*, 112 pp647–61.

Thompson, V. A. (1965) Bureaucracy and Innovation. *Administrative Science Quarterly*, 10 pp1–20.

van der Wal, Z. and Huberts, L. W. J. C. (2008) Value Solidity in Government and Business. Results of an Empirical Study on Public and Private Sector Organizational Values. *American Review of Public Administration*, 38:3 pp264–85.

van Thiel, S. (2008) 'Het Lege Nest Syndroom: Ministeries Na Verzelfstandiging' in F. Ankersmit and L. Klinkers (eds) *De Tien Plagen Van De Staat: De Bedrijfsmatige Overheid Gewogen*, pp170–88. Amsterdam: Van Gennep.

van Thiel, S. and van der Wal, Z. (2010) The Effect of Organizational Value Congruence on the Relationship Between Ministries and Quangos. *Public Organization Review*, 10 pp377–97.

van Thiel, S. and Yesilkagit, K. (2011) Good Neighbours or Distant Friends? Trust Between Dutch Ministries and Their Executive Agencies. *Public Management Review*, 13:6 pp783–802.

Veenswijk, M. and Hakvoort, J. L. M. (2002) Public-Private Transformations. Institutional Shifts, Cultural Changes and Altering Identities: Two Case Studies. *Public Administration*, 80:3 pp543–55.

Verhoest, K. (2005) Effects of Autonomy, Performance Contracting, and Competition on the Performance of a Public Agency: A Case Study. *Policy Studies Journal*, 33:2 pp235–58.

Verhoest, K., Peters, B. G., Bouckaert, G. and Verschuere, B. (2004) The Study of Organisational Autonomy: A Conceptual Review. *Public Administration and Development*, 24:2 pp101–18.

Verhoest, K., Roness, P. G., Verschuere, B., Rubecksen, K. and MacCarthaig, M. (2010) *Autonomy and Control of State Agencies: Comparing States and Agencies*, Hampshire: Palgrave Macmillan.

Verhoest, K., van Thiel, S., Bouckaert, G. and Lægreid, P. eds. (2012) *Government Agencies in Europe and Beyond: Practices and Lessons from 30 Countries*, Basingstoke: Palgrave Macmillan.

Verhoest, K., Verschuere, B. and Bouckaert, G. (2007) Pressure, Legitimacy, and Innovative Behavior by Public Organizations. *Governance*, 20:3 pp469–97.

Vigoda-Gadot, E. (2009) *Building Strong Nations: Improving Governability and Public Management*, Aldershot: Ashgate.

Windrum, P. (2008) 'Innovation and Entrepreneurship in Public Services' in P. Windrum and P. Koch (eds) *Innovation in Public Sector Services: Entrepreneurship, Creativity and Management*. Cheltenham: Edward Elgar.

Wooldridge, J. M. (2002) *Econometric Analysis of Cross Section and Panel Data*, Cambridge, MA: MIT Press.

APPENDIX

Table A1: Survey questions used for construction of indexes on managerial autonomy

Strategic personnel management autonomy	Provided that the organization has own staff, can the organization without interference from above (without ministerial or departmental influence) set the general policy for the organization conditions for promotions?
	Provided that the organization has own staff, can the organization without interference from above (without ministerial or departmental influence) set general policy for the level of salaries?
	Provided that the organization has own staff, can the organization without interference from above (without ministerial or departmental influence) set general policy for the way of evaluating personnel?
Strategic financial management autonomy	Can your organization itself shift between the budgets for personnel-running costs without approval from above (ministerial or departmental approval)?
	Can your organization itself set tariffs for services or products without approval from above (ministerial or departmental approval)?
	Can your organization itself shift between the budgets for personnel or running costs on the one hand and investments on the other hand without approval from above (ministerial or departmental approval)?

Econometric estimates

The estimated Tobit model can be written as follows (see e.g. Greene, 2003):

$$Y_i^* = X_i'\beta + \varepsilon_i, \quad \text{with } \varepsilon_i \sim N(0, \sigma^2)$$

where $Y*$ stands either for innovation-oriented culture or the corrected index o. innovation-oriented culture. X represents a matrix of regeressors, β are the parameters that have to be estimated, and ε is the disturbance term.

We have to take some assumptions underlying the Tobit model into account such as normal distributed errors and homoscedasticity, so $\varepsilon \sim N\ 0, \sigma^2$. Departure from homoscedasticity or normality will cause the estimators to be inconsistent (Wooldridge, 2002). To test the normality assumption, we estimate the Tobit model with polynomials (quadratic, cubic) of the fitted values as additional regressors. A Wald test is then performed to check whether these polynomials have jointly significant explanatory power. For all our models, the null hypothesis of normality could not be rejected.

If the assumption of homoscedasticity is violated in Tobit models, regressions may result in inconsistent coefficient estimates. Consequently, we also estimated hetero-scedastic models where we model a heteroscedasticity term. The heteroscedasticity term includes the country dummies. When performing LR-tests on heteroscedasticity for all models, we notice that the null hypothesis (homoscedasticity) cannot be rejected in any of the models. When performing a Wald test on the joint significance of the variables in the heteroscedasticity term, the assumption of homoscedasticity is again satisfied. As a robustness check, we also estimated a generalized linear model (GLM) as proposed by Papke and Wooldridge (1996). More in particular, we estimated the following specification:

$$E(Y|x) = G(\beta_1 + \beta_1 PA + \beta_2 FA + \beta_3 RC + \beta_4 PA \times RC + \beta_5 FA \times RC +$$
$$\beta_6 SERVICES + \beta_7 AGE + \beta_8 TYPE + \beta_9 BUDGET +$$
$$\beta_{10} SIZE + \beta_{10} COUNTRY)$$

whereby $G(.)$ is specified as a logistic function, i.e. $G(z) = \exp(z)/(1 + \exp(z))$. As this kind of regression leads to similar results as those of the Tobit analysis, they are omitted.[1] However it proves that the results of the Tobit model are reliable.

NOTE

1 GLM estimates are available upon request from the author.

FROM HERO-INNOVATORS TO DISTRIBUTED HEROISM

An in-depth analysis of the role of individuals in public sector innovation

A. J. Meijer

A. J. Meijer
School of Governance
Utrecht University
Utrecht
The Netherlands

...ding on the literature on collaborative leadership, this paper explores the roles of individual persons in processes of public innovation. On the basis of a literature review, a heuristic model is developed that consists of roles at different levels (entrepreneurial leadership versus innovation realization) and in different phases (idea generation, selection, testing, scaling-up, and diffusion). The value of this model is explored through an in-depth, longitudinal analysis of a police innovation in the Netherlands. The empirical study underlines the value of the model and shows that, although individual hero-innovators may not exist, distributed heroism does.

INTRODUCTION

The role of individual person in processes of public sector innovation is seen as important but it is still not well understood. Doig and Hargrove (1987, 2) emphasize that much of the literature on public innovation prefers to focus on structural factors since the role of individual persons appears difficult to treat when the researcher's goal is generalization. Although some assume that characteristics of creative individuals could be identified (Roberts and King 1991, 1996), Georgiades and Phillimore (1975) have convincingly argued that the 'hero-innovator' does not exist. This provocative statement, however, does not mean that individuals do not make a difference. Osborne (1998) highlights that the role of individuals needs to be understood within organizational and institutional contexts, and general characteristics of innovative individuals cannot be identified.

Interesting empirical work into the role of individual persons in public sector innovation has been done by Doig and Hargrove (1987) (see also: Schin and McClomb 1998). This research helps to understand the role of entrepreneurial leadership but it puts an emphasis on the roles of executives. Their line of analysis ignores the fact that leadership may be important but, in the end, individuals at the work floor invent and develop these innovations. Little empirical work has been done that connects the roles of entrepreneurial leadership with various other individual innovation roles in the organization. An analysis of this variety of innovation roles can build upon the literature on a distributive leadership (Currie and Lockett 2011; Gronn 2002, 2009; Spillane 2006) that conceptualizes distributive leadership as an activity that is shared, interactive, and emergent. Combining the literature on a public sector innovation and distributed leadership can provide for a richer understanding of the roles of individuals in processes of the public sector innovation.

This paper aims to contribute to the literature on the public sector innovation by presenting an empirical analysis of the shared, interactive, and emergent roles of various individuals in the public innovation. To this end, the paper will analyse the micro-dynamics of a public innovation process over a period of nearly twenty years. We will analyse how a new system for engaging citizens in police investigations was developed and implemented and how it became a standard element in the Dutch policing. The analysis focuses on the role of entrepreneurial leadership and of individuals at various other positions within the organization. Overall, the paper will develop a perspective on a 'distributed heroism' as an alternative to the idea of a 'hero-innovator'.

PUBLIC SECTOR INNOVATION

Innovation in the public sector has long been regarded as 'non-existent' or even 'aberrant' since innovations should come from (elected) politicians and not from bureaucrats (Bernier and Hafsi 2007). This changed in the 1990s with the growing attention for a public management, and the literature on innovation in the public sector has rapidly expanded (Altshuler and Behn 1997; Bekkers et al. 2011a; Hartley 2005;

Korteland 2011; Osborne and Brown 2005; Perri 6 1993; Sørensen and Torfing 2011; Walker 2006). The whole field of innovation studies still pays distribute to Everett Rogers (1995) but the academic understanding of processes of innovation has become much richer. Insights from disciplines such as economy, psychology and business administration have resulted in a variety of theories about innovation.

At its core, innovation is still a disputed term because of its strong normative connotation. Rogers (1995) triggered this dispute by qualifying those who were unwilling to adopt as 'laggards'. The normative orientation comes back in various other perspectives on innovation (for an overview: Brown and Osborne 2005; Osborne and Brown 2011). While Porter (1985) relates innovation to a competitive advantage, Kolb et al. (1979) sees innovation as a form of continuous improvement and Brown and Osborne (2005, 190) highlight that innovation is often regarded as a normative/ideological good that is pursued irrespective of its actual impact on an efficiency or effectiveness. These normative orientations may be useful for practitioners but they are not helpful for the empirical study of innovations. To study innovations in the public sector, we follow Bekkers et al. (2011b, 197) who define this as 'a learning process in which governments attempt to meet specific societal challenges'. The word 'attempt' is important since it underlines that innovations may fail. Bekkers et al. (2011b, 197) indicate that these societal challenges can be met by developing new services, technologies, organizational structures, management approaches, governance processes and policy concepts. Their conceptualization highlights that an innovative public sector can be understood as a desire to create new and meaningful connections between the government and society.

Innovation processes are almost by definition chaotic processes, and stage models should certainly not be regarded as a 'blue print' for the innovation processes. Still, these models have value for analysing chaotic innovation processes since they help to distinguish the different dynamics that innovations run into and, more specifically, they can help to analyse the various roles of individuals in the innovation processes. An important finding in the literature is that there are different dynamics in the various stages of the innovation process (Damanpour 1991; Korteland 2011, 24; Mumford et al. 2002; Oliver 2000; Osborne and Brown 2005, 129), and this idea shows striking similarities with the literature on the phases of the policy cycle (Howlett and Ramesh 1995). Combining these two approaches, we propose the following analytical phases:

- *Idea generation*. In this phase, the idea of transforming the government practices through an innovation is developed. Perceptual barriers play a key role in this barrier: many actors will not be prepared to change the way they have been viewing themselves, others and the world (King 2000, 306).
- *Idea selection*. Out of all the ideas that are being developed within an organization, some are selected for further development. Organizational attention and resources are scarce and hence selection is needed. Political and organizational

barriers are crucial here: the idea needs to compete with other ideas for attention and resources (Morabito 2008).

- *Idea testing*. The idea is developed and tested on a small scale to see whether it 'works' in practice (Oliver 2000, 375). In this phase, the innovation runs into a range of technological, organizational and institutional barriers. Does the technology work? Will people in the organization act as was expected? Does the innovation fit within institutional rules (Meijer and Zouridis 2006)?

- *Idea scaling-up*. A successful test will be followed by scaling-up of the idea to get it implemented on a larger scale and embedded in the organization (Lee and Luykx 2005; Van Mele 2006). In this phase, financial and capacity barriers may prevent the process of innovation from moving forward.

- *Idea diffusion*. If the innovation has been turned into a successful commodity it can now be transferred to other contexts: the process of diffusion and adoption can take place (Korteland 2011; Oliver 2000; Rogers 1995).

The model suggests a linear development but the literature highlights that actual innovation processes may move back and forth between various stages and also bypass some of them (Korteland 2011, 26) – the value of the stage model in acknowledging that the dynamics (and hence the barriers and the role of individual persons) differs over time.

THE ROLE OF INDIVIDUAL PERSONS IN INNOVATION

The idea of a creative genius who thinks up a brilliant idea that brings a range of improvements is appealing and comes back in all kinds of books and films. On the basis of extensive research, Roberts and King (1991, 1996) built a model of the public entrepreneur or 'hero-innovator'. This 'hero-innovator' is tenacious, works long hour, is goal driven, willing to take risks, confident and skilled in using political connections (Brown and Osborne 2005, 172). Doig and Hargrove (1987, 10) identify three sets of capacities that are associated with successful innovators: a capacity to engage in rational analysis, an ability to see new possibilities offered by the evolving historical situation and a desire to make a difference. More down to earth is Bernier and Hafsi's (2007) identification of autonomy, innovation, risk taking, pro-activeness, and competitive aggression as the dimensions that underlie the values and behaviors of entrepreneurs. Roberts and King (1991, 1996) argue that not everyone can be a hero-innovator but, at the same time, people can be taught and stimulated to be more entrepreneurial. This idea of the hero-innovator has been criticized. Osborne (1998) highlights that individual traits may be important but need to be understood within the organizational context and argues that a contingency approach is crucial to understanding the role of individual persons in innovation in the public service organizations.

Much of the innovation literature focuses on individual persons at executive positions in the organization, and this is generally referred to as entrepreneurial leadership (Doig and Hargrove 1987, 7). The entrepreneurial leader has to create a climate that is favourable to the development and realization of new ideas. Doig and Hargrove (1987) emphasize that a strong executive leadership is needed to drive innovations in the public sector through rhetorical leadership and coalition-building. Bekkers et al. (2011b, 213) mention three roles for managers: (1) boundary spanning, (2) protection (political protection, money, safe haven), (3) balancing (values, interests), and Osborne and Brown (2005, 180) identify the role of 'champion', 'supporter' and 'advocate' that are all about creating support and ensuring resources for innovation. The literature conceptualizes entrepreneurial leadership as a complex internal and external task that demands both management and political skill to protect and drive innovation processes and, in that sense, this literature connects well to the literature on managing an organizational change (Fernandez and Rainey 2006).

To insert more precision, one can distinguish between the roles of individual persons at different (hierarchical) levels in the organization since these phases provide for different contexts in the process of innovation. While entrepreneurial leadership is important in all phases of the innovation process, different roles for realizing innovations are presented in the literature and different task domains are connected to these roles:

- *Creators*. Creators are the 'intellectual leaders' who generate the new idea (Knight 1967). They develop new ways of thinking and manage to break through perceptual barriers.
- *Innovation entrepreneurs*. Innovation entrepreneurs manage to connect the idea to an existing problem (Kingdon 2003; Roberts and King 1991, 1996).
- *Test managers*. Test managers are pragmatic leaders: they manage to realize a successful test of the idea (cf. Shenhar and Dvir 1996).
- *Innovation packager*. Innovation packagers are the individuals who embed the innovation into organizational structures and routines (Lee and Luykx 2005; Van Mele 2006).
- *Innovation diffuser*. Diffusers coordinate the large-scale roll-out of innovations (Chryssochoidis and Wong 1998). They create incentives and support for other organizations that will adopt the innovation.

How can we combine these insights about roles in different phases and various roles of entrepreneurial leadership? Although the perspective of distributed leadership has not been developed for analysing (public) innovation processes – it has actually been developed to study school leadership as being distributed between principals and teachers (Spillane 2006) – it may be helpful for understanding the relations between these innovation roles (for a good overview of this literature: Currie and Lockett 2011). This perspective acknowledges that a school leadership is not about one individual performing one role but rather about different individuals that engage in various (shared, interactive, and emergent) leadership activities and roles (Gronn 2002, 2009; Spillane 2006). Gronn (2002) distinguishes between distributed leadership activities – concertive action – and distributed leadership roles – conjoint agency. He identifies three patterns of activity in concertive action: spontaneous collaboration, shared roles and an institutionalization of concertive mechanisms over time. Conjoint agency is about the alignment and synchronization of leadership roles across different individuals (Currie and Lockett 2011). When translating these notions to issues of leadership in public innovation, we need to acknowledge that distributed innovators may also work within different organizations in the forms of collaborative innovation (Sørensen and Torfing 2011). In addition, the literature on innovations suggests that the development of concertive action – from spontaneous collaboration to shared roles and, eventually, an institutionalization of concertive mechanisms – may be connected to the progressive stages of the innovation process (Osborne and Brown 2005). A combination of the literature on distributed leadership of schools and theories of public innovation results in a perspective that acknowledges the distribution of leadership roles over various (hierarchical) levels, in different organizations and in different phases of the innovation process. This perspective helps to transform our understanding of the role of individuals in public innovation from an individualized one (great individuals) to a distributed one (great collaborations).

The distributed leadership perspective stipulates that one hero will not be able to do the job: distributed heroism is needed for successful innovation. The idea of an individual 'hero-innovator' has been replaced by a collection of heroes who play a role at different levels of the organizations and in different phases of the innovation process (see Bernier and Hafsi's (2007) and Ansell and Gash 2012, for similar arguments). In-depth empirical research was conducted to provide a more fine-grained understanding of distributed innovation leadership and to explore the validity and usefulness of the 'distributed heroism perspective'.

CASE INTRODUCTION: CITIZENS NET

To study the role of individual persons in technological innovation, we analysed the development and implementation of an innovation in the Dutch police: Citizens Net. This case selection is biased since we selected a successful innovation but it took a long time before success was realized, and periods of slowing down can provide information about barriers to innovation. The idea for this system originated in Police Department A in the 1990s, and the system was tested on a small scale in 2004 in City A and on a larger scale in 2008 in nine Dutch cities. At the moment, the Citizens Net is being implemented in every Police Department in the Netherlands. The Citizens Net is not only about the use of new technologies but also about substantially different ways of carrying out work processes – existing routines were altered. The innovation fits Bekkers et al.'s (2011b) idea of creating meaningful connections between the government and society: new connections with citizens are thought to contribute to the coproduction of safety.

The Citizens Net is a network of citizens that can be contacted by the police in real time. The basic idea behind the system is that the police contact large groups of citizens over telephone in the 'golden hour' directly after a crime or need for assistance has been reported to ask for information. Directly after a criminal act has been reported or when a person is missing, citizens are contacted on the basis of their geographical characteristics, and they are asked for information. The following message provides an example: 'Two persons related to raid. One dressed in dark clothes. One wearing a forage cap. One carrying a large bag. One Wearing dark sweatpants. One wearing light sweatpants. If you have any information, contact 0800-011' (Police Nieuwegein, 6 August 2009, my translation). Citizen can call the control room to provide the police with information about the whereabouts of the suspects, and this information can directly be used to locate and apprehend them.

The Citizens Net has been evaluated in 2009, and the results are quite positive (Meijer 2013; Van der Vijver et al. 2009). The level of citizens' engagement is high with an average of 4.6 per cent of the population in the first nine cities signing up for participation in the Citizens Net. This is much higher than levels of citizen engagement that are found in decision-making processes and hence indicates that there is a high willingness to cooperate with the police. Van der Vijver et al. (2009: 41–42) have found that the contribution of the Citizens Net to the police work is substantial since 9 per cent of all the cases that were qualified as fit for a Citizens-Net action are solved on the basis of information from this action. Meijer (2013) emphasizes that the number of 9 per cent seems limited in terms of the total number of actions, but it amounts to more than 50 per cent of the successful police actions. Van der Vijver et al. (2009: 54) also found that participation in the Citizens Net had a positive effect on the citizen satisfaction with the police. The innovation is widely seen as a success and therefore nationwide implemented. This paper analyses the role of individuals in the development of this successful innovation.

RESEARCH DESIGN

The research on the development of the Citizens Net started with a thorough document analysis of the Citizens Net to reconstruct and understand its current features. The main part of the empirical research consisted of in-depth interviews with key actors in the process of innovation. Respondents (Rs) were selected according to the snowball method (Biernacki and Waldorf 1981) starting with the current project manager of the Citizens Net. The selection of respondents was ended when the respondents indicated that they thought we had interviewed the key leading actors. This selection resulted in nine respondents (see Table 1).

The interviews were in-depth ones and lasted between 1.5 and 4 hours. Questions were asked about their own roles, the involvement of other actors and their contributions to the process of innovation. The interviews were analysed on the basis of a data

Table 1: List of respondents

Respondent	Relevant positions	Relation to citizens net
R1	Police officer in Police Department A, project manager in Police Department B	Idea generator (1993), initial project manager of Citizens Net (2002–2005)
R2	Police Chief Police Department A, Police Chief Police Department C	Member of the steering committee (2000–2003)
R3	Senior adviser at Police Information Organization	Senior responsible owner of Citizens Net (2008–2009)
R4	Policy Advisers at the Ministry of Internal Affairs, Director at Department of Justice	Financial support of Citizens Net (2000–2012)
R5	Police Chief of Police Department B	Member of steering committee (2000–2012)
R6	Police Manager at Police Department A	Manager at the time of idea development (1997–2000)
R7	Project manager Citizens Net	Project manager of Citizens Net (2005–2011)
R8	Police officer in Police Department D	Project manager in Police Department D (2006–2012)
R9	Mayor of City A	Member of the steering committee (2002–2011)

matrix that focuses on phases of innovation, barriers and drivers and the roles of individual persons. The results have been anonymized both in terms of respondents and in terms of the regional Police Departments and Cities. Additionally, names of other individual persons who were involved but not interviewed were anonymized (NR).

The results of this case study cannot be generalized into other processes of innovation. Processes of innovation have their own dynamisms and are influenced by, among other things, the features of technologies, the specific organizational and institutional settings, legal frameworks etc. Nevertheless, studying a specific process can provide insights in the underlying patterns and help to enhance our understanding of the role of individual persons at the executive and work floor levels in the processes of innovation.

CASE ANALYSIS

Idea generation (1993–1997)

The idea of Citizens Net was developed in 1993 by R1, a police officer in Police Department A, who was going through a period of illness and had plenty of time to think about improvements to the police work. The idea of Citizens Net followed from his experience as a police officer working in the streets. He indicated how he recognized a pattern in the standard police responses to reports about criminal situations such as burglaries: after a call from a citizen the police would rush to the crime location to find that the burglar would already have left. The police was always too late and they failed to use the willingness of the people in the neighbourhood to help the police in fighting crime. R1 started thinking about a system for engaging citizens:

'I started to think about interests, incentives and problems. There is a neighborhood full of people en everybody has a telephone. The problem is that the police keep the information to themselves. It should be possible to send them a message that says: we are looking for such a person. Please contact the police if you see something.' (R1)

R1 was no scientist or intellectual but a police officer who liked to think about improving his work. He was someone with an interest in technology and a belief in technological opportunities but he was no technological expert. One of the other respondents (R9) referred to R1 as the archetypical inventor from Donald Duck: 'Gyro Gearloose'. The other respondents see him as the intellectual father of Citizens Net (R9) and the Citizens Net was his 'baby' (R3).

The idea was written down in a formal memo for his colleagues in 1994. The reactions of his colleagues were positive, and they stimulated him to develop the idea further but there was no executive 'sponsor' (Osborne and Brown 2011, 1342). Top management at Police Department A highlighted that they found the idea highly interesting but due to organizational changes – regional Police Departments were being created – they did not see any opportunities to realize the idea. 'The idea ended up in various drawers' (R1).

Idea selection (1997–2000)

In 1997, there was a new opportunity to bring the idea forward: Police Department A had a departmental innovation award. R1 applied for it and the Citizens Net won the award of 4,000 euro. This award did not bring him a 'sponsor': his direct manager indicated that he still had other priorities. R1 did get some support from his district manager but his position within the organization was not strong enough to have R1 realize the Citizens Net in Police Department A. He started looking elsewhere, and R1 and R6 went to the Netherlands Ministry of Internal Affairs to obtain additional funding for realizing the Citizens Net. The civil servants at the ministry were willing to support the idea if more regional police departments so that it could result in national improvements to the police work.

In this phase, R1 can be qualified as a 'prophet' who went around obtaining support for his idea (R7). He contacted people at other regional departments from his personal networks and who, he thought, would be interested in the idea of the Citizens Net. R2, the chief of Police Department C and NR2, senior policy adviser at Police Department B, indicated that they were willing to cooperate in the development of the Citizens Net. They formed a project team and now serious resources were made available: the Ministry of Internal Affairs supplied

30.000 euros for the development of the Citizens Net. R1 started to work in Police Department B because they had more people working on similar developments than in Police Department A, and they were willing to engage in an experiment.

Idea testing (2000–2007)

City A, in the region of Police Department B, was selected for the pilot project since it was large enough to produce enough interesting situations for the Citizens Net and not too large to create an overflow. While the innovation has thus far been discussed within the police organization, it now moved into a political territory. The mayor of City A was strongly in favour of the Citizens Net and played a key role in creating a political support. Some respondents refer him as a 'standard-bearer': a person who publicly shows that he is in favour of the Citizens Net and manages to create political support for the innovation (R3, R4). Standard-bearing was required since, although most members of the city council supported the development of the innovation, there was resistance from the Greens:

> The chance is considerable that a 'big-brother-is-watching-you' atmosphere is being created, and citizens start mistrusting one another or even endanger themselves. Another probable consequence could be that citizens see themselves as moralists and claim the right to play secret agent. Intolerance, more mistrust and even conflicts can determine the relations. (Green-Left Party 2004)

The mayor of City A managed to convince the majority of the council that these objections were not warranted, and with broad support from the council, the pilot project started in City A in 2004. Administrative and political support for the pilot study had been created, but this did not mean the process moved into silent waters: technical problems became the next obstacle. A small project team consisting of an employee from the control room and a technical person was formed to develop the system, and the project team had to develop a data processing software (with information about citizens and about police actions), communication software (to send voice mail messages to citizens) and a geographical layer (to select receivers for the messages). Because of the technical problems, the start of the project was postponed by a year, and it received much negative publicity (R7).

And after these technical problems had been solved, the project ran into operational obstacles. When the Citizens Net started in May 2004, calls to citizens were only sent out 14 to 17 minutes after the notification. To obtain an up-to-date information, citizens need to receive a message within a couple of minutes of the notification. The control room failed to do this because of other organizational demands. R1 spend much time to convince the control room and superior officers that the Citizens Net would only work if the control room paid attention to these time constraints. He convinced them and managed to bring down the response time back to a few minutes.

All barriers had now been removed and the innovation was put to the test. Citizens Net booked its first success in February 2005: three pickpockets were apprehended with their loot on the basis of information from the Citizens Net. 'This gave a big kick in the control room. (...) I went to the control room with a box with cakes' (R1). More successes followed, and political, management and operational supports continued to grow. The opinions of the citizens were measured in May 2005, a year after the pilot project had started, and all citizens, even the ones who had not participated, had a very positive opinion about the system.

In spite of the success, the steering committee pushed for a new project manager. The steering committee felt that R1 had developed a great idea but was not the right person for realizing it:

> He can inspire some people. Others do not like him at all. He can seem rather strange. Especially people higher up in the hierarchy find him a difficult person. He makes remarks that do not fit within their frames of understanding. (R8)

> He does not have a connecting style of operating. He is obsessed with his own idea. It is his baby. He was not good at listening. Sometimes a person can be too motivated. (R3)

R1 had a different view on this development and felt that the steering committee took him off the project because they did not want it to be successful. In a dramatic gesture, R1 did not only step down from his position but also resigned from the police force, and R7 became the new project manager of the Citizens Net. The new project manager prepared for slowly scaling-up the project when suddenly it got caught in the national political dynamics.

Idea scaling-up (2007–2009)

Until the phase of idea testing, the Citizens Net had been relatively low key. In 2007, Citizen Net was given a boost by the fact that it was mentioned in the official declaration of the new government: 'Citizens Net is to be implemented nationwide.' (Government Declaration 2007) R1's membership of the smallest coalition party (Christian Union) and his direct contacts with the leaders of this party may have played a role in putting the Citizens Net on the political agenda (R4, R7, R9). The inclusion in the official government programme dramatically changed the involvement of the ministry of Internal Affairs in the Citizens Net:

> Since it was mentioned in the Government Declaration, it became an objective that was discussed regularly in the ministerial staff meetings. Issues that are mentioned in the Government Declaration are of the utmost importance. Ministers are held accountable for these issues. (R4)

It also meant that much more money became available for the project: 2 million euro per year until 2011 and 1.6 million euro programme support per year (R4).

The nationwide implementation of the Citizens Net was to be carried out, and a steering committee was formed with members of the police, the Ministry of Internal

Affairs and a representative of local governments. The successful pilot study in City A was to be followed up by new pilots in nine communities. Due to the success in City A, many local governments were interested, and the preparations for the pilot studies were started.

One could assume that political and administrative support and available funding would facilitate the implementation of the Citizens Net but there was also a downside to it: the political and administrative complexities increased because of the need to discuss all issues in the national coordinating bodies of police chiefs; the external complexities increased because the contract with the IT firm was no longer exempted from the European contracting legislation; financial complexities increased since finances from the regional police departments were difficult to obtain; and technological complexities increased because a nationwide system was needed to be developed. The political, administrative, contracting and financial complexities were becoming too much to handle for R7 and a 'senior responsible owner', R3, was appointed to support him. 'He was tougher at the political game than I am' (R7). R3 had to operate strategically at three levels: in contacts with the IT suppliers he needed to ensure that they would deliver a good system within the agreed costs and timeframe; in contacts with the regional Police Departments he needed to make them start working with the system; and in contacts with the ministries he had to ensure that his project was in line with political demands to ensure funding.

Bureaucratic politics was resolved by creating a new project structure with three distinct levels: operational issues, tactical issues and strategic issues. This phase ended with an extensive formal evaluation of the pilot projects in the nine communities. This evaluation led to positive findings: the Citizens Net contributed to the police effectiveness and strengthened citizens' trust in the police (Van der Vijver et al. 2009). The stage was now set for a massive roll-out of the Citizens Net throughout the whole police organization.

Idea diffusion (2009–2012)

From 2009, the Citizens Net was being implemented in a large number of communities all over the country. The project manager R7 managed the national project and obtained executive level support from NI4. The regional departments developed their own innovation dynamics. The experiences in one Police Department D illustrate the process of obtaining support from the management and police officers at the work floor had to start again, quite similar to the previous process in Police Department A and City A. In Police Department D, they started with a pilot project for the Citizens Net in two cities in 2008 and success in the two pilot projects formed the basis for a roll-out of the Citizens Net in nearly every local community within the police department (R8).

Project manager R8 in Police Department D highlighted that he had limited support from the Police Chief but support from another member of the management team enabled him to continue. As was the case in City A, obtaining support from the control room and the police officers in the street was crucial to the success of the Citizens Net.

> We wanted the work floor level to become involved. We did not want them to see it as something from Police Department management but as a 'blue thing'. (...) No management speak but something that works in practice. (...) We went around and visited all teams to tell our story. (...) Our story was: Citizens Net is about catching criminals. (R8)

In Police Department D, the Citizens Net became embedded in a broader programme for changing the work of the police called 'Direct Police Investigations'. Since technology was taken care of by the national programme bureau, realizing the innovation was an organizational challenge:

> It was an organizational and not a technological challenge. We had to get the control room along. And the local governments. The value of the national program bureau was that they supported the technological systems and they facilitated the exchange of experiences between the various Police Departments. (R8)

In 2012, all police departments in the Netherlands have implemented the Citizens Net in most cities but the system has not been rolled out into every city yet.

THE HERO-INNOVATOR DOES/DOES NOT EXIST

This study provided an interesting insight into the relation between entrepreneurial leadership and innovators in the organization. We found that entrepreneurial leaders do not only seek innovators, innovators may also seek entrepreneurial leaders. After meeting much resistance, the idea generator had to move to another police department to find an entrepreneurial leader who was willing to support his idea. For entrepreneurial leadership, this means that 'scouting' innovators with great ideas may be just as important as facilitating innovations within the own organization. When a match between individual persons at the work floor has been realized, the role of entrepreneurial leadership is to a large extent about creating internal and external supports for innovations. The term 'standard bearer' was often used and is similar to the term 'sponsor' (Osborne and Brown 2011, 1342) and the terms of 'champion', 'supporter' and 'advocate' (Osborne and Brown 2005, 180): entrepreneurial leadership is about protecting and supporting the individual persons actually realizing the innovation.

The findings for the role of individual persons in realizing innovations showed that basically three types can be identified that overlap but also differ from our theoretical model: idea generators (creators and innovation entrepreneurs), idea managers (test managers, innovation packagers and innovation diffusers) and idea fighters (who we had not identified in our theoretical model). The *idea generator* is the ideal-typical innovator: the individual who thinks up a great idea, and in this case the creator proved to be a successful innovation entrepreneur as well. The analysis showed that this role was crucial in the first two phases of the innovation process but ran into problems in the third phase – idea testing – and was replaced by the idea project manager. The problems may be related not only to his capacities but also to his sense of ownership of the innovation and the unwillingness to accept that the organization needs to appropriate it. The idea manager is not driven by the desire to innovate the police but rather by the drive to manage projects successfully. This type of project management is complicated and consists of ensuring a top-down support (innovation push), making the people to express their enthusiasm about the innovation (innovation pull) and creating productive networks between various organizations (innovation networks). The idea manager's expertise is crucial to the realization of the innovation of the phase of idea testing but he is not capable of doing the bureaucratic fighting that is needed to protect the innovation against external threats. When the external threats become too much to handle for the idea manager, entrepreneurial leadership appoints an *idea fighter* to protect the innovation. The idea fighter's assistance was called for since entrepreneurial leadership did not have the time to be engaged in this type of fighting for the innovation. The idea fighter should therefore be regarded as a temporary aide to the idea project manager but also to entrepreneurial leadership. The case indicates that a process of innovation seems to require a rebel in the early phase of the innovation process to challenge organizational routines, a conformist in the later phases to position the innovation within these routines and a strategist in the middle phase to direct organizational change. This finding nuances Bernier and Hafsi's (2007) observation that individuals mostly make a difference in the early phases since the case shows that individuals also play a key role in the scaling-up and diffusion of the innovation.

The drawbacks of rebellious innovators receive little attention in the literature, which emphasizes positive attributes of innovators. A literature search yielded only one publication that stated a negative relation between innovators and innovation – ex-innovators as barriers to change (Steere 1972). Most literature highlights positive characteristics of innovators and stresses that sometimes innovators do not get a chance because the management forms a barrier to an innovation. Berkun (2010, 78) indicates that the behaviour of the lone inventor is eccentric, and therefore they are tough examples to learn from. In this specific case of the Citizens Net, the management seemed to regard the inventor as a soldier who returns from a war: out of place and difficult to manage. The fact that a role has been valuable but may form an obstacle to further development has been analysed by Lievegoed in his work on organizational evolution. Lievegoed (1973) highlights that a pioneer plays a key role in the first stage of organizational evolution but may form an obstacle to a further development. The conflict between the inventor and the steering committee can be understood in a similar fashion: the steering committee wanted the innovation to be institutionalized while the innovator wanted to develop it further. This type of conflict is typical for the transition from one stage in organizational development to the next, and it may as well be typical for the transition of one stage in the innovation process to the next. The pioneering phase of the innovation ends, and the institutionalization phase needs a new type of work-floor leadership.

A variety of individual persons at different levels in the organization and in different phases of the innovation process were involved in the innovations, and this study provides insights in factors that play a key role in enabling collaboration between these individuals. The case study highlights three important patterns:

- *Focus on expertise and not on position.* Various persons in the realization of the innovation – R1 and R8 but also an entrepreneurial leader, R6 – show little respect for hierarchical lines. They have more respect for expertise than for formal positions and this attitude helps them to connect in the early phases of the innovation process. This pattern of cross-organizational collaboration that does not follow formal organizational positions has also been identified by Borins 2001).

- *Individual networks.* R1 used his personal networks to obtain support in Police Department A with R6 and when R1 needed the cooperation of two other police regions he contacted two other people from his own network (R2 and NR3). R2 was also a member of an informal, national network with a number of police chiefs to discuss improvements in police work (the Albuquerque Network). Individual networks proved essential to the innovation process (see Lewis et al. 2011 for an in-depth analysis of innovation and networking).

- *Shared perspective on police and society.* The different actors involved also contacted each other on the basis of similarities in their perspectives on police and society. The shared belief in the strength of the idea was important for creating connections between various actors. 'We both wanted to do something about the decay of society. We felt you can start a movement with citizens to do something about it' (R8). The role of shared vision has been acknowledged in the literature on innovation in the public sector (for example: Pearce and Ensley 2004).

This case study highlights that innovation is about connections between individuals in organizations: they cannot bring the innovation to a success by themselves, and they need to build meaningful connection to others. These connections cross organizational and hierarchical boundaries and create spaces for innovation or 'innovation milieux' (Bekkers et al. 2011b, 202).

On the basis of this research, we would argue that the hero-innovator both does and does not exist. R1 is the typical hero-innovator. He has both the characteristics of a hero-innovator that Brown and Osborne (2005, 172) mention (tenacious, works long hour, is goal driven, willing to take risks, confident, and skilled in using political connections) and the capacities mentioned by Doig and Hargrove (1987, 10) (a capacity to engage in rational analysis, an

Meijer, A. and Zouridis, S. (2006) 'E-government is an Institutional Innovation' in V. Bekkers, H. van Duivenboden and M. Thaens (eds) *Information and Communication Technology and Public Innovation. Assessing the ICT-Driven Modernization of Public Administration*. Amsterdam: IOS Press, pp219–29.

Morabito, M. S. (2008) The Adoption of Police Innovation: The Role of the Political Environment. *Policing: An International Journal of Police Strategies and Management*, 31:3 pp466–84.

Mumford, M., Scott, G., Gaddis, B. and Strange, J. (2002) Leading Creative People: Orchestrating Expertise and Relationships. *The Leadership Quarterly*, 13 pp705–50.

Oliver, W. M. (2000) The Third Generation of Community Policing: Moving through Innovation, Diffusion, and Institutionalization. *Police Quarterly*, 3:4 pp367–88.

Osborne, S. P. (1998) Naming the Beast: Defining and Classifying Service Innovations in Social Policy. *Human Relations*, 51:9 pp1133–55.

Osborne, S. P. and Brown, L. (2005) *Managing Change and Innovation in Public Service Organizations*, Milton Park: Routledge.

Osborne, S. P. and Brown, L. (2011) Innovation, Public Policy and Public Services Delivery in the UK. The Word That Would be King? *Public Administration*, 89:4 pp1335–50.

Pearce C. L. & Ensley, M. D. (2004) A Reciprocal and Longitudinal Investigation of the Innovation Process: The Central Role of Shared Vision in Product and Process Innovation Teams (PPITs). *Journal of Organizational Behavior*, 25:2 pp259–78.

Perri 6 (1993) Innovation by Nonprofit Organizations: Policy and Research Issues. *Nonprofit Management and Leadership*, 3:4 pp397–414.

Porter, M. (1985) *Competitive Advantage. Creating and Sustaining Superior Performance*, New York: The Free Press.

Roberts, N. C. and King, P. J. (1991) Policy Entrepreneurs: Their Activity Structure and Function in the Policy Process. *Journal of Public Administration Research and Theory*, 1:2 pp147–75.

Roberts, N. C. and King, P. J. (1996) *Transforming Public Policy: Dynamics of Policy Entrepreneurship and Innovation*, San Francisco, CA: Jossey-Bass.

Rogers, E. M. (1995) *The Diffusion of Innovations*, 4th ed. New York: Free Press.

Schin, J. and McClomb, G. E. (1998) Top Executive Leadership and Organizational Innovation: An Investigation of Nonprofit Human Service Organizations. *Administration in Social Work*, 22:3 pp1–21.

Shenhar, A. J. and Dvir, D. (1996) Toward a Typological Theory of Project Management. *Research Policy*, 25:4 pp607–32.

Sørensen, E. and Torfing, J. (2011) Enhancing Collaborative Innovation in the Public Sector. *Administration and Society*, 43:8 pp842–68.

Spillane, J. P. (2006) *Distributed Leadership*. San Francisco, CA: Jossey-Bass.

Steere, B. F. (1972) Ex-Innovators as Barriers to Change. *Educational Technology-Teacher and Technology Supplement*, 12:5 p63.

Van der Vijver, K., Johannink, R., Overal, K., Slot, P., Vermeer, A., Van der Werff, P., Willekens, H. and Wisman, F. (2009) *Burgernet in de praktijk. De evaluatie van de pilot van Burgernet*, Dordrecht: Stichting Maatschappij, Veiligheid en Politie.

Van Mele, P. (2006) Zooming-In, Zooming-Out: A Novel Method to Scale Up Local Innovations and Sustainable Technologies. *International Journal of Agricultural Sustainability*, 4:2 pp131–42.

Walker, R. M. (2006) Innovation Type and Diffusion: An Empirical Analysis of Local Government. *Public Administration*, 84:2 pp311–35.

Abstract

Public sector organizations are large buyers and, in previous research public sector, have been regarded to be able to affect the market through demand-driven innovation, especially if different public sector entities collaborate with each other. However, what this study shows is that it is not necessary to be big or to collaborate in order to make an impact on the market, as even smaller local authorities have the ability to affect. In fact, it could even be an advantage to be small. The important factor is to think strategically about purchasing and to have knowledge about the market.

INNOVATION IN THE PUBLIC PROCUREMENT PROCESS

A study of the creation of innovation-friendly public procurement

Hans Knutsson
and Anna Thomasson

Hans Knutsson
School of Economics and Management
Lund University
SE-220 07 Lund
Sweden

Anna Thomasson
School of Economics and Management
Lund University
SE-220 07 Lund
Sweden

INTRODUCTION

The EU Public Procurement law is formed in order to reduce trade barriers and to exploit comparative advantages of member states by opening the markets up to competition (Arrowsmith 2010). However, it may actually be inhibiting a competition. Studies conducted in the EU countries show how purchasers within the public authorities regard the legislation to be complicated; therefore, they play it safe in order to avoid situations where bidders involved in a tendering process appeal a contract (Morgan 2008; Schapper et al. 2006). Playing it safe results in an inflexible procurement process that reduces the ability to provide end users with a public service that they demand (Uyarra and Flanagan 2010). Also, smaller actors in the market perceive the legislation to be complicated, inhibiting them from participating in the tendering processes (Karjalainen and Kemppainen 2008). As a consequence, larger suppliers have come to dominate several of the markets for public services. Consequently, instead of opening the markets up to competition, the public procurement law could be regarded as reducing the competition and innovation on several markets.

Besides the regulation and policy issues, there are other factors relating to governance and an organizational level that create obstacles in the public procurement process (Caldwell et al. 2005; Dalpé 1994; Schapper et al. 2006). For example, in the United Kingdom, a recent efficiency review of the central government (Green 2010) showed, among other things, a lack of coordination between the purchasing units within the same government, an inability to leverage the buying power of the government, and a lack of mandate given to the purchaser. These factors contribute to an increase in the complexity of the public procurement process, and make it even more difficult to challenge how the incumbents perceive the public procurement legislation (Erridge and Greer 2002; Morgan 2008).

The public sector is a large buyer of a broad range of goods and, in particular, services. In Sweden alone, the public sector spending in 2009 summed up to almost 30 per cent of the national GNP. At the same time, the Swedish public sector is increasingly squeezed between an ageing population and a shrinking tax base (SKL 2010, 2012). This situation implies a need for innovation. In the literature on innovation, the demand side is regarded as being important since a large demand for new products spurs research and development as well as product and process innovations (Aschhoff and Sofka 2009; Uyarra and Flanagan 2010). Since the public sector plays a significant role in the economy in many countries around the world, this would mean that the public sector has a direct influence on the supply side in an economy (Aschhoff and Sofka 2009; Uyarra and Flanagan 2010).

The EU procurement law thus supports fundamental mechanisms in the European economic system. Yet, at the same time, the law seems to serve as an institutional restriction on innovation. In the light of approaching challenges to the public sector welfare provision, the ability of public authorities to re-think the procurement process is the key. Public authorities need to learn how to demand different things from the suppliers, all within the realm of the public procurement law. The public procurement processes need to be addressed. This is a challenge that most likely requires a break from a risk-averse public-sector procurement culture. That may be especially challenging for the smaller local authorities, lacking sufficient resources to develop internal administrative processes (Knutsson and Thomasson 2010).

The purpose of this article is to describe and analyse how public procurement within small local authorities can, through innovation in the public procurement process, affect competition in the local markets. This study is a first step towards exploring this subject in a larger research project. The results presented in this article are based on a single-case pilot study. The broader aim of the pilot study is to explore possible interesting perspectives for a future research on this topic. Further, the focus is on the role of the purchasing unit within the small local authorities. This is motivated by previous studies, pointing towards the need to change the buyers' procurement process in order to accomplish innovation-friendly procurement. Other levels and actors, though interesting and important for the process, will therefore not be focused on in this article.

The purpose will be fulfilled by applying a framework consisting of theories of process innovation, demand-driven innovation and strategic procurement to the results of a single case study of innovation in the public procurement process of a local authority in Sweden.

The article is organized as follows: In the next section, the theories used for the analysis will be presented and discussed. This is followed by a discussion of the method chosen for this study and a presentation of the empirical data. The penultimate section contains a discussion of the results of the analysis and finally, the article is concluded with a summary of the results and suggestions for further research.

THEORETICAL FRAMEWORK

The concept of innovation

Innovation is a concept related to something new. Innovation is '[the] creation, diffusion, and adoption of good ideas' (Johnson 2010), where the use of the idea is a key-defining aspect. Accordingly, Downs and Mohr (1979) define it '[as] the earliness or extent of use by a given organization of a given new idea, where "new" means only new to the adopting agent, and not necessarily to the world in general' (Downs and Mohr 1979: 385). Thus, the substantive idea of an innovation does not have to be new to everyone, and the creation, diffusion, and adoption of a particular idea do not have to be closely coinciding in time.

Drucker (1985) sees innovation as the feat of an entrepreneur doing something better or cheaper. He proposes that innovators should look systematically for unexpected occurrences, incongruities, process needs, industry and market changes, demographic changes, changes in perception, and new knowledge. This could be related to what Christensen et al. (2006) discuss in terms of 'social innovation'. They argue that 'in the social sector, too much attention is devoted to providing more of the same to narrow populations that are already served' (2006: 94). Replication is a key concept, which is a way for a new solution to gain economic strength. Through 'catalytic innovation', social systems may be altered by meeting the needs of the over- or the under-served and neglected by the existing firms in the marketplace (Christensen et al. 2006).

Innovation does not have to be a new technology or something completely new. It can, as stated above, be a new way of doing things or about spreading and adopting new ideas. When talking about innovation, it concerns, on the one hand, the development of completely new technologies and services (Aschhoff and Sofka 2009; Uyarra and Flanagan 2010) and, on the other hand, a process innovation that refers to innovation in management and work processes (Walker et al. 2011).

Innovation-friendly procurement

The view on innovation has direct ramifications on innovation in a context of public procurement. Public procurement could be seen as a demand-side-oriented tool for stimulating innovation (Aschhoff and Sofka 2009). However, in order to make a demand-driven innovation work, the procurement process in the public sector needs to be conducive to innovation. The concept of innovation-friendly procurement refers to the ability to, by means of the procurement process, be able to enlarge the market for a certain type of product or service to facilitate the emergence of a new standard technology or to change the market structure by making it attractive for new entrances (Uyarra and Flanagan 2010).

With the scale and scope of the public sector, the public procurement could potentially have a substantial impact on how a certain market evolves. This may require the willingness to adapt the procurement process in order to leverage the potential buying power (Green 2010). Green's (*ibid.*) recommendations are based on a commodity setting, where a well-functioning market and the distribution of bargaining power determine the outcome of a tendering process. Moving away from the commodity markets, a different approach would be to develop the procurement process into a more innovation-friendly process. Previous studies, however, show that there are different factors that create obstacles for innovation-friendly procurement in the public sector.

One factor is the EU directives on public procurement, perceived by public sector purchasers as complex and difficult to interpret (Nielsen and Hansen 2001). People working for public sector organizations tend to be risk averse and thus, reluctant to deviate from what is regarded as being the 'right behaviour' (Erridge and Greer 2002). Instead of trying to increase pressure on suppliers or to adapt the content of the procurement to the changing needs and demands of end users, the tendency among public purchasers is to play it safe in order to avoid court appeals. As such, potential suppliers will not be challenged to develop their offerings; however, renewal and innovation suffer. In this way, the EU directives on public procurement inhibit innovation and competition (Morgan 2008; Schapper et al. 2006). Nevertheless, it is important to emphasize that it is not clear whether it is the law per se that inhibits innovation, or rather how incumbent people perceive the law in the purchasing units (Morgan 2008).

It is not only the public purchasing process that is inhibited by the EU directives on the public procurement; actors in the market, especially smaller firms, also perceive the legislation as being complicated (Karjalainen and Kemppainen 2008). Further, the tendering process is complex and extensive, which means that smaller firms do not have sufficient resources to participate in public tendering (Bovis 1998; Karjalainen and Kemppainen 2008). As a consequence, larger corporations have come to dominate several markets for goods and services where public sector authorities are large buyers (Bovis 1998).

Another factor highlighted in the literature is the lack of collaboration between the public organizations; instead, each unit acts separately and individually. Advantages, derived from the joint size and financial impact within organizations as well as between organizations, are lost (Caldwell et al. 2005; Erridge and Greer 2002).

A third factor mentioned is the governance aspect. Governance occurs on several different levels in a society, but the capacity to implement innovative procurement does not exist on all these levels (Uyarra and Flanagan 2010). There can be discrepancies between the goals presented by the national government and the tools and resources available to the authorities (local and national) to accomplish these goals.

A fourth factor is that the public procurement process in itself is complex and subjected to many different and contradictory goals and expectations, ranging from policy goals to quality and price requirements (Dalpé 1994; Schapper et al. 2006). Individuals influence the purchasing process, including the evaluation of the tenders. It is not unusual for different persons to be involved in different parts of the process and for people responsible for managing the procurement process to lack the competence and/or mandate and influence over the resources needed to develop the processes (Matthews 2005; Morgan 2008). In cases where the person responsible for the procurement process works at a different unit or part of the organization, a process development becomes even more complicated. Such a situation implies little or no connection to, and thus knowledge of, the users of the product or service purchased (Matthews 2005; Morgan 2008).

All these factors, ranging from the policy level down to the organizational level, together make the development of the procurement process difficult and complex for the local authorities. Nevertheless, public procurement is an important instrument that could be used to influence the supply of services and goods offered on the market (Uyarra and Flanagan 2010). However, the purchasing local authority has to be able to overcome the above-mentioned obstacles.

Procurement strategies

Innovation in the procurement setting could refer to either (i) the goods and/or services to be contracted do not exist and may therefore not be pre-defined, or

(ii) the way in which the procurement process is executed, i.e. the process is new in one or more parts. Either way, potential suppliers may be challenged. The procurement of innovation asks suppliers to offer something new, whereas an innovative procurement process changes how suppliers are being asked to supply pre-existing solutions in an improved way. In both situations, the market is asked to respond in a new way. This opens up for new actors to take part in the bidding process.

This shows that both the way that the local authority conducts the procurement and the specific demands they make influence the supply side, i.e. available tenders. An innovation-friendly procurement process, thus, requires procurement strategies to be developed and implemented. It is not enough to simply re-think the process; it is also about implementing a new behaviour.

One way to think strategically about the procurement process is presented by Kraljic (1983). Kraljic (1983) has created a typology of procurement, where procurement is shown to be as much about a supply as it is about a demand. When the financial impact of the procurement of a certain product increases, the procurement process gets increasingly important to control – add to that the risk of being left without supply due to a complex supply market. Kraljic (1983) suggests treating different types of purchases differently. However, in the public sector, it is not only about a financial impact, but also about the policy and accomplishing political goals. The public procurement process is in itself a complex process and subjected to different goals and expectations; for example, environmental and social aspects should be considered in the procurement process. This means that, besides focusing on financial impact and market complexity as mentioned by Kraljic (1983), the public procurement process also needs to consider the interest of the politicians.

Theoretical summary

Public procurement is a powerful tool that can be used in order to stimulate market behaviour and to change the market structure by making it more attractive for new entrances. This is called innovation-friendly procurement (Uyarra and Flanagan 2010). However, public procurement is influenced by several factors that together affect the procurement process. What the theories here discussed indicate is how public authorities, through innovation of the public procurement process, can overcome the above-mentioned obstacles and implement a more innovation-friendly procurement strategy.

METHOD

The case study chosen for this article is the Swedish food industry and the procurement of food in one Swedish municipality. The reason for doing a case study was based on the explorative nature of the article; in particular, the need to create a deeper understanding of the public procurement process and its complexities within a market context (Eisenhardt 1989; Yin 2003). Doing a case study also corresponds with the reason for doing a pilot study as a first step towards exploring this topic further and investigating possible perspectives for future research projects. The case study approach enables the researcher to gather information from a wide range of sources such as documents, interviews, and observations (Bryman and Bell 2003; Flyvbjerg 2006). Our study rests most heavily on interviews and discussions with the responsible manager in Klippan municipality. The information gathered from these occasions has been documented continuously in the form of memory notes. The notes have been gradually processed in consecutive contacts with the manager, but also elaborated on and verified by published articles, interviews, and comments about the Klippan procurement. This particular procurement has been widely recognized and awarded in Sweden; moreover, the manager has been conferred with on numerous occasions during industry-wide seminars, workshops, and events in the last 18 months. Our single source of primary data, thus, is extensively complemented by rich secondary data.

The local authority selected was chosen based on the fact that it has recently implanted a new strategy for procurement of food for schools, childcare, and elderly care. The empirical information presented in the article consists of two sets of data. First, we present data regarding the Swedish food industry. These data have been gathered from different statistical databases, mainly data published by the Swedish governmental organization called 'Statistics Sweden' and from industry statistics as well as descriptions in the Delfi Foodservice Guide 2010. Second, we present data on the procurement process in the local authority chosen, the municipality of Klippan. These data are based on interviews with the person responsible for the procurement of food for the local authority and documents from the procurement process. The researchers have met with this person on several occasions and discussed the procurement process. Moreover, the case has gained wide attention in the field of Swedish public procurement and hence widely exposed in various seminars as well as interviews conducted by others. Our respondent, working in a small municipality with scarce resources, is the one person who is responsible for all the steps in the purchasing process and also the one that has all the contacts with the suppliers. This single respondent compensates for the low number of respondents with his/her breadth and depth of knowledge. This is consistent with the purpose of the article.

The analysis of the empirical data was conducted in order to respond to the two parts of the purpose of this study. In order to respond to the first part – that is, how innovation in the procurement process can be accomplished – we needed to have an understanding of innovation with a focus on process innovation and innovation-friendly procurement. Therefore, the theoretical framework was developed with these aspects in mind. Our data regarding the procurement process in Klippan were then applied to this theoretical framework by matching empirical statements to the corresponding concepts. In order to respond to the second part – namely, how innovation in the procurement process influences the market – we conducted a survey of the food industry characteristics and related this to the design and outcome of the procurement process in Klippan.

Since this is a pilot study, we decided to focus on one municipality and on one level in the organization, the purchasing unit. The authors are aware that this limited range of empirical material affects the possible conclusions that can be drawn from the study. Also, the choice to focus on the purchasing unit alone affects the ability to draw conclusions on other levels that could be of interest for the study. However, the authors find it possible to discuss implications for other levels in the analysis and conclusions of this study, especially considering that the purpose of such a discussion is to generate suggestions for a future research.

THE FOOD INDUSTRY AND THE PUBLIC PROCUREMENT PROCESS IN KLIPPAN

The food industry

The Swedish public sector is organized into three levels: a state level, a county level and a municipality level. The majority of public services are organized in twenty-one counties (healthcare and regional development) and 290 municipalities (schools, child-care and elderly care, local infrastructure, and social welfare).

Approximately six million meals are provisioned daily in the public sector, of which 98 per cent are served in counties and municipalities. In 2010, the Swedish foodservice market was worth 28 billion SEK (about 3 billion Euro). Full-range wholesale companies who share two-thirds of the market dominate it. The remaining third of the market is made up of smaller wholesalers, producers or importers selling a narrow range of products directly to customers without intermediaries. Wholesalers supply food and transportation in a bundled offer to customers. There are seven full-range wholesalers. The biggest company has more than 26 per cent of the market, the second biggest 13 per cent, i.e. the two biggest players serve about 40 per cent of the entire Swedish market. The top five full-range wholesalers serve more than 60 per cent of the market. (Delfi Foodservice Guide 2010).

A second distinctive trait of the Swedish food industry is the prevalence of strong stakeholders such as the National Food Administration and the National Board of Health and Welfare. From early on, these government agencies have influenced the way in which food is produced, processed, distributed, handled and served in Sweden. Regulations and controls are pervasive.

A third characteristic is that there is no organization coordinating the counties and municipalities in questions concerning public meals, either in terms of procurement or education, cooking or serving. The formal responsibility of foodservice operations is normally decentralized to individual schools and nursing homes as support functions, whereas the procurement responsibility is centralized to a legal function of the respective county or municipality. Each county and municipality normally employs a foodservice manager who is responsible for the articulation of food needs and the choice of food products. In most municipalities and counties, there is also a dietician responsible for the nutritional status of the elderly. Procurement is conducted in a particular procurement function. In some cases, procurement is arranged with other municipalities or counties in order to achieve economies of scale and higher leverage in tenders through larger procurement volumes.

However, the industry structure is marked by a strong bargaining power of suppliers, a weak bargaining power of customers and, consequently, a close to non-existing rivalry from competition and new entrants. Substitution possibilities are low. The key competitive strength of the full-range wholesalers is the combined offer of a wide range of food products transported to your doorstep regularly, on one single occasion. A very distinctive characteristic of the Swedish foodservice market is that the two biggest suppliers systematically appeal to influence the municipalities' and counties' decisions to award contracts. Since often it is either the number 1 or number 2 tenderer winning the contracts, they seem to be trapped in a bureaucratic head-to-head competition. However, there are suspicions that the two may have a common interest in 'teaching' public authorities to form their procurement processes along such lines that draw large suppliers.

Public procurement for food in Klippan

Klippan is a small municipality in the south of Sweden with 16,600 inhabitants (2010). The municipalities provide a large part of the public services in Sweden, mainly schools, childcare, and elderly care. For these services, Swedish municipalities need to secure the provision of food.

How the provision of food is organized differs between municipalities. However, a common solution is to have a foodservice unit with a responsible manager. This unit organizes the kitchens and the procurement of food. This is the type of organization that is found in Klippan.

Before the latest procurement process, however, the manager decided that it was time to do things differently. The quality of the food provided by one of the big companies had been poor and so was the service level. This decision was the start of a completely new way of thinking and working in the procurement process.

Before the procurement was initiated, the manager of the foodservice unit started, together with a co-worker, to make an inventory of all the food they purchased and then to classify the food into different categories. They ended up with seventeen different categories of food.

As a second step, they went through all the seventeen categories of food and decided what type of quality they wanted specifically – from the percentage of meat in the sausages purchased to the quality of the meat in the meatballs. It was a time-consuming but thorough work, and formed the foundation for the quality specifications that they later used in the tendering process. During this process, they also asked for samples from potential suppliers, which they tested and tasted. They were surprised to see how low the level of quality was and how few of the suppliers that actually fulfilled the requirements they had stated. However, this part of the pre-procurement work provided the manager with a very clear picture of what the market offered, under what conditions the suppliers worked and what quality they provided.

Following this, they wrote a policy about the level of quality of the food served within the municipal services, and had it approved by the municipality executive committee, i.e. the elected politicians. Besides the quality of the food, this policy also contained environmental considerations, e.g. the distance the food delivered to the municipal services were to be transported. Although it was very difficult to refrain from the contents of the policy, the responsible manager regarded this support as being very important. The new policy and quality criteria constituted a major change from the municipality's previous ways of working. Previously, the criteria for selecting a provider was mainly based on price, and no distinction was ever made between different types and qualities of food. Moreover, the procurement encompassed all products in a single, large 'food' category, which made it difficult to contract different suppliers in specific categories of food.

With a new food policy in place, the procurement process was initiated. They decided to divide the procurement into seventeen different parts, one for each major food category. Their demands on the potential suppliers were based on the quality requirements they had elaborated on, along with the general food policy decided upon by the politicians. For example, demands were made that meat and fish should be delivered freshly five times a week.

Each of these seventeen groups was then evaluated separately based on how they fulfilled the requirements. The decision was made to evaluate the tenders in the same way as the previous procurements, but now with a comprehensive set of quality specifications along with explicit political support. Thirty-five per cent of the evaluation was placed on quality and 20 per cent on the fact that the supplier could guarantee the delivery of the exact product ordered. The offered service level and the environmental compliance were given 15 per cent weight each. The last evaluation criterion, in a way symbolically so, was the price. The price was also given a 15 per cent weight.

Then, as a result of the evaluation, Klippan municipality contracted four individual suppliers of food (which later became five). This was a radical change from the earlier procurements, where only one single contract was given to one single supplier. No court appeals were made.

The manager describes the pre-procurement phase as crucial but extremely time-consuming. The tendering process was equally challenging, but mainly due to bidders who overtly ignored the stated quality criteria and offered inferior products instead. All in all, the procurement process meant a great deal of work, but the manager – on a balance – finds it worthwhile. By dividing the tendering into seventeen different categories and by changing the criteria for evaluation, they managed to improve the quality of the food delivered without increasing the costs. Also, by focusing on quality, it turned out that the big companies forming the oligopoly could not, perhaps *would not*, compete. According to the manager, the message he/she got from the big suppliers was that they believed that in the end, the lowest price would be selected. They believed this despite the fact that the criteria were stated differently. Especially the criteria to have fresh meat and fish delivered five times a week became a watershed. The large companies try to push costs by only delivering once a week, which makes it necessary to supply frozen meat and fish. The manager knew this and asked for fresh products. Thus, by learning about the market, changing the procurement process and deciding for himself/herself what he/she wanted to buy, the manager succeeded in having an impact on the market. Accordingly, he/she was no longer stuck in the hands of the oligopoly.

The key success factor was to find criteria that the large companies could not or did not want to fulfil. This was accomplished by doing a thorough analysis of the market before the procurement started. Another important factor was that they decided not to collaborate with other local authorities. By choosing not to collaborate, they were regarded as being small and insignificant. This probably prevented the larger companies from challenging the decision.

The manager stressed the importance of monitoring the deliveries to make sure that they were in accordance with what they ordered. So, after the procurement process ended, she talked to all the kitchens and instructed the personnel to only accept products that were in line with what they had ordered. Everything else was rejected. After about a year, the suppliers had learned and the compliance with the contracts has improved.

DISCUSSION

The results from the Klippan case show how one small municipality can, by re-thinking the procurement process, affect the market and give smaller and more local companies the ability to participate in the procurement process. The case of Klippan supports the fact that public procurement has the ability, by posing demands, to influence the supply in a market and open up the market for new companies (Caldwell et al. 2005; Erridge and Greer 2002; Morgan 2008; Uyarra and Flanagan 2010).

An interesting aspect in the case of Klippan is the fact that the public authority conducting the procurement does not have to be large in order to have an impact on the market. Even a small and seemingly insignificant municipality can have an impact and influence, if not on the whole market, at least on the local market. This is a result that runs contrary to what has been stressed in previous studies (Caldwell et al. 2005; Erridge and Greer 2002; Morgan 2008). It is, thus, not necessary to collaborate. In fact, the manager in Klippan thought that they had an advantage since they did not collaborate.

On the contrary, spreading the ideas to other municipalities could be a better way to make an impact. This has been done in the case of Klippan. Klippan belongs to a regional network where representatives from foodservice units from different munici-palities in the region meet to exchange experiences. By taking part in these meetings, the manager from Klippan has shared her experience with representatives from other local authorities and as a result, others follow suit. This may actually be a more effective way to affect the market than to collaborate for higher volumes and for expected leverage on the buyer power.

Another important conclusion that can be drawn from the case of Klippan is the importance of being able to break with tradition and the risk-averse culture that is common in the public sector organizations (Erridge and Greer 2002). The fact that one manager wanted to change things and make a difference was crucial in the case of Klippan. It was not a political initiative. Instead, the initiative came from the manager, who then got support from the politicians.

The process innovation that took place in Klippan was thus the result of one person's ambition and interest. This is important, especially when considering governance and organizational aspects that have been addressed in the previous studies (Uyarra and Flanagan 2010). Innovation does not always occur where you might think it will occur. Knowledge and determination are important pre-requisites and these were really what spurred the process innovation. Thus, process design seems to be an important aspect of innovation-friendly procurement.

Another aspect that emerges as being important is the political support and the goals that were accomplished through the procurement process. The manager succeeded in anchoring the decision among the politicians and developing a policy that was in line with the political interests. At the same time, he/she managed to keep the costs down.

The results from the case study show the importance of being able to manage the complexity of the multiple goals that are involved in public procurement, which is in line with the results from previous studies (Dalpé 1994; Schapper et al. 2006). The case of Klippan adds, with an indication, that by re-thinking the procurement process, even a small municipality can have an impact on the market. Re-thinking the procurement process is mainly observed as a shift from viewing procurement as an administrative task to procurement as a business activity. The mind-shift begins in somebody's head, and in Klippan, we found just that person.

CONCLUDING REMARKS

The purpose of this study is to explore how local authorities, through innovation in the procurement process, can change the competition in the market. The article summarizes a pilot study with the aim to explore interesting perspectives for a future research on innovation-friendly procurement.

In general, more case studies and studies with a wider scope encompassing more actors in the process are needed in order to see if the results presented herein are supported by the experience from other local authorities.

The results in this article to some extent support the previous research about a demand-driven innovation (Caldwell et al. 2005; Erridge and Greer 2002; Morgan

2008; Uyarra and Flanagan 2010). The results also reveal some important aspects not previously discussed that could be of interest for future research.

For example, this study shows that it is possible for a small local authority to affect the market. What this study also shows is that it is not necessary to be big or to collaborate in order to make a change. It seems like that it actually could be an advantage to be small and seemingly insignificant. This challenges previous assumptions about procurement (Caldwell et al. 2005; Erridge and Greer 2002; Morgan 2008). Instead, it may be more important to have a network through which the innovation can be spread to other public services. This is not discussed in previous research and could be an interesting topic for future studies on innovation-friendly procurement.

Another important contribution of this study is the conclusion that knowledge is crucial for success. This has not been stressed in the previous research. Knowledge about the market, as well as about the needs of the local authority, is necessary in order to secure a value for money in the public procurement process. Another interesting aspect is how one person's ambitions can make all the difference. These aspects need to be considered when discussing and analysing the design and management of the procurement process.

The results are, as stated in the purpose of the article, a first step towards exploring innovation in the procurement process. The results should be regarded as such. More studies of innovation-friendly procurement are necessary in order to better understand how public authorities may influence society through their own business decisions. Future studies could look more into the supply side and see how suppliers react to the changes on the demand side.

It would also be interesting to look into how individual actors taking part in the procurement process act as innovation leaders. This is a topic touched upon only in this article and thus does not fit into the scope of this study. However, it is an interesting topic to develop.

Yet, another interesting topic to look further into is the co-operation between the Swedish municipalities. To co-operate on the demand side seems to be a way to leverage buyer power, but the effectiveness of such initiatives are cautiously questioned in this article.

REFERENCES

Arrowsmith, S. ed. (2010) *EU Public Procurement Law: An Introduction*, EU Project Report, University of Nottingham, Nottingham.

Aschhoff, B. and Sofka, W. (2009) Innovation on Demand – Can Public Procurement Drive Market Success of Innovations? *Research Policy*, 38 pp1235–47.

Bovis, C. (1998) The Regulation of Public Procurement as a Key Element of European Economic Law. *European Law Journal*, 4:2 pp220–42.

Bryman, A. and Bell, E. (2003) *Social Research Methods*, Oxford: Oxford University Press.

Caldwell, N., Walker, H., Harland, C., Knight, L., Zheng, J. and Wakeley, T. (2005) Promoting Competitive Markets: The Role of Public Procurement. *Journal of Purchasing and Supply Management*, 11 pp242–51.

Christensen, C. M., Baumann, H., Ruggles, R. and Sadtler, T. M. (2006) Disruptive Innovation for Social Change. *Harvard Business Review*, December pp94–101.

Dalpé, R. (1994) Effects of Government Procurement on Industrial Innovation. *Technology in Society*, 16:1 pp65–83.

Delfi Foodservice Guide. (2010) *Statistics on the Swedish Foodservice Industry in 2010.*

Downs, G. W. and Mohr L. B. (1979) Toward a Theory of Innovation. *Administration and Society*, 10:4 pp379–408.

Drucker, P. F. (1985) Discipline of Innovation. *Harvard Business Review*, May/June pp67–72.

Eisenhardt, K. M. (1989) Building Theories from Case Study Research. *The Academy of Management Review*, 14:4 pp532–50.

Erridge, A. and Greer, J. (2002) Partnerships and Public Procurement: Building Social Capital through Supply Relations. *Public Administration*, 80:3 pp503–22.

Flyvbjerg, B. (2006) Five Misunderstandings about Case-Study Research. *Qualitative Inquiry*, 12:2 pp219–45.

Green, P. (2010) *Efficiency Review by Sir Philip Green.* Key Findings and Recommendations. Indendent Report, Cabinet Office, UK Government.

Johnson, S. (2010) *Where Good Ideas Come From. The Natural History of Innovation.* New York: Penguin.

Karjalainen, K. and Kemppainen, K. (2008) The Involvement of Small- and Medium-Sized Enterprises in Public Procurement: Impact of Resource Perceptions, Electronic Systems and Enterprise Size. *Journal of Purchasing and Supply Management*, 14 pp230–40.

Knutsson, H. and Thomasson, A. (2010) *Mat För Äldre – Innovativ Upphandling.* Lund: Skånes Livsmedelsakademi.

Kraljic, P. (1983) Purchasing Must Become Supply Management. *Harvard Business Review*, September/October, pp109–17.

Matthews, D. (2005) Strategic Procurement in the Public Sector: A Mask for Financial and Administrative Policy. *Journal of Public Procurement*, 5:3 pp388–99.

Morgan, K. (2008) Greening the Realm: Sustainable Food Chains and the Public Plate. *Regional Studies*, 42:9 pp1237–50.

Nielsen, J. U.-M. and Hansen, L. G. (2001) The EU Public Procurement Regime – Does it work? *Intereconomic*, September/October pp255–63.

Schapper, P. R., Veiga Malta, J. N., Och Gilbert, D. L. (2006) An Analytical Framework for the Management and Reform of Public Procurement. *Journal of Public Procurement*, 6:1, 3 pp1–26.

SKL. (2010) *Future Challenges.* Long-term financing of Swedish Welfare. Stockholm: Swedish Association of Local Authorities and Regions.

SKL. (2012) *The Economy Report.* Municipal Economy 2012–2016. Stockholm: Swedish Association of Local Authorities and Regions.

Uyarra, E. and Flanagan, K. (2010) Understanding the Innovation Impacts of Public Procurement. *European Planning Studies*, 18:2 pp123–43.

Walker, M., Avellaneda, C. N. and Berry, F. S. (2011) Exploring the Diffusion of Innovation among High and Low Innovative Localities: A Test of the Berry and Berry Model. *Public Management Review*, 13:1 pp95–125.

Yin, R. K. (2003) *Case Study Research: Design and Methods* (3rd ed.) Thousand Oaks, CA: Sage Publications.

Abstract

Assessing impacts related to the adoption of an innovation represents a particular challenge. However, the use of innovation in government organizations does have some effects: some intended, others unintended; some desirable, others undesirable. Findings in literature now suggest that the use of innovation in government organizations produces beneficial results for the most part. The purpose of this article is to provide a multidimensional framework for assessing the impacts of innovation on an organization's performance as perceived by individual stakeholders and at organizational level. In particular, this framework is designed to evaluate the impacts resulting from the introduction of electronic medical records, namely an organizational, cultural, and technological innovation that many health care providers are currently undertaking. It provides the results of a comparative analysis carried out in Spain and Italy and discusses the need for a more systematic evaluation assessment of the innovation processes.

EVALUATION OF THE IMPACTS OF INNOVATION IN THE HEALTH CARE SECTOR

A comparative analysis

Maria Cucciniello and Greta Nasi

Maria Cucciniello
Department of Institutional Analysis and Public Management
Bocconi University
Milan
Italy

Greta Nasi
Department of Institutional Analysis and Public Management
Bocconi University
Milan
Italy

INTRODUCTION

Innovation has made a considerable contribution to the modernization of public administration at all levels. However, many authors (Chung and Snyder 1999; Davenport 2000; Kim et al. 2005; Stefanou 2001) argue that measuring its impacts represents a particular challenge.

Multiple approaches to the evaluation of innovation have been discussed and presented in the literature. Most studies are grounded in more traditional efficiency and effectiveness models, whereas others suggest expanding the focus and taking into account more of the social and ideological effects pursued by public sector innovation (Moore 1994, 1995; O'Flynn 2005). Some authors also suggest the need to perform stakeholder analysis in order to depict the value of innovation for individuals and understand how this determines and influences the overall impacts of innovation adoption (Dawes et al. 2009). Great emphasis has been put on broad types of outputs and outcomes. However, some categories of impacts are dependent on the specific context of the adoption of the innovation and on the type of innovation itself. Studies discussing evidence often represent results through a limited number of case studies, using expost and unstructured evaluation methodologies. This is mainly due to the limited diffusion of evaluation frameworks enabling the benchmarking of innovative practices and measurement of opportunity costs. In turn, evidence, in terms of the impacts delivered after the adoption of an innovation and in terms of the elements that can affect these results, remains patchy and methodologically limited (Williams 2011).

In this article, we review literature on the approaches to the evaluation of innovation, discuss the types of results and the factors that influence it, presenting and discussing a multi-dimensional and multi-stakeholder framework designed to assess the impact of innovation adoption. The framework presents the common types of impacts, in terms of efficiency and effectiveness, in addition to context- and innovation-specific ones. In particular, this model has been designed to measure the impacts of complex organizational and technological innovations in the health care sector. The innovation practice under analysis is the adoption of electronic medical record (EMR) systems by health care organizations.

The adoption of an EMR system, namely information systems that manage both the distribution and processing of information required for the patient delivery process (Laerum and Faxvaag 2004), is marked by a high degree of change produced within the organization after its adoption including process integration, redefinition of roles and responsibilities, job content, and pervasiveness of technology throughout the organization. This can be expected to generate impacts such as efficiency, process effectiveness, and better care (Caccia 1998; Pagliari et al. 2005; Wills et al. 2012). However, some authors (Damschroder et al. 2009; Greenhalgh et al. 2005) claim that the speed and depth of any impact may be mitigated or enhanced by how this type of innovation is implemented and by environmental and organizational conditions.

The article also provides evidence emerging from an international analysis carried out in Spain, which is the most advanced region in Europe in terms of EMR adoption, and from some emerging cases in Italy. It closes with recommendations for assessing the impacts of complex technological innovations.

BACKGROUND

Much has been written on the promises of innovation in the public sector (West 2005) and its capacity to contribute to internal government transformation (Tapscott 1997), greater citizen satisfaction (Van Ryzin et al. 2004; Vigoda 2002; Vigoda and Yuval 2003), and enhanced accountability and democracy (Mehdi 2005). Some of the more traditional NPM literature has focused on the expected effects of innovation (Lapsley and Pallot 2000; Walker 2008), whereas other studies have focused on the conse-quences of innovation processes in terms of the types of effects (often by type of innovation or by sector). As regards the latter, the findings often revealed unintended results and significant gaps between the expected and the actual changes (Danziger and Kraemer 1986; Kraemer and Norris 1994; Kling 1978; Kraemer et al. 1981; Northrop et al. 1990; Olson et al. 1998; TerBogt and van Helden 2000). This might not only be due to the time that should naturally elapse between the adoption of innovation and the visibility of any effects, but may also be due to concurrent effects that might influence the outputs or stakeholder behaviour that reshapes outcomes. Moreover, not all countries have developed a culture for measuring the impacts of innovation adoption (Bouckaert 2012), even though this becomes paramount for engaging in innovation processes, especially in times of crisis. We discuss three main aspects of innovation evaluation in order to contribute to the stream of literature on the impacts of innovation adoption, which is the purpose of this article: different approaches to innovation evaluation, the types of outputs and outcomes, and the factors that might influence the actual manifestation of impacts.

Approaches to innovation evaluation

Evaluating innovation adoption represents a core phase in the innovation's lifecycle (Tidd and Bessant 2011). In the private sector, a substantial body of empirical as well as theoreticallyinformed research has developed discussions on return of investment measures, key performance, and success indicators (Birchall et al. 2004). The main motivation for evaluation is the need to monitor profitability results, in turn providing an incentive for further innovation in order to cut costs, improve market share, and create new products and services. Public sector innovation shares some parallel goals, such as efficiency, productivity, and adequacy of programmes and services. Then again, the value of innovation in the public sector differs substantially from its value in the private sector and can be more complex and more difficult to measure (Walker 2008; Walker et al. 2007). On the one hand, as traditional public management literature points out (Boyne 1998; Hood 1991; Hughes 2003; Kelly 1998; Norris and Moore 2005; O'Flynn 2005; Van Dooren et al. 2010), in government operations and its innovation processes, there is a need to focus on economic efficiency, productivity, and effectiveness as measures of performance. Many authors have contributed to this debate by drawing from economic principles, agency theory, decision/control theories, post-industrial and transaction-cost theories, public choice theories, competition and competitive advantage principles. On the other hand, the value of public services may not be adequately addressed by the results deriving from these models, as it should also embed broader, more ideological and social concepts as well. Moore (1994, 1995) suggests the concept of public value, which embeds a multi-dimensional construct that reflects the results of collectively expressed and process- and politically mediated preferences of constituents. Many other authors (Alford 2002; Dawes et al. 2009; Kelly 2002; O'Flynn 2005) have made a contribution to this concept, highlighting that the public sector offers something unique that distinguishes it from the private sector: innovation outputs (i.e. new tutoring school services) represent a vehicle for generating public value by contributing both to the satisfying of individual needs (i.e. a child's education) and public outcomes (i.e. enhancing a community's human capital), thus generating trust and confidence in the government. In turn, this calls for accurate assessment of all the stakeholders involved in the innovation process, their expectations, and actual contribution to its implementation. A contribution in this direction also comes from the new public governance paradigm and the service-dominant logic (Osborne 1998, 2006, 2009, 2010; Osborne et al. 2013). The results of the adoption of innovation depend largely on the collaboration efforts put in place during all the phases of the innovation adoption and the actual co-production of all stakeholders that might mitigate, enhance, or reshape results.

This evidence has major implications. First, the evaluation of innovation adoption goes beyond the constructs of traditional economic and management-oriented theories. Second, there are multiple measures of performance that reflect individual stakeholder value and the overall community value of the innovation adoption. They include some readilyquantifiable outputs and some 'softer' outcomes, such as the quality of services (or processes) involved in the innovation and trust in the government. Third, the results are influenced by the collaborative forms and the stakeholders involved in the implementation process.

Measures of outputs and outcomes

Unlike the private sector, a common output measure, such as sales revenue, does not exist for public sector innovation. Bloch (2010) argues that quantitative output measures of government innovation are sector-specific (i.e. education, social care, health care, and transportation). This is due to the nature of the products and services that the public sector delivers. Problems in identifying indicators are particularly acute for collective services that are not consumed by, or offered to, an individual.

Many initiatives focus on the contribution of innovation to organizational performance in terms of improvements in key output indicators, efficiency, and user evaluation of services, in line with productivity and effectiveness models. Efficiency can be measured in terms of the accuracy of information, timeliness, and cost savings, or the reduction of red tape/reduction of the administrative burden (Kraemer and Norris 1994; Norris and Moon 2005; Northrop et al. 1990). In the case of the implementation of EMR systems, some of the most highly investigated impacts are related to efficiency and organizational effectiveness measures. Some authors (Pagliari et al. 2007; Van Der Loo et al. 1994) argue that EMRs could increase efficiency in terms of time savings since data is not collected and recorded on multiple occasions, the relevant information about a patient's history can be shared more quickly, reducing geographical barriers, and so improving continuity of care. In turn, this improves efficiency in communication, reduces process fragmentation (Protti and Peel 1998), and might facilitate the formulation of a patient's synopsis and diagnosis, which could lead to potential cost savings (Joos et al. 2006). Abdelhak (1996) and Wills et al. (2012) further elaborate on the contribution of EMRs, suggesting the overall organizational changes associated with implementation of EMRs facilitate the integration of care processes, resulting in the reduction of redundant activities, contributing to shorter hospital stays and potentially improved organizational performance.

The evaluation of service may be external, based on a customer satisfaction survey, or internal, based on employee satisfaction. Some of these measures are qualitative (i.e. when employees and users are asked) even if they can offer a more comprehensive view of all the dimensions to be taken into consideration. Furthermore, they 'can get close to the social actors' meanings and interpretation, to their accounts of the social interaction in which they have been involved' (Blaikie 2000). However, this limits the degree to which the measurement can be generalized but is helpful for 'understanding phenomena within their context uncovering links among concepts and behaviors and generating and refining theory' (Bradley 2007).

Innovation adoption also contributes to public sector outcomes. Such outcomes depend on the type of innovation and are related to the degree of transformation of the innovation process (Nasi 2008; Osborne and Brown 2005). Since most innovation initiatives pursue an ultimate public value or social scope, outcomes are often associated with sociallyrelated measures, such as social cohesion, equality, reduced crime, poverty reduction, increased literacy and graduation rates, improved continuity of care, or enhanced social capital. However, a single innovation initiative can only partially and often indirectly contribute to the enhancement of such measures. This is due to the concurring responsibility of other stakeholders that can influence the manifestation of results and outcomes (Bouckaert 2012). In addition, a particular innovation may be introduced in order to improve a certain aspect of the public sector, but have spill-over effects on the rest of the system. This impact may or may not be measured. A more limited way to measure the outcome of innovation is by assessing intangible benefits at the organizational level, such as improvements to the image of the organization and the services it delivers, boosting its legitimacy and trust among users or other stakeholders (Zhang et al. 2005).

This evidence has multiple implications. First, some results are common across sectors and types of innovation, such as efficiency and productivity measures. However, others are context-specific and depend on the type of innovation.

Factors that might influence the impacts of innovation

Multiple elements may shape the speed, intensity, and types of innovation impacts. Some environmental, institutional and organizational conditions, as well as an organization's characteristics, input and process-related variables, have been seen to be associated with innovation adoption and diffusion (Fountain 2001; Loof and Heshmati 2002; Studer 2005). Although most studies have hypothesized that the innovation inputs have a positive influence on the innovation output, empirical evidence has only been found in a few cases (Klomp and Van Leeuwen 2001; Loof and Heshmati 2002). Similarly, the relationship between process-related factors and the innovation output has only been found for some factors, as mentioned earlier in this section. Loof et al. (2002) suggest that these mixed results could be caused by the shortcomings of existing models for the proper handling of the complexity of the innovation and by the shortcomings of the available datasets. This is particularly true for health care, since this sector presents high degrees of complexity. Also, mitigating effects might be related to particular types of innovation. In the case of innovation processes associated with the adoption of technology, other factors may influence their diffusion, such as the organizational determinants of technology acceptance and use (Kanter et al. 1992), technological characteristics (Hwa Hu et al. 2000; Tornatzky and Fleischer 1990), and financial factors (Borzekowski 2003; Wang et al. 2002).

Second, the design and execution of value-generating mechanisms associated with the implementation process represent a key factor in the diffusion and scaling-up of innovation (Damschroder et al. 2009; Greenhalgh et al. 2005). Many authors suggest multiple domains of influence (Fitzgerald et al. 2002; Fixsen et al. 2005): intervention characteristics, inner setting (i.e. the hospital's structure, culture, and working habits), outer setting, characteristics of the individuals involved and the process of implementation. Dawes et al. (2009) further elaborated on this, suggesting that multiple stakeholders have interests in the innovation process that do not necessarily converge with its goals. They might also have the capacity to influence the innovation process. In turn, this might result in the redefinition of innovation boundaries and the actual results, including the failure of the innovation adoption (Greenhalgh and Russell 2010). Many evaluation models do not clearly identify different stakeholders (Van Der Meijden et al. 2003), although this can represent a powerful element when predicting some types of impacts. According to Westbrook and Georgiou (2009), major professional groups, such as physicians and research groups within health care organizations, have high levels of autonomy, are tribal in their behaviour and operate in hierarchical structures, whereas safe and effective work is dependent upon horizontal work co-ordination, particularly strong collaboration between professional groups. As a consequence, their participation in the implementation of a complex innovation that affects the organizational environment, like EMR adoption, might strongly influence its trajectory and affect results.

To summarize, much study and discussion has focused on the impacts of innovation in the public sector. It seems clear that complex innovations should not be conceived as a 'corporate commodity' with the sole objective of operational efficiency and with a preset budget based on benchmarking. Innovation is a strategic resource with organizational objectives, whose results are not separable from the organization's results and the contribution to public sector outcomes. Furthermore, there are multiple stakeholders affected by an innovation process that might represent non-converging interests. This has three implications. First, they might expect diverging types of impacts. Second, since they have different expectations, they might contribute more or less proactively to the innovation process. Third, evidence remains patchy and methodologically limited in terms of the impacts delivered after the adoption of an innovation by stakeholders and in terms of the elements that can affect these results (Williams 2011).

For these reasons, this article hopes to contribute to the discussion by outlining a multidimensional framework that aims to capture the impacts of the adoption of organizational and technological innovations in health care on stakeholders and at the organizational level.

Towards a multi-dimensional and multi-stakeholder framework for impact assessment in health care

Innovation in health care is crucial. However, there is a need for solid performance measurement and impact assessment to depict its contribution to the efficiency of health care delivery, patient- and other stakeholder satisfaction and the overall performance of the health care system.

Focusing on the implementation of EMRs, many studies discuss the expected contribution to the improvement of the health care organization's performance by the adoption of EMRs (Caccia 2008; Hillestad et al. 2005), which is not limited to productivity measures resulting from the automation of activities and the role of technology in assisting human-executed process, but also encompasses process integration, care effectiveness, motivation of internal stakeholders (physicians, nurses, and staff), and contributes to the overall performance of an organization (Lau et al. 2012;

López et al. 2010; Thompson et al. 2009). Most of these positive promises do not find adequate evidence in existing studies. Some debate exists in the field of medical informatics (Nirel et al. 2010). However, the recent focus on improving the quality of public services, especially those related to health care services and cost containment, has led many scholars, practitioners, and policy-makers to advocate more comprehensive and systemic innovation processes supported by both technical and organizational integration (Burns 1998) and in this context the role of information technology in health care becomes paramount. For this reason, there is a need to develop adequate models to capture the impacts of these types of innovation, which are still difficult to predict (Rye and Kimberly 2007).

De Moore (1993: 11) suggests 'the necessity for integration of (organizational) systems and communication of information in the health care sector becomes evident when studying the variety of interested parties, the multitude of applications and their importance'. The emergence of this scenario, where clinical information is considered a strategic variable in managing care activities, has become the focus of theoretical models of alignment of organizational processes and information flows described in literature (Buccoliero et al. 2002; Waegemann 2002), the design of practical research on clinical information systems and effective implementations (Berg 1997, 2004; Walker 2005), even if there has been little investment in this field in recent years due to several issues, such as institutional, organizational, and project management capabilities (Hunt 1998).

Some authors, (Ammenwerth et al. 2003), state that it is currently complicated to measure the impacts of EMR implementation because of the complexity of the object observed, the project implementation, and the motivation of the health care provider to perform an evaluation study. Some countries with a tradition for performance measurement have been addressing the need to frame impact models for organizational and technological innovation (Baum et al. 2000) that move beyond a cost-benefit analysis and measure organizational performance. Attempts to depict multi-dimensional frameworks also come from the European Union, which introduced the eGovernment Economics Project – eGEP – measurement framework (European Commission 2006). This type of framework has high implementation costs and presents reliability limits since it is based on secondary data collection. Our aim is to depict a comprehensive framework that can actually support the assessment of improvements in organizational performance in a flexible and user-friendly manner. This should also represent a useful tool for supporting decision-making by practitioners. In fact, most health care providers are still wondering to what extent a large organizational investment, in terms of financial and human resources as well as cultural and process reengineering, aimed at introducing complex technological innovations such as EMR systems, can effectively help to improve corporate performance.

The formulation of a multi-dimensional and multi-stakeholder framework built on measures of innovation is common to several sectors, like more traditional efficiency and effectiveness measures.

In addition, it embeds context and sector-specific impacts as well as other measures like innovation-type specific effects. A sector-specific impact of this type of innovation relates to *clinical governance*, defined as concerns about the excellence of clinical care linked to accountability, professional responsibility, clinical audit, quality improvement, and quality assurance (Shaw 2006). Smith (1996), Kelly (1998), and Goodman (2000) conducted a research focusing specifically on *clinical governance* and showed that the adoption of EMRs can facilitate and support clinical decisions. Furthermore, according to Neame and Olson (1998), there is a recognized need to share clinical information in order to improve the integrity, continuity, safety, and speed of the delivery of patient care. This is linked to organizational effectiveness and the capacity to reduce *medical errors* (Doran and DePalma 1996) by providing more accurate and prompt clinical information. Littlejohns et al. (2003) used an evaluation survey to demonstrate that EMRs may give health care professionals greater accessibility to patient-related information through improved handling of medical records. This in turn enhances the efficiency of hospital management and improves patient safety by avoiding potential errors in care processes and support activities (Abdelhak 1996; Bates et al. 1999; Cannon and Allen 2000; Henry et al. 1998; McShane 1999).

Other sector-specific impacts are related to *patient empowerment*. Tsai and Starren (2001) stated that patient interaction with EMRs has the potential to reduce the frequency of clinical visits and improve health care outcomes. Chin (1995) and Wright (1997) argued that the introduction of new communication technologies offers different ways to interact with patients and provide higher-quality care.

Finally, some impacts are related to the type of innovation and the quality of supporting services, including accurate information management and information system reliability.

The framework represents four main impact dimensions: efficiency, organizational effectiveness, clinical governance, and quality of supporting services.

- Efficiency includes measurements of the effects of EMRs in terms of the quality of information, time, and cost savings.
- Effectiveness includes variables that identify the contribution of EMRs to process integration, risk management, and improvement of patient care processes such as diagnosis and therapeutic activities.
- Clinical Governance comprises a group of effects produced on clinical activities in terms of clinical audits, accountability in the management of access and exchange of medical information, and in terms of professional development through education and communication efforts.
- Quality of supporting services refers to the impacts of EMRs in offering reliability of the information system, in facilitating continuity of care, and in enhancing patient empowerment.

The framework aims to measure the effects of EMRs on the performance of an organization by looking disjointedly at these categories, which affect different spheres of the health care organization, its community, and the local territory more generally. However, it sets the basis for ascertaining the overall aggregate value of the effects of EMRs on the performance of an organization by combining the different dimensions using a set of algorithms.

Each dimension is, in turn, divided into fifteen impact categories and a total of forty-one indicators. Each of the indicators, if relevant, has been customized to meet the expected results of each of the main stakeholders influenced by this innovation: namely physicians, nurses, staff (including top management and administration), and patients.

The framework (Table 1) was designed to be easily applied to different contexts and different types of health care providers, as it is based on a set of easy-to-measure indicators and on impact features that can be collected in different timeframes (short-, medium-, and long-term) based on when the effects are expected to be revealed, according to evidence in literature (Bayer et al. 2007; Lee et al. 2005). Since mitigating factors might shape the expected results, the methods developed to apply the frame-work take into account the following issues:

Table 1: The framework

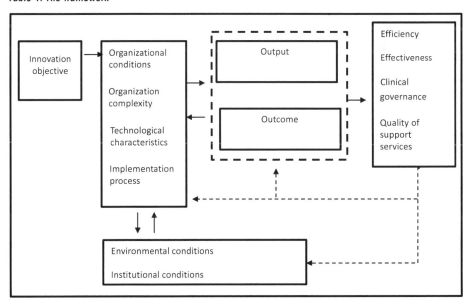

- Nature, complexity of health care organizations according to the type of care provided (i.e. acute care, primary care, etc), and the types of specialties offered (mono vs. multi) and the status of the information system prior to the adoption of EMRs;
- Types of stakeholders and attitude towards innovation and technology;
- Time elapsed since the initial adoption of the innovation.

This also facilitates benchmarking within the same organization in a longitudinal manner and across organizations.

METHODS

The framework was used on three Spanish hospitals, which is the most advanced region in Europe in terms of EMR adoption, and two emerging cases in Italy. These settings were selected based on several criteria (context, types of organization, and status of EMR adoption) with the aim of capturing impacts of organizational and technological innovation perceived by different stakeholders at the organizational level.

Here is a brief overview of the cases (more details in Table 2):

- Context: Italian and Spanish health care organizations are subject to different institutional frameworks. Furthermore, the two Italian cases, a regional health authority and an acute hospital, are located in two different regions. In the Italian context, health care is a regional function and the organizations selected are located in two regions with different health care strategies and governance structures. The three Spanish hospitals are all located in the region of Catalonia, which endorses an overall strategy for the continuity of care and e-health.
- Types of organizations: the health care providers have different corporate characteristics and degrees of complexity: the regional health authority provides acute hospital and primary care services; the hospitals have different sites that not only provide acute care at one or more centres, but may also provide long-term care and some are part of larger organizations.
- Status of EMR adoption: at the time of assessment, one organization was just starting the implementation process (regional health authority); the Italian hospital had been using EMRs for 2 years and were still implementing some features, whereas the three Catalonian hospitals had been using EMRs for more than 6 years.

A multiple-method strategy was selected as the research method for the analysis of these case studies, in particular the triangulation method of using multiple, independent

Organization	Italian regional health authority	Italian acute hospital	Catalonian hospital 1	Catalonian hospital 2	Catalonian hospital 3
Number of structures*	1	1	2*	1	1
Number of beds	1,500	1,450	732	643	213
Number of workers	3,690	4,000	4,900	2,127	850
Number of wards using EMR	90	50	61	21	8
Number of total wards	95	90	61	21	8
Number of authorized users	2,000	1,000	5,800	2,866	700
Average of daily access	1,150	900	1,350	800	250
Patient workflow phases supported	Acceptance; Integrated scheduling, and order management; Diaries – physician, nurse, pharmaceutical therapy; Discharge phase and patient follow-up	Acceptance; Integrated scheduling, and order management; Diaries – physician, nurse, pharmaceutical therapy; Discharge phase and patient follow-up; Continuity of care	Acceptance; Integrated scheduling, and order management Diaries – physician, nurse, pharmaceutical therapy; Discharge phase and patient follow-up; Continuity of care	Acceptance; Integrated scheduling, and order management Diaries – physician, nurse, pharmaceutical therapy; Discharge phase and patient follow-up; Continuity of care	Acceptance; Integrated scheduling, and order management Diaries – physician, nurse, pharmaceutical therapy; Discharge phase and patient follow-up; Continuity of care

Note: *Number of structures: the Catalonian hospital 1 has two main separate locations across the region.

measures of one phenomenon in order to provide 'a more integrated picture of a phenomenon' (Hantrais 2005).

A paper questionnaire with closed and open questions was constructed to evaluate EMR impacts. Quantitative data was collected in order to measure the perceived impacts on the four different dimensions identified above. Based on previous studies (Greenhalgh et al. 2004), health care service research increasingly uses questionnaire tools in order to get data that can be compared across studies, for instance about user involvement (Hallvard and Faxvaag 2004) or patient satisfaction with services (Howie et al., 1998). Furthermore, in this type of research, self-completion questionnaires are widely used since they offer several advantages (Lærum and Faxvaag 2004; Thompson 2003; Van Hook et al 1996). This type of data collection also assures the possibility to get honest responses, to increase the comparability of answers across different groups, such as different health care providers, and to conduct quantitative and statistical analysis to describe and compare answers.

The methods include tools to assess impacts and instruments to capture any mitigating effects. Here is a summary of the methods adopted:

- Self-completion questionnaires about the organization and the EMRs to control for environmental and other conditions that might affect the innovation implementation and shape its intended results, and to provide:
  - an assessment of the organization's context;
  - the patient workflow phases that EMRs are meant to support;
  - the status of the implementation of the EMR system and its features;
- Sets of customized, self-completion questionnaires on the impact dimensions, designed to control for socially desirable answers and get multiple perspectives on the perceptions of impacts based on multiple direct and indirect users of the system. Furthermore, they aimed to identify the impacts perceived by the main stakeholders (physicians, nurses, administration – mainly Board Members, CIOs and controllers – and patients);
- Sets of self-completion questionnaires designed to provide information about user behaviour and characteristics, focusing on the use of EMRs in daily tasks and on computer experience and literacy;
- Semi-structured interview formats to be used when interviewing key actors in the project of EMR implementation;
- Document scrutiny and analysis of other relevant information, such as organization and strategic documents and study reports to triangulate or integrate responses.

The data was collected in autumn 2011.

All the questionnaires, grids, and interview formats were prepared in Italian, English, and Spanish with a common codebook to avoid potential processing errors.

Data was collected on three wards at each health care provider (Gastroenterology, Cardiology and Pulmonology), since they can be considered a representative sample of the health care providers, in general, due to their size in terms of beds, patients and number of employees.

As mentioned above, there are many powerful stakeholder groups within health care organizations, each of which can influence the ultimate success or failure of a system (Lapsley and Llewellyn 1998). However, the selection of the key actors for data collection related to this article was based on certain characteristics (Bryman 2008) in order to include a diversity of roles and responsibilities:

— Profile: clinicians, nurses, administrative staff, and patients – representing the categories of stakeholders who are most involved in the adoption and use of EMR;
— Number of years working for the organization: at least since the adoption of the EMR system.

According to Hoinville, 'as a rule of thumb, we must try to ensure that the smallest subgroup has at least 50 cases' (Hoinville et al. 1977: 61) and our sample can be broken down into two separate subgroups based on the two areas investigated.

For this reason, based on this sampling model (Hoinville et al. 1977), thirty questionnaires were distributed to clinicians and thirty to nurses at each Italian and Catalonian hospital in order to get at least fifty questionnaires for each subgroup. Concerning more qualitative data and information, several semi-structured interviews were carried out at each hospital (about five clinicians and five nurses) randomly selected from the people who filled in the questionnaire. Furthermore, the Chief Information Officer (CIO), the Controller, and members of the Directorates of Medical Services were also involved in some interviews to gain additional information on the EMR project. At this stage, patients were not involved in the analysis. Data was processed using statistical software and the case benchmark was achieved using a set of algorithms to control the weighting factors identified.

Since the focus of this article is on the impacts of EMR in inpatient settings, because of limited reporting space, we are only including an overview of the implementation process and of the perceived impacts on the four dimensions identified above. Further analysis can be conducted in order to fully understand the factors influencing EMR adoption and how these can influence the impacts produced within the different settings analysed. In particular, we focused on perceptions and did not use accessible quantitative data, since we were interested in also capturing the level of change by comparing the current situation with the previous one in order to obtain a longitudinal analysis. However, this will be further extended and will be the subject of further research.

FINDINGS

The organizations considered are subject to different institutional frameworks, have different corporate characteristics and degrees of complexity, and are currently at different stages of adoption.

The comparison between the Italian and Catalonian cases is useful in order to understand what to expect at different times after the implementation of EMR systems. The two Italian cases are relatively similar when it comes to the intensity of the effects on the different dimensions since they are still in the early phases of EMR adoption, whereas the Catalonian cases reveal the medium- and longer-term impacts of EMR adoption.

Another way to analyse and discuss results arising from this research could have been to compare individual Italian and Catalonian examples, but this would have led to other types of considerations, whereas we aim to illustrate the results emerging from the application of the framework on the introduction of EMRs and to discuss the evidence taken from several organizations in two different contexts.

An initial overview of our findings reveals different degrees of intensity in the perception of all impacts (Figure 1). The Catalonian hospitals are more confident in declaring the effects of EMRs across the different categories of impacts compared to the Italian providers; this may be due to the fact that collection of the Catalonian data took place 6 years after implementation and the results, in terms of the perception of effectiveness and the effects on clinical governance, are in line with what is described in literature, since such effects usually appear in the medium to long run.

However, a closer look at the details of the analysis reveals some interesting findings.

Efficiency

The impacts on efficiency show different results for the Italian and Catalonian health care providers (Figure 2). The Italian health care providers had the greatest impact in

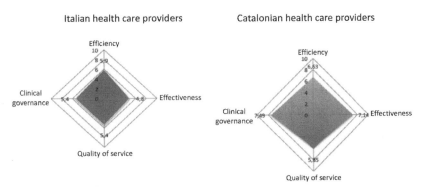

Figure 1: An overview of results

158

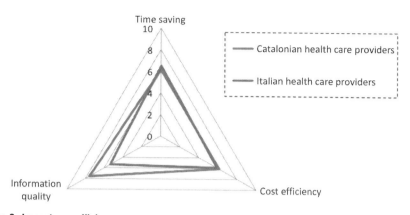

Figure 2: Impacts on efficiency

terms of the time saved, which in turn is considered to have an overall effect on costs. For example, nurses claim that the time spent for getting results from different laboratories has been reduced by up to 40 per cent compared to the time spent before the adoption of the system. Moreover, there has been a reduction in the time taken by the nursing staff to fill in information and data about patients during their admission and to complete daily reports. Time spent on both activities decreased by over 50 per cent. According to clinicians, the waiting time for X-ray results (images or reports) since order and exposure fell by 45 per cent.

These results were somewhat expected since efficiency, especially in terms of time savings, is perceived immediately after EMR implementation, especially when shifting from an existing situation where clinical information and patient records were generally collected and managed on paper, as was the case with the Italian health care providers. In fact, the majority of respondents in Italy agreed that the adoption of an EMR system produced cost savings. These were mainly perceived through the huge reduction of paper-based records and through an improved system of information sharing, leading to savings in terms of printing costs.

However, there are some differences between the two Italian cases with regard to their perception of time saving. At the Italian acute hospital, which has been using the system longer, the time saved is apparently a less obvious effect of EMRs. This was investigated further through semi-structured interviews: the respondents (clinicians and nurses) stated that they take it for granted that EMRs produce information in real time. Similarly, Catalonian hospitals have routinized the time savings and the printing costs and the respondents express efficiency impacts, mainly in terms of enhanced efficiency in the production of useful information for work purposes and for decision-making activities.

Additionally, multiple assessments make it possible to keep track of the evolving nature of impacts within this dimension, which evolves due to the fact that short-term effects (such as time savings) tend to be forgotten once the system becomes a daily tool for supporting patient care processes. According to this last consideration, the results in terms of time savings appear to be less relevant in Catalonia, where health care providers consider the quality of information to be the most important impact on efficiency in terms of the accuracy, completeness, ease of understanding, and reliability of data. This can also be due to the specific organizational characteristics, since the hospitals may also provide long-term care and some are part of larger organizations and the quality of information acquires a major role.

Effectiveness

As expected, Italian health care providers do not show much evidence in terms of the EMR's impact on effectiveness (Figure 3). However, results in terms of impacts on risk management are mainly linked to the presence of alerts. Both nurses and clinicians recognize that the adoption of the EMR system helps to provide all of the patient's information relating to previous admissions, and this helps interaction and communication between members of the staff: they can access the same information about previous admissions and be aware of particular problems such as diabetes or allergies. Nurses sustain that the use of the EMR system has reduced the number of incorrect drug

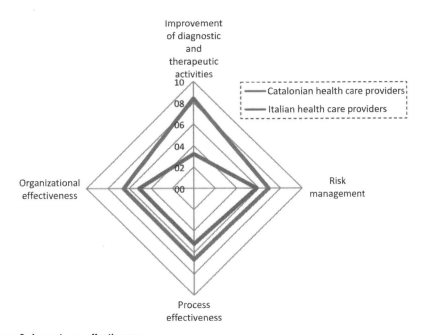

Figure 3: Impacts on effectiveness

administrations per year by 4 per cent, resulting from the misunderstanding of hand-written prescriptions.

Furthermore, clinicians have perceived an improvement in terms of better interaction with patients and in terms of the impacts on health care processes, because saving time promotes the decision-making process (especially at the diagnosis level). This leads to the perception of a potential impact on the overall effectiveness of the quality of care.

Clinicians in Catalonia found a positive effect in terms of improvements to diagnosis, treatment-, and service-related activities. This has led to organizational changes that currently allow for enhanced hospital admission planning and, according to clinicians, also produced a 20 per cent drop in the length of hospitalization. Of course, this may also be due to other elements but, according to clinicians, the new system has played a major role. Furthermore, clinicians claim the EMR system produces more accurate diagnosis and treatment and fewer errors in prescribing tests and compiling reports.

In the Catalonian case, they refer to the integration of information at all phases of patient workflows within the same organization and, in some cases, with continuity of care across hospitals and primary care centres. This comprehensive medical information not only provides the health care provider with alerts, it also offers useful information for reducing different types of errors and avoiding unnecessary, or redundant, invasive clinical tests.

These results may be due to the existing level of expertise within the health care organization. The Catalonian Hospitals, in fact, can count on a competent information technologies (IT) project leader and a team with professional knowledge of the organization. On the other hand, in the two Italian cases, external IT consultant groups played a key role: they had the benefit of technical knowledge, but were less aware of the inner context, thus reducing the potential for producing effective changes at the organizational level.

Clinical governance

The most significant effect on clinical governance refers mainly to the opportunity offered by EMRs to clearly identify who is accessing, managing, and exchanging medical information about patients at all times (Figure 4). Clinicians at Catalonian hospitals argue that the adoption of the EMR system reduced the number of cases in which decisions are postponed due to information unavailability by 25 per cent. The analysis showed that the adoption of EMRs can facilitate and support clinical decisions: the number of steps in the decision-making process fell by 35 per cent. This results from simultaneous organizational and information process reengineering.

This also has a positive effect on the degree of accountability of clinical personnel, considered a fundamental component of high-quality health care organizations, and this helped to improve patient confidence and trust in the services provided.

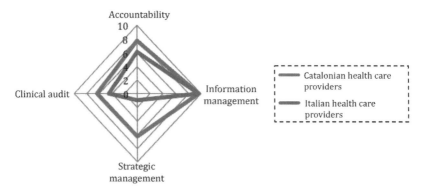

Figure 4: Impacts on clinical governance

The Catalonian hospitals pointed to some interesting results in terms of the effects on clinical auditing: clinicians reveal that using EMRs enabled them to collect useful information for enhancing health care support services, leading to patients having an enhanced perception of quality when they are discharged from the hospital.

The results in terms of clinical governance, defined in terms of clinical care linked to professional responsibility, quality improvement, and quality insurance, could have been influenced by the managerial attitude toward change that characterizes the study settings. The Catalonian Hospitals, in fact, created huge user involvement during the implementation phases, recognizing ICT as a fundamental tool for clinical operations, whereas there was a lack of communication and user involvement during the adoption phase in the two Italian hospitals, resulting in a degree of scepticism and resistance among users during the implementation phase (especially at the Regional Health Authority).

Quality of support services

According to all the clinicians and nurses included in the analysis, the EMR systems adopted in Italy and Catalonia can be considered reliable and assure continuity of access to medical information, for the people authorized to use it, 7 days a week, 24 hours a day (Figure 5). However, some concerns were raised in the Italian cases, especially by the nursing staff, with regard to the trade-off between confidentiality issues and the need to log on with individual IDs without slowing down patient care. This may not necessarily be due to the availability of laptops or other devices on the wards, but rather to the fact that Italian health care providers are still at the early stages of adoption and some information (mainly the nurses' and pharmaceutical therapy diaries) must be managed on paper, whereas other information is stored online.

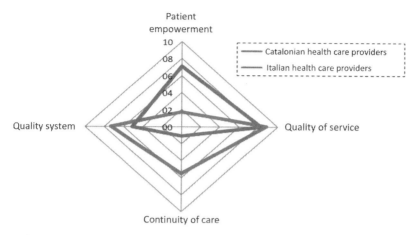

Figure 5: Impacts on quality of support services

Interesting findings concern how Italian clinicians perceive the potential of EMRs for leading to a higher awareness of patient empowerment, particularly the possibility of greater patient involvement in processes due to the increased availability of information.

In Catalonia, physicians perceive the opportunity offered by EMRs in terms of continuity of care because the Catalonian e-health strategy goes beyond hospital-based EMR systems, as mentioned above, and aims for information-sharing across the region, mainly with regard to hospitals and primary care centres. This result could have been influenced by specific organizational characteristics, in fact the three hospitals analysed in the Spanish context have different sites providing acute care as well as long-term care.

DISCUSSION AND CONCLUSION

This article contributes to the stream of research on the evaluation of the adoption of innovation by providing a framework that takes into account the peculiarities of measuring impacts in the public sector and embedding common measures as well as context- and innovation-specific measures. The decision to use mixedmethodologies raises concerns in terms of the limits to the analysis, since it assesses both readily quantifiable results, such as time savings, and discusses softer outcomes, such as quality of care through perception. However, it offers an initial contribution leading in the direction of more comprehensive frameworks and suggests future research opportunities.

This model was tested in Italy and Catalonia using the assessment framework based on four main dimensions of impacts. The findings of the research contribute to existing literature on organizational innovativeness since current studies focus mainly on individual case studies or individual dimensions of innovation performance. In fact, by assessing all dimensions of impacts at all times, it is possible to identify the perceptions of stakeholders with regard to the impacts of innovation by demonstrating that different factors might influence their perceptions.

In particular, certain organizational conditions, the organization's characteristics, and the process of implementation adopted were found to be particularly important in this study.

First, organizational arrangements: the innovation project in the hospitals in Catalonia appears to benefit from a close relationship between clinical professionals and project designers, whereas Italy suffers from the lack of involvement of professionals in the development of innovation projects.

Second, the levels of existing expertise in terms of innovation processes within the organization: this led to the focus on user needs at the organizational level at the Catalonian Hospital and to more technical and formal attention on the introduction of IT in the Italian cases.

Third, the extent of user involvement in the innovation project and the degree of readiness to change marked the Catalonian Hospitals more than the Italian providers.

Lastly, the implementation process adopted: the project at the two Italian organizations was marked by a 'top-down approach', with no promotion of participation by personnel in the process from the selection phase. In contrast, the Catalonian hospitals adopted a 'bottom-up approach' marked by a participatory process for implementing and managing the EMR system. This represents a distinctive way to generate and improve commitment to the project within the organization that also influences the impacts produced in terms of effectiveness and clinical governance. Conversely, if imposed, this process can generate user frustration and can impact the implementation process and on the overall use of the system.

Adopting complex innovation that affects an organization's structure and culture, work processes, behaviour, and communication channels can be considered one of the most difficult and challenging tasks to overcome.

Although there are no major financial motivations, unlike the private sector, it is very important to explore the successes and failures of these processes to build up a knowledge base on innovation practices. Failures, in particular, may help in several ways: first, by helping us to understand the innovation process and the barriers and facilitators of innovation, rather than assuming that innovation leads inexorably to improvements (Hartley 2005). Measures and guidelines to promote active 'change management' at all system levels, may facilitate better implementation of technological and organizational innovation and EMRs in particular.

The model described here enables the monitoring of the impacts of innovation occurring in different time frames and affecting different spheres of the organization's performance and would contribute greatly to literature.

In this sense, the findings are mainly in line with our assumptions during the drafting of our model. In particular, complex innovations produce multiple effects on several spheres of an organization's performance and are revealed at different times after adoption. This suggests the need to systematically and repeatedly collect data on the impacts of this innovation, ideally starting from a pre-adoption situation and continuing in the long run. Furthermore, particular attention to assessment is needed during the implementation process to investigate the nature and direction of the effects and put prompt and well-timed actions in place that may contribute by reducing potential gaps.

However, the study has also some limitations since it presents evidence from a small number of selected cases, chosen with the aim of providing diversity in contexts, while assessing EMR projects at different stages of implementation and usage. This limit may be overcome by extending the sample and repeating the assessment at a future time.

REFERENCES

Abdelhak, M. (1996) *Health Information Management of a Strategic Resource*, Philadelphia, PA: W.B. Saunders Company.

Alford, J. (2002) Defining the Client in the Public Sector: A Social-Exchange Perspective. *Public Administration Review*, 62:3 pp337–46.

Ammenwerth, E., Mansmann, U., Iller, C. and Eichstädter, R. (2003) Factors Affecting and Affected by User Acceptance of Computer-Based Nursing Documentation: Results of a Two-Year Study. *Journal of the American Medical Informatics Association*, 10:1 pp69–84.

Bates, D. W., Teich, J. M., Lee, J., Seger, D., Kuperman, G. J., Ma'Luf, N., Boyle, D. and Leape, L. (1999) The Impact of Computerized Physician Order Entry on Medication Error Prevention. *Journal of the American Medical Informatics Association*, 6:4 pp313–21.

Baum L., Christopher H. and Di Maio, A. (2000) *Gartner's Four Phases of E-Government Model*, http://www.gartner.com [accessed March 2013].

Bayer, S., Barlow, J. and Curry, R. (2007) Assessing the Impact of a Care Innovation: Telecare. *System Dynamics Review*, 23:1 pp61–80.

Berg, M. (1997) 'On Distribution, Drift and the Electronic Medical Record: Some Tools for a Sociology of the Formal' in *Proceedings of the Fifth Conference on European Conference on Computer-Supported Cooperative Work*, Lancaster, UK: Kluwer Academic Publishers, pp141–56.

Berg, M. (2004) *Health Information Management*, London: Routledge.

Birchall, D., Tovstiga, G., Morrison, A. and Gaule, A. (2004) *Innovation Performance Measurement: Striking the Right Balance*, London: GRIST.

Blaikie, N. (2000) *Designing Social Research: The Logic of Anticipation*, Malden, MA: Polity Press.

Bloch, C. (2010) *Towards a Conceptual Framework for Measuring Public Sector Innovation, Module 1 – Conceptual Framework*, Aarhus: The Danish Centre for Studies in Research and Research Policy.

Borzekowski, R. (2009) Measuring the Cost Impact of Hospital Information Systems: (1987–1994). *Journal of Health Economics*, 28:5 pp938–49.

Bouckaert, G. (2012) 'Public Sector Performance: Managing Governments by the Numbers' in G. Tria and G. Valotti (eds) *Reforming the Public Sector: How to Achieve Better Transparency, Service, and Leadership*. Washington, DC: Brookings Institution Press.

Boyne, G. A. (1998) Bureaucratic Theory Meets Reality: Public Choice and Service Contracting in U.S. Local Government. *Public Administration Review*, 58:6 pp474–84.

Bradley, E. H., Curry, L. A. and Devers, K. J. (2007) Qualitative Data Analysis for Health Services Research: Developing Taxonomy, Themes, and Theory. *Health Services Research*, 42:4 pp1758–72.

Bryman, A. (2008) *Social Research Methods* (2nd edn), Oxford: Oxford University Press.

Buccoliero, L., Caccia, C. and Nasi, G. (2002) *Il Sistemainformativodell'azienda Sanitaria*, Milan: McGraw-Hill Italia.

Burns, F. (1998) *Information for Health*, Leeds NHS Executive, A1103.

Caccia, C. (2008) *Management Deisistemiinformativi in Sanità*, Milan: McGraw-Hill Italia.

Cannon, D. S. and Allen, S. N. (2000) A Comparison of the Effects of Computer and Manual Reminders on Compliance with a Mental Health Clinical Practice Guideline. *Journal of American Medical Information Association*, 7 pp196–203.

Chin, H. L. and McClure, P. (1995) 'Evaluating a Comprehensive Outpatient Clinical Information System: A Case Study and Model for System Evaluation' in *Proceedings of the Annual Symposium on Computer Application in Medical Care*, American Medical Informatics Association, pp717–21. IEEE Computer Society Press.

Chung, S. and Snyder, C. (1999) 'ERP Initiation – A Historical Perspective' in *Proceedings of the Americas Conference of Information Systems* (AMCIS '99). AMCIS: Milwaukee, WI.

Cooper, R. B. and Zmud, R. W. (1990) Information Technology Implementation Research: A Technological Diffusion Approach. *Management Science*, 36:2 pp123–39.

Damschroder, L. J., Aron, D. C., Keith, R. E., Kirsh, S. R., Alexander, J. A. and Lowery, J. C. (2009) Fostering Implementation of Health Services Research Findings into Practice: A Consolidated Framework for Advancing Implementation Science. *Implementation Science*, 4:1 pp50.

Danziger, J. N. and Kraemer, K. L. (1986) *People and Computers: The Impact of Computing on End Users in Organizations*. New York, NY: Columbia University Press.

Davenport, T. H. (2000) The Future of Enterprise System-Enabled Organizations. *Information Systems Frontiers*, 2:2 pp163–80.

Dawes, S. S., Cresswell, A. M. and Pardo, T. A. (2009) From "Need to Know" to "Need to Share": Tangled Problems, Information Boundaries, and the Building of Public Sector Knowledge Networks. *Public Administration Review*, 69:3 pp392–402.

De Moore, G. (1993) 'Standardisation in Health care Informatics and Telematics in Europe: CEN 251 Activities' in G. J. De Moor, C. J. McDonald and J. Van Goor (eds) *Progress in Standardization in Health care Informatics*. Amsterdam: IOS Press.

Doran, B. and DePalma, J. A. (1996) Plan to Assess the Value of a Computerized Documentation System: Adaptation for an Emergency Department. *Advanced Emergency Nursing Journal*, 18:1 pp63–73.

European Commission. (2006) *eGovernment Economics Project (eGEP) Measurement Framework Final Version*, DG Information Society and Media, European Commission, Bruxelles.

Fitzgerald, L., Ferlie, E., Wood M. and Hawkins, C. (2002) Interlocking Interactions, the Diffusion of Innovations in Health Care. *Human Relations*, 55 pp3–19.

Fixsen, D. L., Naoom, S. F., Blase', K. A., Friedman, R. M. and Wallace, F. (2005) *Implementation Research: A Synthesis of the Literature*. Tampa, FL: University of South Florida, Louis de la Parte Florida Mental Health Institute, The National Implementation Research Network.

Fountain, J. (2001) *Building the Virtual State*, Washington, DC: Brookings Institution Press.

Goodman, N. (2000) Accountability, Clinical Governance and the Acceptance of Imperfection. *Journal of the Royal Society of Medicine*, 93:2 pp56–8.

Greenhalgh, T., Robert, G., Macfarlane, F., Bate, P. and Kyriakidou, O. (2004) Diffusion of Innovations in Service Organizations: Systematic Review and Recommendations. *Milbank Quarterly*, 82:4 pp581–29.

Greenhalgh, T., Robert, P. Bate, P., Kyriakidou, O., Macfarlane, F. and Peacock, R. (2005) *Diffusion of Innovations in Health Service Organisations: A Systematic Literature Review*, Oxford: Blackwell.

Greenhalgh, T. and Russell, J. (2010) Why Do Evaluations of eHealth Programs Fail? An Alternative Set of Guiding Principles. *PLoS Medicine*, 7:11 ppe1000360.

Hantrais, L. (2005) Social Policy. *Public Administration and Public Policy – New York*, 113 pp557–72.

Hallvard and Faxvaag. (2004) Task-oriented Evaluation of Electronic Medical Records Systems: Development and Validation of a Questionnaire for Physicians. *BMC Medical Informatics and Decision Making*, 4:1 pp1–16

Hartley, J. (2005) Innovation in Governance and Public Services: Past and Present. *Public Money and Management*, 25:1 pp27–34.

Henry, S. B., Douglas, K., Galzagorry, G., Lahey, A. and Holzemer, W. L. (1998) A Template-Based Approach to Support Utilization of Clinical Practice Guidelines Within an Electronic Health Record. *Journal of the American Medical Informatics Association*, 5:3 pp237–44.

Hillestad, R., Bigelow, J., Bower, A., Girosi, F., Meili, R., Scoville, R. and Taylor, R. (2005) Can Electronic Medical Record Systems Transform Health Care? Potential Health Benefits, Savings, and Costs. *Health Affairs*, 24:5 pp1103–17.

Hoinville, G., Jowell, R. and Associates. (1977) *Survey Research Practice*, London: Heinemann.

Hood, C. (1991) A Public Management for All Seasons? *Public Administration*, 69:1 pp3–9.

Howie, J. G., Heaney, D. J., Maxwell, M. and Walker, J. J. (1998) A Comparison of a Patient Enablement Instrument (PEI) Against Two Established Satisfaction Scales as an Outcome Measure of Primary Care Consultations. *Family Practice*, 15:2 pp165–71.

Hughes, O. E. (2003) *Public Management and Administration: An Introduction* (3rd edn), New York, NY: Palgrave.

Hunt, D. (1998) Computer-Based Clinical Decision Support Systems. *Journal Administration Medical Association*, 280:15 pp1339–46.

Hwa Hu, J. P., Chau, P. Y. K. and Liu Sheng, O. R. (2000) 'Investigation of Factors Affecting Health care Organization's Adoption of Telemedicine Technology' in *System Sciences, 2000. Proceedings of the 33rd Annual Hawaii International Conference*. IEEE Computer Society Press.

Joos, D., Chen, Q., Jirjis, J. and Johnson, K. B. (2006) 'An Electronic Medical Record in Primary Care: Impact on Satisfaction, Work Efficiency and Clinic Processes' in *AMIA Annual Symposium Proceedings*, 2006 pp394–398. IEEE Computer Society Press.

Kanter, R., Stein, B. A. and Jick, T. D. (1992) *The Challenge of Organizational Change: How Companies Experience It and Leaders Guide It*, New York, NY: Free Press.

Kelly, G. (1998) Patient Data, Confidentiality and Electronics. *British Medical Journal*, 316 pp718–9.

Kelly, G., Mulgan, G. and Muers, S. (2002) *Creating Public Value: An Analytical Framework for Public Service Reform*. Discussion Paper Prepared by the Cabinet Office Strategy Unit, UK.

Kelly, R. M. (1998) An Inclusive Democratic Polity, Representative Bureaucracies, and the New Public Management. *Public Administration Review*, 58:3 pp201–8.

Kim, Y., Lee, Z. and Gosain, S. (2005) Impediments to Successful ERP Implementation Process. *Business Process Management Journal*, 11:2 pp158–70.

Kling, Rob. (1978) *The Impacts of Computing on the Work of Managers, Data Analysts, and Clerks*. Irvine, CA: University of California–Irvine, Public Policy Research Organization.

Klomp, L. and Van Leeuwen, G. (2001) Linking Innovation and Firm Performance: A New Approach. *International Journal of the Economics of Business*, 8:3 pp343–64.

Kraemer, K. L., Dutton, W. H. and Northrop, A. (1981) *The Management of Information Systems*, New York, NY: Columbia University Press.

Kraemer, K. L. and Norris, D. F. (1994) 'Computers in Local Government' in *The 1994 Municipal Yearbook*. Washington, DC: ICMA, pp3–13.

Lærum, H. and Faxvaag, A. (2004) Task-Oriented Evaluation of Electronic Medical Records Systems: Development and Validation of a Questionnaire for Physicians. *BMC Medical Informatics and Decision Making*, 4:1 pp1–16.

Lapsley, I. and Llewellyn, S. (1998) Markets, Hierarchies and Choices in Social Care. *Management*, 12:4 pp29–38.

Lapsley, I. and Pallot, J. (2000) Accounting, Management and Organizational Change: A Comparative Study of Local Government, *Management Accounting Research*, 11:2 pp213–29.

Lau, F., Price, M., Boyd, J., Partridge, C., Bell, H. and Raworth, R. (2012) Impact of Electronic Medical Record on Physician Practice in Office Settings: A Systematic Review. *BMC Medical Informatics and Decision Making*, 12:1 pp10.

Lee, S. Y. T., Gholami, R. and Tong, T. Y. (2005) Time Series Analysis in the Assessment of ICT Impact at the Aggregate Level–Lessons and Implications for the New Economy. *Information and Management*, 42:7 pp1009–22.

Littlejohns, P., Wyatt, J. C., and Garvican L. (2003) Evaluating Computerised Health Information Systems: Hard Lessons Still to be Learnt. *British Medical Journal*, 326:7394 pp860–63.

Lööf, H. and Heshmati, A. (2002) Knowledge Capital and Performance Heterogeneity: A Firm-Level Innovation Study. *International Journal of Production Economics*, 76:1 pp61–85.

Lööf, H., Heshmati, A., Asplund, R. and Nåås, S. O. (2002) *Innovation and Performance in Manufacturing Industries: A Comparison of the Nordic Countries*. 457 SSE/EFI Working Paper Series in Economics and Finance. The Economic Research Institute, Stockholm School of Economics.

Lopez, D. M., Blobel, B. and Gonzalez, C. (2010). Quality Evaluation of Health Information System's Architectures Developed Using the HIS-DF Methodology. *Studies in Health Technology and Informatics*, 156 pp21–31.

McShane, L. (1999) *Community Development in Health and Social Services: The Craigavon and Banbridge experience*, Guilford: Craigavon and Banbridge Community Health & Social Services Trust.

Mehdi, A. (2005) Digital Government and Its Effectiveness in Public Management Reform. *Public Management Review*, 7:3 pp465–87.

Moore, M. (1994) Public Value as the Focus of Strategy. *Australian Journal of Public Administration*, 53:3 pp296–303.

Moore, M. (1995) *Creating Public Value: Strategic Management in Government*, Cambridge, MA: Harvard University Press.

Mulgan, R. (2003) *Holding Power to Account: Accountability in Modern Democracies*, Basingstoke: Palgrave.

Nasi, G. (2008) *L'attuazionedell'e-Government in Italia: Retoricao Realtà?* Milano: Egea

Neame, R. and Olson, M. (1998) How Can Sharing Clinical Information Be Made to Work? *Medinfo*, 9:1 pp315–18.

Nirel, N., Rosen, B., Sharon, A., Blondheim, O., Sherf, M., Samuel, H. and Cohen, A. D. (2010) The Impact of an Integrated Hospital-Community Medical Information System on Quality and Service Utilization in Hospital Departments. *International Journal of Medical Informatics*, 79:9 pp649–57.

Norris, D. F. and Moon, M. J. (2005) Advancing E-Government at the Grassroots: Tortoise or Hare? *Public Administration Review*, 65:1 pp64–75.

Northrop, A., Kraemer, K. L. Dunkle, D. and King, J. L. (1990) Payoffs from Computerization: Lessons Over Time. *Public Administration Review*, 50:5 pp505–14.

O'Flynn, J. (2005) *A Public Value Framework for Contractual Governance*, PUBLIC, Issue 07. Barcelona: ESADEs Institute of Public Management.

Olson, O., Guthrie, J. and Humphrey, C. (1998) 'International Experiences with "New" Public Financial Management (NPFM) Reforms: New World? Small World? Better World?' in O. Olson, C. Humphrey and J. Guthrie (eds) *Global Warning: Debating International Developments in New Public Financial Management*. Oslo: Cappelen Akademisk Forlag As.

Osborne, S. (1998) Naming the Beast Delivering and Classifying Service Innovation in Social Policy. *Human Relations*, 51 pp1133–54.

Osborne, S. (2006) The New Public Governance? *Public Management Review*, 8 pp377–88.

Osborne, S. (2009) Delivering Public Services: Are We Asking the Right Questions? *Public Money & Management*, 29:1 pp5–7.

Osborne, S. (2010) *The New Public Governance?: Emerging Perspectives on the Theory and Practice of Public Governance*, Oxford: Taylor & Francis.

Osborne, S. and Brown, K. (2005) *Managing Change and Innovation in Public Service Organizations*, New York, NY: Routledge.

Osborne, S. P., Radnor, Z. and Nasi, G. (2013) A New Theory for Public Service Management? Toward a (Public) Service-Dominant Approach. *The American Review of Public Administration*, 43 pp135–58.

Pagliari, C., Detmer, D. and Singelton. P. (2007) Potential of Electronic Personal Health Records. *British Medical Journal*, 335 pp330–33.

Pagliari, C., Sloan, D., Gregor, P., Sullivan, F., Detmer, D., Kahan, G.P, Oortwijn, W. and MacGillivray, S. (2005) What Is eHealth: A Scoping Exercise to Map the Field. *Journal of Medical Internet Research* 7:1 ppe9.

Protti, D. and Peel, V. (1998) Critical Success Factors for Evolving a Hospital Toward an Electronic Patient Record System: A Case Study of Two Different Sites. *Journal of Health care Information Management*, 12:4 pp29–38.

Rye, C. B. and Kimberly, J. R. (2007) The Adoption of Innovations by Provider Organizations in Health Care. *Medical Care Research and Review*, 64:3 pp235–78.

Shaw, N. T. (2006) Clinical Governance and Laboratory Medicine: Is the Electronic Medical Record Our Best Friend or Sworn Enemy? *Clinical Chemical Laboratory Medicine*, 44:6 pp712–18.

Smith, R. (1996) What Clinical Information do Doctors Need? *British Medical Journal*, 313 pp1062–8.

Stefanou, C. J. (2001) A Framework for the Ex-Ante Evaluation of ERP Software. *European Journal of Information Systems*, 10:4 pp595–21.

Studer, M. (2005) The Effect of Organizational Factors on the Effectiveness of EMR System Implementation: What Have We Learned. *Electronic Health Care*, 4:2 pp92–98.

Tapscott, D. (2008) The Digital Media and the Reinvention of Government. *Canadian Public Administration*, 40:2 pp328–45.

TerBogt, H. and Van Helden, G. J. (2000) Accounting Change in Dutch Government: Exploring the Gap Between Expectations and Realizations. *Management Accounting Research*, 11:2 pp263–79.

Thompson, A. G. (2003) Questioning Practices in Health Care Research: The Contribution of Social Surveys to the Creation of Knowledge. *International Journal for Quality in Health Care*, 15:3 pp187–88.

Thompson, D., Johnston, P. and Spurr, C. (2009) The Impact of Electronic Medical Records on Nursing Efficiency. *Journal of Nursing Administration*, 39:10 pp444–51.

Tidd, J. and Bessant, J. (2011) *Managing Innovation: Integrating Technological, Market and Organizational Change*, New York, NY: Wiley.

Tornatzky, L. G. and Fleischer, M. (1990) *The Process of Technological Innovation*, Lanham, MD: Lexington Books.

Tsai, C. C. and Starren, J. (2001) Patient Participation in Electronic Medical Records. *JAMA: The Journal of the American Medical Association*, 285:13 pp1765.

Van der Loo, R. P., van Gennip, E. M. S. J., Bakker, A. R., Hasman, A. and Rutten, F. F. H. (1994) 'Evaluation of Automated Information Systems in Health Care: An Approach to Classify Evaluative Studies' in *Proceedings 12th Medical Informatics Europe*, 1994, Lisbon: EFMI.

Van der Meijden, M. J., Tange, H. J., Troost, J. and Hasman, A. (2003) Determinants of Success of Inpatient Clinical Information Systems: A Literature Review. *JAMA: The Journal of the American Medical*, 10 pp235–43.

Van Dooren, W., Bouckaert, G. and Halligan, J. (2010) *Performance Management in the Public Sector*, London: Routledge.

Van Hook, M. P., Berkman, B. and Dunkle, R. (1996) Assessment Tools for General Health Care Settings: PRIME-MD, OARS, and SF-36. *Health & Social Work*, 21 pp230–34.

Van Ryzin, G. G., Muzzio, D., Immerwahr, S., Gulick, L. and Martinez, E. (2004) Drivers and Consequences of Citizen Satisfaction: An Application of the American Customer Satisfaction Index Model to New York City. *Public Administration Review*, 64:3 pp331–41.

Vigoda, E. (2002) Administrative Agents of Democracy? A Structural Equation Modeling (SEM) of the Relationship between Public Sector Performance and Citizenship Involvement. *Journal of Public Administration Research and Theory*, 12:2 pp241–72.

Vigoda, E. and Yuval, F. (2003) Managerial Quality, Administrative Performance and Trust in Governance: Can We Point to Causality? *Australian Journal of Public Administration*, 62:3 pp12–25.

Waegemann, C. P. (2002) *Status Report 2002: Electronic Health Records*, Boston, MA: MRI.

Walker, J. M. (2005) Electronic Medical Records and Health Care Transformation. *Health Affairs*, 24:5 pp1118–20.

Walker, R. M. (2008) An Empirical Evaluation of Innovation Types and Organizational and Environmental Characteristics: Towards a Configuration Framework. *Journal of Public Administration Research and Theory*, 18:4 pp591–15.

Walker, R. M., Damanpour, F. and Avellaneda, C. N. (2007) Combinative Effects of Innovation Types on Organizational Performance: A Longitudinal Study of Public Services. *Paper given at the Academy of Management Meeting*, Philadelphia, PA.

Wang, B., Burke, D. and Wan, T. (2002) 'Factors Influencing Hospital Strategy in Adopting Health Information Technology' *Paper presented at 2002 Annual Research Meeting, Health Services Research, From Knowledge to Action*, Washington, DC.

West, D. M. (2005) E-Government and the Transformation of Service Delivery and Citizen Attitudes. *Public Administration Review*, 64:1 pp15–27.

Westbrook, J. I. and Georgiou, A. (2009) The Impact of Mobile Handheld Technology on Hospital Physicians' Work Practices and Patient Care. *Journal of the American Medical Informatics Association*, 16:6 pp792–801.

Williams, I. (2011) Organizational Readiness for Innovation in Health Care: Some Lessons from the Recent Literature. *Health Services Management Research*, 24:4 pp213–18.

Wright, J. H. and Bloom, A. S. (1997) Computer Assisted Psychotherapy. *The Journal of Psychotherapy Practice and Research*, 6 pp315–22.

Zhang, J., Dawes, S. S. and Sarkis, J. (2005) Exploring Stakeholders' Expectations of the Benefits and Barriers of e-Government Knowledge Sharing. *Journal of Enterprise Information Management*, 18:5 pp548–67.

Abstract

This research focuses on innovation and its diffusion in public services in authoritarian China. A mechanism between vertical government intervention and diffusion of innovation in public services is established by conducting a comparative case study between Sichuan and Tianjin. Administrative commands facilitate the formation of the 'mandatory policy diffusion' that rapidly diffuses policy instruments. Competition in the performance evaluation-based personnel system contributes to the formation of 'championship policy diffusion', which leads to the divergence of policy instruments in neighbouring local governments. Therefore, classic theoretical hypotheses on geographical proximity, competition, and vertical intervention concerning innovation diffusion need to be modified.

MANDATE VERSUS CHAMPIONSHIP

Vertical government intervention and diffusion of innovation in public services in authoritarian China

Xufeng Zhu

Xufeng Zhu
School of Public Policy and Management
Tsinghua University
Beijing
PR China

INTRODUCTION

Researchers have long founded their studies on the traditional belief that the innovation of autonomous governments in decentralized political structures may be construed as 'laboratories of democracy' (Brandeis 1932; Greve 2001; Karch 2007). Therefore, most classic empirical studies on innovation and diffusion focus on the democratic decentralized political regime (Berry and Berry 1990; Bulmer et al., 2007; Collier and Messick 1975; Derthick 1970; Füglister 2012; Hoberg 1991; Nedergaard 2009; Oakley 1998; Peterson and Rom 1990; Radaelli 2000, 2008, 2009; Sigelman et al. 1981; Walker 1969). However, more studies on undemocratic centralized countries without a federal structure, such as authoritarian China (Yang 2006), are highly encouraged (Berry and Berry 1999: 170; Walker et al. 2011: 117). The inter-regional diffusion of innovation in China has evolved greatly since before Mao Zedong's era (Heilmann and Perry 2011). Previous studies concluded that policy experimentations and diffusion among Chinese local governments in economic policies and public services result in economic growth as well as political adaptability to the constantly changing and complicated environment (Heilmann 2008a; Wang 2009). Nevertheless, many are still unfamiliar with the inter-regional diffusion of innovation in China. What are the various mechanisms that promote the diffusion of innovation in the public service sector of China?

This article compares the difference in diffusion patterns of the administrative licensing service innovations between Sichuan and Tianjin in China by conducting field surveys. Chengdu City, the capital of Sichuan Province, first launched the 'one-window parallel licensing system' that greatly enhanced service efficiency. This system was rapidly adopted by the other local governments in Sichuan Province. Alternatively, Tianjin is one of the four provincial-level municipalities (*Zhixiashi*). Nankai District of Tianjin initiated the administrative licensing innovation called 'time-limited permission system', which also greatly improved service efficiency. In subsequent years, Nankai District's innovation was emulated by many other government systems outside Tianjin. Note that the local governments of other districts and counties under the jurisdiction of Tianjin Municipality successively conducted various innovation programmes that aim towards enhancing the efficiency of the administrative licensing service, but none duplicated Nankai District's innovation.

By comparing the diffusion patterns of innovations in Sichuan and Tianjin, a series of theoretical questions can be proposed. What forces produce a significant difference in the diffusion patterns of innovation exercised by different local governments under the same authoritarian political structure? The classic view of policy diffusion states that geographical proximity among local governments results in similar socioeconomic conditions and facilitates the mutual exchange of learning. Although some scholars argue that the classic view of policy diffusion as geographic clustering is often overly limiting, sometimes misleading, and increasingly outdated (Shipan and Volden 2012), no study has reported that geographical proximity exerts a negative effect on policy diffusion in decentralized countries. However, why did none of the neighbouring districts of Nankai adopt its policy instruments to enhance public service efficiency while many local governments outside Tianjin adopted its innovative programme? In democratic decentralized structures, central or superior governments promote the diffusion of local innovation and experimentation to other local governments through mandate measures such as national policies and incentive systems. What roles do the central or superior governments play in the process of their subordinate governments' innovation and diffusion in public service in authoritarian political structures? This article classifies two different diffusion mechanisms of innovation in public service, namely, 'mandatory policy diffusion' and 'championship policy diffusion' to generalize the roles played by the central governments in authoritarian China.

Innovation and diffusion in public services

This study focuses on innovation and diffusion in public services instead of the specific measures taken by governments to deliver public services. In the field of public administration, innovation is a process of creating or developing projects, services, institutions, or policies that are relatively new to the government regardless of whether the same programme has been previously adopted in another place (Boehmke and Witmer 2004; Heywood 1965: 107; Mohr 1969: 112; Rogers 1983; Thompson 1965: 2; Walker 1969; Walker et al. 2002). Innovations in public services specifically refer to products or procedures that public sectors deliver to private sectors and citizens, whereas policy innovations mainly focus on new policy goals, instruments, and strategies, a large part of which are public service oriented (Berry and Berry, 1994; Greenhalgh et al. 2004; Osborne 2002). If a public service innovation is presented in the form of a new policy implemented, we can therefore also call it a policy innovation. Policy diffusion is generally defined as the choices that one government's policy take, as influenced by the choices made by other governments. (Baybeck et al. 2011: 232; Shipan and Volden 2012) Policy innovation is not policy invention. For example, the new policy that government A launches may probably be learned *de facto* from, or influenced by the policy of government B. Therefore, in such a special situation, the adoption of the new policy is a policy innovation to government A, whereas to government B, the earlier adopter of the policy, such a government behaviour of government A can be construed as the policy of government B being diffused (Berry and Berry 1990; Braun and Gilardi 2006: 298; Gilardi 2010; Gray 1973). Moreover, policy diffusion in terms of context can either be a social construction process targeted at policy problems, policy scopes, and policy goals or a process of instrumental learning in which more attention is given to the design and implementation of policy instruments (Hall 1993; Howlett and Ramesh 1993; May 1992).

Most studies focus on the reasons behind the innovations and the mechanisms of inter-regional diffusion. These studies can generally be divided into internal determinant models, horizontal influence models, and vertical intervention models. The internal determinant models assume that specific internal government factors may determine and stimulate government innovations to some extent (Nice 1994). The internal determinants, which include social, economic, political, and historical traditions, traits of leaders, and internal policy networks, among others, are discussed as follows. First, economic development encourages citizens to demand for better public services (Berry and Lowery 1987; Ingram and Mann 1980), which is the reason why local governments in economically developed, industrialized, and urbanized areas are more inclined towards innovation (Walker 1969). Nevertheless, although economic resources are generally important in fuelling policy innovation, the financial situation of the local government has a greater impact on public service innovations (Gray 1974). Second, when pursuing re-election, the innovative behaviour of local politicians is dependent on their election security (Kiewiet and McCubbins 1985). The more unsecured politicians feel, the more willing they are to adopt new deals that are popular with the voters (Berry and Berry 1990; Hays and Glick 1997), and the more likely they are to reject new deals that are widely unacceptable or in conflict with the interest of some voters (Berry and Berry 1992; Mikesell 1978; Mintrom 1997). Third, politicians with high socioeconomic status brought about by higher education, better income, and wealth are more innovative than their counterparts with low socioeconomic status (Rogers 1983). Fourth, internal policy networks promote policy innovations, for example, by facilitating the setting of policy agenda and generating power that strongly supports the policy innovation (Mintrom 1997).

The horizontal influence models explain the major driving forces of government innovation and policy diffusion that come from another government that has no supervisor–subordinate relationship with the adopting government. The first driving factor is the interaction of government officials from different states that may help them learn about an innovative project from its earlier adopter, which is often affected by geographic factors (Füglister 2012; Gray 1973). Such interaction among government officials encourages many states to accept the guidelines of the innovative project of one or more advanced states in their neighbouring areas (Foster 1978; Grupp and Richards 1975; Walker 1969, 1973). Moreover, if a certain government adopts a new policy, its neighbouring governments are more inclined to adopt the same policy (Boehmke and Witmer 2004). With regard to transnational policy diffusion, the effect of geographic proximity in global network positions facilitates policy learning and emulation, resulting in policy convergence (Cao 2012). The second horizontal influential factor is the competition among governments. In USA, competition with other states causes the local government to adopt a new policy (Rogers 1983; Walker 1969). For example, a state may lower its social welfare level to acclimatize itself to the welfare level of its neighbouring areas to avoid being a 'welfare magnet' to the poor (Peterson and Rom 1990). Moreover, a state may adopt the same social policies and economic incentive programmes implemented in its neighbouring states to prevent local residents and enterprises from investing in other states (Berry and Berry 1990; Gray 1994).

Competition among countries over foreign investments and markets also promotes mutual policy learning among them (Elkins et al. 2006; Glick and Hays 1991; Simmons and Elkins 2004). However, aside from policy diffusion among local governments, a government of a country may undertake transnational coercive transfer when it is pressured by the hegemonic power of another country to issue certain policies (Braun and Gilardi 2006; Dolowitz and Marsh 1996; Rose 2005).

In contrast with the horizontal influence models that merely focus on the interaction between innovators and learners, the vertical intervention models introduce a powerful government as the third party, which holds a higher hierarchical position than innovating and learning local governments. Central governments may spread and accelerate innovations from one subordinate government to another with mandate measures, including administrative regulations or incentive policies (Berry and Berry 1999, 2007). In England, which is a democratic and relatively centralized state, many policies implemented by local governments stem from best practices disseminated by the central government through legislation and national-level guidance (Newman et al. 2000; Nutley et al. 2012; Walker et al. 2011). In USA, although all states are entitled to their autonomy, the federal (central) government can also provide strong fiscal incentives to local governments to accelerate the adoption of state policies (Berry and Berry 1999; Moon and Bretschneider 1997; Welch and Thompson 1980).

Most previous empirical studies focused on innovation and inter-regional diffusion in democratic federalist countries. However, recent academic debates have paid more attention to the effect of different political structures on the mechanisms of innovation and diffusion. On the one hand, theoretical evidence argues that, under the federalist structure, decentralization is unlikely to be favourable to the innovative behaviours of local governments because of the local officials' preference to avert risk (Rose-Ackerman 1980). Moreover, innovation as a public good contributes to free riding by other local governments. Therefore, the structure of a centralized system is favourable to the innovation of local governments when they are relatively large in number (Strumpf 2002). On the other hand, some scholars argue that the incentives of political competition for federal office of local officials and the pressure of 'location choices' of residents can offset the risk-averse preference and freeriding, and that the political process in federalist structures continues to present more advantages in terms of innovation than that in unitary structures (Baybeck et al. 2011; Kotsogiannis and Schwager 2004). Unfortunately, the abovementioned controversies are still at the theoretical analysis stage (with mathematical statements) instead of at the stage of empirical study. In this article, I intend to conduct an empirical study on the diffusion of innovation in public services in China, which is an authoritarian country with a large number of diversified local governments and where the central government has great influence on the behaviours of local governments and on the careers of local officials.

Vertical intervention from the central or superior government in authoritarian China is more complicated than that in democratic decentralized countries. For example, the classic vertical influence models only focus on tangible administrative and incentive mandate measures implemented by central governments to promote a specific adoption of innovation. However, in China, local governments may adopt a national policy not because of the economic incentives but to express loyalty to the central authority (Montinola et al. 1996; Shirk 1993). In Mao's era, the Chinese central leaders possessed the authority to reinforce local experimentations without implementing any national policies or incentive programmes and sufficient experience to prove the effectiveness of experimentations (Heilmann 2008b: 15). Moreover, the effectiveness of these local experimentations is based on the encouragement, protection, and promotion of the central authority than on trial and error or spontaneous policy diffusion (Heilmann 2008b: 29). These special characteristics of Mao's era motivate us to study further the mechanisms of the inter-regional diffusion of innovation in post-Mao China since the reform was initiated. Therefore, this research attempts to establish the mechanism between vertical government intervention and patterns of diffusion of innovation in public service fields by conducting a comparative case study.

Authoritarian structure and diffusions of innovation in China

China's authoritarian structure has two main features. The first feature is relevant to the relationship between the central and local governments. China possesses neither classic federalist nor unitary political structures. Vertical administrative centralization and fiscal decentralization coexist. Based on the fiscal system, during the initial stage of reform, the national financial revenues were distributed between the central government and the local governments in the form of fiscal revenue-sharing contracts (Montinola et al. 1996; Oi 1992). Since the establishment of the tax-sharing system in 1994, the financial distribution structure between the central government and the local governments has been stabilized (Tsui 2005). Moreover, the local governments are responsible for the majority of the expenditures for the national social welfare (Caulfield 2006; Chou 2008). With respect to public affairs management, the administrative system dictates that local governments must follow commands and policies from the central or superior governments. Local governments also possess certain autonomy in public affairs management (Chung 1995; Foster 2006).

The second feature focuses on the personnel and career system of the local officials. This system is an undemocratic regime in which local officials are appointed and selected by the central or superior leaders instead of elected by voters. In post-Mao China, with the gradual decline of the personal authority of national leaders and the rise of local governments (Montinola 1996: 72), significant changes in bureaucratic personnel management took place in the selection criteria in the institutional structure (Zhou 1995). Currently, local government officials pay more attention to recognition and positive work evaluation under the performance evaluation system designed by the central and superior governments. Local government officials rely on such an evaluation system in their desire to be promoted, resulting in horizontal competition among officials (Chan and Gao 2008; Gao 2009). Such a career-oriented system for local officials based on performance evaluation tends to push local officials into developing their local economy (Li and Zhou 2005; Maskin et al. 2000; Whiting 2001). This *nomenklatura*-style personnel system leads us to consider that Chinese local government officials are more concerned about the central government instead of the public (Kung and Chen 2011). However, with the recent transition of the Chinese government from an economic-cantered to a people-oriented state, aside from economic indices such as the gross domestic product and fiscal revenue, new indicators of functional targets of some public services, such as education, public health, environment protection, and public security, among others, have been added to the performance evaluation system (Gao 2009; Xue and Zhong 2012).

Unlike local governments under democratic decentralized structures, the targets of innovation and diffusion by Chinese local governments are more complicated. The central government, after evaluating the economic benefits and political risks caused by local government experimentations, has the authority to promote or terminate a project through administrative commands (Cai and Treisman 2006; Heilmann 2008a). Furthermore, the recognition and successful promotion of an innovation by the central or superior governments reflect the performance of local officials who first adopted such innovation. Local governments must also make greater efforts to achieve multiple objectives including developing the economy, increasing fiscal revenues, and saving financial expenditure through policy innovation within the framework of the current vertical decentralized fiscal system. In public service, when a new project is favourable to the local financial condition, other areas will follow suit in such forms as public service outsourcing (Jing 2008) and public–private partnership (Hodge and Greve 2007), which are diffused in many public service fields throughout China. Moreover, apart from focusing on economic development and financial balance, local government officials must also respond prudently to the greater expectations of the society, the market, and the public according to the enriched government performance system (Ngok and Zhu 2007; Walker and Wu 2010).

In light of the policy innovation and experimentation of subordinate governments, the central or superior governments may adopt two major intervention methods to impose the necessary effect: (1) intervention with administrative command and (2) competition with performance evaluation.

Administrative commands, including administrative instructions, policies, regulations, rules, and institutional systems, among others, come from the central or superior governments. The central or superior governments may promote a public service system successfully experimented on by a certain local government in pilot sites by issuing a specific administrative command. The mandatory policy diffusion strongly promoted by the administrative commands of the central or superior governments and the coercive transfer discussed in the previous literature are different. Coercive transfer occurs when a powerful country, as the early adopter of an institutional policy, forces other countries to adopt such policy against the willingness of the latter's state leaders and domestic citizens. Conversely, mandatory diffusion reflects a triangular relationship in which the central or superior government as the third party can force a local government to learn the policy innovation of a pilot area through administrative commands.

An innovation from a certain local government can be rapidly diffused to different areas nationwide through administrative commands. However, if administrative commands are too tight, they may block the flexible adaption of an innovation to local conditions. As a result, an innovation of policy instruments in one area may not always be successful when implemented in other areas. For instance, the Chinese basic medical insurance system for urban workers and the rural pension system have been popularized nationwide through central administrative commands after the successful pilot experimentations of the local governments. However, the outcomes of the diffusion of the two innovations are completely different. With stable financial support, the nationwide promotion of the basic medical insurance system for urban workers in 1998 became successful, and it was regarded as a landmark for the full coverage target of the basic medical insurance in China (Lin et al. 2009; Liu 2002). On the contrary, the promotion of the rural pension system failed soon after it was popularized nationwide in 1995 because of financial decentralization and the limited administrative capacity of local governments (Béland and Yu 2004; Shi 2006).

Unlike the mandatory diffusion of innovation directly intervened by the central or superior governments through administrative commands, the performance evaluation of the superior government indirectly influences the innovation behaviours of local officials. Economic development, improved public service performances, and the recognition of the superior government of the local innovations may collectively increase the probability of promoting officials in the subordinate local governments. Therefore, in the pursuit of rare promotional opportunities, local governments compete with one another in an all-dimensional performance.

Under the performance evaluation system, the innovation and policy-learning behaviours of local governments are referred to as 'championship policy diffusion'. When a certain local government is the first adopter of a policy project that enhances a certain dimension of performance, officials in the neighbouring local governments, bound by performance competition under the jurisdiction of the same superior government, follow the same policy goal to achieve identical performance. However, as the learner, the neighbouring government under the jurisdiction of the same superior government shows reluctance to emulate the policy instrument of the local government that took the lead in using it to avoid being regarded as the 'follower' of the innovation. On the contrary, the neighbouring government prefers to discover new policy instruments to be considered the 'pioneering adopters' of the innovation. The discovery of such a new policy instrument not only can ensure that the adopter does not yield to its opponent in the performance competition but instead facilitates the adopter in drawing attention and concern from the superior governments to the new policy instruments.

Although, in most cases, the inter-regional diffusion of innovation in USA is derived from competition hypotheses, 'competitive policy diffusion' under the federalist structure differs greatly from the 'championship policy diffusion' caused by the competition between local governments in China. Under the federalist structure, the voters who mainly influence local government behaviours are more concerned with the outcome of the policy instead of whether their government is the pioneer adopter of such policy. In complicated situations, state politicians strive to seek shorter means of formulating new policies and are thus are more inclined to select solutions that have been proven effective and promising (Walker 1969). Therefore, the competition among local governments in federalist structures tends to result in the convergence of policy goals and instruments. On the contrary, the championship policy diffusion between neighbouring local governments engaged in performance competition in China is more inclined towards the convergence of policy goals but to the divergence of policy instruments. Unsurprisingly, if two local governments under the jurisdiction of different superior governments are not involved in performance evaluation competition, the learner is likely to duplicate directly the policy instrument from other areas to improve its performances. Therefore, the learner will play the role as the pioneering adopter of the new policy within its own area.

METHODOLOGY AND DATA COLLECTION

This research focuses on innovation in public service to enterprises at the local level and different mechanisms of diffusion among Chinese local governments. 'Business invitation and investment attraction' are important indicators of performance evaluation in China because of the financial revenues they contribute. If a new corporation registers in a certain local government, it will promote benefits such as local economy, investment, taxes, and job opportunities. Consequently, it means that other areas will lose these opportunities. At the initial stage of China's 'reform and opening up', the central government established special economic zones in some coastal open cities to allow these areas to implement special preferential policies to attract many investors. However, in other areas where similar preferential policies were not provided but were merely driven by the mindset 'no preferential policy but excellent service', the local governments strove to promote the reform of public service and management, optimizing the local investment environment and thereby ultimately obtaining the competitive advantages in attracting external and foreign investments. One of the important sectors that provide public service to enterprises is the administrative licensing services for corporate registration.

In the past, the procedures for administrative licensing for corporate registration were cumbersome and known for their inefficiency. For example, if an enterprise wanted to complete its registration procedures, it must transact with numerous government departments located in different downtown areas. At the onset of the twenty-first century, the Chinese central government issued many policy documents and required local governments to reform the administrative licensing service. Consequently, local governments set up their respective administrative licensing service centres in response to the call of the central government to provide enterprises and residents with concentrated administrative licensing services. However, the central policy did not stipulate reform target and solutions or offer any evaluation standards and incentive measures to assess any reform initiatives. Under such a flexible reform background, local governments differed greatly in terms of pilot solutions, speed, and effectiveness in local administrative licensing reforms (Zhu and Jiao 2012).

The methodology of this comparative case study followed the criteria of 'theoretical replication', that is, contrasting results for anticipatable reasons (Yin 2009: 54). A comparative case study of administrative licensing service reforms in Sichuan and Tianjin was applied to demonstrate the diverse mechanisms of diffusion patterns of innovation in public service. There are important similarities between the two cases. Both Sichuan and Tianjin are provincial-level local governments in China. Sichuan is one of the provinces located in the inland area of China, and Tianjin is one of four provincial-level municipalities located in the eastern coast of the country. Local governments under the Sichuan and Tianjin jurisdictions attempted an administrative licensing service innovation that achieved great success in both cases, winning the same national local government innovation reward in different years. There are also substantial differences in the nature of diffusion of innovation in the two regions where different mechanisms of vertical intervention from superior governments were applied. However, as regional variations are common in China, many other differences between Sichuan and Tianjin could affect the diffusion mechanisms of innovation among local governments. In this regard, the research design should be understood as an exploration through two different cases rather than as a rigorous case comparison.

The methods used to collect data for this study include interviews, observations, conferences, and documentary evidence. In the last three years, a group of researchers, including two students and myself, interviewed 27 officials at the superior city level and in administrative licensing service centres, related experts, and businessmen. In 2009, I interviewed two leaders in the Tianjin Government General Office who are in charge of administrative licensing services in Tianjin. In April 2010, I was invited at a government consultation meeting on the reform of administrative licensing services in Tianjin, where I interviewed the Director of the Administrative Licensing Service Center of Heping District and the former Director of the Administrative Licensing Service Center of Nankai District who was in charge of the 2004 Nankai innovation. In July 2010, a national conference on 'administrative licensing service innovation' was held by the Chinese Public Administration Society and Tianjin Government, where several local officials from Tianjin (including different districts), Chengdu City of Sichuan, Beijing

City, Dalian of Liaoning Province, Chongqing City, and others were semi-structured interviewed. In addition, during the field study in Tianjin between 2010 and 2011, I observed the Administrative Licensing Service Center of Tianjin City as well as those of Hexi and Heping districts.

Between 2011 and 2012, we travelled to Sichuan Province three times to interview related officials and businessmen. The administrative licensing service reform in Chengdu City was initiated and managed by Hu Changnian, who was then Deputy Secretary-General of the General Office of Chengdu Government. Unfortunately, he died in a plane crash in Yichun City, Heilongjiang Province on 24 August 2010. Nevertheless, we managed to interview the Deputy Director and two division directors of the Chengdu Administrative Licensing Service Center. Then, we visited and interviewed two businessmen whose firm was registered in the Chengdu Administrative Licensing Service Center. Furthermore, we visited three counties in Sichuan Province, where we interviewed the Party Secretary and the Director of the Party General Office of Chengxiang County, County Chief of Danba County, and Budgeting Director of the Financial Bureau of Batang County.

Other empirical data for this research were collected from papers in conference proceedings, government policies, websites, and media news. The proceedings of the 2010 National Conference on Administrative Licensing Service Innovation held in Tianjin provided numerous cases of innovations in administrative licensing services throughout China. The conference papers presented by local officials and related scholars became a valuable documentary evidence for the study. We also searched original government policy documents on administrative licensing service reforms in official websites of local governments. Moreover, the Chinese Local Government Innovation Award was launched and organized by the Central Compilation and Translation Bureau of China, which has established a website called 'China Innovations' (www.chinainnovations.org/). All awarded local government innovations are presented in the 'Database of Innovations' in the website, where the innovations in administrative licensing services in Chengdu and Nankai are listed and introduced in detail. In addition, the author presented the draft of the paper in four international and domestic academic conferences held in Beijing, Tianjin, Chengdu, and Macao to obtain critiques and suggestions from other scholars. Table 1 summarizes the collected data.

Mandatory policy diffusion: Sichuan case

Innovation in Chengdu City

Administrative licensing service reform is a key reform of the Chinese government in promoting the transition of China from economic management functions to market-oriented service and in creating an excellent development environment. The State Council made the overall implementation of the national administrative licensing reform in October 2001. Chengdu City in Sichuan Province began its administrative

Table 1: Summary of data collection

Data collection methods
Interviews (*n* = 27)
Leaders in superior governments (*n* = 2)
Heads in local governments and party committees (*n* = 4)
Heads of local administrative licensing service centres (*n* = 11)
Staff in local administrative licensing service centres (*n* = 4)
Experts (*n* = 4)
Businessmen (*n* = 2)
Conferences (*n* = 6)
Government consultation seminar (*n* = 1)
National government conference (*n* = 1)
Academic conferences (*n* = 4)
Locations of observation in local administrative licensing service centres (*n* = 3)
Documents (conference proceedings, government documents, websites, media presentations)

licensing reform by combining the requirements for a 'standardized service government'. The reform achieved remarkable results such as simplified approval procedures and an improved approval internet system. In 2004, the full implementation of the *Administrative Licensing Law* led Chengdu City to establish the first Government Affairs Service Center for a joint provincial and municipal administrative office. The centre first established the 'one-station' administrative licensing with marked advantages, such as the unified acceptance of corporate registration as all relevant departments work in the same hall. One-station licensing reduces hassle and saves energy on the part of enterprises and of citizens during the registration process. Prior to the reform implementation, the period allotted for processing a registration application of an enterprise in Chengdu City was 58 working days. After implementing the 'one-station' service reform, the processing period was cut to nine working days. However, one-station service did not change the administrative licensing procedure, which still involves a number of departments approving a licence for each item. Therefore, administrative licensing still undergoes a complicated procedure involving complex formalities and a longer corporate registration waiting period, which may affect the efficiency of administrative work and obstruct the improvement of the Chengdu investment environment.

In June 2007, the State Council officially approved the establishment of the Experimental Area of Urban–Rural Comprehensive Development Reform in Chengdu City and required the city to reform the overall structure and encourage innovations in key fields. Thus, Chengdu City initiated the 'one-window parallel licensing system' reform project to establish a highly efficient and citizen-friendly administrative licensing service model. The reform for corporate registration in the city involves the following process: (1) an enterprise applicant submits the application documents to one window only (instead of the previous multiple windows in the one-station service procedure), and (2) the application documents are transferred to the relevant departments inside the window. This solution does not necessarily involve enterprise applicants to transact in every step because the offices are the ones that process the applications. The government affairs service centre remodels and stream-lines the administrative licensing procedures through the following: (1) conducting the series connection of any licensing step with the legal cause-and-effect relationship and (2) conducting the parallel connection of any licensing step without the legal cause-and-effect relationship. The new procedures are automatically processed online; thus, the process is characterized by the following: (1) parallel licensing and an internet system, (2) two-way interaction between the government affairs service centre and the applicants, (3) data transmission to the relevant licensing authorities, (4) online inquiry of applicants, and (5) real-time monitoring and supervision on the part of the management departments.

The 'one-window parallel licensing' reform project of Chengdu City has greatly enhanced the administrative licensing services efficiency. The guaranteed processing period for corporate registration has been shortened to two working days from the original nine working days. During the trial period of the project from July to September 2007, the average processing time was approximately three hours and twenty-two minutes, with the minimum processing time reaching only one hour and eight minutes, thus becoming the new national record. The project was awarded the 2007 Chinese City Management Progress Award, won First Prize in the Chengdu City Science and Technology Progress, and was an awardee in the Fourth Chinese Local Government Innovation Award.

Diffusion under administrative command

With this successful public service innovation, the Sichuan Provincial Government integrated the administration command-based promotion of the Chengdu City 'one-window parallel licensing' service (particularly the corporate registration 'one-window parallel licensing') into its diffusion process. On 28 April 2008, the Sichuan Provincial Communist Party Committee and the People's Government jointly promulgated the *Decision of Sichuan Provincial Communist Party Committee and People's Government on Strengthening the Building of the Administrative Effectiveness of Enterprises and Institutions*. The promulgation requires the Communist Party Committees and the People's Governments of all cities (prefectures) and counties (cities and districts) to draw and learn from the reform solution of the Chengdu City Government Affairs Service Center and to implement the corporate registration parallel connection approval project. All municipal governments within Sichuan Province (prefectures) are then ordered to conduct a parallel licensing service reform in subordinate local governments through government commands. To date, all local governments within the jurisdiction of

Sichuan Province conduct corporate registration parallel licensing service projects. The administrative licensing service innovation of Chengdu City has also been popularized in local governments in other provinces and municipalities. The corporate registration 'one-window parallel licensing' approval system has been diffused to Putian City in Fujian; Yichang City in Hubei; Xining City in Qinghai; Shantou City in Guangdong; Weihai City in Shandong; Yuhang District, Hangzhou City, and Cangnan County; Wenzhou City in Zhejiang; and in other places across China.

Championship policy diffusion: Tianjin case

Innovation in Nankai District

After the promulgation of the *Administrative Licensing Law* in 2004, the Tianjin Municipal Government successively issued numerous documents on the administrative licensing service reform that governments at the district and county levels within the entire municipality must implement. However, these documents did not provide a unified reform solution for local governments in the entire municipality. Moreover, the municipal government did not issue any administrative directives or policies for promoting the successful reform experience within the districts and counties under its jurisdiction. In 2005, the Chinese central government particularly designated the Tianjin Binhai New Area (TBNA) as the Experimental Area of Comprehensive Reform. As a result, the central government honourably gave TBNA a series of preferential policies to attract corporate investments related to land, finance, and taxes, among others. Consequently, other local governments in Tianjin adopted the philosophy of 'no preferential policy, but excellent service' and initiated the enhancement of quality and efficiency of public service provided to enterprises. In recent years, with the strong promotion of the Tianjin Municipal Government of the administrative licensing service reform and the once-created loose institutional environment, administrative licensing service centres in all districts (counties) successively issued their respective administrative licensing service reform solutions for corporate registration.

Among all districts (counties) under the jurisdiction of Tianjin Municipality, Nankai District was the first local government to develop an administrative licensing innovation solution independently. Prior to 2002, Nankai District introduced several basic initiatives, including a concentrated handling procedure to enhance administrative licensing efficiency. However, enterprises were confronted with a number of problems in handling the corporate registration procedure. These problems can be categorized into two types: (1) difficulty in handling the procedure within the prescribed time limit and (2) approved projects lacking the necessary planning. The Nankai District Administrative Licensing Service Center succeeded in developing a set of electronic licensing software in 2002 using Internet technology, and it was put into official operation in January 2003. The centre advanced the Time-Limited Permission System in February 2004 to integrate the handling procedure into the requirements of the

Administrative Licensing Law. This system specifies that the matter accepted by administrative licensing departments should be automatically deemed as implied permission or tacit consent if no approved or declined decision is made beyond the prescribed processing period (three days) or if the processing period is not extended based on legal procedure.

The administrative licensing reform of Nankai District greatly enhanced the efficiency of corporate registration. In the past, approximately 45 days were required to complete one corporate registration in Tianjin. After Nankai District implemented an administrative licensing service reform in 2002 and established the Time-Limited Permission System in 2004, the processing period for one corporate registration was shortened to less than three days. In 2003, for the first time, the total number of registered private industrial and commercial enterprises exceeded that of Heping and Hexi districts, both of which are former leaders in this aspect. From 2003 until the TBNA was reconstructed and integrated into a large administrative district in 2009, Nankai District ranked first among all the districts and counties in Tianjin (Tianjin Statistics Bureau 2003–2009). In 2006, the Time-Limited Permission System in the administrative licensing service reform of Nankai District won the Third Chinese Local Government Innovation Award.

Divergence under competition

Under strong competitive pressure from the administrative licensing service reform of Nankai District, all other districts and counties in Tianjin initiated their respective administrative licensing service reforms. In June 2004, the Administrative Licensing Service Center of Hexi District was officially established to implement the 'One-station Concentrated Office' for administrative licensing affairs. In March 2005, Hexi District implemented the system of District Mayor Reception Service Day for Enterprises, and the Deputy District Mayor in-charge of the economy assigned the consultation and procedure-handling services to enterprises and individuals applying for corporate registration or intending to invest in the district. Hexi District successively launched effective service initiatives such as appointment handling, key project green channel, and duty supervisor ushering for handling. The district also successively established two systems, namely, the Investment Project Joint Licensing and the Enterprise Registration Joint Licensing, in January 2008 and February 2009, thereby enhancing the handling efficiency of the two services up to 80 per cent and 70 per cent, respectively. In January 2009, the centre led in obtaining an ISO 9001:2008 Quality Management System certificate for entire Tianjin, standardizing and optimizing the operating procedure for corporate registration licensing. In July 2009, Hexi District began to implement an administrative licensing chief representative system. After a series of reforms and innovations, the district successfully shortened the licensing time limit to 3.2 days on average, with the fastest approval time limit of 2.3 days.

For a long time, Heping District was the economic and political centre of all other districts and counties within Tianjin Municipality. Heping was also the leader in attracting businesses and investments in Tianjin. However, since 2003, Nankai District, Hexi District, and the TBNA have surpassed Heping District in terms of economic leadership. Under this competitive pressure, the Administrative Licensing Service Center of Heping District implemented the Full-Service Agency System. This system involves public-service outsourcing in which the government outsources (with compensation) administrative licensing service affairs to intermediary companies. In turn, the intermediary companies provide a whole-process agency service for handling corporate registration and registration change procedures. In the beginning, the Full-Service Agency System operation encountered resistance from other Heping District administrative departments, resulting in limited improvements in administrative licensing approval. The Administrative Licensing Service Center of Heping District established the 'ongoing log system' to solve the problems. Under this system, intermediary companies were empowered to supervise the administrative licensing services process. The combination of Full-Service Agency and ongoing log facilitates procedure handling efficiency through the reduction of the processing period from the original one and a half months or so to two to three days. More private commercial and industrial enterprises have applied for corporate registration with remarkable improvement in administrative licensing service efficiency in Heping District. Since the implementation of the reform in 2007, the number of private industrial and commercial enterprises in Heping District recovered significantly and became stable, with an increase noted every year (for a detailed case study, see Zhu and Jiao 2012).

Aside from the aforementioned central urban districts (i.e. Nankai, Hexi, and Heping districts), other districts and counties within Tianjin Municipality initiated reforms in their respective administrative licensing services. For example, Hedong District adopted the 'Four Systems' (i.e. Window Service System, Service Commitment System, First Acceptance Responsibility System, and Accountability System); Hongqiao District adopted the 'Four Networks' (i.e. Intranet, Extranet, Joint Approval Special Network, and Departmental Approval Business Special Network) and 'Four Systems' (i.e. Administrative Approval Operating System, Joint Approval System, Municipal and District Two-tier Interaction System, and Administrative Approval Efficiency Supervision System); Dongli District established the 'Three Platforms' (i.e. Administrative Licensing Service Platform, Business Supporting Service Platform, and Family Network Service Platform); and Wuqing District established the 'Four Platforms' (i.e. Administrative Licensing Service Platform, Administrative Efficiency Supervision Platform, Elements Distribution Platform, and Social Service Platform), among others. After Nankai District took the lead in implementing an administrative licensing service reform, all other districts and counties within Tianjin Municipality exerted greater efforts to conduct their respective innovation initiatives, with a resolution to enhance public service efficiency and quality to attract businesses and investments. However, although the Time-Limited Permission System of Nankai District had gained unanimous recognition from officials and enterprises and had won the national award, none of the other local governments in the areas under the Tianjin Municipality jurisdiction adopted the system. Furthermore, none of the administrative licensing service reform projects that the Tianjin districts and counties used were the same. Interestingly, however, Wenzhou City in Zhejiang, Wuhan City in Hubei, Tanshan City in Hebei, Liyang City in Jiangsu, Shuangyashan City in Heilongjiang, and other cities nationwide employed and learned from the advanced experience of Nankai District and successfully established their respective Time-Limited Permission Systems, modelled after the Nankai District system.

Summary of the comparative case studies

The comparative case study of the administrative licensing service innovations in Sichuan and Tianjin as well as their respective diffusion processes enables us to discover and verify the two different diffusion patterns of public service innovation that the superior governments in China adopt as an intervention means. In the case of Sichuan, considering the success of the Chengdu Administrative Licensing Service Center, the provincial government popularized the Chengdu innovation throughout Sichuan Province in the form of administrative commands, a process that can be called 'mandatory policy diffusion'. The method of higher authorities in popularizing local government innovation through administrative commands or instructions is extremely efficient for policy diffusion. According to the Sichuan Provincial Government requirements, all local governments within Sichuan Province must complete a corporate registration parallel licensing system reform within a few years. The Tianjin Municipal Government, for its part, did not impose administrative commands on local governments to adopt a specific administrative licensing institutional arrangement. The public service innovation and diffusion by local governments within Tianjin complied with a 'championship policy diffusion' arising from the challenge of a performance evaluation system. The economic performance competition among local governments encourages the exertion of greater efforts to promote public service reforms in all local governments within Tianjin to attract businesses and investments. After Nankai District took the initiative to launch a public service innovation and greatly enhanced public service efficiency, other local governments, pressured by economic competition to attract external or foreign investments, initiated public service reforms with comparable policy goals. Innovation itself is a political performance of local governments. Therefore, all local governments refused to imitate the innovative institutional arrangement of other local governments under the jurisdiction of the same superior government. They were willing to initiate their own innovative projects. Local decision makers strove to be 'the pioneering adopter' of a certain innovation in the neighbouring areas, hoping to receive commendation from the superior government.

CONCLUSION

This article proposes a theoretical explanation of the diffusion of public service innovation within authoritarian China. The authoritarian structure in China demonstrates two features: (1) the coexistence of vertical administrative centralization and fiscal decentralization and (2) the official personnel system based on performance evaluation, which results in horizontal competition among local government officials. Moreover, with the changes in the governance ideology of the central government, the performance evaluation system continues to be updated and enriched, thereby affecting the behaviours of local governments.

Unique vertical intervention measures that the Chinese central and superior governments implemented have converted our beliefs on traditional theories on the diffusion of innovation. In general, the characteristics that drive innovation adoption in China cannot be simply labelled as top down and bottom up. Based on the comparative studies of public service innovations in Sichuan and Tianjin, different diffusion patterns of innovation in public service are adopted by the subordinate local governments under various vertical intervention mechanisms that the central or superior governments implemented under one authoritarian structure. The central or superior governments promote innovations in public service through administrative commands based on the benefits and risks of local government innovations. Administrative commands from the superior government facilitate the formation of the 'mandatory policy diffusion' among local governments. This action results in the hasty achievement of diffusion for policy goals as well as policy instruments within the time limit that the administrative commands prescribe. In addition, mandatory policy diffusion does not leave considerable room for local adjustments and flexibility. Although the Sichuan case of mandatory policy diffusion presented in this article was quite successful, it does not imply that flexibility is not necessary in all cases of governance through administrative commands.

The competition for performance evaluation by superior governments contributes to the formation of 'championship policy diffusion' among local governments under the jurisdiction of the same superior government. Unwilling to yield to their opponents in terms of performance, local officials are likely to imitate the policy goals of an innovation that a pioneering adopter initiated. However, they will strive to adopt new policy instruments unlike those of others to achieve the same policy goals and to avoid being regarded as mere followers of a certain innovation. Therefore, the championship policy diffusion demonstrates a convergence of policy goals but a divergence of policy instruments. In decentralized countries, traditional geographic hypotheses on policy diffusion argue that a policy innovation tends to spread from one government to the neighbouring geographic states (Berry and Berry 1990; Peterson and Rom 1990). Despite geographic clustering that now appears increasingly outdated because of less communication and travel barriers (Shipan and Volden 2012), scholars never argued that geographic proximity negatively affects policy diffusion and learning. However, performance evaluation in China produces a level of competition that discourages policy diffusion of innovation among neighbouring local governments.

Therefore, the findings of this research encourage us to modify classic theoretical hypotheses on geographical proximity, competition, and vertical intervention concerning innovation diffusion.

China's authoritarianism is such a political structure that has a central government that plays a pivotal role in the process of local government innovation and diffusion. On the one hand, the central government is in a position to manoeuvre administrative measures to popularize a certain local government institutional innovation within a short time. On the other hand, the central government can strongly inspire local governments to try out different policy instruments for similar policy goals through a vertical governmental fiscal decentralization and a horizontal governmental performance competition. Both mechanisms can internalize the learning externality innovation for local governments and contribute in popularizing successful local government innovations to other areas nationwide. Therefore, despite the lack of sufficient autonomy in authoritarian China, local governments continue to have a strong desire for innovation, which endows the entire country with vitality and diversity. More importantly, local governments also provide sufficient policy alternative solutions to the macroeconomic decisions that the central government will formulate in the future.

Public service, as referred to in this research, is mainly involved in the administrative licensing service for enterprises. Business invitation and investment attraction are among the most important contents of performance evaluation for Chinese local governments. Therefore, lower-level or mid-level provincial governments are highly motivated to initiate excellent public service innovations to attract external or foreign investments. An important question then is this: Are the two diffusion patterns of public service suggested in this article applicable to other public service fields or even to other policy fields in China? The important role that the central or superior governments play in conducting the performance evaluation of local governments should be considered. With the behavioural logic of local officials under an authoritarian structure, if the relevant public service performance indicators are incorporated into the performance evaluation systems, the author of the present article predicts that the abovementioned diffusion mechanisms of innovation may be effectively applicable in other public service fields. However, this prediction remains to be further verified using new empirical evidence. In addition, the prevailing research strategy of policy diffusion is based on quantitative methods. However, this research is only a qualitative two-case comparison. We, therefore, look forward to conducting comprehensive quantitative empirical analyses on the policy diffusion in authoritarian China.

ACKNOWLEDGEMENTS

I would like to thank Qiyuan Jiao and Ting Jia for their valuable assistance in field works in Tianjin and Sichuan and all interviewees and referees for this research. I would also like to thank the Management Science Program of National Natural Sciences Foundation of China (70973058) for the sponsorship.

REFERENCES

Baybeck, B., Berry, W. B. and Siegel, D. A. (2011) A Strategic Theory of Policy Diffusion via Intergovernmental Competition. *The Journal of Politics*, 73:1 pp232–47.

Béland, D. and Yu, K. M. (2004) A Long Financial March: Pension Reform in China. *Journal of Social Policy*, 33:2 pp267–88.

Berry, F. S. and Berry, W. D. (1990) State Lottery Adoption as Policy Innovations: An Event History Analysis. *American Political Science Review*, 84:2 pp395–415.

—— (1992) Tax Innovation in the States: Capitalizing on Political Opportunity. *American Journal of Political Science*, 36:3 pp715–42.

—— (1994) Innovation in Public Management: The Adoption of Strategic Planning. *Public Administration Review*, 54:4 pp322–9.

—— (1999) "Innovation and Diffusion Models in Policy Research", in P. A. Sabatier (ed) *Theories of the Policy Process*, Boulder, CO: Westview.

—— (2007) "Innovation and Diffusion Models in Policy Research", in P. A. Sabatier (ed) *Theories of the Policy Process* (2nd edn), Boulder, CO: Westview.

Berry, W. D. and Lowery, D. (1987) *Understanding United States Government Growth: An Empirical Analysis of the Postwar Era*, New York, NY: Praeger Publishers.

Boehmke, F. J. and Witmer, R. (2004) Disentangling Diffusion: The Effects of Social and Economic Competition on State Policy Innovation and Expansion. *Political Research Quarterly*, 57:1 pp39–51.

Brandeis, L. D. (1932) New State Ice Co. v. Liebmann (dissenting) 285 U.S. 262. Available at http://caselaw. lp.findlaw.com/scripts/getcase.pl?court=US&vol=285&invol=262 (accessed 15 July 2012).

Braun, D. and Gilardi, F. (2006) Taking Galton's Problem Seriously: Toward a Theory of Policy Diffusion. *Journal of Theoretical Politics*, 18:3 pp298–322.

Bulmer, S., Dolowitz, D., Humphreys, P. and Padgett, S. (2007) *Policy Transfer in European Union Governance: Regulating the Utilities*, London: Routledge.

Cai, H. and Treisman, D. (2006) Did Government Decentralization Cause China's Economic Miracle. *World Politics*, 58:4 pp505–35.

Cao, X. (2012) Global Networks and Domestic Policy Convergence: A Network Explanation of Policy Changes. *World Politics*, 64:3 pp375–425.

Caulfield, J. L. (2006) Local Government Reform in China: A Rational Actor Perspective. *International Review of Administrative Sciences*, 72:2 pp253–67.

Chan, H. S. and Gao, J. (2008) Performance Measurement in Chinese Local Governments. *Chinese Law & Government*, 41:2–3 pp4–9.

Chou, B. K. P. (2008) Does 'good governance' matter? Civil Service Reform in China. *International Journal of Public Administration*, 31:1 pp54–75.

Chung, J. H. (1995) Studies of Central-Provincial Relations in the People's Republic of China: A Mid-Term Appraisal. *The China Quarterly*, 142 pp487–508.

Collier, D. and Messick, R. E. (1975) Prerequisites Versus Diffusion: Testing Explanations of Social Security Adoption. *American Political Science Review*, 69:4 pp1299–315.

Derthick, M. (1970) *The Influence of Federal Grants: Public Assistance in Massachusetts*, Cambridge, MA: Harvard University Press.

Dolowitz, D. and Marsh, D. (1996) Who Learns What from Whom: A Review of the Policy Transfer Literature. *Political Studies*, 44:2 pp343–57.

Elkins, Z., Guzman A. T. and Simmons, B. A. (2006) Competing for Capital: The Diffusion of Bilateral Investment Treaties, 1960–2000. *International Organization*, 60:4 pp811–46.

Foster, J. (1978) Regionalism and Innovation in the American States. *Journal of Politics*, 40:1 pp179–87.

Foster, K. W. (2006) Improving Municipal Governance in China: Yantai's Pathbreaking Experiment in Administrative Reform. *Modern China*, 37:2 pp221–50.

Füglister, K. (2012) Where Does Learning Take Place? The Role of Intergovernmental Cooperation in Policy Diffusion. *European Journal of Political Research*, 51:3 pp316–49.

Gao, J. (2009) Governing by Goals and Numbers: A Case Study in the Use of Performance Measurement to Build State Capacity in China. *Public Administration and Development*, 29:1 pp21–31.

Gilardi, F. (2010) Who Learns from What in Policy Diffusion Processes? *American Journal of Political Science,* 54:3 pp650–66.

Glick, H. R. and Hays, S. P. (1991) Innovation and Reinvention in State Policymaking: Theory and the Evolution of Living Will Laws. *Journal of Politics*, 53:3 pp835–50.

Gray, V. (1973) Innovation in the States: A Diffusion Study. *American Political Science Review*, 67:4 pp1174–85.

—— (1974) Expenditures and Innovation as Dimensions of Progressivism: A Note on the America States. *American Journal of Political Science*, 18:4 pp693–9.

—— (1994) 'Competition, Emulation and Policy Innovation' in L. Dodd and C. Jilson (eds) *New Perspectives in American Politics*. Washington, DC: Congressional Quarterly Press.

Greenhalgh, T., Robert, G., Macfarlane, F., Bate, P. and Kyriakidou, O. (2004) Diffusion of Innovations in Service Organizations: Systematic Review and Recommendations. *The Milbank Quarterly*, 82:4, pp581–629.

Greve, M. S. (2001) Laboratories of Democracy: Anatomy of a Metaphor. *Federalist Outlook*, http://www.aei.org/article/politics-and-public-opinion/elections/laboratories- of-democracy/ (accessed 15 July 2012).

Grupp, F. W., Jr. and Richards, A. R. (1975) Variations in Elite Perceptions of American States as Referents for Public Policy Making. *American Political Science Review*, 69:3 pp850–8.

Hall, P. A. (1993) Policy Paradigms, Social Learning, and the State: The Case of Economic Policymaking in Britain. *Comparative Politics*, 25:3 pp275–96.

Hays, S. P. and Glick, H. R. (1997) The Role of Agenda Setting in Policy Innovation: An Event History Analysis of Living Will Laws. *American Politics Quarterly*, 25:4 pp497–516.

Heilmann, S. (2008a) Policy Experimentation in China's Economic Rise. *Studies in Comparative International Development*, 43:1 pp1–26.

—— (2008b) From Local Experiments to National Policy: The Origins of China's Distinctive Policy Process. *The China Journal*, 59 pp1–30.

Heilmann, S. and Perry, E. J. (2011) *Mao's Invisible Hand: The Political Foundations of Adaptive Governance in China*, Cambridge, MA: Harvard University Asia Center.

Heywood, S. J. (1965) Toward a Sound Theory of Innovation. *The Elementary School Journal*, 66:3 pp107–14.

Hoberg, G. (1991) Sleeping with an Elephant: The American Influence on Canadian Environmental Regulation. *Journal of Public Policy*, 11:1 pp107–31.

Hodge, G. A. and Greve, C. (2007) Public–Private Partnerships: An International Performance Review. *Public Administration Review,* 67:3 pp545–58.

Howlett, M. and Ramesh, M. (1993) Patterns of Policy Instrument Choice: Policy Styles, Policy Learning and the Privatization Experience. *Review of Policy Research,* 12:1–2 pp3–24.

Ingram, H. M. and Mann, D. E. (1980) *Why Policies Succeed or Fail*, London: Sage.

Jing, Y. (2008) Outsourcing in China: An Exploratory Assessment. *Public Administration and Development*, 28:2 pp119–28.

Karch, A. (2007) *Democratic Laboratories: Policy Diffusion among the American States*. Ann Arbor, MI: University of Michigan Press.

Kiewiet, D. R. and McCubbins, M. D. (1985) Congressional Appropriations and the Electoral Connection. *Journal of Politics*, 47:1 pp59–82.

Kotsogiannis, C. and Schwager, R. (2004) On the Incentives to Experiment in Federations. *Journal of Urban Economics*, 60:4 pp484–97.

Kung, J. K.-S. and Chen, S. (2011) The Tragedy of the Nomenklatura: Career Incentives and Political Radicalism during China's Great Leap Famine. *American Political Science Review*, 105:1 pp27–45.

Li, H. and Zhou, L. A. (2005) Political Turnover and Economic Performance: The Incentive Role of Personnel Control in China. *Journal of Public Economics*, 89:9–10 pp1743–62.

Lin, W., Liu, G. G. and Chen, G. (2009) The Urban Resident Basic Medical Insurance: A Landmark Reform towards Universal Coverage in China. *Health Economics*, 18:S2 pp83–96.

Liu, Y. (2002) Reforming China's Urban Health Insurance System. *Health Policy*, 60:2 pp133–50.

Maskin, E., Qian, Y. and Xu, C. (2000) Incentives, Scale Economies, and Organization Forms. *Review of Economic Studies*, 67:2 pp359–78.

May, P. J. (1992) Policy Learning and Failure. *Journal of Public Policy*, 12:4 pp331–54.

Mikesell, J. L. (1978) Election Periods and State Tax Policy Cycles. *Public Choice*, 33:3 pp99–l05.

Mintrom, M. (1997) Policy Entrepreneurs and the Diffusion of Innovation. *American Journal of Political Science*, 42:3 pp738–70.

Mohr, L. B. (1969) Determinants of Innovation in Organizations. *The American Political Science Review*, 63:1 pp111–26.

Montinola, G., Qian, Y. and Weingast, B. R. (1996) Federalism, Chinese Style: The Political Basis for Economic Success in China. *World Politics*, 48:1 pp50–81.

Moon, M. J. and Bretschneider, S. (1997) Can State Government Actions Affect Innovation and Its Diffusion? An Extended Communication Model and Empirical Test. *Technological Forecasting and Social Change*, 54:1 pp57–77.

Nedergaard, P. (2009) Policy Learning Processes in International Committees: The Case of the Civil Servant Committees of the Nordic Council of Ministers. *Public Management Review*, 11:1 pp23–37.

Newman, J., Raine, J. and Skelcher, C. (2000) *Innovation and Best Practice in Local Government*, London: The Stationery Office.

Ngok, K. and Zhu, G. (2007) Marketization, Globalization and Administrative Reform in China: A Zigzag Road to a Promising Future. *International Review of Administrative Sciences*, 73:2 pp217–33.

Nice, D. C. (1994) *Policy Innovation in State Government*, Ames, IA: Iowa State University Press.

Nutley, S., Downe, J., Martin, S. and Grace, C. (2012) Policy Transfer and Convergence within the UK: The Case of Local Government Performance Improvement Regimes. *Policy & Politics*, 40:2 pp193–209.

Oakley, A. (1998) Public Policy Experimentation: Lessons from America. *Policy Studies*, 19:2 pp93–114.

Oi, J. C. (1992) Fiscal Reform and the Economic Foundations of Local State Corporatism in China. *World Politics*, 45:1 pp99–126.

Osborne, S. P. (2002) *Voluntary Organizations and Innovation in Public Services*, New York, NY: Routledge.

Peterson, P. and Rom, M. C. (1990) *Welfare Magnets: A New Case for a National Standard*, Washington, DC: Congressional Quarterly Press.

Radaelli, C. M. (2000) Policy Transfer in the European Union: Institutional Isomorphism as a Source of Legitimacy. *Governance*, 13:1 pp25–43.

—— (2008) Europeanization, Policy Learning, and New Modes of Governance. *Journal of Comparative Policy Analysis*, 10:3 pp239–54.

—— (2009) Measuring Policy Learning: Regulatory Impact Assessment in Europe. *Journal of European Public Policy*, 16:8 pp1145–64.

Rogers, E. M. (1983) *Diffusion of Innovations*, New York, NY: Free Press.

Rose, R. (2005) *Learning from Comparative Public Policy: A Practical Guide*, New York, NY: Routledge.

Rose-Ackerman, S. (1980) Risk Taking and Reelection: Does Federalism Promote Innovation? *Journal of Legal Studies*, 9 pp593–616.

Shi, S. J. (2006) Left to Market and Family – Again? Ideas and the Development of the Rural Pension Policy in China. *Social Policy and Administration*, 40:7 pp791–806.

Shipan, C. R. and Volden, C. (2012) Policy Diffusion: Seven Lessons for Scholars and Practitioners. *Public Administration Review*, 72 pp788–96.

Shirk, S. J. (1993) *The Political Logic of Economic Reform in China*. Berkeley, CA: University of California Press.

Sigelman, L., Roeder, P. W. and Sigelman, C. K. (1981) Social Service Innovation in the American States: Deinstitutionalization of the Mentally Retarded, *Social Science Quarterly*, 62 pp503–15.

Simmons, B. A. and Elkins, Z. (2004) The Globalization of Liberalization: Policy Diffusion in the International Economy. *American Political Science Review*, 98:1 pp171–89.

Strumpf, K. S. (2002) Does Government Decentralization Increase Policy Innovation? *Journal of Public Economic Theory*, 4:2 pp207–41.

Thompson, V. A. (1965) Bureaucracy and Innovation. *Administrative Science Quarterly*, 10:1 pp1–20.

Tianjin Statistics Bureau, *Tianjin Statistic Yearbooks (2003–2009)*. Beijing: China Statistics Press.

Tsui, K. Y. (2005) Local Tax System, Intergovernmental Transfers and China's Local Fiscal Disparities. *Journal of Comparative Economics*, 33:1 pp173–96.

Walker, J. L. (1969) The Diffusion of Innovations among the American States. *The American Political Science Review*, 63:3 pp880–99.

——— (1973) Comment: Problems in Research on the Diffusion of Policy Innovations. *The American Political Science Review*, 67:4 pp1186–91.

Walker, R. M., Avellaneda, C. N. and Berry, F. S. (2011) Exploring the Diffusion of Innovation Among High and Low Innovative Localities. *Public Management Review*, 13:1 pp95–125.

Walker, R. M., Jeanes, E. and Rowlands, R. (2002) Measuring Innovation – Applying the Literature-Based Innovation Output Indicator to Public Services. *Public Administration*, 80:1 pp201–14.

Walker, R. M. and Wu, J. (2010) Future Prospects for Performance Management in Chinese City Governments. *Administration & Society*, 42:S1 pp34–55.

Wang, S. (2009) Adapting by Learning: The Evolution of China's Rural Health Care Financing. *Modern China*, 35:4 pp370–404.

Welch, S. and Thompson, K. (1980) The Impact of Federal Incentives on State Policy Innovation. *American Journal of Political Science*, 24:4 pp715–29.

Whiting, S. (2001) *Power and Wealth in Rural China: The Political Economy of Institutional Change*, Cambridge: Cambridge University Press.

Xue, L. and Zhong, K. (2012) Domestic Reform and Global Integration: Public Administration Reform in China over the Last 30 Years. *International Review of Administrative Sciences*, 78:2 pp284–304.

Yang, D. (2006) Economic Transformation and Its Political Discontents in China: Authoritarianism, Unequal Growth, and the Dilemmas of Political Development. *Annual Review of Political Science*, 9 pp143–64.

Yin, R. K. (2009) *Case Study Research: Design and Methods*, London: Sage.

Zhou, X. (1995) Partial Reform and the Chinese Bureaucracy in the Post-Mao Era. *Comparative Political Studies*, 28:3 pp440–68.

Zhu, X. and Jiao, Q. (2012) 'New Public Management' in China at the Local Level: Competition-Driven Local Public Service Reform in Tianjin. *Lex Localis – Journal of Local Self-Government*, 10:2 pp153–70.

Abstract

Faced with an increasingly challenging environment, nonprofit organizations (NPOs) must behave innovatively and act in a result- or performance-oriented manner. In this article, we explore the extent to which NPOs behave innovatively (in their management and service delivery), and the factors that determine this innovative behaviour. We conducted our research in the main subsectors of the Flemish nonprofit sector (education, welfare, health and the sociocultural sector). The results presented here are based on a survey of 170 NPO managers. We found that the organizations within our sample claim that innovations occur to a fairly large extent. We have, however, discovered differences in innovative behaviour between subsectors. In addition, we found that there are many forces at work when trying to explain innovative behaviour in NPOs and different forms of innovative behaviour also seem to have different explanations.

DETERMINANTS OF INNOVATIVE BEHAVIOUR IN FLEMISH NONPROFIT ORGANIZATIONS

An empirical research

Bram Verschuere, Eline Beddeleem and Dries Verlet

Bram Verschuere
Faculty of Economics and Business Administration
Ghent University & University College Ghent
Ghent, Belgium

Eline Beddeleem
Faculty of Business Administration and Public Administration
Ghent University College & Ghent University
Ghent, Belgium

Dries Verlet
Faculty of Business Administration and Public Administration
Ghent University College & Ghent University
Ghent, Belgium

INTRODUCTION

One of the biggest challenges nonprofit organizations (NPOs) are confronted with is the rapidly changing environment in which they operate. As public service deliverers, NPOs are subject to a trend similar to public sector modernization, as a result of the confrontation with more demanding customers, limited resources, technological breakthroughs, increased accountability requirements and so on. Increasingly, NPOs have to prove they work efficiently, effectively and in line with the overall mission, in order not to lose legitimacy in the eyes of their stakeholders (Verschuere and Cantens, 2009). Generally, we see that classical answers and strategies often do not offer a way out to meet the challenges. As Osborne (1998b: foreword) states: 'Across the world there are increasing pressures on voluntary organisations to improve the quality and effectiveness of public services through innovation and change' and 'the innovative capacity of voluntary organisations has become a touchstone for their role in providing public services'. Also Bezemer *et al.* (2006) see a need for strategic renewal because of an increasing environmental turbulence for NPOs. With this article we will make an attempt to answer two research questions: (1) to what extent do NPOs in Flanders (Belgium) show innovative behaviour, and (2) how can we explain why NPOs act as observed? The latter question will be addressed by testing theoretical assumptions about innovative behaviour in NPOs. In this article, we do not present results of a longitudinal research. Instead, we examine whether NPOs actually behave innovative at present, and under what conditions. In the remainder of this article, we first define our central research concept: innovative behaviour in NPOs. Second, we present our theoretical framework. Third, we discuss our research design and the operationalization and measurement of our variables. Fourth, the empirical results are presented. We conclude with a discussion of our findings.

INNOVATIVE BEHAVIOUR IN NPOs

Paulsen (2006) states that 'paradigms like the New Public Management have been associated with the introduction of market mechanisms in the public sector, including concepts such as entrepreneurialism, innovation and customer responsiveness in the delivery of public services'. This trend also seems to apply to private NPOs that are delivering public services on behalf of government. Increasingly, NPOs fulfil their tasks and roles in a result- or performance-oriented way and thus adopt and/or implement innovations, aimed at improving their results (e.g. De Steur *et al.*, 2009; Toepler, 2004; Zan, 2000). Based on a review of existing literature, we can argue that innovative behaviour may emerge on two levels in NPOs: innovations in their management and innovations in their service delivery.

Organizations may firstly be innovative in terms of service delivery. Osborne (1998b) developed a typology of change and innovation and tested this classification within the context of voluntary and non-profit organizations in the personal social services in Britain. In his classification, Osborne makes a distinction between two domains in which organizational changes can occur: on the level of services (offering existing services vs. the creation of new services) and on the level of the clients of the organization (serving an existing end-user group vs. serving a new end-user group). Organizations may also be innovative from a managerial point of view. Many authors (Dart, 2004; Davis *et al.*, 2011; De Steur *et al.*, 2009; Dolnicar *et al.*, 2008; Eikenberry and Kluver, 2004; Evans *et al.*, 2005; Lindgren, 2001; Toepler, 2004) claim that NPOs are forced to operate more market-oriented and thus adopt methods, techniques, approaches and values of the market. On the level of innovation in management, De Steur *et al.* (2009) observed a strong evolution towards a more professional management in NPOs.

DETERMINANTS OF (INNOVATIVE) BEHAVIOUR IN NPOs

In recent years, more attention has been devoted to the question which factors impede or encourage innovative behaviour in nonprofit and public organizations (e.g. Bezemer *et al.*, 2006; Laegreid *et al.*, 2009; Osborne, 1998b; Osborne *et al.*, 2008; Verbruggen *et al.*, 2011). In order to answer the question about the factors that determine innovative behaviour in NPOs, we rely on different theoretical perspectives, from which hypotheses can be derived. This allows us to identify relevant variables and to assess the relative strength of these variables for explaining innovative behaviour. Broadly spoken, innovative behaviour can originate in the environment of the organization, or in the organization itself.

Environmental Explanations for Innovation

A first set of theoretical perspectives considers the environment of the organization as the major driver for behaviour of and in organizations (Hult, 2003). Institutional theory (DiMaggio and Powell, 1991) claims that socially created norms exist within the environment of organizations. To receive legitimacy and support from their environment, organizations must try to conform to those norms. According to this theory, actors behave as they are supposed to act, in a manner that is acceptable in the environment of the organization. DiMaggio and Powell (1991) assume that organizations in the same organizational field become more similar to one another because of existing socially created norms in that field ('isomorphic change'). Therefore, we expect that *organizations in different subfields of the nonprofit sector (here: welfare, health, education and the socio-cultural sector) will show different levels and patterns of innovative behaviour, because they face different isomorphic pressures.*

DiMaggio and Powell (1991: 67) identified 'three mechanisms through which institutional isomorphic change occurs'. 'Mimetic isomorphism' is about norms that are spread through imitation: organizations tend to model themselves after similar organizations in their field that they perceive to be successful. From this, we can infer that *organizations engage in innovative behaviour, because people within the organization have seen innovations in other organizations, where it led to better results.* 'Normative isomorphism' stems primarily from professionalization (DiMaggio and Powell, 1991: 67). Two aspects of professionalization are important sources of isomorphism. One is 'the resting of formal education and of legitimation in a cognitive base produced by university specialists', the second is 'the growth and elaboration of professional networks that span organizations and across which new models diffuse rapidly' (DiMaggio and Powell, 1991: 70). Hence, *organizations engage in innovative behaviour, because people within the organization have seen or learned innovations during training, information sessions, etc.* A third form of isomorphic change is called 'coercive isomorphism' (DiMaggio and Powell, 1991: 67). In the institutional environment, there are formal rules, procedures and systems that apply to the organization. We can assume that an important coercive power for NPOs is the government, as many NPOs, especially in a European continental country like Belgium (Anheier, 2005), rely largely on government funding and perform tasks on behalf of government. Therefore, we expect that *the more government is forcing or encouraging an NPO to innovate, the higher the extent of innovative behaviour within the NPO will be.*

According to Verbruggen *et al.* (2011: 8), 'coercive isomorphism has been and can be linked to resource dependence in the case of nonprofit organizations because both loci of power (at least partially) coincide, as the government is the institution that sets the rules as well as controls important resource flows'. Therefore, we can combine this third form of isomorphic pressure with resource dependency theory (Pfeffer and Salancik, 2003). According to this theory, organizations may be dependent on other actors in their environment (like government) for the necessary resources to have their task performed. The greater this resource dependence, the lower the autonomy of the dependent organization will be. Therefore, by combining resource dependency theory and coercive isomorphism, we can assume that *the larger the relative share of government revenue in the total budget of the NPO, and the more government forces or encourages innovative behaviour, the more the NPO will engage in innovative behaviour, because this behaviour is in compliance with the requirements of the strategic resource provider.*

Organizational Explanations for Innovation

The cultural-institutional theoretical perspective (Thoenig, 2003) claims that organizations bring values into their organization and therefore gradually develop into 'institutions'. This way, an organization will develop its own unique and informal character. Contrary to the institutional theory discussed above, organizations do not mirror themselves to the environment to assess the level of appropriateness. Here, appropriate behaviour is something that originates in the internal organizational culture.

197

First, the age of the organization can be linked to organizational culture. The older the organization, the stronger the institutionalized identity of the organization, because older organizations have had the opportunity to develop a distinct identity over time (Verhoest *et al.*, 2010). Behaviour that is incompatible with established norms and values will probably be rejected. We assume that the stronger the institutionalized organizational identity, the greater the likelihood of resistance to change and renewal within the organization. As such, we expect that *the older the organization, the less the NPO will engage in innovative behaviour, because older organizations are more likely to have a strong organizational identity and therefore a greater resistance to change.* Following this line of reasoning, the commitment to certain values can be an important driver for organizational behaviour. Hermans and Vranken (2010a: 5) state that an innovative welfare organization has three characteristics: 'it chooses for collaboration, it recognizes the importance of knowledge and the sharing of knowledge and it allows users to participate in policy making'. Participation of users seems essential to launch innovations and to test its results, because 'by involving users, there arises a natural and direct flow of feedback' (Hermans and Vranken, 2010a: 40). In order to innovate, new knowledge is necessary and therefore learning is important. Collaboration is important because innovation is not an easy challenge and by working together one can achieve more (Hermans and Vranken, 2010b). According to Hermans and Vranken (2010a), an organization can strengthen its innovative capacity by addressing these three issues. We assume that a first step in addressing these issues lies in the recognition of their importance (considering these issues as important values). Because these three issues lead to the enhancement of the innovative capacity of organizations, we call the commitment to these three values having 'an innovative culture'. Hence, we can assume that *the more the organizational culture reflects values such as participation, learning and collaboration, the more the NPO will engage in innovative behaviour, because addressing these matters increases the innovative capacity of the organization.*

Another theoretical perspective is based on 'a logic of consequence', which interprets organizational action as a rational choice (March, 1994). The idea that actions are rational and that people calculate the costs and benefits of actions before deciding what to do, is known as rational choice theory (Scott, 2000). From a rational choice perspective, actors will do what is in their interest. They will calculate the outcomes of the different behavioural options they have, and choose that behaviour that will lead to the optimal outcome. According to such a calculus-logic, we can assume that decision makers in NPOs make rational choices and therefore act according to a logic of interest of the organization. As such, *an organization will engage in innovative behaviour, because this behaviour is considered beneficial for the organization.*

A final theoretical perspective (Egeberg, 2003) considers the importance of the formal organizational structural features for organizational behaviour. One idea is that organizations need enough internal capacity (in terms of financial and human resources), to be able to develop desired behaviour. An indicator of structural capacity is the size of the organization. Larger organizations will have a greater internal capacity and expertise. The expectation is than that *the larger the organization, the more the NPO will engage in innovative behaviour, because the organization has the structural capacity to do so: it is able to mobilize those resources that are necessary to be able to behave in one or another way (here: innovation).*

EMPIRICAL RESEARCH: SAMPLE AND DATA

Our units of analysis are private NPOs in Flanders. We selected organizations within the main subsectors of the Flemish nonprofit sector (education, welfare, health and the socio-cultural sector). We limited ourselves to service-delivery organizations, as opposed to NPOs with a mainly expressive function (Anheier, 2005), and organizations with a certain degree of professionalism. The latter means that they are entities subsidized by government and have at least one paid staff member. In each subsector, we have chosen one exemplary type of organization: secondary schools (education), residential care facilities for elderly people (welfare), general hospitals (health) and museums (socio-cultural). The research population consist of all entities in Flanders that meet the criteria above (private NPO, Flemish, service delivery as main task and a certain degree of professionalism). This cross-sector research creates the opportunity to focus on common trends (and/or differences) in different sectors.

As research strategy, we chose the survey approach, because of the possibility to collect quantitative data (Denscombe, 2007), which are currently lacking for Flemish NPOs concerning the theme of innovation. We constructed a questionnaire based on an extensive literature review and performed a pilot of our questionnaire (both with academics and practitioners). With the eventual questionnaire, we built a web-based survey[1] that was sent to the managers of 833 organizations, during the summer of 2010. We surveyed the managers, because they have a view on the organization as a whole (key-informant method). A final response rate of 20.4 per cent was obtained by December 2010. The presence of the four sub-sectors within our sample can be seen in Table 1 (per cent in sample).

Table 1: Presence of the four sub-sectors within total sample

	Total	Residential care facilities for elderly people	General hospitals	Museums	Secondary schools
N population surveyed	833	297	55	23	458
N in sample (% of population surveyed)	170 (20.4%)	55 (18.5%)	17 (30.9%)	12 (52.2%)	86 (18.8%)
% in sample	100%	32.4%	10%	7.1%	50.6%

We examined the respresentativeness of our sample (in terms of distribution between the different subsectors in our research) with the Chi-squared test, to see whether the actual sample is a good representation of the intended research population. These checks show that there are no significant problems with the respresentativeness according to the sector the organization is situated in.[2] Approximately half of the organizations in our sample are secondary schools (50.6 per cent of the sample), the second largest group in our sample are the residential care facilities for elderly people (32.4 per cent of the sample).

Measurement of the Dependent Variables

For operationalizing innovative behaviour in management, we relied on several sources that consider the trend of 'managerialism' and also made it measurable (De Steur *et al.*, 2009; Rigby and Bilodeau, 2009; Verhoest *et al.*, 2003, 2010a,b; Windels and Christiaens, 2006). Based on this literature review, we selected five managerial subsystems: strategic management, quality management, human resource management, financial management and stakeholder management and listed a range of items that can be seen as 'result-oriented' and 'innovative' in the management of organizations. The managerial subsystems and items we selected were subject to a pilot in both practice and the academic world. In our survey, we asked respondents to what extent these items occur within their organization.[3] Although each item in the questionnaire is interesting in itself, we focus primarily on the question to what extent the responses for each item within a certain management discipline are related (validity of scales). We found, for example, that organizations that are involved in strategic long-range planning often also use a SWOT analysis. In order to find out whether all items point at one theoretical construct, we conducted factor analysis (principal component analysis). In addition, we checked for the reliability of the scale by looking at the value for Cronbach's Alfa. In Table A1, the results of these factor and reliability analyses can be found. Based on these analyses, we created five indexes (one for each management subsystem), by adding up the scores for the items under a management subsystem and dividing this sum by the total number of items within that management subsystems. This way, we obtain a score between 0 and 1 for each management discipline. These five indexes are our five (dependent) variables to measure innovative behaviour within the management of organizations.

To classify innovations in service delivery, we mainly relied on the work of Osborne (1998a). Like Osborne (1998a), we distinguish between the development of new services and the serving of new target groups. Osborne also mentioned that the most common classification is that based on whether the innovation is a new process for providing existing products or services, or a new product/service itself. Therefore, we also consider the development of new work processes as a way to behave innovatively in service delivery. In our questionnaire, we asked respondents to report whether they had been involved (since 2000) in these three practices: the development of new services, the serving of new target groups and the development of new work processes. This way, we included three (dependent) variables to measure innovative behaviour in service delivery, with each time a score between 0 and 1 for each innovation in service delivery.[4]

Measurement of the Independent Variables

Above, we identified a number of possible determinants of innovative behaviour in NPOs. Here, we will discuss the measurement of these (independent) variables. In Table A2, the descriptive statistics of these variables can be found. The variable *sector*, which consists of four categories (schools, museums, residential homes for the elderly and hospitals), will be used to measure the organizational field in which isomorphism may occur. *Isomorphism* is measured indirectly via our questionnaire. We asked respondents to indicate the importance[5] of several motives for innovative behaviour within the organization (separately for innovation in management and innovation in service delivery), like 'we have seen innovations in other organizations, where it led to better results' (imitation) and 'certain innovations were handed, taught to us during training, information sessions, etc.' (professionalization, learning). In addition, the motives 'government encouraged us to innovate' and the motive 'government forced us to innovate' were included in these two questions (encouragement from government and coercion from government).

In order to measure governmental *resource dependence*, we asked respondents to indicate the relative share of government revenue within the overall budget for 2010.[6] Based on this question, we created a new variable with three categories.[7] To measure the extent to which an organization has an *innovative culture* (earlier described by us as the commitment to three values: participation, learning and collaboration), we asked respondents to indicate to what extent the organization can identify with these three values.[8] To construct our variable innovative culture, we added up the scores for participation, learning and collaboration and divided this sum by three. The figures in Table A1 show that this is a reliable and valid scale. For measuring *age of the organization*, we asked respondents in which period the organization was created.[9] Based on this variable we constructed another variable, with one additional category (don't know – no answer). Concerning rational choice motives for innovative behaviour, we asked respondents to indicate the importance[10] of motives which are indicative for *self-interest driven calculation* (again separately for innovation in management and innovation in service delivery): 'a desire to grow/to learn' and 'a desire to achieve better results'. In order to measure the importance of calculus-driven innovations in service delivery, two motives were included in the questionnaire: 'to meet increasing demands of users (that have become better informed, more demanding, etc.)' and 'to meet increased demand for services'. In order to create these two variables of self-interest driven calculation (one for innovation in management and another for innovation in service delivery), we added up the scores for the included items and divided this sum by the total number of items. The figures in Table A1 show that we can construct reliable and valid scales. *Organizational size* is measured as the total number of staff members in 2010 and as the total budget of the organization in 2010. To measure the number of staff within the organization, we asked respondents to indicate the number of paid staff (FTE) with a master degree, with a bachelor degree and with no or another degree. We created the variable total number of paid FTE in 2010 by adding up the numbers of these three categories. To avoid outliers, we converted this variable to a variable with four categories.[11] In our questionnaire, we asked for the total budget of the organization in 2010. We converted this variable to a variable with four categories.[12]

EMPIRICAL RESEARCH: RESULTS

We first discuss the extent to which the organizations within our sample are innovative in their management and service delivery. We also take into account differences between the four sub-sectors within our sample. Second, we search for possible determinants of innovative behaviour, by means of bivariate and multivariate analysis.

RQ1: How innovative are Flemish NPOs?

Table 2 shows descriptive statistics for our dependent variables, taking into account all organizations within our sample.

Generally we see that for the organizations in our sample, these innovations occur to a fairly large extent. When only considering innovations in service delivery, we see that

Table 2: Descriptives of dependent variables (innovative behaviour)

Dependent variables	Mean	SD	N	Min	Max
Innovation in management					
Strategic management	.63	.26	141	.00	1
Quality management	.64	.24	149	.10	1
Human resource management	.61	.19	131	.20	1
Financial management	.60	.25	139	.00	1
Stakeholder management	.59	.26	142	.00	1
Innovation in service delivery					
Developing new services	.59	.27	133	.00	1
Serving new target groups	.53	.28	134	.00	1
Developing new work processes	.68	.23	135	.00	1

Table 3: Results of the ANOVA and post-hoc test for the dependent variables

	ANOVA (factor = sector)		Post-hoc test, mean (SD)				Scheffe-test
	F-value	Significance	Residential care facilities for elderly people	Hospitals	Museums	Schools	(*p < .10, **p < .05, ***p < .01)
Strategic management	5.07	.002	.68 (.23)	.72 (.23)	.79 (.23)	.55 (.27)	R > S*; M > S*
Quality management	26.16	.000	.79 (.16)	.81 (.15)	.47 (.25)	.52 (.21)	R > M***; R > S***; H > M***; H > S***
HR management	5.71	.001	.69 (.17)	.53 (.17)	.56 (.19)	.57 (.20)	R > S***; R > H**
Financial management	3.64	.015	.68 (.23)	.61 (.19)	.63 (.21)	.53 (.27)	R > S**
Stakeholder management	.15	.933	.57 (.27)	.60 (.21)	.60 (.22)	.60 (.27)	–
New services	1.25	.296	.60 (.28)	.70 (.21)	.61 (.18)	.55 (.28)	–
New target groups	4.69	.004	.56 (.28)	.65 (.18)	.70 (.16)	.44 (.29)	M > S**; H > S*
New work processes	3.35	.021	.72 (.19)	.80 (.17)	.58 (.24)	.64 (.25)	–

Table 4: Bivariate analysis between categorical independent variables and dependent variables, by means of one-way ANOVA: the significance values

ANOVA (significance)	Strategic management	Quality management	HR management	Financial management	Stakeholder management	New services	New target groups	New work processes
The relative share of government revenue in the total budget, in categories	**.051**	**.040**	.912	.717	.894	**.054**	.830	.229
Total number of FTE, in categories	.762	.077	**.019**	**.038**	**.038**	.178	.393	.186
The total budget of the organization, in categories	**.028**	**.001**	.180	.101	.840	.356	.537	.304
Age of the organization	.220	.387	.327	.158	.459	.182	.624	.165
Sector, in categories	**.002**	**.000**	**.001**	**.015**	.933	.296	**.004**	**.021**

Table 5: Bivariate analysis between metric independent variables and innovations in management, by means of Pearson Correlations

$**p < .01$, $*p < .05$	A	B	C	D	E	F	G	H	I	J	K
A. Strategic management	1	.430**	.416**	.390**	.319**	.048	.168	-.043	.171	.135	.332**
B. Quality management		1	.461**	.323**	.222**	.019	.302**	.110	.199*	.064	.204*
C. HR management			1	.402**	.431**	.216*	.289**	.135	.171	.268**	.398**
D. Financial management				1	.340**	.249*	.286**	.186*	.329**	.248**	.443**
E. Stakeholder management					1	.332**	.106	.199*	.141	.288**	.313**
F. Innovative culture						1	.345**	.088	.214*	.334**	.347**
G. Encouragement from government							1	.382**	.297**	.130	.362**
H. Coercion from government								1	.251**	.143	.067
I. Imitation									1	.469**	.230**
J. Professionalization										1	.173*
K. Self-interest											1

the organizations within our sample are mostly engaged in the development of new work processes (.68). The lowest mean value corresponds with the serving of new target groups (.53). Concerning innovations in management, we see that quality management has the highest mean value (.64), followed by strategic management (.63). Stakeholder management has then the lowest mean value (.59). When looking at interrelationships between our dependent variables, we can see whether a distinction between innovation in management and service delivery can be made. The correlation coefficients in Table 5 (A–E) indicate that our variables for innovation in management are strongly interrelated. The same applies for the variables of innovation in service delivery (see Table 6). Principal component analysis also shows that our five indexes for innovations in management point at one theoretical construct and that our three variables for innovation in service delivery share one underlying dimension.[13] These analyses indicate that a theoretical distinction between innovation in management and service delivery is justified. As a consequence, it would be possible to create one variable for innovation in management and one for innovation in service delivery. We have chosen, however, to maintain the distinction between innovations in different managerial subsystems and to differentiate between various forms of innovative behaviour in service delivery, in order to see if there are different explanations for these different forms of innovative behaviour.

In addition, we can look whether there are significant differences in innovative behaviour, according to the sector to which organizations belong. Therefore, we conducted one-way ANOVA (Table 3), an analysis where group averages are compared (Slotboom, 1987).

The F-value for ANOVA and its corresponding significance value indicate significant differences in innovative behaviour between the different sub-sectors in our sample,

Table 6: Bivariate analysis between metric independent variables and innovations in service delivery, by means of Pearson Correlations

$**p < .01, *p < .05$	A	B	C	D	E	F	G	H	I
A. New services	1	.710**	.592**	.211*	.321**	.203*	.241**	.271**	.540**
B. New target groups		1	.536**	.107	.331**	.143	.240**	.228*	.473**
C. New work processes			1	.249*	.205*	.219*	.311**	.196*	.488**
D. Innovative culture				1	.298**	.104	.245*	.432**	.149
E. Encouragement from government					1	.560**	.234*	.272**	.356**
F. Coercion from government						1	.359**	.249**	.152
G. Imitation							1	.660**	.192*
H. Professionalization								1	.263**
I. Self-interest									1

Table 7: Results linear regressions model, standardized beta (Enter method)

Standardized coefficients Beta (*p < .10, **p < .05, ***p < .01)	Strategic management	Quality management	HR management	Financial management	Stakeholder management	New services	New target groups	New work processes
Sector (ref. = museums)								
Schools	-.54***	-.002	-.14	-.49***	-.17	-.11	-.60***	.08
Hospitals	-.26	.54***	-.09	-.26	-.01	.02	-.23	.30*
Residential care facilities for elderly people	-.34	.63***	.24	-.22	-.20	-.15	-.28	.33*
The relative share of government revenue in the total budget of the organization (ref. = don't know – no answer)								
A low share (< 75%)	.20	-.04	-.25	-.01	-.35**	-.04	-.20	.13
A high share (≥ 75%)	-.01	-.08	-.06	-.04	-.34**	-.06	-.12	.04
Encouragement from government	-.01	.13	.05	.02	.08	.23*	.30**	-.05
Coercion from government	-.11	.11	.09	.17*	.21**	-.02	-.07	-.05
Mimetic isomorphism: innovation as imitation	.28**	.01	.07	.12	-.001	.10	.17	.28**
Normative isomorphism: innovation as professionalization/learning	.10	.10	.23**	.19*	.20*	.06	.15	-.18
Self-interest	.17	-.05	.14	.21**	.19*	.33***	.18*	.23**
Total number of FTE (ref. = don't know – no answer)								
A low number of FTE (< 50)	-.13	.06	.29**	-.29**	.17	.12	-.13	-.19
A moderate number of FTE (50–100)	-.11	.11	.19	.004	.35**	.08	-.11	-.08
A high number of FTE (> 100)	.08	.09	.31**	.06	.43***	.33**	.27**	.03

(continued)

Table 7: (Continued)

Standardized coefficients Beta (*p < .10, **p < .05, ***p < .01)	Strategic management	Quality management	HR management	Financial management	Stakeholder management	New services	New target groups	New work processes
The total budget of the organization (ref. = don't know – no answer)								
A small budget (< 2,000,000 €)	−.19	−.02	−.15	−.22*	.08	−.12	−.17	−.09
A moderate budget (2,000,000–5,000,000 €)	−.04	−.05	.12	.05	.14	.002	.06	−.04
A big budget (>5,000,000 €)	.13	.10	.02	.03	.06	.003	−.07	.05
Innovative culture	.12	.24**	.20	.23**	.33***	.12	.06	.39***
Adj. R^2	.25	.39	.28	.30	.30	.24	.32	.26
Significance	.003	.000	.001	.000	.000	.000	.000	.001
N	84	95	88	95	95	94	95	95

except for stakeholder management and the development of new services (usually, a significance level of less than .05 is considered significant). The post-hoc test shows that residential care facilities for elderly people (R) and museums (M) score significantly higher than schools (S) in terms of strategic management. Residential care facilities for elderly people and hospitals (H) score significantly higher than museums and schools in terms of quality management. On the subject of human resource management, residential care facilities for elderly people score significantly higher than hospitals and schools. Concerning financial management, residential care facilities for elderly people score significantly higher than schools. Concerning innovations in service delivery, significant differences occur within the serving of new target groups. Museums and hospitals score significantly higher than schools when it comes to the serving of new target groups. The variable sector can also contribute to explaining differences within the development of new work processes, but the differences between the specific sectors were not significant (p-value of $> .10$), so not included in this table.

RQ2: Possible explanations for innovative behaviour of NPOs

For examining the bivariate relation between our categorical independent variables (sector, age of the organization, etc.) and innovative behaviour, we conducted one-way ANOVA and looked at the significance values (Table 4). A significance level of less than .05 (figures in bold) indicate that the corresponding variable contributes significantly to explaining differences in that particular innovation variable.

We see that, with the exception of 'age of the organization', all independent variables have a significant relationship with one or more dependent variable. We see for example significant differences in the level of strategic management depending on the relative share of government revenue in the total budget of the organization, the total budget of the organization and the sector to which the organization belongs. For investigating the bivariate relationship between metric variables, correlation analyses can be used. We made one correlation table for innovations in management and one for innovations in service delivery, as both have their 'own' independent variables (the importance of different motives was asked separately for innovations in management and innovations in service delivery).[14] In Table 5, correlations are displayed between our metric independent variables and our five variables for innovation in management (figures in bold indicate significant relationships). We notice that all independent variables have one or more positive and significant relationship with a dependent variable.

Table 6 shows the correlations between the metric independent variables and our three variables for innovation in service delivery (figures in bold indicate significant relationships). Here, we also see that all independent variables have one or more positive and significant relationship with a dependent variable (here: innovations in service delivery).

In order to test the explanatory value of the independent variables for the innovative behaviour of organizations, we performed regression analysis. The observed associations are not causal relationships *ipso facto*. They only denote to what extent the variance in the dependent variables can be explained by the independent variables in the analysis. A causal relationship would imply different measurements from the same respondents throughout time (McClendon, 1994). In the bivariate analysis, we discovered that only one variable (the age of the organization) does not contribute to explaining differences in innovative behaviour. All other independent variables will be used in multiple regression analysis. Because some of these independent variables were categorical variables, we transformed them into dummy variables to be able to put them into a regression model as independent variables.[15] Our multiple regression model was tested for each dependent variable (five variables for innovation in management and three variables for innovation in service delivery). Again, each regression was performed with the independent variables that corresponded with innovations in management or innovations in service delivery. The results of the multiple regression analysis can be found in Table 7.

In all eight regressions, there appears to be a significant relationship between our regression model and the dependent variable (significance $< .05$). Our regression model can explain 25 per cent (adj. R^2) of the variance within strategic management. We see that schools score significantly lower in terms of strategic management. In addition, we notice that imitation leads to higher scores for strategic management. Thirty-nine per cent of the variance within quality management can be explained by our model. Hospitals and residential care facilities for elderly people score significantly higher in terms of quality management. Also having an innovative culture contributes to higher scores on our quality management index. The regression model explains 28 per cent of the variance within human resource management. Higher levels of professionalization lead to higher scores in terms of HR management. Also the number of FTE can help to explain differences within HR management. Both a low number and a high number of FTE contribute significantly and positively to explaining differences within HR management. Also the beta-coefficient for a moderate number of FTE is positive (but not significant). These findings can be interpreted with respect to the reference category (don't know – no answer). Because these three categories have a positive beta-coefficient, it must be the reference-category that has a negative value. From this, we can deduce that respondent who don't know or who are not willing to indicate the number of FTE within their organization, will score low in terms of HR management. The regression model is able to explain 30 per cent of the variance within financial management. It seems that schools significantly score lower on our index for financial management. We also note that coercion from government and professionalization lead to higher scores in terms of financial management. Also the motive of self-interest (a desire to grow, or to achieve better results) contributes to higher scores in terms of financial management. Apparently, small organizations (with a low number of FTE and a small budget) score lower in terms of financial management. Finally, having an innovative culture also contributes to higher scores on the financial management index. We see that our model can explain 30 per cent of the variance within stakeholder management. Government revenue in general leads to lower scores in terms of stakeholder management. Coercion from government leads to higher scores regarding stakeholder management. In addition, the variables professionalization, the desire to grow or to achieve results (self-interest) and having an innovative culture all lead to higher scores in terms of stakeholder management. Also the number of FTE can help to explain differences within stakeholder management. Both a moderate number of FTE and a high number of FTE lead to higher scores on our index for stakeholder management. The beta-coefficient for a high number is however higher and more significant, so we can argue that the higher the number of FTE within the organization, the more the organization will engage in stakeholder management.

Concerning innovations in service delivery, our model is able to explain 24 per cent of the variance within the development of new services. Apparently, encouragement from government leads to the development of new services. Also a motive of self-interest leads to the development of new services. In addition, we can observe that a high number of FTE within the organization contributes to the development of new services. The model explains 32 per cent of the variance within the serving of new target groups. Schools score significantly lower when it comes to the serving of new target groups. Further, encouragement from government, self-interest and a high number of FTE contribute to the serving of new target groups. Finally, 26 per cent of the variance within the development of new work processes can be explained by our model. Hospitals and residential care facilities for elderly people score significantly higher when it comes to the development of new work processes. Imitation, self-interest and having an innovative culture seem to contribute to the development of new work processes in NPOs.

DISCUSSION AND CONCLUSIONS

Our research may add to the literature of (determinants of) innovative behaviour by NPOs by its empirical scope (European NPOs) and by its method (quantitative survey-data from a sample of 170 NPOs), although we acknowledge limitations in our research: the use of perceptual data from a single source (CEO's perceptions of the situation in their organization), and the measurement of the 'formal' adoption of innovations (e.g. 'the use of a SWOT-analysis'), without taking into account any 'informal' aspects of innovation in organizations (e.g. regularly reflection on strengths, weaknesses, of the managerial practice applied in the organization). Still, our analysis allows us to draw some conclusions in answer to our two research questions.

First, our results show that the organizations within our sample seem to claim that innovations occur to a fairly large extent. This is consistent with the findings of Bezemer et al. (2006), who showed that NPOs initiate strategic renewal (internal reorganizations, approaching new target groups, entering into strategic alliances, etc.) and thus proactively anticipate developments and opportunities in their environment. In our research, NPOs claim that innovative behaviour is strongly developed, both in terms of managerial innovation and in terms of innovative service delivery. Only the serving of new target groups seems not to happen very often. This confirms the statement of Osborne (1998a: 91) that 'wholly new client groups rarely come into existence' and that 'this is probably a product of the "particularism" of nonprofit organizations'. There are differences, however, between subsectors. Our research shows that residential care facilities for elderly people and hospitals tend to be more innovative, compared to museums and secondary schools (especially with regard to innovations in management). This may be explained by the fact that the first two are subject to large quality requirements that are controlled by subsidizing governments, more than this is the case for schools and (certainly) museums. Part of this quality control involves proof of innovative and modern management (e.g. client satisfaction and quality planning).

Second, we found that a considerable number of independent variables, both from an environmental and from an organizational perspective, contribute to explaining differences in innovative behaviour. This suggests that ideas from several theoretical perspectives combined may explain to what extent NPOs behave innovatively.

From an environmental perspective, the sector to which the organization belongs is an important driver for organizational innovation. It seems that institutional factors (legislation, governmental requirements, etc.) that are particular for one sector may urge organizations in that sector for innovation. We also observed that NPOs indicate that forces in their environment urge them to innovate, or are examples to innovate (isomorphistic behaviour). We discovered a positive relationship between encouragement from government and the development of new services and the serving of new target groups. These observations confirm the results of Verbruggen et al. (2011: 8), who state that 'compliance with government requirements is often a major driver for organizational behaviour'. On the level of innovations in service delivery, this observation is consistent with the findings of Osborne (1998a) and Osborne et al. (2008), who found that strong institutional pressures (like policy frameworks) were found to be at work in innovative organizations. Contrary to what we assumed, and to what other authors found (Osborne, 1998a), we did not observe an association between the level of government revenue and innovative behaviour. A possible explanation might be that all organizations in our sample receive a great deal of government funding (a feature of the Flemish NPO-sector as a whole). This results in a low variance of the scores of the organizations on this variable, which can explain the absence of a statistical relationship with the variables of innovative behaviour. Another explanation could be that a high level of government revenue is an inhibitory factor for innovation, as government revenue goes together with government requirements and therefore does not allow much flexibility.

From an organizational perspective, rational behaviour seems to be an important driver for innovative behaviour. Organizations claim to engage in innovative behaviour because this behaviour is considered beneficial for the organization: they expect future benefits like organizational growth and better results. Also size, as an organizational structural feature, seems to explain innovative behaviour. We found that NPOs with a high number of FTE, of which we assume to have capacity to innovate, claim higher scores for several innovations. This observation contrasts with other recent research for public and non-profit organizations, that found no relationship between the size of the (public and/or NPO) organization and innovative behaviour (Bezemer *et al.*, 2006; Laegreid *et al.*, 2009). Finally, we observed significant relationships between having an innovative culture (in this research defined as a culture that acknowledges the importance of participation, learning and collaboration) and innovative behaviour.

To conclude, we have evidence that Flemish NPOs are quite innovative, and that the level of their innovative behaviour can be explained by a variety of environmental and organizational factors. This may direct future research in the direction of multi-theoretical research designs that can test the relative explanatory value of competing theories, instead of working with a single-theory design. Moreover, from a conceptual point of view, future research should take into account the heterogeneity of the concept of innovation. Innovation in service delivery, and innovation in different managerial systems, may differ within one and the same organization or sector. And, as we showed, also explanations of innovative behaviour of organizations may differ, depending on what 'kind' of innovation is under scrutiny.

NOTES

1 For constructing and sending the survey, we relied on Qualtrics (www.qualtrics.com).

2 A Chi^2 value of 15.5 was obtained, with a *p*-value of .002. The value for Chi^2 indicates that there is a small difference in the distribution between sectors in the planned versus the actual sample. The *p*-value is the criterion to assess whether this difference is statistically significant. With samples of this size, a *p*-value of more than 0.001 indicates that the realized sample is a good reflection of the research population (differences are not statistically significant) (ISPO, 1998).

3 On a five-point scale, ranging from 'not' (1) to 'to a large extent' (5). To ensure standardization, we recoded all scales in our research to scales with values between 0 and 1.

4 A seven-point scale, ranging from 'not at all' (1) to 'to a large extent' (7). We recoded this scale to a scale with values between 0 and 1. A score of 0 indicates that the organization was not involved in this practice, a score of 1 means that the organization was to a large extent involved in this practice.

5 On a five-point scale, ranging from 'not important at all' (1) to 'very important' (5). We recoded this scale to a scale with values between 0 and 1.

6 Possible answer categories were: no share (1); 1–10 per cent (2); 11–24 per cent (3); 25–49 per cent (4); 50–74 per cent (5); 75–100 per cent (6).

7 These categories are 'low' (< 75 per cent), 'high' (≥ 75 per cent) and a category 'don't know – no answer'.

8 On a seven-point scale, ranging from 'not important at all' (1) to 'very important' (2). We recoded this scale to a scale with values between 0 and 1.

9 The possible answer categories were: after 2000, 1990–2000, 1980–1990, 1970–1980, 1960–1970, 1950–1960 and before 1950.

10 On a five-point scale, ranging from 'not important at all' (1) to 'very important' (5). We recoded this scale
to a scale with values between 0 and 1.

11 These categories are 'low' (< 50), 'moderate' (50–100), 'high' (≥ 100) and a category 'don't know – no
answer'.

12 These categories are '< 2,000,000 €', '2,000,000–5,000,000 €', '> 5,000,000 €' and a category 'don't
know – no answer'.

13 When considering the five indexes for innovation in management, only one component (that explains 50.41
per cent of the total variance) was extracted. When considering the three variables for innovation in service
delivery, only one component (that explains 74.18 per cent of the total variance) was extracted. Principal
Component Analysis of all eight innovation-variables together resulted in two underlying components.

14 See the operationalization of the independent variables.

15 Descriptive statistics of these dummy variables can be found in Table A3.

REFERENCES

Anheier, H. (2005) *Nonprofit Organizations. Theory, Management, Policy*, London & New York: Routledge.

Bezemer, P. J., Volberda, H. W., van den Bosh, F. A. J. and Jansen, J. J. P. (2006) Strategische vernieuwing in
nederlandse nonprofitorganisaties. *Maandblad voor Accountancy en Bedrijfseconomie*, 80:4 pp190–7.

Dart, R. (2004) Being "Business-Like" in a Nonprofit Organization: A Grounded and Inductive Typology.
Nonprofit and Voluntary Sector Quarterly, 33:2 pp290–310.

Davis, J. A., Marino, L. D., Aaron, J. R. and Tolbert, C. L. (2011) An Examination of Entrepreneurial
Orientation, Environmental Scanning, and Market Strategies of Nonprofit and For-profit Nursing Home
Administrators. *Nonprofit and Voluntary Sector Quarterly*, 40 pp197–211.

De Steur, D., Heene, A. and Carels, B. (2009) *Social Entrepreneurship: Management Development in East-Flanders,
Belgium. Overview and Challenges*, Economic Council of Province East-Flanders.

Denscombe, M. (2007) *The Good Research Guide for Small-Scale Social Research Projects*, Buckingham: Open
University Press.

DiMaggio, P. J. and Powell, W. W. (1991) *The New Institutionalism in Organizational Analysis*, Chicago: University
of Chicago Press.

Dolnicar, S., Irvine, H. and Lazerevski, K. (2008) Mission or Money? Competitive Challenges Facing Public
Sector Nonprofit Organisations in an Institutionalised Environment. *International Journal of Nonprofit and
Voluntary Sector Marketing*, 13 pp107–17.

Egeberg, M. (2003) 'How Bureaucratic Structure Matters: An Organizational Perspective' in: B. G. Peters and J.
Pierre (eds), *The Handbook of Public Administration*, London: Sage.

Eikenberry, A. M. and Kluver, J. D. (2004) The Marketization of the Nonprofit Sector: Civil Society at Risk?
Public Administration Review, 64:2 pp132–40.

Evans, B., Richmond, T. and Shields, J. (2005) Structuring Neoliberal Governance: The Nonprofit Sector,
Emerging New Modes of Control and the Marketisation of Service Delivery. *Policy and Society*, 24:1
pp73–97.

Hermans, K. and Vranken, R. (2010a) Zet je licht op groen voor zorginnovatie. Praktijkboek, Vlaams
Welzijnsverbond.

Hermans, K. and Vranken, R. (2010b) Zorginnovatie in welzijn. Project stelt gebruikersgerichte zorgdoelen
centraal. *Tijdschrift voor welzijnswerk*, 34:306 pp44–56.

Hult, K. M. (2003) 'Environmental Perspectives on Public Institutions' in B. G. Peters and J. Pierre (eds) *The
Handbook of Public Administration*, London: Sage.

Laegreid, P., Roness, P. G. and Verhoest, K. (2009) 'Explaining Innovative Culture and Behaviour of State
Agencies'. Presented at the *EGPA Annual Conference*, Malta, 2–5 September, pp1–30.

Lindgren, L. (2001) The Non-profit Sector Meets the Performance-Management Movement. A Programme-Theory Approach. *Evaluation* 7:3 pp285–303.

March, J. G. (1994) *A Primer on Decision Making. How Decisions Happen*, New York: The Free Press.

McClendon, J. (1994) *Multiple Regression and Causal Analysis*, Itsca/Illinois: Peacock.

Osborne, S. P. (1998a) Naming the Beast: Defining and classifying service innovations in social policy. *Human Relations*, 51:9 pp1133–54.

—— (1998b) *Voluntary Organizations and Innovation in Public Services*, London/New York: Routledge.

Osborne, S. P., Chew, C. and Mc. Laughlin, K. (2008) The Once and Future Pioneers? The Innovative Capacity of Voluntary Organisations and the Provision of Public Services: A Longitudinal Approach. *Public Management Review* 10:1 pp51–70.

Paulsen, N. (2006) 'New Public Management, Innovation, and the Non-Profit Domain: New Forms of Organizing and Professional Identity', in M. Veenswijk (ed) *Organizing Innovation: New Approaches to Cultural Change and Intervention in Public Sector Organizations*, Amsterdam: IOS Press, pp15–28.

Pfeffer, J. and Salancik, G. R. (2003) *The External Control of Organizations: A Resource Dependence Perspective*, Stanford, CA: Stanford University Press.

Rigby, D. and Bilodeau, B. (2009) *Management Tools and Trends 2009*, Bain & Company.

Scott, J. (2000) 'Rational Choice Theory' in G. Browning, A. Halci and F. Webster (eds) *Understanding Contemporary Society. Theories of the Present*, London: Sage.

Slotboom, A. (1987) *Statistiek in woorden. De meest voorkomende termen en technieken*, Groningen: Wolters-Noordhoff.

Thoenig, J. C. (2003) 'Institutional Theories and Public Institutions: Traditions and Appropriateness' in B. G. Peters and J. Pierre (eds) *The Handbook of Public Administration*, London: Sage.

Toepler, S. (2004) Conceptualizing Nonprofit Commercialism: A Case Study. *Public Administration and Management: An Interactive Journal*, 9:4 pp1–19.

Verbruggen, S., Christiaens, J. and Milisk, K. (2011) Can Resource Dependence and Coercive Isomorphism Explain Nonprofit Organizations' Compliance With Reporting Standards? *Nonprofit and Voluntary Sector Quarterly* 40:1 pp5–32.

Verhoest, K., Roness, P. G., Verschuere, B., Rubecksen, K. and Mac. Carthaigh, M. (2010a) *Public Sector Organizations. Autonomy and Control of State Agencies. Comparing States and Agencies*, Basingstoke: Palgrave Macmillan.

Verhoest, K., Verschuere, B. and Bouckaert, G. (2003) Agentschappen in Vlaanderen: Een beschrijvende analyse. Spoor Bestuurlijke Relaties, Steunpunt beleidsrelevant onderzoek. Bestuurlijke organisatie Vlaanderen.

Verhoest, K., Verschuere, B., Meyers, F. and Sulle, A. (2010b) Performance of public sector organisations: Do managerial tools matter? P. Laegreid and K. Verhoest (eds) *Governance of Public Sector Organizations. Proliferation, Autonomy and Performance*, Basingstoke: Palgrave McMillan.

Verschuere, B. and Cantens, N. (2009) *Social governance: Behoorlijk bestuur in de non-profit sector*, Brugge: Die Keure.

Windels, P. and Christiaens, J. (2006) Management Reform in Flemish Public Centres for Social Welfare: Examining Organisational Change. *Local Government Studies*, 32:4 pp389–411.

Zan, L. (2000) Managerialisation processes and performance in arts organisations: the Archaelogical Museum of Bologna. *Scandinavian Journal of Management*, 16 pp431–54.

Appendix

Table A1: Reliability and validity of scales ('innovation in management', 'self-interest' and 'innovative culture'

				Innovation in management		
				Components with eigenvalue		Component
	CA^a	N	Cum %^{b}	> 1	Communalities^c	matrix^d
Strategic management	.792	141	82.87	1		
Strategic long-range planning					.829	.910
The use of a SWOT-analysis					.829	.910
Quality management	.846	149	64.90	1		
Pursuing a quality policy					.623	.789
Quality planning					.694	.833
The use of a quality model					.583	.764
Hiring a quality employee or a quality steering committee, exclusively responsible for quality management					.645	.803
The use of a quality manual					.699	.836
Financial management	.816	139	64.92	1		
Financial long-range policy planning, coupled with the strategic long-range planning					.532	.730
Working with a result-oriented budget					.754	.868
Conducting an internal audit on the financial performance of the organization					.719	.848
Conducting an external audit on the financial performance of the organization					.591	.769
HR management	.796	131	55.21	1		
Pursuing an HR-policy, integrated in the strategic policy of the organization					.595	.771
The assessment of employees based on results and/or competencies					.541	.736
Pursuing a training policy					.532	.729

(*continued*)

Table A1: (*Continued*)

	CA[a]	N	Cum %[b]	Components with eigenvalue > 1	Communalities[c]	Component matrix[d]
				Innovation in management		
Pursuing a diversity policy, concerning own staff					.536	.732
The empowering of employees					.557	.746
Stakeholder management	.769	142	81.24	1		
Informing stakeholders (through newsletter, website, etc.)					.812	.901
Questioning stakeholders (personnel-/customer surveys, discussion groups,...)					.812	.901
Self-interest (for innovation in management)	.755	136	80.40	1		
A desire to grow/learn					.804	.897
A desire to achieve better results					.804	.897
Self-interest (for innovation in service delivery)	.786	117	82.45	1		.824	.908
Meeting the requirements of users/clients (that have become better informed, more demanding, etc.)					.824	.908
To meet increased demand for service delivery						
Innovative culture	.725	100	64.63	1		
Participation					.580	.761
Collaboration					.739	.860
Learning					.620	.787

Notes: [a]Scales are reliable at the .700 level (value for Cronbach's alpha). [b]The extent to which the factor contributes to explaining the total variance. [c]The extent to which the factor can explain the variance within the different variables. [d]The factor loadings.

Table A2: Descriptives of independent variables

Independent metric variables	Mean	SD	N	Min	Max
Innovative culture	.80	.15	100	.34	1
Encouragement from government					
for innovation in management	.49	.24	132	.00	1
for innovation in service delivery	.47	.22	117	.00	1
Coercion from government					
for innovation in management	.53	.26	133	.00	1
for innovation in service delivery	.51	.26	117	.00	1
Imitation					
for innovation in management	.58	.24	132	.00	1
for innovation in service delivery	.61	.22	118	.00	1
Professionalization					
for innovation in management	.64	.20	133	.00	1
for innovation in service delivery	.63	.21	118	.00	1
Self-interest					
for innovation in management	.78	.19	136	.00	1
for innovation in service delivery	.74	.19	117	.13	1
Independent categorical variables	Per cent				
The relative share of government revenue in the total budget, in categories					
Less than 75%	25.9				
75% or more	25.9				
Don't know – no answer	48.2				
Total number of FTE, in categories					
low (< 50)	13.5				
Moderate (50–100)	21.8				
High (> 100)	17.6				
Don't know – no answer	47.1				
The total budget of the organization, in categories					
< 2,000,000	16.5				
2,000,000–5,000,000	10.6				
> 5,000,000	12.9				
Don't know – no answer	60.0				
Age of the organization, in categories					
After 2000	14.7				
1990–2000	11.8				
1980–1990	13.5				
1970–1980	7.1				
1960–1970	2.9				
1950–1960	1.8				
Before 1950	17.1				
Don't know – no answer	31.2				

Table A3: Descriptives of dummy variables

	Per cent	
	0	*1*
The relative share of government revenue in the total budget of the organization		
A low share (< 75%)	74.1	25.9
A high share (≥ 75%)	74.1	25.9
Total number of FTE		
A low number of FTE (< 50)	86.5	13.5
A moderate number of FTE (50–100)	78.2	21.8
A high number of FTE (> 100)	82.4	17.6
The total budget of the organization		
A small budget (< 2,000,000)	83.5	16.5
A moderate budget (2,000,000–5,000,000)	89.4	10.6
A big budget (> 5,000,000)	87.1	12.9

Increasing employees' innovative work behaviour is a complex process of developing an internal climate supportive of idea generation and realization through use of financial, participative, and decentralization mechanisms. This article investigates the effectiveness of these managerial mechanisms in a public versus private context. In a survey in Scandinavia, 8,310 full-time employees were split into public and private employees and analysed with regression models for differences in effectiveness. From the results, two distinct perceptions emerged. Public employees perceive innovative work behaviour as extra-role behaviour to be compensated for. Private employees recognize innovative work behaviour as necessary behaviour for career advancement.

EXPLORING MANAGERIAL MECHANISMS THAT INFLUENCE INNOVATIVE WORK BEHAVIOUR

Comparing private and public employees

Rune Bysted and Kristina Risom Jespersen

Rune Bysted
Department of Economics and Business
Aarhus University
Aarhus
Denmark

Kristina Risom Jespersen
Department of Economics and Business
Aarhus University
Aarhus
Denmark

INTRODUCTION

Innovative work behaviour is found to increase individual job performance and ensure effective organizational processes (Janssen 2000; Yuan and Woodman 2010). Organizational performance is positively affected by the innovative work behaviour of employees (Baer et al. 2003; Janssen 2001). Scholars agree that innovative work behaviour concerns a voluntary willingness by employees to perform on-the-job innovation (Dorenbosch et al. 2005).

Innovative work behaviour literature holds two views: efficiency-oriented and social-political. The efficiency-oriented perspective is founded on a rational view on innovation decisions, where organizational improvements result from employees' practices. The efficiency-oriented perspective assumes that innovative behaviour of employees is positive for the organization (Yuan and Woodman 2010). The social-political perspective became significant as employees' innovative behaviour introduced two negative interpersonal work consequences (Yuan and Woodman 2010). Though there was efficiency improvement, innovative work behaviour increased work-related conflicts and decreased general job satisfaction (Cheng et al. 2010; Shalley et al. 2000). The social-political view is focused on interpersonal relationships in organizations and the influence of innovative work behaviour on them. Employees engaged in innovative work behaviour send a signal statement within the organization to peers and to management. These employees take on the role of active innovators in the organization (Janssen 2000; Zhang and Bartol 2010a).

From both the views on innovative work behaviour, the key to successful innovative work behaviour is whether the internal climate that management creates motivates employees to engage in innovation (Alpkan et al. 2010; Amabile 1988; Dorenbosch et al. 2005). Employees act in organizations on the basis of expected consequences of their behaviour (positive and negative) (Yuan and Woodman 2010). Similar to earlier studies of innovative work behaviour, this article adopts the perspective that it is through organizational practices that management can promote, stimulate, and support employees' innovative work behaviour (Burroughs et al. 2011; Cohen and Levinthal 1990; Dorenbosch et al. 2005; Scott and Bruce 1994; Tuominen and Toivonen 2011; Zhang and Bartol 2010a). The organizational practice perspective of innovative work behaviour concentrates on mechanisms applied by management to support employees' innovative efforts (Dorenbosch et al. 2005; Oldham and Cummings 1996). In order to motivate innovative work behaviour among employees, management uses a variety of participative, decentralization, and traditional financial mechanisms (Alpkan et al. 2010; Burroughs et al. 2011; Scott and Bruce 1994; Zhang and Bartol 2010a, 2010b). In other words, innovative work behaviour requires that managers participate actively to ensure the presence of these factors (Lassen et al. 2009).

In addition, an entrepreneurial climate is contingent on factors such as support, incentives, structures, resources, and risk-taking (Alpkan et al. 2010). These factors constitute the framework in which management and employees may perform innovative work behaviour. In this regard, private and public organizations define ends of business contexts in which internal climates supporting entrepreneurial activity are to be created (Klein et al. 2010). In relation to innovation, public organizations innovate in a political environment, where competitive advantages or performance improvements are not permitted by pure market pursuit of objectives (Oliver and Holzinger 2008). Goals are defined through political processes, often resulting in being misaligned with individual work performance and organizational goals (Georgellis et al. 2011; Rainey 1999). The typical innovative demand on public employees then is to apply the resources for creation of innovative output as described by the top of the organization, i.e. the political system (Klein et al. 2010). In addition, public organizations are characterized by a wealth of procedures and regulations that give a high level of control and a low level of flexibility (Boyne 2002; Klein et al. 2010). It is these conditions that set the framework for the innovative efforts of public employees. For public employees, this means that their form of creative output is defined narrowly. In public organizations, the dominant form of creative output is process innovation (Bartlett and Dibben 2002). Private organizations, on the other hand, innovate in dynamic environments, where the competitive advantage is maintained and developed only through continuous adaptation to external changes (Fauchart and Keilbach 2009; Ren and Guo 2011). The private work context is consequently characterized by a high level of flexibility (Bessant 2003). Individual and organizational goals are aligned (Klein et al. 2010). The innovative process and implementation is initiated at all organizational levels, based on both internal and external creative inputs. Consequently, private organizations do not have one dominant form of creative output but rather a diversified portfolio of innovation types contingent on the innovation objectives of the organization (Leiponen and Helfat 2010).

As such, it seems reasonable to assume that private and public managers operate under different conditions when applying participative, decentralization, and financial mechanisms to support employee innovative work behaviour. Managers have to consider the differences between private and public sector contexts (Boyne 2002; Klein et al. 2010). Rather than investigating the direct effect of participative, decentralization, and financial mechanisms on employees' level of innovative work behaviour, the article focuses on a comparison of the effectiveness of these mechanisms among public and private employees. The addressed research question is: Do participative, decentralization, and financial mechanisms influence the innovative work behaviour of private and public employees differently? Specifically, the private/public sector is treated as a moderating context significant for managers' successful creation of an internal climate supportive of innovative work behaviour with participative, decentralization, and financial mechanisms.

We argue that the exploration of managerial mechanisms in creating an internal climate of innovation contributes to two streams of management research. First, we find that the public and private sector context is significant for the ability of managerial mechanisms to influence the level of innovative work behaviour among employees. Management disciplines from private organizations have been increasingly implemented in the public sector. Yet, research finds that this adoption is not superior for public organizations, and the transformation of public organizations, typically implicit, assumes that the private sector has well-designed practices (Rainey 1999). Also, private and public organizations continue to attract two different segments of employees, motivated by different factors (Georgellis et al. 2011). In sum, very little is known about the innovative behaviour of public employees (Rainey 1999; Sørensen and Torfing 2011), and innovative work behaviour has primarily been studied from a private perspective (Janssen 2000, 2003, 2005; Scott and Bruce 1994). Hence, we find that there is a gap in literature pertaining to knowledge on differences in management mechanisms for private and public employees' innovative work behaviour. The aim of this article is to provide insights to fill this gap.

Second, this study responds to a call for an analysis of how management mechanisms can be applied for designing supportive mechanisms focused on increasing innovative work behaviour (Burroughs et al. 2011; Tuominen and Toivonen 2011). In a recent review of innovation management literature, mechanisms for increased employee creativity and ideation were listed as a topic for future research (Hauser et al. 2006). As this study focuses on mechanisms for increased innovative behaviour, the insights given in the article add to this amalgamation of research fields. Management mechanisms have positive and negative effects on employee creativity and innovativeness (Yuan and Woodman 2010; Zhang and Bartol 2010a). A key issue seems to be the contingencies attached to the context structures (Baer et al. 2003). This study examines the differences in the effect of management mechanisms. Hence, we aim to fill a part of this gap in extant literature.

The study is built on a survey of employees in public and private organizations in Denmark, Norway, and Sweden. The sample consists of 8,310 full-time employees (3,743 public and 4,567 private), randomly selected from different industries and subsectors. In order to ensure unbiased and representative results, the sample is post stratified so that gender, age, education, and geography are representative for the labour market.

HYPOTHESES DEVELOPMENT

Scholars agree that employee creativity and innovation are important to innovativeness, effectiveness, and survival (Amabile et al. 1996; Shalley et al. 2009; Yuan and Woodman 2010; Zhang and Bartol 2010a). The objective of innovative work behaviour is value creation in organizations and is achieved through two types of employee behaviour: creativity-oriented work behaviour and implementation-oriented work behaviour (Dorenbosch et al. 2005). This article holds two propositions. First, management may create an internal environment supportive of innovative work behaviour through the use of participative, decentralization, and financial mechanisms. Second, the effectiveness of these various mechanisms is moderated by the context in which they are applied. In this article, context is investigated at the macro level in the form of the public and private sectors. Both propositions will be elaborated in the following hypotheses development.

Financial mechanisms

Financial mechanisms are classic motivators used by management to induce employee motivation. Use of financial mechanisms as a motivating mechanism is also found in the literature on innovative work behaviour (Klein and Sorra 1996). The historic use of financial mechanisms in organizations necessitates its inclusion. The interesting aspect of financial mechanisms is that an employee's motivation shifts from intrinsic to extrinsic (Deci et al. 1999). Research on motivation of an individual shows that the ability of financial mechanisms to motivate new behavioural practices is low because employee engagement shifts from interest (intrinsic) to trade (extrinsic) (Burroughs et al. 2011; Eisenberg 1999). This is important because intrinsic motivation is regarded as a necessary condition for innovative work behaviour (Baer et al. 2003; Grant and Berry 2011; Zhang and Bartol 2010a). However, this does not imply that financial mechanisms are ineffective for management. The many online competitions of innovation with money prizes stress the ability of financial mechanisms to engage people in innovation (Jespersen 2011). When money prizes are linked to specific performance objectives, financial mechanisms may become effective (Georgellis et al. 2011). However, research has shown that the loss of intrinsic motivation offsets these benefits of financial rewards (Burroughs et al. 2011; Grant and Berry 2011). In congruence with this, there is an ongoing theoretical discussion of the innovativeness resulting from innovation contests (Di Gangi et al. 2010; Sawhney et al. 2005; Terwiesch and Xu 2008). The point made is that money prizes may communicate a clear relation of behaviour, performance and reward, but at the same time. there is a loss of personal drive to be creative (Shalley et al. 2000). As such. it seems reasonable to propose that the derived net effect of money prizes, such as salary bonuses on employees' innovative work behaviour, is negative. Thus, it is hypothesized that

H1a: Financial mechanisms relate negatively to employees' innovative work behaviour.

For the moderating effect of the private/public sector context on the effectiveness of financial mechanisms, such as salary bonuses, the clear link of behaviour, performance, and reward is central. Innovation literature has shown that money prizes motivate people to engage in innovation contests (Jespersen 2011). An explanation is the clear performance–reward connection created by money prizes. Private employees are more likely to have well-defined individual performance indicators linked tightly to organizational profit, whereas public employees deploy resources for better performance on public objectives (Georgellis et al. 2011; Klein et al. 2010). Public objectives are, for example, public health care or public schooling, but these objectives do not state the performance indicators for the individual employee. However, helping to fulfil such objectives intrinsically motivates people to work in the public sector (Boyne 2002; Georgellis et al. 2011). In congruence with this, a study of public management effectiveness demonstrated that financial mechanisms did not create behavioural changes or influence the work behaviour of public employees (Verhoest et al. 2007). It was found that the effect of money prizes does not crowd out the effect of intrinsic motivation for public employees (Georgellis et al. 2011). Yet, performance objectives are ill-defined in public organizations relative to private organizations (Klein et al. 2010; Rainey 1999). As such, it seems reasonable to propose that money prizes may positively influence public employee's innovative work behaviour because money prizes create goal clarity on how to fulfil public objectives. Because public employees lack goal clarity, money prizes will give this positive effect relative to private employees already working with a high level of goal clarity. Based on the goal clarity created by money prizes or salary bonuses that add to public employees' already higher levels of intrinsic motivation, it is hypothesized for this sector context that

H1b: Financial mechanisms relate positively to employees' innovative work behaviour.

Decentralization mechanisms

Decentralization mechanisms are job elements designed and used by managements concerned with the decentralization of decision power to the employees and actualizing the decisions (Alpkan et al. 2010). Managers are to use decentralization mechanisms to add a feeling of concern and ownership of the problems confronting employees in the workplace (Dorenbosch et al. 2005). A feeling of ownership is important for motivating employees. Management may encourage employee participation through the creation of employee autonomy (Alpkan et al. 2010; Hennessey and Amabile 2010; Janssen 2000; Lee 2008; Shalley et al. 2000) and/or through employee competence development (Coombs and Bierly 2006). An organizational environment characterized by autonomy provides employees with the necessary decision latitude for the development of new innovative ideas (Janssen and Van Yperen 2004). Autonomy provides employees with the space to be creative and experimental with improvements as an outcome (Alpkan et al. 2010; Lee 2008; Sundbo 2001). Creating conditions for autonomy is important, because autonomy increases an intrinsic motivational state

(Hennessey and Amabile 2010; Shalley et al. 2000). Innovative work behaviour research has documented that innovation builds on employees' intrinsic motivation to be innovative (Grant and Berry 2011). Competence development is also a decentralization mechanism that managers may use to motivate employee innovation. Employees' creative abilities are stimulated through competence development (Laine and Laine 2012). Organizations investing in competence development realize a higher innovation outcome and a higher level of organizational learning (Acur et al. 2010). Research has shown that when people feel more competent, their task enjoyment and motivation increase (Burroughs et al. 2011; Dahl and Moreau 2002). Competence development creates human growth (Ryan and Deci 2000). Based on the ability of autonomy and competence development to intrinsically motivate employees' innovative work behaviour, it is hypothesized that

H2a: Autonomy and competence development relate positively to employees' innovative work behaviour.

Decentralization mechanisms can be expected to work with varying degrees of success for managers in public/private sector contexts. Specifically related to autonomy is the difference in bureaucracy and control between private and public organizations (Boyne 2002). Due to institutional constraints and external political influence, managers in the public sector are often said to administer less autonomy to employees and lower-level managers (Boyne 2002; Rainey 1999). As such, it is likely that the level of autonomy that public management can offer public employees may not be significant enough for this mechanism to effectively increase their innovative work behaviour. However, this does not imply that public employees do not regard autonomy as a motivating factor. The point made is that private employees are more likely to experience an organizational practice of true autonomy relative to public employees working in and serving a political system. For competence development as a mechanism for managers to motivate innovative work behaviour, the variation in the public/private sectors is most likely to pertain to the purpose and form of innovation. The constant pressure to adapt to environmental dynamics for private organizations results in a greater innovation portfolio (Leiponen and Helfat 2010). In public organizations, the innovation focus resembles that of a cost-efficiency view, rendering dominance to process innovation (Hartley 2005). Public organizations are challenged because of very complex objects and bureaucratic structures (Klein et al. 2010). Consequently, it seems likely that the competence development offered to employees would differ between public and private organizations, with the latter being focused more on entrepreneurial competences. This would lead to creative competence development among private employees, and it would create a higher motivational state of innovative work behaviour than experienced by public employees. Hence, it is proposed that decentralization mechanisms positively influence employee innovation but that the private

226

sector context creates a higher positive moderation of this effect. Thus it is hypothesized that

H2b: Autonomy relates positively to employees' innovative work behaviour of private employees over
that of public employees.
H2c: Competence development relates positively to employees' innovative work behaviour of private
employees over that of public employees.

Participative mechanisms

A relationship between the organization and the employee characterized by support and
trust is important for innovative work behaviour (Scott and Bruce 1994). Management
may create a psychologically safe organizational environment with regard to innovative
work behaviour to apply participative mechanisms. Two mechanisms that management
can use to gain participation from employees are innovation trust and recognition
(Burroughs et al. 2011; Pieterse et al. 2010; Spreitzer 1995; Zhang and Bartol 2010a).
The underlying perception that management has to influence is the risk that employees
associate with innovative work behaviour (Yuan and Woodman 2010). Innovative work
behaviour is a risky behavioural effort (Lee 2008), as employees pushing innovative
ideas for change challenge the established work goals, work methods, task relationship,
informal norms, and expectations that employees have of one another (Janssen et al.
2004). Colleagues and supervisors can be expected to resist changes for the following
reasons: their tendency to avoid the insecurity and stress surrounding change, their
habits and preferences for familiar practices, to avert cognitive dissonance, and their
general interest and commitment in the established framework (Cowan et al. 2011;
Janssen 2003). Thus, uncertainty of innovation emerges because innovative ideas
challenge the status quo. To reduce the associated threat of innovative work behaviour,
the organizational purpose of innovation should be clearly communicated. A mechanism
to create trust and support is the use of management recognition for innovative work
behaviour process and not the outcome (Clegg et al. 2002; Dobni and Luffman 2000).
Recognizing employees' idea generation attempts and employee resources spent on
implementation-oriented behaviour creates an internal climate in which failure and
success become equal. Subordinates who report having a high-quality relationship with
managers characterized by support and trust report a higher level of innovative work
behaviour (Scott and Bruce 1994). Such high-quality leadership helps allocate the
necessary political resources that decrease the risks (Yuan and Woodman 2010). In
conjunction with this, managers also need to address the organizational employee-to-
employee relationship, as the perceived risk of innovation also results from potential
conflicts originating from internal tensions between employees with a high level of
innovative work behaviour and their co-workers with a low level of innovative work
behaviour (Janssen 2003; Shih and Susanto 2011). Employees having a high level of

227

innovative work behaviour are attractive to job market and hence are less risk averse. Employees possessing a lower level of innovative work behaviour, on the other hand, regard innovation as a threat (Martin et al. 1981; Shih and Susanto 2011), as innovations introduced by colleagues may threaten their job security (Cheng et al. 2010). The perception and reaction of others in the organization is important as this influences the potential actor (the individual employee) who puts himself in the spotlight (Yuan and Woodman 2010). The point made is that management can positively influence employee innovation through recognition and attention to the employee. Important for this is a climate that secures high levels of trust and safety felt by the employee when engaging in innovative tasks. Psychological incentives, in particular, stimulate employees in performing creative job tasks (Chang and Liu 2008; Spreitzer 1995). Psychologically motivated employees have a feeling of mastering innovative job tasks (Zhang and Bartol 2010a). Therefore, it is hypothesized that

H3a: Innovation, trust, and recognition relate positively to employees' innovative work behaviour.

The public/private sector differences that moderate the effect of participative mechanisms are related to the perception of the risk associated with innovation in public and private organizations. Private employees are disposed to more dynamic and changing environments compared to public employees (Boyne 2002; Rainey 1999). In the private work climate, efficiency and innovation are part of business and of maintaining competitiveness. Private employees on a career path seek to stick out from the group and become noticed by management. In the public system, politicians address the issue of efficiency through the issue of labour cost and replacement of human labour with technology (Sparrow and Sparrow 2006). The associated risk of innovative work behaviour is manifested institutionally in the public sector. Public organizations innovate for a system in which the rhetoric of innovation is that innovation is used within the same sentences as downsizing the public sector (Klein et al. 2010; Rainey 1999). It follows that innovation in public organizations is often regarded by employees as a reduced number of workplaces. This results from primary processes and administrative innovations as the public sector has no opportunity to expand business areas (Boyne 2002). Process innovations, in particular, is found to increase uncertainty (Cheng et al. 2010), and employees supplying such innovations to public organizations stick out in the organization through demonstrated innovative work behaviour. This represents a risk for public employees, and thus mechanisms that reduce the perceived risk of innovation will be more important for public employees. In addition, research has documented that public employees are less risk-averse than private employees (Boyne 2002), and this also indicates that the risk-reducing mechanisms are relatively more important for public employees compared to private employees. Consequently, safety and positive recognition is more likely to motivate public rather than private employees. Hence, the differences of public and private organizations lead to the following hypotheses:

H3b: Innovation trust relates positively to employees' innovative work behaviour of public employees over that of private employees.

H3c: Recognition relates positively to employees' innovative work behaviour of public employees over that of private employees.

RESEARCH METHOD

Data collection

Data was collected in Denmark, Norway, and Sweden in January 2011. The survey is an integrated part of the European Employee Index.[1] The respondents were randomly selected from different industries and subsectors. In order to participate in the survey, respondents had to qualify on all of the following screening criteria: 18 years or older, more than 25 hours of paid work per week, not self-employed, and active on the labour market (currently employed). To ensure unbiased and representative results, the sample was pre-stratified by gender, age, education, and geography in accordance with the Scandinavian labour market. The survey was sent to a panel of respondents. A total of 8,310 respondents, equivalent to 60 per cent of the panel, completed the questionnaire. In a previous study, this approach gave an effective response rate at around 20 per cent (Eskildsen et al. 2004). The questionnaire was self-reported. In particular, consistency has been demonstrated between self-reported and non self-reported scales in relation to innovative work behaviour (Janssen and Van Yperen 2004).

Variable measurement

The scales used in this study were developed based on earlier academic work, and the questions have been translated into Danish, Swedish, or Norwegian by professionals. The questionnaire has been pre-validated by two professionals in the field of survey analysis and one academic scholar. Further, the survey was validated and a pilot test was carried out in a Danish firm, with approximately 300 employees, which induced some modifications to the survey. All questions identified in academic literature were answered by giving a number on a Likert agreement scale (1 = fully disagree, 10 = fully agree). Correlations and Cronbach's alpha for the constructs are shown in Table 1.

Innovative work behaviour was conceptualized as two behavioural phases for employees to undertake: idea generation and idea realization. The scale for innovative work behaviour is based on the work of Janssen (2001) and Scott and Bruce (1994). Idea generation is reflected by three items: 'I create new ideas for improvements', 'I often search out new working methods, techniques, or instruments', and 'My ideas generate original solutions to problems'. Idea realization is reflected by four items: 'I transform innovative ideas into useful applications', 'I try to introduce innovative

Table 1: Correlations and Chronbach's alpha (α)[a,b]

	1	2	3	4	5	6	7	8	α	Mean	Std.
Salary bonuses (1)	.793								.719	5.64	2.21
Recognition (2)	.591	.931							.871	6.01	2.75
Innovation trust (3)	.354	.490	.852						.847	7.25	1.92
Safety (4)	.338	.335	.311	n.a.					n.a.	2.05	.68
Autonomy (5)	.446	.546	.520	.359	.828				.886	7.50	2.01
Competence dev. (6)	.535	.700	.500	.358	.618	.861			.939	5.75	2.49
Idea generation (7)	.223	.298	.476	.192	.417	.359	.889		.875	6.70	1.97
Idea realization (8)	.217	.305	.488	.210	.422	.345	.852	.910	.934	6.69	2.10
AVE	.628	.868	.726	n.a.	.685	.742	.790	.828			
Composite reliability	.835	.929	.889	n.a.	.914	.945	.919	.951			

Notes: Values in italics are descriptive numbers.
[a]Root AVE is placed in the diagonal.
[b]Correlations between factors are all significant at a .05 significance level.

ideas into the work environment in a systematic way', 'I work actively on trying to test new ideas', and 'I focus on promoting the positive elements of new ideas'. *Financial mechanism* was conceptualized as money prizes connected to performance. Management gives money prizes in the form of salary bonuses linked to performance. This construct was measured by three questions developed on the basis of Cardinal (2001). The three questions are 'clear connection between performance and financial rewards', 'salary compared to similar jobs', and 'perquisites compared to similar jobs'. *Participative mechanisms* are measured by two constructs: recognition and innovation trust. Recognition focuses on managerial actions towards making innovative work behaviour a safe investment. Therefore, recognition is measured by a recognition construct and a safety measure ('safety in employment'). Recognition by management was measured by two items (Cardinal 2001): 'clear connection between performance and appreciation' and 'departmental appreciation of good performance'. The construct innovation trust was measured with four questions inspired by the work of Clegg et al. (2002): 'I am sure that my ideas will be taken seriously by my colleagues', 'I am sure that my colleagues will listen to my ideas', 'I feel respected by my colleagues', and 'I know that I will benefit from a good idea even though I have presented it to my colleagues first'. *Decentralization mechanisms* are measured by two constructs: competence development and autonomy. Competence development is measured by three items based on the work of Spreitzer (1995) and Zhang and Bartol (2010a): 'opportunities for professional and personal development', 'high attention to professional advancement', and 'continuous focus on professional advancement'. Autonomy is measured by four items inspired by Zhang and Bartol (2010a): 'necessary decision latitude for job decisions', 'sufficient influence on job tasks', 'impact on job tasks to perform', and 'clear expectations of job tasks'.

Control variables

This study includes a range of control variables. We include the following dichotomous variables: *'Do you have formal employee responsibilities'* measures whether the respondent is a manager or an employee, and the respondent can choose (Yes/No). *'Gender'* is measured by (Male/Female). *'Age'* is measured by the following groups (18–29 years/30–39 years/40–49 years/50–59 years/60 and above). *'Last accomplished education'* is measured by the following groups (ground school/high school/1–2 years' additional education/3–4 years' additional education/5 years or more of additional education). Age and Education is transformed to a scale 1–5, and in the analysis, this scale is transformed to the variation from the mean. *'Work experience'* is measured as the number of years in the current job position. In the analysis, this is transformed to the variation from the mean. In addition to this, we control for the country in the collection process (Denmark/Norway/Sweden).

Analyses

Initially, the data was tested for validity. For addressing discriminant validity, confirmatory factor analysis and Average Variance Extracted (AVE) are evaluated. The confirmatory factor analysis (CFA) showed a close fit between the observed and the postulated covariance structure of the data (CFI: 0.943; and RMSEA: 0.063), AVE showed a high level of variance explained by the constructs, and, in addition to this, root AVE should be higher than the correlation with other latent variables. All these three measures show appropriate discriminant validity (Hulland 1999). The convergent validity is addressed by Cronbach's alpha and supplemented by composite reliability (Fornell and Larcker 1981) that both should exceed (0.7) (Hulland 1999). Both these measures indicate convergent validity. Table 1 show factor mean, standard deviation, Cronbach's α, AVE, composite reliability, and correlations.

To test the hypotheses, hierarchical regression analysis was applied (Baron and Kenny 1986). This approach was preferred as hierarchical regression models allow the inclusion of moderating effects induced by the private/public sector context investigated in our study. The interaction terms were calculated using a centred approach. The regressions were performed with Huber–White correction (robust regressions) in STATA 12.0, meaning that the coefficients are robust in relation to heteroscedasticity. Further, the regressions do not indicate multicollinearity with VIF factors smaller than 5 and mean values of 2.51 for both idea generation and idea realization. The hierarchical regression analysis was performed in two steps, analysing the two phases of innovative work behaviour: idea generation and idea realization. This procedure is in congruence with previous empirical work on innovative work behaviour, including moderating effects (Janssen 2003). Furthermore, we find that our discriminant analysis and low VIF estimates support this distinction, but as expected, Table 1 shows a high correlation between the two phases. The results are shown in Tables 2 and 3. In addition, a set of control variables were included in the analyses (see Tables 2 and 3). In comparison with previous studies of innovative work behaviour (Chen and Aryee 2007; Janssen 2000, 2005; Miron et al. 2004; Vinding 2006), the control variables were not found to bias the results, thereby enabling a discussion of results against existing theory and empirical findings.

In order to control for the potential single-source problem in this study and to control for common-method variance, a Harman's one-factor test was used to address the issue of common-method variance (Schriesheim 1979). This common factor explains around 26 per cent of the variance of the included variables. This is slightly higher than similar studies (Li and Atuahene-Gima 2001; Scott and Bruce 1994) controlling for common-method. Common-method bias is thus not a significant problem for this study. However, large multivariate regression models as analysed in this study are conservatively affected by common-method variance. If the data of this model suffers from common-method variance, the slope estimates decrease as a larger number of measured variables suffering from common-method variance (CMV) are included (Siemsen et al. 2010). In addition, the interaction effects induced by the context are, in particular, central in our study. Interaction effects are found to be deflated because of common-method variance (Evans 1985; Siemens et al. 2010). Overall, the analyses of this article are not driven by common-method variance, and the estimates are considered as robust, taking into account that the estimates will be conservatively affected by potential common-method variance.

RESULTS

The aim of the article was to explore managerial mechanisms that influence the innovative work behaviour of private and public employees. The results in Tables 2 and 3 below are elaborated in relation to the developed hypotheses.

In Hypothesis 1, financial mechanisms were proposed to negatively influence employee innovative behaviour. The results in Tables 2 and 3 show that financial mechanisms do not influence employees' idea generation (creativity), but do decrease idea realization (implementation) ($\beta_{finance} = -.05$). As such, salary bonuses seem not to influence employee creativity but to induce a tentative residence towards the implementation of innovation. Hence, Hypothesis 1a is partly supported. The sector moderation in Hypothesis 1b was that public employees' innovative behaviour would more likely be

Table 2: Dependent variable idea generation[a,b]

	Model 1	Model 2	Model 3
	Std. β	Std. β	Std. β
Control			
Employee/Manager (1 = employee)	−.19[***]	−.11[***]	−.11[***]
Gender (1 = female)	−.04[***]	−.05[***]	−.05[***]
Age	.05[***]	.02[a]	.01
Work experience	−.02[*]	−.04[**]	−.04[**]
Education	.10[***]	.06[***]	.06[***]
Norway	−.03	−.03	−.04
Sweden	−.01	.00	.00
Financial mechanism			
Salary bonuses		−.02	−.02
Decentralization mechanism			
Autonomy		.19[***]	.19[***]
Competence development		.09[***]	.12[***]
Participative mechanism			
Recognition		−.04[*]	−.06[**]
Safety		.01	−.02
Innovation trust		.33[***]	.35[***]
Sector context			
Public/private (1 = public)		.01	.01
Sector moderation			
Financial mechanism			
Public × Salary bonuses			.01
Decentralization mechanism			
Public × Autonomy			.01
Public × Competence dev.			−.04[*]
Participative mechanism			
Public × Recognition			.04[*]
Public × Safety			.04[*]
Public × Innovation trust			−.03[a]
F	73.78	153.06	100.92
Df	7	13	20
R^2	.0543	.2887	.2904
ΔR^2		.2344	.0017

Notes:[a]$p < .1$; [*]$p < .05$; [**]$p < .01$; [***]$p < .001$.
[b]Using the robust estimation technique, the sum of squared residuals are not relevant inputs for the F-test, as these residuals are corrected; therefore, significance of the ΔR^2 *is not calculated.*

Table 3: Dependent variable idea realization[a,b]

	Model 1	Model 2	Model 3
	Std. β	Std. β	Std. β
Control			
Employee/Manager (1 = employee)	$-.18^{***}$	$-.11^{***}$	$-.11^{***}$
Gender (1 = female)	$-.04^{***}$	$-.05^{***}$	$-.05^{***}$
Age	$.07^{***}$	$.03^{**}$	$.03^{**}$
Work experience	$-.03^{*}$	$-.05^{***}$	$-.05^{***}$
Education	$.09^{***}$	$.04^{***}$	$.04^{***}$
Norway	.01	.01	.01
Sweden	$.03^{*}$	$.04^{***}$	$.04^{***}$
Financial mechanism			
Salary bonuses		$-.03^{*}$	$-.05^{**}$
Participative mechanism			
Recognition		$-.01$	$-.03$
Safety		$.02^{a}$	.00
Innovation trust		$.36^{***}$	$.36^{***}$
Decentralization mechanism			
Autonomy		$.20^{***}$	$.21^{***}$
Competence development		$.04^{**}$	$.07^{**}$
Sector context			
Public/private (1 = public)		$.02^{a}$	$.02^{a}$
Sector moderation			
Financial mechanism			
Public × Salary bonuses			$.03^{*}$
Participative mechanism			
Public × Recognition			.02
Public × Safety			$.02^{a}$
Public × Innovation trust			$-.01$
Decentralization mechanism			
Public × Autonomy			$-.01$
Public × Competence dev.			$-.04^{a}$
F	73.75	144.89	102.81
Df	7	13	20
R^2	.0514	.2984	.2996
ΔR^2		.2470	.0012

Notes: $^{a}p < 0.1;$ $^{*}p < 0.05;$ $^{**}p < 0.01;$ $^{***}p < 0.001$.
[b]Using the robust estimation technique, the sum of squared residuals are not relevant inputs for the F-test, as these residuals are corrected; therefore, significance of the ΔR^2 is not calculated.

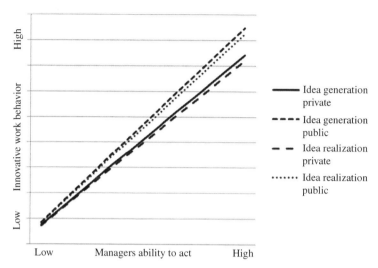

Figure 1: Innovative work behaviour correlated with managers' ability to act

motivated by salary bonuses due to the clear link of behaviour and goal created by installed financial mechanisms. The results show that public employees' willingness to implement new ideas is motivated by salary bonuses ($\beta_{public \times finance}$ = .03), thereby supporting Hypothesis 1b partly. A post hoc analysis on the variable 'to evaluate the connection between work performance and rewards' in the data showed through a t-test of mean differences (Wilks' Lambda: $F(1,7929) = 241.21$) that work performance and reward connection are significantly lower for public ($\mu = 37.95$) than for private employees ($\mu = 48.65$). In other words, public employees have a low performance–reward connection, which salary bonuses can help to increase. The argument of the new public management is that increased management autonomy given from the political level down into the hierarchy of the system would increase the clarity of performance rewards, because management demonstrates an ability to act on employees' inputs (Verhoest et al. 2007). Salary bonuses seem to act as a symbol for managers' ability to act in public organizations. To investigate this further, a post hoc analysis on the role of managers' ability to act on employee innovative behaviour was regressed.[2] The correlation of the variable 'My immediate supervisor shows an ability to act' with innovative work behaviour tested on public and private employees is illustrated in Figure 1. Figure 1 shows that innovative behaviour (idea generation and idea realization) of public employees is motivated more by managers' ability to act rather than the innovative behaviour of private employees. Furthermore, data showed that public managers' ability to act ($\mu = 68.1804$) is evaluated lower than private managers' ability to act ($\mu = 66.9314$) by t-test analysis of mean differences ($t = 2.0665$). As such, the post hoc analyses support our finding that goal clarity could be more effective on public employees' innovative work behaviour relative to private employees.

For an internal climate to support innovative wok behaviour, decentralization mechanisms were hypothesized in H2 to be effective for the increased innovative behaviour of employees. The results show that the decentralization of decision power via autonomy increases employee engagement in all phases of innovative work behaviour (Creativity: $\beta_{\text{Autonomy}} = .19$; Implementation $\beta_{\text{Autonomy}} = .21$). Also, competence development contributes positively to innovative work behaviour (Creativity: $\beta_{\text{Competence development}} = .12$; Implementation: $\beta_{\text{Competence development}} = .07$). As such, Hypothesis 2a is supported by the results. Interestingly, the sector moderating effect pertains to competence development. To illustrate this, we may post hoc calculate the relative difference of the significant regression coefficients in Tables 2 and 3 to demonstrate the relative difference in the effect on public versus private employees. Based on relative differences (Δ), the effect of competence development on innovative work behaviour for public employees is 33 per cent lower on creativity (Δ: $(.12-.04)/.12 = .67$) and is 57 per cent lower on realization (Δ: $(.07-.04)/.07 = .43$) than for private employees. Innovative work behaviour and entrepreneurship literature have established that a higher level of education positively influences individuals' entrepreneurial activities (Goll et al. 2007). An F-test ($F (1,8211) = 255.99$) of the average educational level of public and private employees in the sample finds a significantly higher educational level of public employees. The results in Table 3 show that public employees do capitalize on this proposed entrepreneurial potential. The level of idea realization is higher for public than private employees (Implementation: $\beta_{\text{public}} = .02$). The level of idea generation, however, does not differ between public and private employees. Hence, the reduced effect of competence development on public employees' innovative work behaviour can be described as the insignificance of high educational level interacting with new education (competence development) (Melly 2005).

In H3, participative mechanisms were hypothesized to positively influence employee innovative work behaviour. Management can expect increased innovative work behaviour if they succeed in creating a safe climate in which employees feel secure and comfortable about innovation (H3a). The results in Tables 2 and 3 show mixed coefficients. Innovation trust is a main driver of innovative work behaviour in Tables 1 and 2 (Idea generation: $\beta_{\text{Innovation trust}} = .35$; Idea realization: $\beta_{\text{Innovation trust}} = .36$). However, recognition is insignificant in the analysis. Hence, Hypothesis 3a is partly supported. With regard to the sector differences, especially for public employees, creativity seems likely to be generated through experienced recognition (Creativity: $\beta_{\text{recognition}} = .04$; $\beta_{\text{safety}} = .04$). Hence, Hypothesis 3c is supported, whereas Hypothesis 3b is not supported. Innovation trust is not moderated by sector context. In congruence with previous research, we find that management may increase employee innovative work behaviour through the use of participative mechanisms (Spreitzer 1995; Zhang and Bartol 2010a).

N.B.

DISCUSSION AND CONCLUSIONS

Employees' innovative work behaviour is essential in public and private organizations. The purpose of the article was to explore differences in three managerial mechanisms argued to be important for creating conditions for innovative work behaviour. The article is among the first quantitative studies to compare the influence of incentive mechanisms on the innovative work behaviour of public and private employees. Management can apply financial, decentralization, and participative mechanisms to increase innovative work behaviour in their organizations. However, the results demonstrated that the effectiveness of these mechanisms depends on managerial traits and organizational innovative objectives. These major findings are elaborated below.

The first finding emerging from our study pertains to the efficiency-oriented perspective, stating that innovative changes are supplied if rewarded (Burroughs et al. 2011). Our results showed that public employees respond well to clear performance rewards. This result has two possible interpretations within the efficiency-oriented perspective. One of them has to do with public employees' perception of innovative work behaviour. They need to be paid to behave in this particular way. Literature refers to this perception as the 'extra-role' syndrome (Dorenbosch et al. 2005; Janssen 2000). The view taken by public employees is that innovative work behaviour is beyond their job description and, therefore, something extra, for which they need to be rewarded for separately. Public employees perceive innovative work behaviour as risky behaviour; hence it has to be ordered and paid for by the system (Morrison et al. 2011; Yuan and Woodman 2010). The second explanation may be the clear performance–reward connection that salary bonuses (money prizes) create. Goal clarity is a motivating factor for innovation (Amabile et al. 1996), but in particular for public employees, there is a lack of clear goals (Bozeman and Kingsley 1998). Consequently, as our results demonstrate that salary bonuses (money prizes) become motivational because they represent a link between performance and goal. Both the 'extra-role' syndrome and the goal clarity interpretation can be explained by the institutional characteristics framing public innovation efforts. Public employees view innovation work behaviour as initiated and driven by the system. One explanation may be that the regulations and rules in the public system need to be ready to handle the change stemming from innovation. The more bureaucratic is the system, the less changeable it is (Boyne 2002). There is no reward for public employees' innovative work behaviour if the system is not ready for the change, and the innovative behaviour of an employee may even challenge his/her co-worker relations (Cheng et al. 2010; Shih and Susanto 2011). Because innovation is driven top–down, innovative work behaviour becomes extra-role behaviour, for which employees need a clear signal to supply, i.e. when public managers demonstrate an ability to act and install salary bonuses for innovative behaviour. As such, it seems reasonable to argue that the 'extra-role' syndrome among public employees is nurtured by the lack of goal clarity in public organizations. However, as our results demonstrated in Figure 1, public organizations have the opportunity to change this by providing public middle managers with a greater ability to act. Hence, managers' ability to act is the first step towards increased public innovative work behaviour. This argument is in congruence with the new public management theory (Verhoest et al. 2007), but our findings add to this discussion by addressing explicitly the current perception of innovative work behaviour as extra-role behaviour.

Another insight emerging from the results is the perception of innovative work behaviour by private employees. In Tables 2 and 3, participative mechanism in the form of autonomy and competence development was particularly effective for private employees' innovative work behaviour. These results indicate that private employees – to a larger extent than public employees – regard innovative behaviour as part of the opportunity window for career advancement. Innovative work behaviour is perceived by private employees as an organizational measurement of individual performance and worth investing in as a career enhancer (Alpkan et al. 2010). Dorenbosch et al. (2005) noted that innovative work behaviour covers two behavioural outcomes: 'extra-role behaviour' and 'doing-more-than-required'. Based on our results, we argue that private employees regard innovative work behaviour as a deliberate personal choice of doing more than required. Though 'extra-role' and 'doing-more-than-required' have been treated as the same in innovative work behaviour literature, our results contribute to this research string by demonstrating that innovative work behaviour seems to be perceived very differently by public and private employees. Furthermore, the two perspectives react very differently to managerial mechanisms aiming at motivating innovative behaviour in organizations. As the research before us too has pointed out, public organizations should take care in directly implementing managerial practices from private organizations (Rainey 1999).

A third finding emerging from the results is the importance of the social-political environment for innovative work behaviour. Both private and public employees are more likely to be innovative in climates characterized by innovation trust. One explanation for this finding may be that the financial austerity in the current economy has created an intense focus on creating bottom-line savings. To honour this goal, organizations focus on innovations that reduce or simplify processes. Efficiency innovations is the name of this current innovation focus that seems to create a demand for innovation trust from employees, according to our results. In particular, the results show that public employees' creative performance requires managerial recognition and a feeling of employment safety in order to decrease the risk associated with innovative work behaviour – a finding in congruence with literature (Unsworth and Clegg 2010). Hence, public managers need to reassure their employees in order for them to engage in innovation activities. Based on these findings, our comparison of public and private employees adds insights to the challenges facing management in regard to employees' innovative efforts. It seems that public managers face a larger task in creating a secure and comfortable internal climate. However, security and avoidance of threats limit the attention of individuals, thereby inhibiting the exploration of novel ideas and, in turn, making performed creativity less innovative (Sauermann and Cohen 2010). Reducing the riskiness of innovative work behaviour may enhance the number of employees involved in innovative work behaviour, but it also limits the performed innovativeness, as a large number of new ideas can impede implementation (Hansen and Birkinshaw 2007). Due to this contradiction, it seems likely that innovative work behaviour in public organizations cannot be increased as long as the innovative activity only benefits the system. Hence, another conclusion of this study is that the macro-level characteristics of public sector innovation inhibit the innovative work behaviour of public employees.

Finally, our study also contributes to management practices. There is a pressure on management to ensure internal climates supportive of innovative work behaviour. Public employees react to a demand of increased innovative work behaviour from a social-political perspective and treat innovative work behaviour as risky business (Hartley 2005; Klein et al. 2010). These behavioural differences have managerial implications when incentive mechanisms are used to increase innovative behaviour in an organization. First, innovative work behaviour is a performance signal to employees. However, the expected reward for this performance is very different for private and public employees. Private employees expect career progressions, whereas public employees react positively on clear goal expectations (financial prizes) for behavioural changes. Second, job security works differently in the public and private sector. Public employees experience more motivation for innovative behaviour when feeling higher employment safety. This is in alignment with general theory underlining the importance of job security in the public sector (Crewson 1997). Job security, in particular, has been argued to be important as a moderating variable for empowering employees (Georgellis et al. 2011; Spreitzer 1995). Thus, job security does not crowd out creative performance for public employees. Safety and innovation trust are important for management, creating a safer inner climate for innovation in public organizations as these elements reduce the negative tensions that may follow from innovative work behaviour (Shih and Susanto 2011; Tierney 1997). This difference is considered important from a managerial perspective, as it challenges the way downsizing and balancing budgets are communicated in public organizations. In the context of financial austerity, it may be more suitable to initiate innovative work behaviour through empowerment of employees using autonomy and competence development as forwarded by the results in this article.

Research limitations

Despite the many interesting insights emerging from our results, there are limitations to our study. Though we analysed differences between public and private organizations, the study is limited by having to treat public and private employees as equal and, at the same time, as two ends on a continuum, when private and public organizations are diverse and, at times, share characteristics. However, we find that our large sample, split across several subsectors, compensates for this challenge. Yet, it is true that management should use the results with care to the specific characteristics of their organizational focus and objectives with innovative behaviour.

Among other limitations of our study is its cross-sectional nature with a self-reported design. We have, however, shown that the common-method bias is not above critical levels stated in literature, but caution should naturally be given to this aspect. In addition, our conclusions are limited by small size of some of the effects. Yet, the aim of our article was to explore the differences in the effectiveness of financial, participative, and decentralized mechanisms on increased innovative behaviour. We established effects but call for other studies to work more in depth with each individual mechanism as to give a more thorough explanation of the underlying aspects related to innovative work behaviour.

Despite these limitations, we find that our study contributes new insights on some of the challenges faced by public organizations aiming at increased innovative work behaviour among their employees to help in the development of the next generation of the welfare system.

NOTES

1 European Employee Index © is gathered by Ennova A/S.

2 First, we regressed the simple regression mode with $y = b_1 + b_2 x_2 + b_3 x_3 + b_4 zx_3 + e$. Y is a vector of innovative work behaviour, x_2 is a vector of all control variables, and x_3 is the variable '.ability to act', with z as sector difference. For idea generation, the slopes of this regression $b_3 = .148$ ($p = .000$) and $b_4 = .023$ ($p = .035$). For idea realization, the slopes of this regression $b_3 = .144$ ($p = .000$) and $b_4 = .021$ ($p = .037$). Figure 1 illustrates these regressions. To validate this correlation, we also added x_3 to the analyses of the conceptual model to ensure independence of this framework. These regressions confirmed the positive interaction of sector and 'nearest managers' ability to act' on innovative work behaviour without creating collinearity to the results in Tables 2 and 3.

ACKNOWLEDGEMENTS

The authors greatly appreciate the thoughtful comments from the editor, Stephen P. Osborne, and two anonymous reviewers. In addition, Ennova A/S is acknowledged as an important supportive partner for the research project.

REFERENCES

Acur, N., Kandemir, D., De Weerd-Nederhof, P. C. and Song, M. (2010) Exploring the Impact of Technological Competence Development on Speed and NPD Program Performance. *Journal of Product Innovation Management*, 27: pp915–29.

Alpkan, L., Bulut, C., Gunday, G., Ulusoy, G. and Kilic, K. (2010) Organizational Support for Intrapreneurship and its Interaction with Human Capital to Enhance Innovative Performance. *Management Decision*, 48: pp732–55.

Amabile, T. M. (1988) A Model of Creativity and Innovation in Organizations. *Research in organizational behaviour*, 10: pp123–67.

Amabile, T. M., Conti, R., Coon, H., Lazenby, J. and Herron, M. (1996) Assessing the Work Environment for Creativity. *The Academy of Management Journal*, 39: pp1154–84.

Baer, M., Oldham, G. R. and Cummings, A. (2003) Rewarding Creativity: When Does it Really Matter? *The Leadership Quarterly*, 14: pp569–86.

Baron, R. M. and Kenny, D. A. (1986) The Moderator Mediator Variable Distinction in Social Psychological-Research – Conceptual, Strategic, and Statistical Considerations. *Journal of Personality and Social Psychology*, 51: pp1173–82.

Bartlett, D. and Dibben, P. (2002) Public Sector Innovation and Entrepreneurship: Case Studies from Local Government. *Local Government Studies*, 28: pp107–21.

Bessant, J. (2003) *High-Involvement Innovation*, Chichester: John Wiley & Sons.

Boyne, G. A. (2002) Public and Private Management: What's the Difference? *Journal of Management Studies*, 39: pp97–122.

Bozeman, B. and Kingsley, G. (1998) Risk Culture in Public and Private Organizations. *Public Administration Review*, 58:2 pp109–18.

Burroughs, J. E., Dahl, D. W., Moreau, C. P., Chattopadhyay, A. and Gorn, G. J. (2011) Facilitating and Rewarding Creativity During New Product Development. *Journal of Marketing*, 75:4 pp53–67.

Cardinal, L. B. (2001) Technological Innovation in the Pharmaceutical Industry: The Use of Organizational Control in Managing Research and Development. *Organization Science*, 12: pp19–36.

Chang, L. C. and Liu, C. H. (2008) Employee Empowerment, Innovative Behaviour and Job Productivity of Public Health Nurses: A Cross-Sectional Questionnaire Survey. *International Journal of Nursing Studies*, 45: pp1442–8.

Chen, Z. X. and Aryee, S. (2007) Delegation and Employee Work Outcomes: An Examination of the Cultural Context of Mediating Processes in China. *Academy of Management Journal*, 50: pp226–38.

Cheng, C.-F., Lai, M.-K. and Wu, W.-Y. (2010) Exploring the Impact of Innovation Strategy on R&D Employees' Job Satisfaction: A Mathematical Model and Empirical Research. *Technovation*, 30: pp459–70.

Clegg, C., Unsworth, K., Epitropaki, O. and Parker, G. (2002) Implicating Trust in the Innovation Process. *Journal of Occupational and Organizational Psychology*, 75: pp409–22.

Cohen, W. M. and Levinthal, D. A. (1990) Absorptive Capacity: A New Perspective on Learning and Innovation. *Administrative science quarterly*, 35:1 pp128–152.

Coombs, J. and Bierly, P. (2006) Measuring Technological Capability and Performance. *R&D Management*, 36: pp421–38.

Cowan, R., Sanditov, B. and Weehuizen, R. (2011) Productivity Effects of Innovation, Stress and Social Relations. *Journal of Economic Behavior & Organization*, 79: pp165–82.

Crewson, P. E. (1997) Public-service Motivation: Building Empirical Evidence of Incidence and Effect. *Journal of Public Administration Research and Theory*, 7: pp499–518.

Dahl, D. W. and Moreau, P. (2002) The Influence and Value of Analogical Thinking During New Product Ideation. *Journal of Marketing Research*, 39:1 pp47–60.

Deci, E. L., Koestner, R. and Ryan, R. M. (1999) A Meta-Analytic Review of Experiments Examining the Effects of Extrinsic Rewards on Intrinsic Motivation. *Psychological bulletin*, 125: p627.

Di Gangi, P. M., Wasko, M. and Hooker, R. (2010) Getting Customers' Ideas to Work for You: Learning from Dell How to Succeed with Online User Innovation Communities. *MIS Quarterly Executive*, 9: pp213–28.

Dobni, C. B. and Luffman, G. (2000) Market Orientation and Market Strategy Profiling: An Empirical Test of Environment-Behaviour-Action Coalignment and its Performance Implications. *Management Decision*, 38: p503.

Dorenbosch, L., Engen, M. L. and Verhagen, M. (2005) On-the-Job Innovation: The Impact of Job Design and Human Resource Management through Production Ownership. *Creativity and Innovation Management*, 14: pp129–41.

Eisenberg, J. (1999) How Individualism-Collectivism Moderates the Effects of Rewards on Creativity and Innovation: A Comparative Review of Practices in Japan and the US. *Creativity and Innovation Management*, 8: pp251–61.

Eskildsen, J. K., Westlund, A. H. and Kristensen, K. (2004) Measuring Employee Assets – The Nordic Employee Index. *Business Process Management Journal*, 10: pp537–50.

Evans, M. G. (1985) A Monte Carlo Study of the Effects of Correlated Method Variance in Moderated Multiple Regression Analysis. *Organizational Behavior and Human Decision Processes*, 36: pp305–23.

Fauchart, E. and Keilbach, M. (2009) Testing a Model of Exploration and Exploitation as Innovation Strategies. *Small Business Economics*, 33: pp257–72.

Fornell, C. and Larcker, D. F. (1981) Evaluating Structural Equation Models with Unobservable Variables and Measurement Error. *Journal of Marketing Research*, 18: pp39–50.

Georgellis, Y., Iossa, E. and Tabvuma, V. (2011) Crowding Out Intrinsic Motivation in the Public Sector. *Journal of Public Administration Research and Theory*, 21: p473.

Goll, I., Johnson, N. B. and Rasheed, A. A. (2007) Knowledge Capability, Strategic Change, and Firm Performance: The Moderating Role of the Environment. *Management Decision*, 45: pp161–79.

Grant, A. M. and Berry, J. W. (2011) The Necessity of Others is the Mother of Invention: Intrinsic and Prosocial Motivations, Perspective Taking, and Creativity. *The Academy of Management Journal (AMJ)*, 54: pp73–96.

Hansen, M. T. and Birkinshaw, J. (2007) Innovation Value Chain. *Harvard Business Review*, 85:6 p121.

Hartley, J. (2005) Innovation in Governance and Public Services: Past and Present. *Public Money and Management*, 25: pp27–34.

Hauser, J. R., Tellis, G. J. and Griffin, A. (2006) Research on Innovation: A Review and Agenda for Marketing Science. *Marketing Science*, 25: pp687–717.

Hennessey, B. A. and Amabile, T. M. (2010) Creativity. *Annual Review of Psychology*, 61 pp569–98.

Hulland, J. (1999) Use of Partial Least Squares (PLS) in Strategic Management Research: A Review of Four Recent Studies. *Strategic Management Journal*, 20: pp195–204.

Janssen, O. (2000) Job Demands, Perceptions of Effort-Reward Fairness and Innovative Work Behaviour. *Journal of Occupational and Organizational Psychology*, 73: pp287–302.

Janssen, O. (2001) Fairness Perceptions as a Moderator in the Curvilinear Relationships Between Job Demands, and Job Performance and Job Satisfaction. *Academy of Management Journal*, 44: pp1039–50.

Janssen, O. (2003) Innovative Behaviour and Job Involvement at the Price of Conflict and Less Satisfactory Relations with Co-workers. *Journal of Occupational and Organizational Psychology*, 76: pp347–64.

Janssen, O. (2005) The Joint Impact of Perceived Influence and Supervisor Supportiveness on Employee Innovative Behaviour. *Journal of Occupational and Organizational Psychology*, 78: pp573–9.

Janssen, O., Van De Vliert, E. and West, M. (2004) The Bright and Dark Sides of Individual and Group Innovation: A Special Issue Introduction. *Journal of Organizational Behaviour*, 25: pp129–45.

Janssen, O. and Van Yperen, N. W. (2004) Employees' Goal Orientations, the Quality of Leader-Member Exchange, and the Outcomes of Job Performance and Job Satisfaction. *Academy of Management Journal*, 47: pp368–84.

Jespersen, K. R. (2011) Online Channels And Innovation: Are Users Being Empowered And Involved? *International Journal of Innovation Management*, 15: pp1141–59.

Klein, K. J. and Sorra, J. S. (1996) The Challenge of Innovation Implementation. *The Academy of Management Review*, 21: pp1055–80.

Klein, P. G., Mahoney, J. T., Mcgahan, A. M. and Pitelis, C. N. (2010) Toward a Theory of Public Entrepreneurship. *European Management Review*, 7:1 pp1–15. http://onlinelibrary.wiley.com/doi/10.1057/emr.2010.1/abstract (accessed June 3, 2013).

Laine, M. O. J. and Laine, A. V. O. (2012) 'Open Innovation, Intellectual Capital and Different Knowledge Sources' In *Proceedings of the European Conference on Intellectual Capital*, January, Ispwich, MA, pp239–45.

Lassen, A. H., Waehrens, B. V. and Boer, H. (2009) Re-orienting the Corporate Entrepreneurial Journey: Exploring the Role of Middle Management. *Creativity and Innovation Management*, 18: pp16–23.

Lee, J. (2008) Effects of Leadership and Leader-Member Exchange on Innovativeness. *Journal of Managerial Psychology*, 23: pp670–87.

Leiponen, A. and Helfat, C. E. (2010) Innovation Objectives, Knowledge Sources, and the Benefits of Breadth. *Strategic Management Journal*, 31: pp224–36.

Li, H. Y. and Atuahene-Gima, K. (2001) Product Innovation Strategy and the Performance of New Technology Ventures in China. *Academy of Management Journal*, 44: pp1123–34.

Martin, T. N., Price, J. L. and Mueller, C. W. (1981) Job-Performance and Turnover. *Journal of Applied Psychology*, 66: pp116–9.

Melly, B. (2005) Public-Private Sector Wage Differentials in Germany: Evidence from Quantile Regression. *Empirical Economics*, 30: pp505–20.

Miron, E., Erez, M. and Naveh, E. (2004) Do Personal Characteristics and Cultural Values that Promote Innovation, Quality, and Efficiency Compete or Complement Each Other? *Journal of Organizational Behaviour*, 25: pp175–99.

Morrison, E. W., Wheeler-Smith, S. L. and Kamdar, D. (2011) Speaking Up in Groups: A Cross-level Study of Group Voice Climate and Voice. *Journal of Applied Psychology*, 96: p183.

Oldham, G. R. and Cummings, A. (1996) Employee Creativity: Personal and Contextual Factors at Work. *Academy of Management Journal*, 39:3 pp607–34.

Oliver, C. and Holzinger, I. (2008) The Effectiveness of Strategic Political Management: A Dynamic Capabilities Framework. *The Academy of Management Review ARCHIVE*, 33: pp496–520.

Pieterse, A. N., Van Knippenberg, D., Schippers, M. and Stam, D. (2010) Transformational and Transactional Leadership and Innovative Behaviour: The Moderating Role of Psychological Empowerment. *Journal of Organizational Behaviour*, 31: pp609–23.

Rainey, H. G. (1999) Using Comparisons of Public and Private Organizations to Assess Innovative Attitudes Among Members of Organizations. *Public Productivity & Management Review*, 23:2 pp130–49.

Ren, C. R. and Guo, C. (2011) Middle Managers' Strategic Role in the Corporate Entrepreneurial Process: Attention-Based Effects. *Journal of Management*, 37: pp1586–610.

Ryan, R. M. and Deci, E. L. (2000) Self-determination Theory and the Facilitation of Intrinsic Motivation, Social Development, and Well-Being. *American Psychologist*, 55: pp68–78.

Sauermann, H. and Cohen, W. (2010) *What Makes them Tick? Employee Motives and Firm Innovation*. NBER Working Paper. Cambridge: NBER.

Sawhney, M., Verona, G. and Prandelli, E. (2005) Collaborating to Create: The Internet as a Platform for Customer Engagement in Product Innovation. *Journal of interactive marketing*, 19: pp4–17.

Schriesheim, C. A. (1979) The Similarity of Individual Directed and Group Directed Leader Behavior Descriptions. *The Academy of Management Journal*, 22: pp345–55.

Scott, S. G. and Bruce, R. A. (1994) Determinants of Innovative Behaviour: A Path Model of Individual Innovation in the Workplace. *The Academy of Management Journal*, 37: pp580–607.

Shalley, C. E., Gilson, L. L. and Blum, T. C. (2000) Matching Creativity Requirements and the Work Environment: Effects on Satisfaction and Intentions to Leave. *Academy of Management Journal*, 43: pp215–23.

Shalley, C. E., Gilson, L. L. and Blum, T. C. (2009) Interactive Effects of Growth Need Strength, Work Context, and Job Complexity on Self-Reported Creative Performance. *Academy of Management Journal*, 52: pp489–505.

Shih, H. A. and Susanto, E. (2011) Is Innovative Behavior Really Good for the Firm? Innovative Work Behavior, Conflict with Coworkers and Turnover Intention: Moderating Roles of Perceived Distributive Fairness. *International Journal of Conflict Management*, 22: pp111–30.

243

Siemsen, E., Roth, A. and Oliveira, P. (2010) Common Method Bias in Regression Models with Linear, Quadratic, and Interaction Effects. *Organizational Research Methods*, 13: pp456–76.

Sørensen, E. and Torfing, J. (2011) Enhancing Collaborative Innovation in the Public Sector. *Administration & Society*, 43:8 pp842–68.

Sparrow, R. and Sparrow, L. (2006) In the Hands of Machines? The Future of Aged Care. *Minds and Machines*, 16: pp141–61.

Spreitzer, G. M. (1995) Psychological Empowerment in the Workplace – Dimensions, Measurement, and Validation. *Academy of Management Journal*, 38: pp1442–65.

Sundbo, J. (2001) *The Strategic Management of Innovation*, Cheltenham: Elgar.

Terwiesch, C. and Xu, Y. (2008) Innovation Contests, Open Innovation, and Multiagent Problem Solving. *Management Science*, 54: pp1529–43.

Tierney, P. (1997) The Influence of Cognitive Climate on Job Satisfaction and Creative Efficacy. *Journal of Social Behavior and Personality*, 12: pp831–47.

Tuominen, T. and Toivonen, M. (2011) Studying Innovation and Change Activities in Kibs Through the Lens of Innovative Behaviour. *International Journal of Innovation Management (IJIM)*, 15: pp393–422.

Unsworth, K. L. and Clegg, C. W. (2010) Why Do Employees Undertake Creative Action? *Journal of Occupational and Organizational Psychology*, 83: pp77–99.

Vinding, A. L. (2006) Absorptive Capacity and Innovative Performance: A Human Capital Approach. *Economics of Innovation and New Technology*, 15: pp507–17.

Verhoest, K., Verschuere, B. and Bouckaert, G. (2007) Pressure, Legitimacy, and Innovative Behavior by Public Organizations. *Governance*, 20: pp469–97.

Yuan, F. R. and Woodman, R. W. (2010) Innovative Behaviour in the Workplace: The Role of Performance and Image Outcome Expectations. *Academy of Management Journal*, 53: pp323–42.

Zhang, X. and Bartol, K. M. (2010a) Linking Empowering Leadership and Employee Creativity: The Influence of Psychological Empowerment, Intrinsic Motivation, and Creative Process Engagement. *The Academy of Management Journal (AMJ)*, 53: pp107–128.

Zhang, X. and Bartol, K. M. (2010b) The Influence of Creative Process Engagement on Employee Creative Performance and Overall Job Performance: A Curvilinear Assessment. *Journal of Applied Psychology*, 95: pp862–73.

Abstract

Internationally, the public sector is adopting social media applications (e.g. Twitter and social networking services (SNS)) to harness cutting-edge information technology (IT) developments, but we know little about what drives the diffusion of these applications. In this paper, I adapt the Berry–Berry policy and innovation diffusion model to explain the diffusion and assimilation of government microblogging, supplementing its four dimensions (learning, competition, upper-tier mandate and public pressure) with organizational resources and capacity. Data on 282 prefecture-level cities in China are employed to test several theoretical hypotheses empirically. Horizontal competition is found to be significantly and positively associated with the assimilation of government microblogging, although the other three dimensions are found not to be its key antecedents. Consistent with the study's hypotheses, the results support the significantly positive effects of fiscal resources and IT capacity. Municipal wealth, size and administrative ranking are also positively and significantly correlated with the number of government microblogs.

DIFFUSION AND ASSIMILATION OF GOVERNMENT MICROBLOGGING

Evidence from Chinese cities

Liang Ma

Liang Ma
School of Humanities, Economics, and Law
Northwestern Polytechnical University
127 West Youyi Road, Xi'an, Shaanxi 710072
China
Nanyang Centre for Public Administration
Nanyang Technological University
50 Nanyang Avenue, Singapore 639798
Singapore

INTRODUCTION

At the cutting edge of information technology (IT) development, Web 2.0 technologies and social media applications (e.g. Twitter, social networking services (SNS) and so forth) are enabling netizens and organizations to communicate and collaborate freely, openly and actively (McAfee, 2009). The rapid development of social media applications is also helping governments to better communicate with their peers and citizens (Hrdinová et al., 2010; Reddick and Wigand, 2010), and many scholars and government officials have posited Government 2.0 as the new shape of government (Eggers, 2007). The public sector in numerous countries and regions has adopted and leveraged these technologies to improve public service quality and elicit public participation, and government agencies in China are pioneers in this regard (Thomler, 2011). Government agencies at all levels throughout the country have launched official microblogs in the past two years (Ma, forthcoming 2012). As of the end of 2011, government agencies and civil servants had launched 50,561 official microblogs on China's four dominant microblogging platforms, a 776.58 per cent increase over the beginning of the year, according to the *2011 China Government Microblog Assessment Report* released on 8 February 2012 by the E-Government Research Center (2012) at the China National School of Administration.[1] If 2010 can be regarded as Year One of the microblogging era, then 2011 is the first year of the government microblogging era in China. The unprecedented interest in and enthusiasm for microblogging amongst Chinese government agencies raises an interesting research question. What is driving the rapid diffusion and widespread assimilation of government microblogging in China?

As a technology that is new to public organizations, the spread of microblogging lends itself to investigation from the perspective of innovation adoption and diffusion (Rogers, 2003). However, because microblogging and other social media applications are new to the Chinese government, their diffusion has yet to be studied systematically, with two notable exceptions. Mergel (2011) analysed the diffusion of social media applications amongst federal departments and agencies in the United States based on interview data and found both upper-tier mandates and peer learning to be driving their spread. Ma (forthcoming 2012) examined the diffusion of microblogging across Chinese municipal police bureaus, and his findings partially support the significant effects of government size, the Internet penetration rate, regional diffusion effects and upper-tier pressure.

In this paper, I further investigate the assimilation of government microblogging, which is defined as the process of deploying this new technology by organizational parties and members after its initial acquisition. Organizations may adopt an innovation but not fully deploy it, and it is thus essential to examine the post-adoption behaviour of organizations and the assimilation of innovation by their members (Fichman and Kemerer, 1999). One of the paper's major contributions is its development of a comprehensive model to test diverse explanations of government microblogging diffusion. The theories of organizational IT innovation adoption (Jeyaraj et al., 2006) and policy diffusion (Berry and Berry, 1999, 2007; Lee et al., 2011; Walker et al.,

2011) are synthesized into a conceptual framework in which learning, competition, public pressure, upper-tier mandate and organizational resources and capacity are argued to be positively associated with such diffusion. Data on more than 280 prefecture-level cities in China are employed to test five theoretical hypotheses empirically, and the findings partially support the theoretical framework. I also compare the findings with prior studies of e-government and other IT innovations, revealing government microblogging to have both similar and distinct attributes.

As this is the first empirical study of the diffusion and assimilation of microblogging amongst local governments, its findings have both theoretical and practical implications. The results extend and confirm the theoretical arguments of policy and innovation diffusion, in that the spread of government microblogging is driven by similar antecedents to other technology and policy innovations (Berry and Berry, 1999, 2007). I also find distinct explanations for government microblogging diffusion, thus offering a foundation for its differentiation and comparison in future examinations. My empirical findings also have policy implications for governments that wish to advance the spread of microblogging and other social media technologies across the public sector.

The remainder of the paper is structured as follows. I first introduce the theories of innovation adoption and diffusion and propose several hypotheses deserving of empirical testing. I then report the data and methods employed in the study, followed by a discussion of its primary findings. After presentation of the study's theoretical contributions and policy implications, the paper concludes with a discussion of its limitations and of future research avenues.

THEORY

An innovation is something new to its adopters (herein public organizations), no matter how many of their peers have previously adopted it (Walker, 1969). Innovation diffusion is the process by which an innovation spreads over time across the members of a social system (e.g. organizations or jurisdictions) (Rogers, 2003). Organizations may adopt an innovation symbolically rather than using it in reality, thus resulting in an adoption–implementation gap. Innovation assimilation is the actual use and deployment of an innovation by organizational members after its adoption (Fichman and Kemerer, 1999). Going beyond the mainstream innovation adoption research paradigm to analyse the assimilation of an innovation is crucial, because it is the actual deployment of an innovation that may affect organizational performance (Anderson et al., 2004).

Many theories have been developed to further understanding of innovation adoption, and it is vital that we also integrate diverse theoretical perspectives to explain fully what drives innovation diffusion and assimilation (Crossan and Apaydin, 2010). Berry and Berry (2007) synthesized the literature on policy and innovation diffusion across diverse disciplines and developed a theoretical model that comprehensively explains the diffusion of government innovation. Their model comprises four dimensions, namely, learning, competition, mandate or norms and citizen pressure (Berry and Berry, 2007). Motivation and pressure deriving from peers, competitors, upper-tier authorities and jurisdictional citizens drive governments to adopt specific policies and innovations. Interestingly, the global explanation of policy and innovation diffusion coincides with the upward, downward and outward outreach of the Moore government strategic management framework (Moore, 1997). The Berry–Berry model has received extensive support from recent empirical studies on the development and diffusion of cross-country e-government (Lee *et al.*, 2011) and British local government innovations (Walker *et al.*, 2011). Thus, I believe it is appropriate to employ the model to explain the diffusion and assimilation of government microblogging.

I adapt the Berry–Berry framework to propose theoretical hypotheses to explain such diffusion and assimilation across government agencies. All four of its dimensions concern the external motivational bases of policy and innovation diffusion, thus failing to incorporate the underlying intra-jurisdictional characteristics that transform motivation and pressure into adoption action. Mohr (1969) argued that organizational innovation is a multiplicative function of motivations, resources and barriers. Although motivation and a propensity to innovate are crucial for adoption decision-making, the resources to overcome barriers are also important antecedents (Berry, 1994). Accordingly, I supplement the Berry–Berry framework with intra-governmental attributes, specifically organizational resources and capacity, to better understand the diffusion of government microblogging. Meta-analysis has identified organizational resources and capacity, particularly IT infrastructure and large-scale investment, as key antecedents to organizational IT innovation adoption (Jeyaraj *et al.*, 2006). Evidence from South Korea also suggests that management capacity has positive effects on government innovation (Kim and Lee, 2009). In sum, to explain the diffusion and assimilation of government microblogging in fully, it is essential that we incorporate organizational resources and capacity into the theoretical model.

Competition

Governments compete with one another to attract the flow of financial and human capital necessary to fuel economic growth (Dobbin *et al.*, 2007). The interdependence of governments may drive the convergence of policy and practice, which is the key determinant of policy and innovation diffusion (Berry and Baybeck, 2005). When neighbouring or socioeconomically similar peers have adopted specific innovations, governments may be inclined to adopt these or similar practices to regain advantages or mitigate disadvantages (Berry and Berry, 1999, 2007). In addition to intergovernmental competition in the economic arena, this study also examines the career tournament amongst government officials from the political perspective. China's authoritarian party-state system grants central and upper-tier party committees the personnel management authority to appoint local officials, and thus the career tournament amongst local governments within a specific jurisdiction may trigger intense political and economic competition (Bo, 2002; Landry, 2008). Accordingly, local government officials may treat their counterparts in the same jurisdiction as competitors and threats to career advancement (Li and Zhou, 2005). With regard to the adoption decision, I employ the average number of microblogs launched by other cities within the jurisdiction (excluding the focal city) to capture intergovernmental competition effects.

> H1: The average number of government microblogs launched in adjacent cities within a jurisdiction is positively correlated with the number of government microblogs launched in the focal city.

Learning

Social learning is a key process by which governments adopt policy and innovation, because it reduces the extraordinary risk and cost of innovation (Berry and Berry, 2007), and learning and imitation are key drivers of international policy transfer and convergence (Dobbin *et al.*, 2007). Social learning is distinct from economic competition, and disentangling these two dimensions are important for theoretical development (Boehmke and Witmer, 2004). Economic competition is restricted to jurisdictions' adjacent counterparts, whereas IT developments allow governments to overcome geographic limitations to learn from many sources other than their peers (Rogers, 2003). Prior studies employ the number of international organizations in which a country participates to capture its national government's potential to learn from abroad (Lee *et al.*, 2011). Successful practices generate followers and spur spread, and governments in developing countries and regions are keen to learn from their developed counterparts. China is no exception, with its governments eager to learn from more developed countries and regions internationally, particularly the United States and Hong Kong (Chien and Ho, 2011; Christensen *et al.*, 2008). International sister city agreements facilitate municipal cooperation and exchange in a variety of fields, with participants benefitting from the learning and imitation of their twinned counterparts (Cremer *et al.*, 2001). Similar to previous studies, I employ the number of international sister cities to gauge the learning orientation and channels of municipal governments.

> H2: The number of international sister city relationships enjoyed by a municipality is positively correlated with the number of government microblogs launched by that municipality.

Vertical mandate

Upper-tier mandates or political norms play a key role in shaping a government's propensity to adopt specific policies and practices (Berry and Berry, 2007). Coercion from international organizations and upper-tier governments may push governments lower down the scale to adopt the innovations these power holders advocate (Dobbin et al., 2007). I posit that vertical mandates are important for policy and innovation diffusion in China, as the country's authoritarian unitary system renders lower-level governments heavily dependent on the policies and grants of upper-tier authorities (Chung, 2000). Satisfying the requirements of upper-level governments may also help government officials to win the cut-throat career tournament in which they are engaged (Li and Zhou, 2005). If upper-tier authorities advocate, support or adopt social media applications, then lower-tier governments are likely to introduce microblogging quickly. I employ the number of microblogs launched by provincial government departments to measure the degree of the top-down mandate.

H3: The number of microblogs launched by provincial government departments is positively correlated with the number of government microblogs launched by the cities within that province.

Public pressure

When particular policies have been adopted in neighbouring jurisdictions, informed citizens may demand that their government immediately adopt similar policies if they believe them to be beneficial to their welfare (Berry and Berry, 2007). Public pressure plays a key role in policy and innovation diffusion, and citizens may push governments to adopt the innovations they prefer. Furthermore, the network externality effect of IT applications requires a vast Internet population (Katz and Shapiro, 1986), and a large percentage of highly educated netizens is pivotal to the success of any social media application. Although both enterprises and individual citizens are crucial constituencies for governments, this paper focuses on the public because the majority of microbloggers are individual citizens (Ma, forthcoming 2012). A municipality's Internet penetration rate and human capital are used to measure public pressure, as they are two of the key components of public pressure (Lee et al., 2011).

H4a: The municipal Internet penetration rate is positively correlated with the number of government microblogs launched in a city.

H4b: Municipal human capital is positively correlated with the number of government microblogs launched in a city.

Organizational resources and capacity

Resources and capacity are interrelated but distinct concepts. Resources are the tangible and intangible assets available for organizational use (Barney, 1996), whereas capacity (or capabilities) refers to an organization's ability to acquire and deploy resources

(Teece *et al.*, 1997). Slack resources have been identified as a key antecedent to organizational innovation (Damanpour, 1991), and fiscal health is also reported to be positively associated with the adoption of public management innovation (Berry, 1994). Large-scale investment in IT infrastructure is crucial to the development and success of e-government and other IT applications (Jeyaraj *et al.*, 2006), and wealthy governments with abundant resources are likely to adopt IT innovations earlier (Moon and Norris, 2005). Institutional capacity has also been identified as important to e-government development (Tolbert *et al.*, 2008). Management capacity as an umbrella concept is also one of the most important drivers of government innovation (Kim and Lee, 2009). As microblogging is at the cutting edge of IT development and application, its adoption requires sufficient resources and support in addition to managerial reorientation and restructuring (Ma, forthcoming 2012). The transformation from Government 1.0 to 2.0 is also dependent on the level of e-government development (Eggers, 2007). Here, I employ the fiscal health and performance of urban e-government to gauge a municipal government's level of resources and capacity, respectively.

H5a: Municipal fiscal health is positively correlated with the number of government microblogs launched in a city.

H5b: Municipal e-government performance is positively correlated with the number of government microblogs launched in a city.

METHODS

Sample and data

I test the foregoing hypotheses in the context of local governments in China. China is a unitary country with a strongly authoritarian governance system and is structured into five administrative tiers. The central government coordinates twenty-three provinces (including Taiwan), four municipalities (Beijing, Shanghai, Tianjin and Chongqing), five autonomous regions (of which Tibet is one) and two special administrative regions (Hong Kong and Macau). Below the provinces are more than 280 prefectures and prefecture-level cities (e.g. Suzhou), followed by almost 3000 counties, county-level cities and districts. Towns and sub-districts are at the lowest administrative level, and beneath them are highly autonomous villages and communities. The country's dramatic transformation in the wake of the reform and opening-up policy launched in the late 1970s has seen the extensive delegation of authority from the central government to local governments, with governments at each level afforded the ability to make relatively more independent decisions than in the past (Chung, 2000). Local governments have adopted numerous technological and administrative innovations in the past few decades and have achieved marked improvements in public service performance (Wu *et al.*, forthcoming 2012). Thus, local governments can be treated as independent innovation adopters in examination of their official microblogging launch behaviour.

I employ data from the full population of Chinese prefecture-level cities to examine the drivers of microblogging diffusion empirically. These cities are appropriate for the current study because they provide a sufficiently large sample, exhibit a high degree of involvement in government innovation and allow reasonable comparability (Chien, 2010). Although China is also home to provincial- and county-level cities, its prefecture-level cities enjoy greater equivalence and are thus more conducive to assessment and comparison (China Association of Mayors, 2010). Policy diffusion researchers have called for studies that go beyond mainstream state-level analysis to dig more deeply into local governments, where innovations emerge and spread relatively frequently and rapidly (Berry and Berry, 2007; Zhang and Yang, 2008). Most prior studies on e-government development and the adoption and diffusion of other innovations focus on city-level governments (Moon and Norris, 2005), thus affording ease of comparison with the findings of the current study.

I obtain the government microblogging data from weibo.com (Sina), a dominant microblogging platform in China that lists all authenticated government microblogs by functional sector (e.g. police or public health) and region (province or prefecture-level city) and is updated in a timely fashion, thus enabling me to collect data on their distribution.[2] Although it would be ideal to collect these data by monitoring all accessible microblogging platforms, doing so is not possible.[3] In any case, previous studies have reported weibo.com to be the predominant microblogging platform in China, accounting for more than half of all registered microbloggers (Ma, forthcoming 2012). A sample survey also revealed that government agencies that launch a microblog on one platform (e.g. weibo.com) usually mirror it on another (e.g. t.qq.com [Tencent]) to encompass netizens registered on different platforms.[4]

The data on the study's independent variables come primarily from the *China City Statistical Yearbook* compiled by the National Bureau of Statistics of China (NBSC) (2011) and from relevant statistics and reports. The data on the dependent variable were collected at the end of 2011, whereas most of the independent variables were measured at the end of 2010, the most recent year for which these data were available. Such an approach was also helpful in mitigating the reverse causality problem. There were 283 prefecture-level cities at the time of data collection, but the final sample for analysis includes 282 cities owing to missing data on Lhasa, the capital of Tibet. The conceptualization, operationalization and data sources of all variables are reported in Appendix (see Table A1).

Dependent variable

The dependent variable is the assimilation of government microblogging at the municipal level. Different from the traditional dichotomy of innovation adoption, I employ the actual use of IT innovation as my measure of assimilation. Assimilation of a specific innovation is usually measured by the percentage of the social system or organizational members who have adopted it (Fichman and Kemerer, 1999; Rogers, 2003; Zhang and Yang, 2008). The total number of microblogs launched by municipal government agencies and approved by the microblogging service provider is employed to measure the assimilation of government microblogging in each city. The underlying assumption of my measurement approach is that the potential population of microblogging adopters in each city is equivalent and comparable because of China's unitary administrative system and the similar structuring of local governments nationwide.

Independent variables

Competition

As previously noted, cities may be inclined to compete with their counterparts in the same jurisdiction to win the economic and political competition between them. I employ the average number of microblogs launched by other cities in the province (excluding the focal city) to measure the effects of intergovernmental competition.[5] Although some scholars suggest employing geographic information systems or spatial models to examine inter-jurisdictional competition (Berry and Baybeck, 2005), the methods used herein dominate the mainstream research (Berry and Berry, 2007; Boehmke and Witmer, 2004). A recent test of the Berry–Berry model in the global e-government development arena applied the same measure (Lee et al., 2011). Hence, I believe my measure satisfactorily captures the competition effects of government microblogging diffusion.

Learning

The government sectors of cities with more overseas sister cities have relatively more channels through which to communicate with and learn from their international counterparts. Similar to other studies (Lee et al., 2011), the current study employs the number of international sister cities recorded by the China International Friendship Cities Association (CIFCA) to gauge the learning orientation and channels of urban governments.[6] The CIFCA updates these statistics annually, and I use the latest accumulative data to calculate the measure. It would be ideal to compile data on communications and learning amongst Chinese cities to measure these learning effects, but such data are not accessible. In any case, learning is a propensity that is inherited in specific cities (Dobbin et al., 2007), and it can thus be assumed that municipalities with more international sister cities have a greater tendency to connect with and learn from other domestic cities.

253

Vertical mandate

The intermediate upper-tier authority for city governments, that is, provincial government departments, exerts the strongest influence on policy decision-making. The attitude and propensity of these departments toward microblogging may thus affect municipal governments' adoption decisions to a large extent. If provincial government departments have launched official microblogs, then municipal governments may be more inclined to follow their example.[7] Accordingly, I use the number of microblogs launched by provincial government departments to measure the top-down mandate. Provincial government microblogs are geographically registered in provincial capital cites, and I thus employ the total number of government microblogs launched in these cities minus the number of city-level government microblogs as the number of provincial government microblogs. Accordingly, the number of government microblogs in provincial capital cities is the total number of government microblogs minus the number of provincial government microblogs.

Public pressure

Informed citizens with a high level of human capital may be the dominant force pushing the government to innovate. I thus adopt the Internet penetration rate and percentage of highly educated citizens to measure public pressure, in line with prior studies (Lee et al., 2011).

Organizational resources and capacity

I create two measures to gauge municipal government resources and capacity. First, fiscal health is measured by the difference between fiscal revenue and expenditure divided by fiscal expenditure, the methods developed by Berry (1994). The larger the measure, the healthier the municipal fiscal system. Second, municipal e-government performance is employed to gauge government IT capacity based on the government website performance assessment results compiled by the China Software Testing Center (CSTC, 2011). The most authoritative e-government assessment body in China, the CSTC assesses the websites of governments across diverse levels and regions annually in terms of the key dimensions of online service, interactive properties and information disclosure. I use its comprehensive score to measure municipal e-government performance.

Control variables

Several geographic, socioeconomic and demographic attributes of the sample cities are taken into account in estimating the models discussed in Results section. First, municipal gross domestic product (GDP) per capita as a measure of economic wealth is controlled in the model. Generally speaking, wealthier governments are more inclined to adopt innovations owing to their resource endowment (Mohr, 1969; Tolbert et al., 2008).

Second, I control the total municipal population size as a proxy of jurisdictional size. Prior studies suggest that government size plays an important role in eliciting innovation adoption (Ma, forthcoming 2012; Moon and Norris, 2005; Tolbert et al., 2008). Larger cities with more public sector departments may have the potential to launch more microblogs.

Third, several strategically important cities in China (e.g. Shenzhen) are granted extra authority by the central government, although they are also prefecture-level cities (Chien, 2010; Chung and Lam, 2004). Similarly, provincial capital cities may also enjoy greater autonomy owing to their proximity to provincial authorities. Greater administrative authority may enable municipal governments to adopt innovations more autonomously or, conversely, it may render them more cautious and risk-averse. I create two dummies for the fifteen sub-provincial cities[8] and twenty-seven provincial capital cities in the sample to control for the effects of a city's administrative rank.

Finally, cities located in particular geographic regions, namely, the coastal and inland provinces, enjoy distinct resources and opportunities, and this disparity may affect their innovative propensity. To control for these geographic effects, I create two dummies for the eastern and western regions, taking the central region as the reference group.[9]

Analytical methods

Multivariate regression analysis is applied to test the hypotheses proposed herein, and several controls are included to eliminate alternative explanations. The dataset is cross-sectional in nature, and the dependent variable is a count outcome. Linear regression models (e.g. ordinary least squares (OLS)) may result in biased estimates when the dependent variable is a count outcome because of the violation of the normal distribution assumption, and these models are thus inappropriate for analysis in this study (Long and Freese, 2006). Models specifically designed for regressions with count data are preferable, and many alternatives could have been employed.[10] The Poisson regression model is unsuitable for analysis, however, because it does not take heterogeneity into account. The negative binomial regression model resolves this problem and is thus appropriate for our purposes (Long and Freese, 2006). The government sectors of all prefecture-level cities can launch official microblogs, and the sample covers the entire population. Thus, the number of government microblogs launched by municipal governments does not suffer from the dispersion problem deriving from left-censoring and sampling bias, rendering zero-inflated and zero-truncated models unsuitable for the current analysis (Long and Freese, 2006). For all of these reasons, I employ the negative binomial regression model to test the study's hypotheses.

RESULTS

The descriptive statistics and correlations of the variables are reported in Table A2 of Appendix. The distribution of the number of municipal government microblogs exhibits substantial variance across cities. Some cities, such as Chengdu in the northwestern province of Sichuan, have launched more than 400 such blogs, whereas others, such as Songyuan in the northeastern province of Jilin Province, have yet to adopt any. The average number of government microblogs launched by prefecture-level cities is thirty-four, and its standard deviation is over fifty, thus implying a large variation deserving of further explanation. There are also substantial variations amongst the independent variables, which could be employed to explain the variance in government microblogging assimilation.

The correlation metrics reported in Table A2 show the number of government microblogs to be positively and significantly correlated with all of the independent variables, providing preliminary support for the hypotheses. Generally speaking, the independent variables are weakly interrelated, and all of the correlations are less than 0.700. The variance inflation factors (VIFs) of the independent variables are all less than 3.00, much lower than the standard value of 10.00 recommended for diagnosis of regression multicollinearity (Belsley *et al.*, 2004).

I first enter all of the control variables into Model 1. I then enter the four dimensions of the Berry–Berry model (Model 2) separately and add the resources and capacity dimension (Model 3) without the control variables. The four dimensions with the control variables are entered into Model 4, and the full model (Model 5) is finally used to test the hypotheses. The preliminary results reported in Table 1 show that the theoretical framework is partially supported by the empirical test. The likelihood ratio (LR) χ^2 for all five models are statistically significant at the 0.0000 level, thus suggesting that the models' explanatory power is non-zero. When the other variables are omitted in Model 2, the four dimensions advocated by Berry and Berry (1999, 2007) all have significantly positive effects on the diffusion of government microblogging, thus strongly supporting their predictive power. Their explanatory power is reduced when alternative explanations are taken into account, as evidenced by Models 3–5. The pseudo R^2 for the models with the four dimensions are 0.0593 (Model 2) and 0.0755 (Model 4), whereas those for the models that include organizational resources and capacity improve substantially to 0.0698 (Model 3) and 0.0825 (Model 5), respectively. Thus, the findings support my adaptation of the Berry–Berry model to explain the diffusion and assimilation of government microblogging.

In all five models, horizontal competition measured by the average number of government microblogs launched by adjacent cities in the same province has significantly positive effects on the number of municipal government microblogs, thus providing support for H1.

Horizontal learning measured by the number of international sister cities is positively and significantly associated with government microblogging assimilation in Models 2

Table 1: Results of negative binomial regression models

Variable	Model 1	Model 2	Model 3	Model 4	Model 5
Competition		0.00951***	0.00719***	0.0113***	0.00881***
		(0.00228)	(0.00228)	(0.00306)	(0.00301)
Learning		0.0774***	0.0380**	0.00994	−0.00779
		(0.0148)	(0.0161)	(0.019)	(0.0189)
Mandate		0.0160***	0.00906**	0.00282	0.000157
		(0.00425)	(0.00426)	(0.0047)	(0.00459)
Human capital		0.00745*	−0.0003	0.00169	−0.00089
		(0.00446)	(0.00437)	(0.00469)	(0.00457)
Netizens		1.701***	0.692	0.285	0.142
		(0.561)	(0.578)	(0.637)	(0.62)
Fiscal health			0.933***		1.028***
			(0.319)		(0.366)
E-government			0.0206***		0.0156***
			(0.00518)		(0.00522)
GDP per capita	0.106***			0.0869***	0.0391
	(0.02)			(0.0233)	(0.0242)
Population size	0.571***			0.479***	0.461***
	(0.0852)			(0.0938)	(0.0934)
Sub-provincial city	0.029			−0.0331	−0.152
	(0.257)			(0.276)	(0.275)
Provincial capital city	0.833***			0.928***	0.677***
	(0.193)			(0.241)	(0.244)
Eastern city	0.536***			0.138	0.14
	(0.126)			(0.157)	(0.155)
Western city	−0.171			−0.126	0.0471
	(0.126)			(0.128)	(0.131)
Constant	−0.642	1.657***	2.120***	−0.554	−0.0781
	(0.525)	(0.193)	(0.364)	(0.535)	(0.565)
Ln α	−0.475***	−0.391***	−0.486***	−0.536***	−0.599***
	(0.0861)	(0.0848)	(0.0864)	(0.0871)	(0.088)
N	282	282	282	282	282
Log likelihood	−1199.612	−1211.7175	−1198.1507	−1190.8726	−1181.8224
LR χ^2	177.01***	152.79***	179.93***	194.48***	212.58***
Pseudo R^2	0.0687	0.0593	0.0698	0.0755	0.0825

Notes: Standard errors are in parentheses; ***$p < 0.01$, **$p < 0.05$, *$p < 0.10$.

and 3, but its effects become insignificant when the control variables are entered simultaneously in Models 4 and 5. The sign of horizontal learning is even reversed in Model 5, becoming negative, because of its high degree of correlation with some of the control variables (e.g. the sub-provincial city dummy). Thus, H2 is not supported by the results.

Upper-tier mandate measured by the number of microblogs launched by provincial governmental departments is significantly and positively correlated with the dependent variable in Models 2 and 3, in which the control variables are omitted, but its effects become insignificant in those that incorporate these variables (i.e. Models 4–5). I thus fail to find evidence supportive of H3.

Municipal human capital is positively associated with the number of government microblogs, but this association is statistically significant only in Model 2. Its sign even reverses, turning negative, when the organizational resources and capacity dimension and the control variables are added in Models 3 and 5. Similarly, the municipal Internet penetration rate is positively and significantly correlated with the dependent variable only in Model 2, although its sign is consistently positive in Models 3–5. The two public pressure hypotheses, H4a and H4b, thus obtain no support from the results.

Finally, both measures of organizational resources and capacity, that is, municipal fiscal health and e-government performance, have significantly positive effects on the number of government microblogs. The regression coefficients of both measures are statistically significant at the 0.01 level, thus indicating that they are powerful predictors of the assimilation of government microblogging. These findings provide strong support for H5a and H5b.

The control variables in Model 1 explain a small portion of the variance in the dependent variable. Municipal wealth measured by per capita GDP is positively and significantly correlated with the number of government microblogs, but its effects become insignificant when other independent variables are entered (Model 5). Jurisdictional size measured by the total population size is found to be positively and significantly associated with government microblogging assimilation in all five models. The two dummy variables measuring municipal administrative ranking have different effects on the number of government microblogs. The provincial capital city dummy is found to have significantly positive effects, and the sub-provincial city dummy to have insignificant and unstable effects. Finally, a city's geographical attributes matter little with regard to its adoption of government microblogging, and the two dummies for eastern and western cities are insignificantly correlated with the dependent variable in all of the models except for the eastern city dummy in Model 1.

DISCUSSION

The results reported in this paper show the diffusion and assimilation of government microblogging in the Chinese municipal context to be driven by diverse antecedents. Of the four dimensions summarized in the Berry–Berry model, intergovernmental competition provides the best explanation of such diffusion and assimilation. The intense competition amongst local governments in China is shaped by both the economic and political contests (Landry, 2008; Li and Zhou, 2005), which provide substantial incentives for governments to adopt innovation in pursuit of competitive advantage.

Intergovernmental learning is found to have no significant effects on government microblogging assimilation, which can be attributed to the limitations of its measurement. The number of international sister cities a municipality has constitutes only an available channel of learning. Whether its government actually deploys that channel depends on other exogenous factors. Furthermore, although they lag behind in other arenas, Chinese governments have been pioneers in harnessing social media applications, in contrast to governments in Western countries such as Australia, which still treat microblogging tools with scepticism if not outright scorn (Thomler, 2011). Accordingly, international learning channels may be a poor predictor of the former's adoption of new technologies. The development of differentiated measures for specific types of innovation is pivotal to disentangling and comparing the effects of social learning and economic competition (Boehmke and Witmer, 2004; Lee et al., 2011).

Although both vertical and horizontal diffusion effects are found to influence the diffusion of government innovation, I find horizontal competition to outperform vertical mandate. Statistics show China's central ministries and provincial government departments to have launched official microblogs later and much less frequently than their counterparts at lower levels (e.g. prefecture, county and town) owing to political sensitivity and risk aversion (E-Government Research Center, 2012). It is local governments at lower levels that are driving the government microblogging bandwagon. In other words, bottom-up emergence is relatively more important than top-down promotion in explaining the spread of government microblogging in China (Ma, forthcoming 2012). It is recommended that future studies explore the competing effects of both vertical diffusion mechanisms when relevant data become available (Shipan and Volden, 2006).

The two public pressure hypotheses explain little of the diffusion and assimilation of government microblogging, which can be attributed to the characteristics of IT innovation. The boundless nature of the Internet and its applications means that government microblogs can attract numerous followers from every corner of the globe rather than being restricted to their own jurisdictions. As an increasingly important source of breaking news, microblogs have also become a platform for the gathering of diverse populations. For instance, when the official microblog of the Beijing Police Department debuted on 1 August 2010, it attracted more than 230,000 followers, but only about one-fifth of them were from Beijing, with the remainder coming from all over the country and even from abroad, according to media reports.[11] Thus, jurisdictional pressure from the citizenry is not the sole external driver of government microblogging assimilation. It is left to future research to develop more accurate measures of the size and propensities of microbloggers. Another explanation for the public pressure hypotheses' lack of explanatory power is the authoritarian nature of the Chinese government system, which lacks an effective bottom-up accountability mechanism. The results imply that the country's authoritarian municipal government officials respond actively to the upper-tier authorities who are in charge of their fiscal grants and career prospects, but do not feel accountable to their citizens who are *de facto* ignored by the current government system (Landry, 2008). This explanation coincides with recent observations of local government dysfunction in public service delivery and calls for a more citizen-centred and service-oriented public management approach.

The Berry–Berry model is well able to explain the diffusion of different types of government innovation, for example, policy, management and technological innovations, although it originates in the policy diffusion research tradition. Recent studies suggest that the model is able to explain some types of innovation but not others, which this study's findings confirm. For example, although the model is able to explain the diffusion of total innovation satisfactorily, its performance becomes unsatisfactory for specific types of organizational innovation (Walker *et al.*, 2011). In addition, it can predict the development of e-government but not that of e-democracy (Lee *et al.*, 2011). I find robust support for the Berry–Berry model's explanatory power in the diffusion and assimilation of government microblogging, but when fiscal resources and IT capacity are considered that power is substantively reduced. Competition, vertical mandate and learning are found to have significant effects, but public pressure must be dropped from the list. The model's explanatory power is further weakened when jurisdictional control variables are taken into account, with competition alone found to make a difference. As noted, I find intergovernmental competition to be the most important predictor of government microblogging diffusion, with learning and upper-tier and public pressure having little effect on its variance.

The diffusion and assimilation of government microblogging are driven by different components of the variables considered herein, and the results imply that future studies would be advised to expand the Berry–Berry framework to better predict the dynamics of innovation diffusion. My adaptation of the framework constitutes a first step, and future research should further refine this study's models to capture the authentic nature of such diffusion. The results show the addition of organizational resources and capacity to improve the Berry–Berry model's explanatory power considerably, thus supporting my adaptation of and confirming the importance of organizational resources and capacity for IT innovation adoption (Jeyaraj *et al.*, 2006). Although microblogging is a free IT innovation, its healthy operation requires large-scale investments in managerial attention, time, and energy and organizational human capital and infrastructure (Ma, forthcoming 2012). Fiscal health and IT capacity play different roles in eliciting the diffusion of government microblogging. Resource slack is an essential prerequisite of IT innovation, whereas IT capacity is one of the key components of innovation success (Tolbert *et al.*, 2008). Finally, government microblogging's dependence on organizational resources and capacity also explains the significantly positive effects of municipal wealth and size.

Several limitations of this study merit discussion and suggest directions for future research. As a temporal dynamic process, public sector post-adoption behaviour would better be examined separately to distinguish the different phases and contingencies of innovation diffusion. The diffusion and assimilation of government microblogging could be analysed with a time-series dataset to mitigate the estimation limitations of the cross-sectional dataset used here, and future studies could retest my findings when such a dataset becomes available. Furthermore, I do not examine the interaction effects of the independent variables on the diffusion of government microblogging, and it is suggested that future studies analyse the issue as a multiplicative function (Mohr, 1969). Finally, the microblogging linkages of government agencies may evoke large-scale diffusion and assimilation, the effects of which should be examined in future research. For instance, Internet opinion leaders and the microblogs of well-known governments and officials with great influence may also serve as effective catalysts to spur an extensive and rapid spread (Ma, forthcoming 2012).

CONCLUSION

The diffusion and assimilation of government microblogging are examined empirically in this paper, and the Berry–Berry model of innovation and policy diffusion is adapted and tested using data on more than 280 prefecture-level cities in China. The findings suggest that horizontal competition is significantly and positively correlated with the number of government microblogs, whereas intergovernmental learning, upper-tier mandate and public pressure have only insignificant effects. Fiscal health and IT capacity are also found to have significantly positive effects on the assimilation of government microblogging. My findings confirm my rationale for adapting the Berry–Berry model to better understand the diffusion of IT innovation amongst municipal governments in China. They also suggest that governments that face intense horizontal competitive pressure and are equipped with sufficient resources and capacity are much more likely to adopt microblogging. I believe this study contributes to the literature by offering a robust explanation of the rapid but uneven spread of microblogging across governments and to practice by helping governments to better understand the diffusion of new IT technologies.

ACKNOWLEDGEMENTS

A previous version of this paper was presented and granted the best paper prize at the Public Management Research Conference: 'Seeking Excellence in a Time of Change', held at Fudan University in Shanghai on 26 May 2012. I would like to thank the conference committee members and participants, particularly Yixin Dai, Alfred Tat-Kei Ho and Richard M. Walker, for their helpful comments and suggestions. The comments from the two anonymous reviewers of the paper are also appreciated, and I am grateful to the journal's editor, Stephen P. Osborne, for his editorial assistance. I would like to appreciate the editors at Armstrong-Hilton Ltd for language polishing.

NOTES

1 Due to Internet censorship, Facebook and Twitter are not accessible in China. The country's four dominant government microblogging platforms are weibo.com (Sina), t.qq.com (Tencent), t.people.com.cn (*People's Daily* Online) and t.home.news.cn (Xinhua News Agency). My interview with a rapporteur from the E-Government Research Center in April 2012 revealed that Sina and Tencent are the two most prominent platforms, and, accordingly, the centre plans to drop the other two from future assessments. As of the end of 2011, the total number of official microblogs launched by government agencies and officials in China had reached 32,358 and 18,203, respectively, increasing from 27,400 and 17,393 at the beginning of the year.

2 The list of all verified government microblogs on the weibo.com platform is accessible at http://verified.weibo.com/gov/. To search the microblogging portal comprehensively, I use Teleport Pro, excellent webspidering software developed by Tennyson Maxwell Information Systems, Inc. This software can be obtained from http://www.tenmax.com/teleport/pro/home.htm

3 My interview with a rapporteur from the E-Government Research Center (2012) revealed that the centre to have collaborated with the four microblogging platforms to obtain these data, which are kept secret by bilateral agreement. Furthermore, data at the city level are also not classified or reported.

4 This strategy is also adopted by most US federal agencies, as reported by Mergel (2011).

5 I treat the competition effects of cities with no peers in the same province (e.g. Xining) as equal to zero.

6 The CIFCA dataset, which is sponsored by the Chinese People's Association for Friendship with Foreign Countries (CPAFFC), is accessible at http://english.cifca.org.cn/default.aspx

7 My interviews with local officials also revealed that risk-reverse government sectors may be reluctant to launch official microblogs unless upper-tier authorities also launch microblogs or permit them to do so.

8 Five ordinary cities (Dalian, Qingdao, Ningbo, Xiamen and Shenzhen) and ten provincial capital cities (Harbin, Changchun, Shenyang, Jinan, Nanjing, Hangzhou, Guangzhou, Wuhan, Chengdu and Xi'an) constitute the fifteen sub-provincial cities.

9 The standard socioeconomic trichotomy divides China into eastern, central and western regions. The eleven eastern provinces, Beijing, Fujian, Guangdong, Hainan, Hebei, Jiangsu, Liaoning, Shandong, Shanghai, Tianjin and Zhejiang, are commonly regarded as developed regions, whereas the twelve western provinces, Chongqing, Gansu, Guangxi, Guizhou, Inner Mongolia, Ningxia, Qinghai, Shaanxi, Sichuan, Tibet, Xinjiang and Yunnan, are relatively less developed. The eight central provinces, Anhui, Heilongjiang, Henan, Hubei, Hunan, Jiangxi, Jilin and Shanxi, fall between their eastern and western counterparts geographically and socio-economically.

10 For instance, the Poisson regression model, negative binomial regression model, zero-inflated Poisson regression model, zero-inflated negative binomial regression model, zero-truncated Poisson regression model and zero-truncated negative binomial regression model are all relevant to the count data regression model.

11 Beijing police microblog draws much attention, 29 November 2010, *China News*: http://www.china.org.cn/china/2010-11/29/content_21442622.htm

REFERENCES

Anderson, N., Dreu, C. K. W. D. and Nijstad, B. A. (2004) The Routinization of Innovation Research: A Constructively Critical Review of the State-of-the-Science. *Journal of Organizational Behavior*, 25:2 pp147–73.

Barney, J. B. (1996) The Resource-Based Theory of the Firm. *Organization Science*, 7:5 p469.

Belsley, D. A., Kuh, E. and Welsch, R. E. (2004) *Regression Diagnostics: Identifying Influential Data and Sources of Collinearity,* 2nd ed. Hoboken, New Jersey: John Wiley & Sons, Inc.

Berry, F. S. (1994) Innovation in Public Management: The Adoption of Strategic Planning. *Public Administration Review*, 54:4 pp322–30.

Berry, F. S. and Berry, W. D. (1999) 'Innovation and Diffusion Models in Policy Research' in P. A. Sabatier (ed.) *Theories of the Policy Process.* Boulder: Westview Press, 169–200.

—— (2007) 'Innovation and Diffusion Models in Policy Research' in P. A. Sabatier (ed.) *Theories of the Policy Process,* 2nd ed. Boulder: Westview Press, 223–60.

Berry, W. D. and Baybeck, B. (2005) Using Geographic Information Systems to Study Interstate Competition. *American Political Science Review*, 99:4 pp505–19.

Bo, Z. (2002) *Chinese Provincial Leaders: Economic Performance and Political Mobility Since 1949*, Armonk, NY: M.E. Sharpe.

Boehmke, F. J. and Witmer, R. (2004) Disentangling Diffusion: The Effects of Social Learning and Economic Competition on State Policy Innovation and Expansion. *Political Research Quarterly*, 57:1 pp39–51.

Chien, S.- S. (2010) 'Prefecture and Prefecture-Level Cities-Political Economy of Administrative Restructuring' in J. H. Chung and T.-C. Lam (eds) *China's Local Administration: Traditions and Changes in the Sub-National Hierarchy.* London: Routledge, 127–48.

Chien, S.- S. and Ho, B. (2011) Globalization and the Local Government Learning Process in Post-Mao China: A Transnational Perspective. *Global Networks*, 11:3 pp315–33.

China Association of Mayors. (2010) *State of China Cities 2010/2011: Better City Better Life*, Beijing: Foreign Language Press.

Christensen, T., Dong, L. and Painter, M. (2008) Administrative Reform in China's Central Government – How Much 'Learning from the West'? *International Review of Administrative Sciences*, 74:3 pp351–71.

Chung, J. H. (2000) *Central Control and Local Discretion in China: Leadership and Implementation During Post-Mao Decollectivization*, New York: Oxford University Press.

Chung, J. H. and Lam, T.-c. (2004) China's "City System" in Flux: Explaining Post-Mao Administrative Changes. *The China Quarterly*, 180 pp945–64.

Cremer, R. D., De Bruin, A. and Dupuis, A. (2001) International Sister-Cities: Bridging the Global-Local Divide. *American Journal of Economics and Sociology*, 60:1 pp377–401.

Crossan, M. M. and Apaydin, M. (2010) A Multi-Dimensional Framework of Organizational Innovation: A Systematic Review of the Literature. *Journal of Management Studies*, 47:6 pp1154–91.

CSTC. (2011) *Performance Assessment of Government Websites in China 2011*, Beijing: China Software Testing Center.

Damanpour, F. (1991) Organizational Innovation: A Meta-Analysis of Effects of Determinants and Moderators. *Academy of Management Journal*, 34:3 pp555–90.

Dobbin, F., Simmons, B. and Garrett, G. (2007) The Global Diffusion of Public Policies: Social Construction, Coercion, Competition, or Learning? *Annual Review of Sociology*, 33:1 pp449–72.

Eggers, W. D. (2007) *Government 2.0: Using Technology to Improve Education, Cut Red Tape, Reduce Gridlock, and Enhance Democracy*, Lanham: Rowman & Littlefield Publishers, Inc.

E-Government Research Center. (2012) *2011 China Government Microblogging Assessment Report*, Beijing: The E-Government Research Center, China National School of Administration.

Fichman, R. G. and Kemerer, C. F. (1999) The Illusory Diffusion of Innovation: An Examination of Assimilation Gaps. *Information Systems Research*, 10:3 pp255–75.

Hrdinová, J., Helbig, N. and Peters, C. S. (2010) *Designing Social Media Policy for Government: Eight Essential Elements*, Albany, NY: Center for Technology in Government, University at Albany, SUNY.

Jeyaraj, A., Rottman, J. W. and Lacity, M. C. (2006) A Review of the Predictors, Linkages, and Biases in it Innovation Adoption Research. *Journal of Information Technology*, 21:1 pp1–23.

Katz, M. L. and Shapiro, C. (1986) Technology Adoption in the Presence of Network Externalities. *Journal of Political Economy*, 94:4 pp822–41.

Kim, S. E. and Lee, J. W. (2009) The Impact of Management Capacity on Government Innovation in Korea: An Empirical Study. *International Public Management Journal*, 12:3 pp345–69.

Landry, P. F. (2008) *Decentralized Authoritarianism in China: The Communist Party's Control of Local Elites in the Post-Mao Era*, New York: Cambridge University Press.

Lee, C.- p., Chang, K. and Berry, F. S. (2011) Testing the Development and Diffusion of E-Government and E-Democracy: A Global Perspective. *Public Administration Review*, 71:3 pp444–54.

Li, H. and Zhou, L.- A. (2005) Political Turnover and Economic Performance: The Incentive Role of Personnel Control in China. *Journal of Public Economics*, 89:9–10 pp1743–62.

Long, J. S. and Freese, J. (2006) *Regression Models for Categorical Dependent Variables Using Stata,* 2nd ed. College Station, TX: Stata Press.

Ma, L. (forthcoming 2012) The Diffusion of Government Microblogging: Evidence from Chinese Municipal Police Bureaus. *Public Management Review*, doi: 10.1080/14719037.2012.691010. Available at http://dx.doi.org/10.1080/14719037.2012.691010 (accessed 18 September 2012).

McAfee, A. (2009) *Enterprise 2.0: New Collaborative Tools for Your Organization's Toughest Challenges*, Boston: Harvard Business School Press.

Mergel, I. (2011) '"A Mandate for Change": Diffusion of Social Media Applications among Federal Departments and Agencies'. The 11th Biennial Public Management Research Conference. Syracuse, NY.

Mohr, L. B. (1969) Determinants of Innovation in Organizations. *American Political Science Review*, 63:1 pp111–26.

Moon, M. J. and Norris, D. F. (2005) Does Managerial Orientation Matter? The Adoption of Reinventing Government and E-Government at the Municipal Level. *Information Systems Journal*, 15:1 pp43–60.

Moore, M. H. (1997) *Creating Public Value: Strategic Management in Government*, Cambridge, MA: Harvard University Press.

National Bureau of Statistics of China. (2011) *China City Statistical Yearbook 2010*, Beijing: Chinese Statistics Press.

Reddick, C. G. and Wigand, F. D. L. (2010) 'Adoption of Web 2.0 by Canadian and US Governments' in R. Sharda and S. Voß (eds) *Comparative E-Government*. New York: Springer, 161–81.

Rogers, E. M. (2003) *Diffusion of Innovations,* 5th ed. New York: Free Press.

Shipan, C. R. and Volden, C. (2006) Bottom-up Federalism: The Diffusion of Antismoking Policies from Us Cities to States. *American Journal of Political Science*, 50:4 pp825–43.

Teece, D. J., Pisano, G. and Shuen, A. (1997) Dynamic Capabilities and Strategic Management. *Strategic Management Journal*, 18:7 pp509–33.

Thomler, C. (2011) Can Microblogging Save or Destroy Governments? *Government in the Lab* [online]. Available at http://govinthelab.com/can-microblogging-save-or-destroy-governments/ (accessed 4 September 2012).

Tolbert, C. J., Mossberger, K. and McNeal, R. (2008) Institutions, Policy Innovation, and E-Government in the American States. *Public Administration Review*, 68:3 pp549–63.

Walker, J. L. (1969) The Diffusion of Innovations among the American States. *The American Political Science Review*, 63:3 pp880–99.

Walker, R. M., Avellaneda, C. N. and Berry, F. S. (2011) Exploring the Diffusion of Innovation among High and Low Innovative Localities – A Test of the Berry and Berry Model. *Public Management Review*, 13:1 pp95–125.

Wu, J., Ma, L. and Yang, Y. (forthcoming 2012) Innovation in the Chinese Public Sector: Typology and Distribution. *Public Administration*, doi: 10.1111/j.1467-9299.2011.02010.x. Available at http://dx.doi.org/10.1111/j.1467-9299.2011.02010.x (accessed 18 September 2012).

Zhang, Y. and Yang, K. (2008) What Drives Charter School Diffusion at the Local Level: Educational Needs or Political and Institutional Forces? *Policy Studies Journal*, 36:4 pp571–91.

Appendix

Table A1: Summary of the variables

Category	Variable	Description	Source
Dependent variable	Microblogs	The number of municipal government microblogs registered in a city	Sina platform and author's calculation
Independent variables	Competition	The average number of microblogs launched by other cities in the same province	Sina platform and author's calculation
	Learning	The accumulative number of international sister cities	CIFCA
	Mandate	The number of microblogs launched by provincial government departments	Sina platform and author's calculation
	Human capital	The percentage of highly educated municipal citizens	NBSC
	Netizens	Internet penetration rate, measured by the number of households with Internet access divided by the total population	NBSC
	Fiscal health	The difference between fiscal revenue and expenditure divided by fiscal expenditure	NBSC
	E-government	The total score of the municipal government website performance assessment	CSTC
Control variables	GDP per capita	GDP divided by total population size. The values are divided by 10,000 when entered in the regressions	NBSC
	Population size	Total year-end population size	NBSC
	Sub-provincial city	Dummy variable $= 1$ for sub-provincial cities and 0 for other cities	/
	Provincial capital city	Dummy variable $= 1$ for provincial capital cities and 0 for other cities	/
	Eastern city	Dummy variable $= 1$ for cities located in the eastern region and 0 for other cities	/
	Western city	Dummy variable $= 1$ for cities located in the western region and 0 for other cities	/

Table A2: Descriptive statistics and correlation metrics

	N	Mean	S.D.	Min	Max	1	2	3	4	5	6	7	8	9	10	11	12	13
Microblogs	283	34.922	50.323	0	435	1												
Competition	283	34.932	23.613	0	111.583	0.319	1											
Learning	283	3.855	4.625	0	28	0.460	0.249	1										
Mandate	283	30.212	13.480	3	58	0.155	0.330	0.062	1									
Human capital	282	11.690	13.816	1.010	100	0.328	0.238	0.393	0.169	1								
Netizens	283	0.266	0.108	0.1	0.728	0.391	0.220	0.626	0.116	0.367	1							
Fiscal health	282	−0.532	0.235	−0.933	0.091	0.465	0.447	0.582	0.279	0.560	0.538	1						
e-government	283	38.763	12.961	12.570	80.720	0.482	0.346	0.577	0.305	0.414	0.491	0.566	1					
GDP per capita	282	3.548	3.651	0.519	36.870	0.349	0.228	0.413	0.190	0.655	0.483	0.649	0.437	1				
Population size	282	5.842	0.669	3.082	7.110	0.264	0.184	0.296	0.311	−0.088	0.158	0.023	0.294	−0.198	1			
Sub-provincial city	283	0.053	0.224	0	1	0.395	0.063	0.663	0.042	0.346	0.501	0.335	0.468	0.379	0.216	1		
Provincial capital city	283	0.095	0.294	0	1	0.332	−0.151	0.563	−0.076	0.263	0.492	0.336	0.332	0.158	0.198	0.460	1	
Eastern city	283	0.346	0.477	0	1	0.318	0.677	0.282	0.497	0.361	0.255	0.541	0.363	0.321	0.161	0.159	−0.034	1
Western city	283	0.297	0.458	0	1	−0.149	−0.317	−0.209	−0.329	−0.155	−0.185	−0.364	−0.337	−0.131	−0.228	−0.085	0.079	−0.473

Note: The absolute values of correlations larger than 0.130 are statistically significant at the 95% level.

Index

INDEX

assimilation of 247–8, 253, 256, 259–61; horizontal learning and 256–7; launching of 252–3; learning and 249, 253; organizational resources for 250–1, 254; public pressure and 250, 254; vertical mandate and 249–50, 254
Government Performance Project 5–6
Granger causality 92
Gray, Phillip 45
green-washing 34
gross domestic product (GDP) 254–5, 258

hard result control 97
Harman's one-factor test 232
harmful research 36
health care system. *See also* Innovation evaluation; Institutional logics: Canadian 49; Catalonian 158–63; communication in 55, 151; innovation evaluation in 150–4 (*See also* Electronic medical record (EMR)); institutional logics in, shifts in 51
Hedong District 186
Heping District 186
hero-fighter 127
hero-implementer 127
hero-innovator 115, 124–7
heroism, distributed 127
hero-standard-bearer 127
heteroscedasticity 111
Hexi District 185–6
high financial management autonomy 102, 104–5
high involvement innovation 75
high-performing agency 26
high personnel management autonomy 104
high result control 104
Holy Grail, quest for the 28
homoscedasticity 111
Hongqiao District 186
horizontal competition 256
horizontal control 93–4
horizontal diffusion of innovation 259
horizontal learning 256–7
human agency 53
human capital 250, 254, 258
human proclivity 36
human resource management 200, 210
hybrid organization 51–2

ICT. *See* Information and communication technologies (ICT)
idea fighters 124–5
idea generator 124–5
idea managers 124–5
ideas: diffusing 115; generation of 114, 124, 235–6; for improvement 229; new 230; realization of 229–30, 232, 235–6; scaling-up 115; selection of 114–15; testing 115
ideas competitions 76
implementation-oriented innovative work behaviour 223–4
improvement, ideas for 229
incremental innovation 3
individual person's role in public innovation 113, 115–17, 124–5
information and communication technologies (ICT) 75, 162
information technology (IT) 245; assimilation and 253; development of 246; innovation in 246–8, 251, 260; investment in 251
inherently incompatible institutional logics 51
innovation. *See also* specific types of: administrative 52; ancillary 3–4; benefits of 26; bottom-up 58–9; capacity for 31, 198; catalytic 133; collaborative 69, 75; connectivity formation for 71–4; consequences of 2; crowd 75–6; customer responsiveness and 195; defining 52; democratization of 75; due to external environment 2; efficiency 238; empirical scrutiny of 1; employee 226–7; entrepreneurial 32; entrepreneurial leadership in 124; entrepreneurship and, link between 31, 34–5; ethical problem of 40, 43; failures of 26–7; follower of 178; general theory of 31; implementation process for 53–4; implementing 53–4; importance of 26; incremental 3; informal aspects of 211; innovator's role in 125–6; input 52; institutional logics and 52; inter-organizational 3; in IT 246–8, 251, 260; in management 206, 209; market 52; in Nankai District 180; occurrence of 3; open 75; organisation-environment boundary 4; organizational 52, 212, 251; pioneering adopters of 178, 187; policy 69–70; principles for 27; process 3,

271